SuperCharged Web Browsers

SuperCharged Web Browsers

Cheryl Kirk

CHARLES RIVER MEDIA, INC.
Rockland, Massachusetts

Executive Editor: Jenifer L. Niles
Interior Design/Comp: Barbara Northcott
Cover Design: Marshall Henrichs
Printer: InterCity Press, Rockland, Ma

CHARLES RIVER MEDIA, Inc.
P.O. Box 417, 403 VFW Drive
Rockland, MA 02370
781-871-4184
781-871-4376(FAX)
chrivmedia@aol.com
http://www.charlesriver.com

This book is printed on acid-free paper

SuperCharged Web Browsers
by Cheryl Kirk
    ISBN 1-886801-04-5
    Printed in the United States of America

98 99 00 01 7 6 5 4 3 2 First Printing

CHARLES RIVER MEDIA titles are available for site license or bulk purchase by institutions, user groups, corporations, etc. For additional information, please contact the Special Sales Department at 781-871-4184.

Contents

Appendix: About the CD-ROM

Introduction

In This Chapter

- What this book is about
- Who this book is for
- What you'll find in this book
- What you won't find in this book
- Conventions used in the book

What This Book Is About

Most likely you've picked up this book because you want to know how to supercharge your favorite Web browser, be it Netscape Navigator or Internet Explorer. But you're not quite sure what that means or how to go about it. You've learned how to click from one Web page to the next. You've seen some nifty colorful pages, sprinkled with crisp colorful pictures. You've seen advertisements that flash and dance across your screen. But you've heard there's more to Internet life than just static Web pages and a few colorful, rudimentarily animated pages. And you want to know what that "more" is.

Maybe you've overheard the couple standing in line in front of you at the grocery store go on and on about the latest Bob Dylan album cut they heard over the Internet. Maybe your teenage son spends hours using your computer to fly through animated worlds killing aliens, or your daughter begs you to let her spend just a few more minutes chatting with friends online. Or maybe you've been using the Internet more and more in your business and are simply longing for someone to show you an easier way to view, edit, and work collaboratively with those clients or co-workers who are millions of miles away. Or just maybe you've heard about "plug-ins" and want to know how you can use and incorporate them into your own Web pages.

If any of the above are the case, you've picked up the right book. Keep reading, and soon you'll embark on a fantastic journey whereby you'll learn how to supercharge your Web browser, adding new features you probably never thought of adding. And in turn you'll make the time you spend browsing the Internet not only more productive, but also more fun and exciting. Plus, you'll learn how to turn your Web browser into the single most important application on your computer, capable of doing more than you ever would have imagined.

This book is primarily about adding what are called "plug-ins" or "ActiveX" options to your Web browser. In very nontechnical terms this simply means that this book is about adding additional functions to your Web browser. Plug-ins or ActiveX options are simply additional programs you choose to add to your browser that offer features your browser wouldn't normally have. Plug-ins help you view, see, hear, fly through, share or enjoy different types of data files you might run across while cruising through the Internet. And this book shows you not only what the best plug-ins are, but also how real people like you are using them, what they're using them for, and ways you too can incorporate the use of plug-ins not only into your own Web pages but also within a company network.

WHO THIS BOOK IS FOR

This book is really for anybody that is on the Internet using graphical Web browsers such as Netscape Navigator or Internet Explorer. (So tell all your friends to go out and buy their own copy right now!) But it's also for those people who are

- Web page developers
- Network administrators who deploy Netscape Navigator or Internet Explorer onto their Intranets
- Users interested in developing their own plug-ins but want first to learn from the best and the worst examples
- Super-users, nerds, power-users, or those who spend all their waking hours on the Internet and want to add more spice to their browsing time
- Casual users who want to do more than just browse static Web pages, but don't want to fool with IRC chat clients, VRML browsers, separate sound or movie players, or other specialized client software

Throughout this book you'll notice the writing style isn't cluttered with too many technical terms, and that's on purpose. The Internet is inherently easy to use, and it's my feeling that any book closely related to the topic of the Internet should be just as easy to read and understand. So don't worry; you won't be overwhelmed with a lot of techno-jargon. Learning about, installing, using, and adding plug-ins is not a tremendously complex subject. But if you are a technical type, you won't be underwhelmed either with a lot of nonsensical information. There's plenty of technical information here, specifically in Chapter 4-Getting Down to Business Installing Plug-Ins, Chapter 6-Using Plug-Ins on an

Intranet, Chapter 8-But Wait, I Use AOL or CompuServe!, Chapter 11-The Big Plug-In and ActiveX FAQs, and Chapter 12-The Big Plug-In Tips List.

What You'll Find in This Book

You'll find a LOT in this book. Not only will you get one of the most comprehensive lists of plug-ins for both Netscape Navigator and Internet Explorer available, but I've rated each plug-in according to how easy they are to use and what useable function they offer. I also segmented out the list so those of you using Netscape can quickly find the plug-ins you need, and those of you using Internet Explorer can do the same. Plus, the enclosed CD-ROM contains the top most useful and needed plug-ins available at your fingertips. And for those plug-ins that aren't on the CD, I've made it easy for you to quickly locate them by providing you with an entire Web page-based list of links that take you directly to those Web sites that contain the most recent plug-ins.

Chapter 1: Plug-Ins? ActiveX? What's It All About?

This chapter serves as your official introduction to Netscape Navigator plug-ins and Internet Explorer ActiveX plug-ins. You'll learn what plug-ins do, the difference between a plug-in and a helper application, and how plug-ins for Netscape are different than plug-ins for Explorer. You'll learn the three different ways plug-ins can be displayed, and you'll also learn where some of the best spots to find plug-ins are, along with the hardware, software, and bandwidth requirements you'll need to run the majority of plug-ins available. If you've never worked with plug-ins before, this is the place to start. If you just want to size up your system and find quick pointers to where you can get the most popular plug-ins, you might also check this chapter out.

Chapter 2: A Quick Tour of Plug-Ins

Once you've got a solid idea of the what's, where's, and how's of plug-ins, I'll take you on a tour of plug-ins and you'll see firsthand a few in action. You'll see everything from plug-ins that play video, to those that stream audio, to those that work with external applications such as Microsoft Office, providing full Internet/desktop integration. You'll see the different ways plug-ins are displayed and why developers would choose one display option over another. And you'll learn how to tell what plug-ins you have installed inside your computer. By the time you finish this chapter, you should have a good grasp of exactly the difference between Navigator and Internet Explorer plug-ins and how they both function.

CHAPTER 3: WHAT PEOPLE ARE DOING WITH PLUG-INS

Most books about plug-ins you'll find on the store shelves these days simply list what the plug-in is, what it does, and then shows you a few screen shots of how the plug-in looks. But not with this book; no sir. In this book you'll get much more. I'll go beyond just the fluff, and show you exactly what real people are doing with real plug-ins, and the real problems and real solutions these plug-ins have solved. In this chapter you'll see for yourself what people use, what they like about plug-ins, and the pitfalls they've run into. This chapter isn't just a sales pitch for a particular group of plug-ins, either. It's down-and-dirty information on what works, what doesn't, and what you should expect in terms of how plug-ins function in the real world. You'll learn how Jane is able to share and publish documents across the Internet, allowing others to comment and change information at will. You'll learn about Harry, who needed to get financial information out to a group of people, then conduct real-time conferences about that information. I'll introduce you to Sam, who simply wanted to offer some interactivity on his site so people would keep coming back for more. You'll see firsthand how several small and large companies save big bucks just by using a few simple plug-ins. If you are thinking of adding plug-ins to your Web site or to your Intranet, you might peruse this chapter to get some ideas of how people view, work with, understand, and either love or hate all sorts of different plug-ins and ActiveX controls.

CHAPTER 4: GETTING DOWN TO INSTALLING PLUG-INS

Once you've seen these things in action you'll probably be ready to get some installed into your own system. In this chapter I'll show you exactly how to do that. You'll learn how to find, download (or take off the CD-ROM), then install both Netscape and Internet Explorer plug-ins. You'll also learn how to size up a plug-in to see if your system is capable of handling any additional load the plug-in will add to your system. You'll also learn what all those licensing agreements are about, and what programs you need to uncompress plug-ins should they come your way compressed. Finally you'll learn how to manage all the plug-ins and external files you'll collect on your plug-in journey. By that time you'll be ready to learn more about other options available to you if you happen to be using Microsoft's Internet Explorer browser.

Chapter 5: All about ActiveX Controls

Although Netscape does have the majority of the browser market, there's no doubt Microsoft is coming up fast with its Internet Explorer browser. With the promise of true Windows 95 desktop integration, nifty features like subscriptions, Channels, and the Active Desktop, Internet Explorer already has converted many a Netscape user. What's more, not only can Internet Explorer use a wide variety of Netscape plug-ins, it also offers ActiveX—a kind of plug-in like technology that extends the reach of the browser to just about every application on your computer. In this chapter you'll learn exactly what ActiveX is, how it works, how you can tell if a Web site offers ActiveX controls, and how you can find and implement ActiveX technology within your own site. After you've learned all about ActiveX options, the next chapter will help you understand exactly how to implement both plug-ins and ActiveX controls within a company's internal network.

Chapter 6: Using Plug-Ins and ActiveX on an Intranet

Plug-ins can actually make the corporate or company network user more productive, and in this chapter I'll show you exactly how to accomplish this. You'll learn which plug-ins are "must haves" in the corporate network environment, which ones to stay away from, and how to handle multiple installations across a network. You'll also get an idea of which plug-ins work best, how to prevent users from causing their own problems when using plug-ins, and how to train people on the use of plug-ins within a corporate Intranet. If you're interested in innovative ways to save your company money and yourself some time, you need to read this chapter.

Chapter 7: But Wait! I Use AOL, CIS...

Millions of people connect through the Internet using a wide variety of commercial information service providers such as America Online, CompuServe, or the Microsoft Network. And each system uses it's own specialized software to make that connection. Unfortunately, in many cases this specialized software can pose numerous problems if you want to utilize plug-ins. In this chapter I'll cover exactly what you need to know if you are using one of these services and want to add plug-ins to your online experience. I'll also cover some of the problems you might encounter running older AOL, CIS, or MSN connection software, and some of the work-arounds you can do if you insist on living in the past and don't want to upgrade to the latest versions.

CHAPTER 8: CREATING WEB PAGES USING PLUG-INS AND ACTIVEX

Up to this point you've been the user, not the creator, of Web pages that incorporate plug-ins. In this chapter you'll learn exactly how to create Web pages that offer plug-ins in all their different forms. And you'll learn how to redesign your site to accommodate a wide variety of plug-ins. Although this chapter assumes you know a little bit about the Web page programming language, HTML, we'll start at the beginning and work our way up to some pretty advanced HTML and Javascript programming. For real novices, the first section of this chapter should be relatively easy to understand. For those more advanced types, the second portion of this chapter should provide you with some nifty code that will make your site sizzle.

CHAPTER 9: THE BIG NETSCAPE LIST

This is the big list of Netscape Navigator plug-ins, categorized by type, ranked by usability, and listed with all the pertinent information such as manufacturer's name, Web page address, system requirements, version numbers, and more. If you want to forgo all the reading and dive right into the doing but don't know where to go for the type of plug-ins you want, this is the chapter for you. Each plug-in is ranked and each is given a quick review. Each review shows what the plug-in looks like, and gives you an idea of what you'll need to do to install it. I guarantee you, this will be the most thumbed-through, used chapter in the book.

CHAPTER 10: THE BIG ACTIVEX LIST

This chapter contains basically the same information as Chapter 9, but with one distinct difference—this chapter lists all the ActiveX controls for Internet Explorer. Once you come across a site that employs ActiveX controls, you have instant access to any ActiveX control regardless of whether you're using Internet Explorer 3.0 or 4.0.

CHAPTER 11: THE BIG PLUG-IN AND ACTIVEX FAQS

You've read about, seen, played with, installed, and developed Web pages for plug-ins. But by now you probably have all sorts of questions about all types of popular plug-ins. Well, this is the chapter that will answer all those questions. Remember, no question is too dumb or too technical, and this chapter runs the gamut of questions both novices and experts have about plug-ins. Maybe you have problems installing a plug-in, or maybe you have a quick question about how to tag a full-screen plug-in on a Web page. If that's the case, this is where you find your answers.

Chapter 12: The Big Plug-In and ActiveX Tips List

I love quick tips, like the kind you read in computer magazines. Just little snippets of information, little gems of timesaving information that can make your life just that much easier. Well here in this chapter you'll find those little tips that make working with, using, installing, or finding plug-ins easier. Arranged first by general tips, then detailed by plug-in manufacturer, you'll find a treasure trove of useful information. No tip is longer than a couple of paragraphs, and none is more involved than just making a few mouse clicks or changing a few lines in a registry file. If you already know lots about plug-ins and just want some handy hints, this is the chapter for you.

Chapter 13: The Big Plug-In and ActiveX Web Site List

This is the big list of not only the company Web sites that offer free and pay-for plug-ins but also the sites that cater specifically to information such as development of plug-ins, reviews of plug-ins, discussions of plug-ins, and examples of new plug-ins in action. If a Web site has anything to do with plug-ins, this is the place you'll find it.

Appendix: The CD-ROM

This appendix holds all the information you'll need to use the enclosed CD-ROM. It also contains the licensing agreements for each of the products included. If you need instructions on installing the software from the CD-ROM, here's the place to go.

What You Won't Find in This Book

By now you should realize that this book is almost entirely about browser plug-ins and how they can supercharge your browsing experience. It's not a book about learning all the intricacies of your Web browser application. Nor is it a book about searching the Web, configuring your e-mail client, finding your perfect mate, or learning how to post to newsgroups. Nor is it about developing plug-ins. If you're thinking about developing plug-ins, consider this your primer. If you want to develop your own plug-ins, I suggest you check out the Netscape developer's site at *http://developer.netscape.com*, or Microsoft's ActiveX site at *http://www.microsoft.com/activex*. Both of these sites contain everything you need in order to learn how to develop plug-ins for the different browsers, assuming you already have some programming experience.

You also won't find recipes for chocolate cake, floor plans for a multilevel home, remedies for bee stings, or directions to the stars' homes.

CONVENTIONS USED IN THIS BOOK

To make it easier to understand here are a few conventions that will be used throughout this book.

Offers a helpful or neat little trick you can use.

Points out useful information.

Lets you know when you might run into trouble.

IN SUMMARY...

By now you should be champing at the bit to supercharge your browser. This chapter should have given you an idea of where you'll find the information you need to do just that. You may decide to read the book from start to finish or simply use it as a reference guide when you need to find that perfect plug-in. If you're like me and have a tendency to jump around, picking and choosing chapters to read on a whim, you can always come back to this chapter and use it as a quick reference guide. Whatever method you use, hopefully you now have a clear view of where this book will lead you. If you have any questions, feel free to e-mail me at *ckirk@alaska.net*. I'll be happy to answer any questions you might have or guide you to the right place to find the answer. If you're ready to get going, turn the page, and watch as your Web browser transforms itself over the course of this book.

CHAPTER

1

Plug-Ins? ActiveX? What's It All About?

You might have noticed the gaps in your browser. Maybe the bookmark feature wasn't everything you wanted it to be. Maybe you wanted to view Microsoft Office documents without having to launch the entire Office suite. Perhaps you wanted a personal information manager you could use within your browser. And of course you probably wanted instant access to your favorite search site without having to call up a Web page every time you wanted to search. Or perhaps you wanted some way to respond automatically to those spamming e-mail messages, demanding to be taken off their advertising lists. Or maybe you just wanted some way to hear your favorite radio talk show while you browse the rest of the Web. If you can identify with any of these scenarios, you need to learn how to supercharge your browser, and supercharging your browser means learning about the wonderful world of plug-ins.

WHAT DOES SUPERCHARGING YOUR BROWSER REALLY MEAN?

Supercharging your browser is a relatively simple thing to do if you use the plug-in technology of Netscape and Internet Explorer. Supercharging your browser actually means adding new functionality to the browser, which it wasn't originally programmed to have, but can be added because of the way the browser has been programmed. And this special programming, called plug-ins, allows you to plug new features into your browser without being a programmer yourself. Just remember, the concept of plug-ins is a relatively easy one to grasp if you don't let the technology get in the way. You don't have to be a programmer, nor do you have to know much more than how to download files or click a few buttons.

WHAT YOU'LL LEARN HERE

In this chapter you'll learn all about the plug-in concept. The actual process of implementing plug-ins into your system will be covered in subsequent chapters. What you should concentrate on here is grasping the concepts and imagining what functionality you might want to add. Once you see how plug-ins work, what forms they take, the features they offer, how relatively easy they are to incorporate, you'll soon come to realize this technology, although not highly touted, is worth learning. And better still, it doesn't cost an arm and a leg, requires little technical knowledge, and opens up new avenues to your browsing experience.

TIP

If you're already familiar with plug-ins and are on the hunt for an interesting article on the nature of plug-ins, check out Wired's *"Webmonkey" column at http://www.hotwired.com/Webmonkey/plugins/96/35/index1a.html. Columnist Luke Knowland outlines what he thinks makes a plug-in a good plug-in, and which plug-ins "suck" and "don't suck." He even gives you a brief rundown of the good, the bad, and the ugly. We'll talk more specifically about what makes a good plug-in later in this chapter.*

Little did you know when you first installed Netscape Navigator or Internet Explorer you were actually installing a kind of electronic Lego set. Your browser, the foundation, lets you snap on new parts—plug-ins. The plug-ins are the extra pieces, the building blocks, for adding those capabilities the browser didn't come with. You can snap in place any plug-in you want, any time you want. And in most cases, plug-ins snap into place in just a few seconds. Plug-ins in their most basic form let you add all sorts of new functionality to your browser, building upon an already solid foundation. You control exactly what you want, building up your browser as you see fit.

NOTE

You might also have heard the term "plug-in" used when referring to other programs such as Adobe Photoshop. Photoshop also employs "plug-in" technology, pieces of software code you can add to Photoshop to give it additional capabilities. You will probably see more and more applications employ the use of plug-in technology in the future, since it gives both the user and the developer control over adding new features and options.

That's really the crux of the plug-in concept. You simply "plug-in" little programs into your browser. It doesn't seem that revolutionary until you consider the whole concept of plug-ins in general is pretty darn important for both Netscape and Microsoft, and any company that develops plug-ins. Both companies allow you the freedom to enhance your browser as you see fit. And better still, the browser never goes out of style or loses its ability to be upgraded. It's not a closed-end product like many other applications you have on your hard drive; you can always add new features to it regardless of how old the actual program might be. If there's something lacking in either browser, plug-ins open up a whole new programming world where developers can quickly and easily develop new features not found in either Navigator or Explorer. And this means programmers will continually develop for both browsers for a long time. The browser is essentially open ended and can continually be improved for a relatively low cost.

TIP

If you're looking to develop plug-ins for Navigator, make sure you check out the Netscape Plug-Ins Software Developer's Kit at http://home.netscape.com/comprod/development_partners/plugin_api/index.html.

The Concept of Plug-Ins in Action

But how does this whole concept of Lego-like electronic building blocks work and how do you plug these new features into your browser? First, let's start by understanding how the Web browser works and what it's really doing. Web browsers take a text file, read special instructions placed in that file, called HyperText Markup Language (or HTML) tags, then display the result on your screen. These HTML tags tell your browser how to format the text and where to find the graphics files stored on a computer server that the HTML tags point to, eventually displaying all text and graphics on your computer screen together. These text files that make up Web pages are usually named using certain file extensions such as .HTML, .HTM, or .ASP. You've probably noticed these file extensions when you browse the Web. For example, if you go to *http://www.ptialaska.net/~radio/index.html.*, you'll see a Web page like that in Figure 1.1. And of course this Web page is actually just a text file

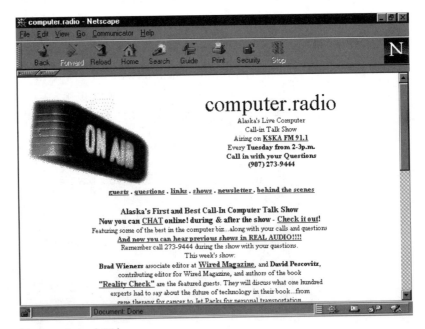

Figure *A simple Web page.*
1.1

that tells your browser how and where to display the text and where to pick up the graphics.

But Web browsers can also understand and display a limited range of graphics files such as GIF or JPG. GIF files are mainly line-drawing type graphics, whereas JPG files are usually photos. Anytime your browser comes across one of these file types, it displays it in your browser window just like it would text. Based on where the designer of the Web page placed the graphic, it can show up anywhere on the page, next to text, underneath it, or on top. The designer programs exactly where the graphic should be placed in the Web page.

What happens when a browser doesn't understand a file format? Say you run across a Corel Draw file, a Word Perfect file, or an Excel spreadsheet—all special formats, not just text files that can contain different formats and graphics. What happens then?

One of several things can happen. First, the browser will check to see if the file format can be displayed through the use of a plug-in—essentially additional programming you've added to your browser. If there is no plug-in capable of displaying that file type, your browser will check to see if a helper application—an external program which operates separate from the browser—is assigned to the file format. If that's the case, the helper application will launch and display the file, again separate from the Web browser. If neither a plug-in nor a helper application can handle the file format, your browser will alert you with a dialog window telling you it can't read the file but if you'd like, you can save the file and open it later with another application. If you've done much Web surfing, I'm sure you've run across such a dialog window as displayed in Figure 1.2.

Sounds simple, doesn't it? Whether it's your Web browser, a helper application, or a plug-in, it's all essentially about displaying a particular type of file. That file may be static, like a word processing document, or it may be an interactive file, like a streaming audio file or a rolling chat session. Regardless, it's all about taking information from a remote computer and displaying that same information on your computer's screen.

THE NITTY-GRITTY ABOUT PLUG-INS AND HOW THEY WORK

What exactly is a plug-in, besides some strange piece of programming that somehow attaches to your browser and lets you read files you normally wouldn't be able to read? According to Netscape, the manufacturer of the popular Netscape Navigator browser and main instigator of

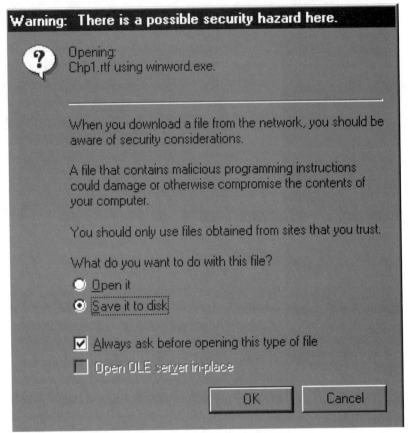

FIGURE *Your browser is telling you it doesn't have the capability to show the file, and no*
1.2 *plug-in or assigned helper application can help out.*

plug-ins, a plug-in is a "...dynamic code module that exists as part of
the Netscape Application Programming Interface for extending and
integrating third-party software into Communicator or Navigator."

The English translation goes more like this: Again, think of your
browser as if it were a basic Lego set. You have all the pieces and parts
you need to create any kind of browser you want, and you can add these
pieces at any time you choose. When you add these pieces, just little
programs (dynamic code modules) that connect into your browser
(through the use of the Netscape Application Programming Interface, or
API), your browser then has more functionality. Once added, these
plug-in programs aren't brought into play or loaded into memory until
you need them, basically when Communicator or Navigator can't open

or display a particular file type on its own and needs to call on the plug-in to open or display the file instead.

The Process of Installing Plug-Ins into Your Browser

Just like the concept of plug-ins, the process of installing a plug-in into your Web browser is pretty simple. When you install a plug-in, the plug-in doesn't actually install directly into the browser. Instead, the plug-in resides in the plug-ins folder which is stored within your browser's own program folder. Figure 1.3 shows you where you can find all the plug-ins currently installed that work with your browser.

When you install a plug-in, it not only places itself in the plug-ins folder, but it installs a kind of notification into your browser to let it know what file type and file extension (or extensions) the plug-in can handle. When the browser runs across a file type or extension which the plug-in is capable of opening up or displaying, it passes control over to the plug-in, and the data is then displayed. Pretty much everything is handled for you once you've installed the plug-in. Most, but not all, plug-ins are installed through a simple installation program, something you'll become familiar within the next chapter.

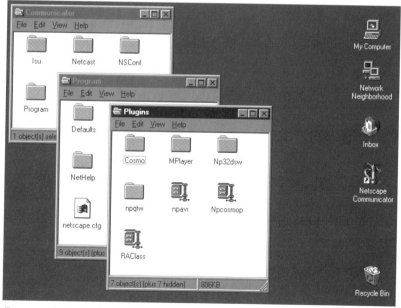

FIGURE *Notice the plug-ins folder? It contains all the plug-ins that work with your cur-*
1.3   *rent browser.*

The information displayed through a plug-in is cross-platform compatible just like Web pages are. That means a Shockwave animation will display on both a Mac- or a Windows-based computer if the proper plug-in is installed.

The only thing you really have to pay attention to is that you download the plug-in for your particular computer and operating system. Although the data they display is cross-platform compatible, a plug-in for a Mac won't work on a Windows 95 computer, and vice versa. If you do download plug-ins from popular download sites such as Shareware.com, make sure you're downloading the plug-in for your type of computer.

What Happens After Installation?

Once you've installed the plug-in and relaunched your browser, the browser checks the plug-in folder to see what plug-ins are installed. However, the browser does not load any of the plug-ins into RAM. Instead, plug-ins are only loaded into RAM when the browser runs across a file type the plug-in can display. Once you move on to another page that no longer needs the plug-in to display information, the plug-in is deleted from RAM, thus freeing up valuable RAM space for other programs you might want to run.

Here's a real world example that might help you understand the value plug-ins really bring to browsers. Say you're working within your company's internal network, and you run across your department's budget, created and saved in an Excel spreadsheet file. You want to view the information in the file. You have two options: either download the entire file, which means saving it to your hard disk then opening it up with Excel, or use a plug-in capable of displaying the spreadsheet in your Web browser window.

Both procedures accomplish the same goal: you can view the information in the spreadsheet. But the plug-in option takes up less memory, takes less time, and most likely will prevent you from accidentally changing any of the data in the spreadsheet. If you use the plug-in method, you don't have to download a thing and you don't have to save the file on your hard drive. And better still, once you're finished viewing the file, you don't have to worry about quitting Excel to free up more useable memory so you can run other programs simultaneously. In the long run, plug-ins not only take up less time, but also take up less computing resources.

Throughout the whole plug-in experience, the browser acts as if the plug-in is simply a part of the browser. When you leave the page, and no longer need the capability the plug-in offers, the browser unloads the plug-in from your computer's RAM or turn-on memory. The memory the plug-in was using is freed-up and made available for other programs to use should they need it. If you didn't know you had a plug-in installed, you probably wouldn't know the difference between it displaying a file and your Web browser displaying a file. The browser and plug-in operate relatively smoothly, giving the unassuming user the appearance that the functionality to read certain file formats is simply built in the browser.

The Three Faces of Plug-Ins

Plug-ins can display all types of files—graphic files, animation files, spreadsheet files, sound files, video files, and so on. Name any type of file, and most likely there's a plug-in that can display it. But different file types call for different ways to display the information. Take the previous example, for instance. A spreadsheet file would require much more screen landscape to display its contents than a simple little sound file might. With a word processing document, you'd probably want the ability to scroll down the page; whereas with an animation file, you certainly wouldn't want to have to scroll to the left to see the animation in action. That would be too distracting.

The programmers who first thought up the concept of plug-ins realized different types of data need different options for displaying content. Some data may need to take up the entire Web browser screen, leaving room only for the standard Web browser navigational tools. Other data may best be displayed almost as if it were embedded into the Web page. Still other plug-in data, like sound files, only need to be heard, not seen. Therefore, plug-ins can display data in one of three forms:

- **Embedded**
- **Full-screen**
- **Hidden**

Embedded simply means the plug-in and the contents of the file display within the Web page itself, looking as if it were simply just another element on the page, oftentimes providing you with either limited or non-existent controls to manipulate the file itself. Yet all the same features of the Web browser stay intact, including the menus at the top, the status bar at the bottom, and any scroll bars that may allow you to scroll up and down the page. A good example of an embedded plug-in is the Real Audio plug-in, which lets you adjust the volume, or control which portion of the streaming audio file you want to listen to. Figure 1.4 is an example of a Real Audio embedded plug-in in action.

Full-screen means the plug-in occupies the full screen of the Web browser window, often bringing with it window controls specific to the particular data type it's displaying. This means the menu items often change to reflect the options the plug-in now provides while displaying the contents of the file. The plug-in may also display new toolbars at the top, bottom or sides for viewing, manipulating, or paging through the file. The Adobe Acrobat reader is a fine example of a full-screen plug-in, one that adds menu bars of its own. The main Web page navigational controls still remain, but some of the other additional toolbar options may close to provide room for the toolbars the plug-in may introduce. Figure 1.5 is an example of what you might see if you had the Acrobat plug-in installed and were looking at an Adobe Acrobat document, commonly referred to as a PDF file.

Hidden plug-ins do pretty much what their name implies; they hide from the user as if they were simply a transparent part of the browser. Most plug-ins that are formatted using the hidden screen option are plug-ins for playing sounds, music, or MIDI files. Unlike their counter-

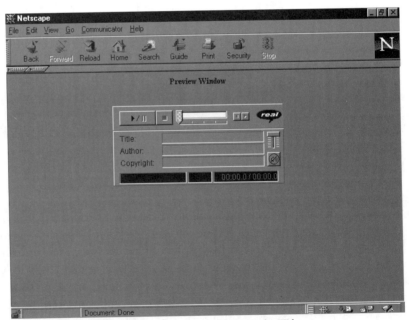

FIGURE *The Real Audio plug-in appears embedded into this Web page.*
1.4

FIGURE   *The Adobe Acrobat plug-in gives you a good idea of what a full-screen plug-in*
1.5   *looks like.*

parts, embedded or full-screen plug-ins, hidden plug-ins don't change
the relative appearance of the screen, and offer no visible controls for
manipulating any portion of the file they are reading or displaying. I'd
show you a screen shot of a hidden plug-in, but then you wouldn't see
anything, now would you?

How Much Do Plug-Ins Cost and Are Any Included?

Here's the good news. Most consumer-based plug-ins are free. And
whether you know it or not, if you're using the latest version of Netscape
Communicator, you already have a whole bunch of plug-ins installed,
including plug-ins that understand the MIME types in Table 1.1.

TABLE 1.1: *Plug-ins installed in Netscape Communicator.*

Type	Used For	File Extension
Video/Unix-msvideo	Playing movies or video files.	.AVI
Audio/Unix-aiff	Playing sound files commonly created on Macintosh or Unix computers.	.AIF, .AIFF, and .AIFC

(Table 1.1 continued)

Audio/Unix-wave	Playing sound files usually created on Windows-based computers.	.WAV
Audio/Basic	Playing sound files usually created on Unix or Windows-based computers.	.AU, .SND
Unix-world/Unix-vrml	Displaying three-dimensional worlds or graphics.	.WRL
Video/QuickTime	Displaying QuickTime movies usually created on Macintosh or Windows-based computers.	.QT, .MOV

For the most part, you can download hundreds of free plug-ins. Those that aren't free usually offer the ability to download time-limited or feature-limited versions so you can check them out before buying them.

The ones you have to buy are pretty much industry specific and run in the neighborhood of about $50 or less. My recommendation to you is NEVER pay for a plug-in until you've tried it out, weighed the cost versus the cost of using a secondary application, and made sure the plug-in works well on your system. Although most popular plug-ins are relatively easy to install and work as advertised, this is not the case with all plug-ins. There are a few that are simply too difficult for the average user to install. Some don't work well with certain other applications installed, and others provide little enhancement over what other free plug-ins or helper applications provide. Chapters 9 and 10 contain lists of those that cost and those that don't.

Internet Explorer's Version of Plug-Ins—ActiveX

Never lacking for that competitive edge, Microsoft has created a kind of plug-in of its own to compete with Netscape's plug-in technology. To the user, the difference isn't that apparent simply because Netscape's plug-in technology and Internet Explorer's own proprietary technology called ActiveX accomplish the same task—they both display files or information that the browser wouldn't otherwise be able to display. You'll see ActiveX controls referred to in much the same way as plug-ins mainly because they function so much like plug-ins. And that's also why you'll find a huge list of ActiveX controls listed in Chapter 10. If you're not interested in the specifics of plug-ins and ActiveX controls, by all means just skip over this section. The key thing to realize is there is a difference, although sometimes subtle. Unlike plug-ins, which are relatively secure, ActiveX controls are far less secure and should be used with great caution.

In some regards, from a programming standpoint, ActiveX controls function in similar fashion. Like plug-ins, they are programming code that the Web page designer inserts into a Web page. And like plug-ins, they are activated only when you, the browser, run across a page containing that particular type of control or file format. And once downloaded to your computer, an ActiveX control acts just like a plug-in. Yet unlike plug-ins, ActiveX controls operate independent of the browser, using their own separate programming architecture. When you think about it, ActiveX controls are actually more like Java applets than plug-ins. And from a real programmer's standpoint, ActiveX controls are basically slimmed down versions of the Object Linking and Embedding standard (OLE) used in Windows and other Microsoft applications, such as Microsoft Office.

You probably have heard about OLE. OLE is in integral part of programs such as Microsoft Office, and is actually a key component of the Windows 95 operating system. OLE allows data seemingly to be passed from one application to another. For example, say you have three different programs: a spreadsheet, word processor, and e-mail program. If all three have OLE built in, you could use one spell checker with all three programs, instead of having one for each. The spell checker would just be another OLE "object" the various programs could call when needed. And when a new spell checker comes out with more words and more features, instead of having to upgrade each application, you only upgrade the one "object," the spell checker.

Since ActiveX is actually just a slimmed down version of OLE, this type of functionality is now brought to your favorite Web browser. So when you view a Web page with a particular ActiveX control or object, that object can, in theory, be used with any OLE-compliant software program. For example, say you run across a great tic-tac-toe ActiveX object. In theory, once you download that module, it could be played not just in a Web page, but also in an Excel spreadsheet; or you could affix it to a Microsoft Word memo and send it to your office mate down the hall.

Unfortunately, like plug-ins, ActiveX controls are not platform independent. Moreover, they aren't entirely safe to use. The level of security ActiveX controls offer is very, very scary. In theory (and in some examples in reality), ActiveX controls could do such disastrous things as format your hard drive, suck all the data out of your checkbook program, or install viruses and Trojan horses without your knowledge. Although Microsoft is instituting the idea of making each ActiveX control use a digital signature, a kind of electronic guarantee the maker of the ActiveX control won't create a control that would wreak havoc on your system, there still is a huge potential for disaster.

Check www.zdnet.com/wsources/content/0597/sec0.html for more information on security problems ActiveX poses.

Navigator can use ActiveX controls, but only with the help of a plug-in called **ScriptActive**. Netscape Communicator 4.0, however, offers full ActiveX functionality. Ironically, most plug-ins created for Netscape Navigator usually work with Internet Explorer. However, you can't bet that all will function properly, so I caution you to read the instructions for installation and double-check any **ReadMe** files that come with the plug-in for information on whether the plug-in will work with Internet Explorer.

As mentioned, if you want to use some of those nifty ActiveX controls but don't want to switch from using Netscape Navigator 3.0 to Internet Explorer, you can download a program called NCompass ScriptActive. This plug-in enables Netscape to fully interact with ActiveX controls within the Netscape browser. You can download a ten-day trial version of NCompass ScriptActive from NCompass Labs at http://www.ncompasslabs.com/scriptactive/. A full working version of ScriptActive sells for $21.

One special feature of ActiveX controls is that unlike plug-ins, which usually require you to run some sort of setup program in order for them to become available to your Netscape browser, ActiveX controls are automatically installed on your system. When you run across a site and view data that utilizes them, the control will automatically be installed if you don't already have it. You don't need to run a setup program or restart your browser; they immediately install and become active the moment you view a site that uses a particular control. That's why ActiveX controls, although somewhat like plug-ins, more resemble Java applets. Just like Java applets, there is no installation process and the minute you run across a page using Java, the Java applet starts to play or function.

Internet Explorer, like Netscape Navigator, comes equipped to view and play many of the standard audio and video file formats now available on the Internet, including AVI files, QuickTime movies, MPEG video, WAV, AU, AIFF, and MPEG audio.

Throughout this book I'll refer to plug-ins and ActiveX controls sometimes synonymously. Yet in the listings you'll find in Chapters 9 and 10, I'll clearly note which are which, since you want to be especially careful when implementing ActiveX technology into your Internet Explorer browser due to the security issues.

WHERE DO YOU GET PLUG-INS?

Chapters 9 and 10 encompass a huge listing, complete with reviews of just about every useful plug-in I could find and many ActiveX controls as well. But if you're itching to get started and want to search out a few plug-ins on your own, Table 1.2 lists four spots where you're bound to find a ton of plug-ins, most for free, some available at a cost.

TABLE 1.2: *Some great places for plug-ins.*

Name	Location	Comments
Browsers.com	http://www.browsers.com	Excellent location for finding the most popular plug-ins for your particular browser.
Shareware.com	http://www.shareware.com	It's a searchable index for not just plug-ins but also shareware, freeware, and demo software programs. It lets you search by computer, operating system, keyword, or type of file.
Netscape	http://www.netscape.com	Netscape started the concept of plug-ins and maintains a running list of all plug-ins available for all platforms including Unix, Mac, and Windows.
Browser Watch's Plug-In Plaza	http://browserwatch.internet.com/plug-in.html	Lists virtually every plug-in known to man with links to locations to download them. Segments them out by operating system. Be aware the listings take a long time to display.

Want to know what plug-ins you already have installed in your browser? Try typing "about:plugins" in the **Location** *field of your browser, or choose* **About Plug-ins** *from the* **Help** *menu.*

What You Need To Run Most Plug-Ins

If you can run Navigator or Explorer, you can pretty much run any plug-in for either application. However, if you plan to run many of the multimedia plug-ins, you definitely will need multimedia hardware capable of playing sound, music, or voice recordings. A standard 486 PC is capable of running a large majority of plug-ins.

But besides a PC, what else do you need to run a plug-in? To make it easier to understand whether your computer will work with a majority of plug-ins, I've created two tables of computer configurations, one for playing the majority of non-multimedia plug-ins (Table 1.3), and the other for playing multimedia intensive plug-ins (Table 1.4).

Table 1.3: *Configuration for non-multimedia-intensive plug-ins.*

Component	Size/Type	Comments
Computer	486/66Mhz or above	Slower 486s can function just fine, but may run relatively slow depending upon the amount of memory or number of plug-ins.
Video System	VGA	The better the monitor, the more colors it can display, and the niftier things look.
Hard Disk	At least 10MB available	More, if you plan on adding lots of plug-ins.
RAM Memory	16-32MB	Again, the rule of thumb is the more plug-ins, the more RAM you should have.
Modem	28.8 baud or above	Depending upon the plug-in, the bandwidth really doesn't matter that much.
Operating System	Windows 95	Because of the built-in TCP/IP options and the 32-bit capabilities, this makes it a much better operating system than the DOS/Windows 3.1 environment.

TABLE 1.4: *Configuration for multimedia-intensive plug-ins.*

Component	Size/Type	Comments
Computer	Pentium 120 or above	MMX technology will help with graphically oriented plug-ins.
Sound Card/Speakers	8-bit sound card, 16-bit if you want to use Internet telephony, allowing you to talk and hear another person at the same time. Speakers that offer relatively clear response.	SoundBlaster-compatible is something you want to look for in a sound card since most sound-oriented programs and plug-ins use this standard interface for working with and playing sounds through sound cards.
Video System	VGA	The better the monitor, the more colors it can display, and the niftier things look. And of course, the bigger the monitor, the better.
Hard Disk	At least 100MB available	You should have enough space for temporary files, especially for nonstreaming audio and video plug-ins.
RAM Memory	32-64MB	Multimedia plug-ins work well with lots of RAM to work within.
Modem	56K	Ask your service provider what type of 56K modem they are using, either 56K Flex or X2 technology. You should get the same modem and possibly model as your service provider to prevent incompatibilities.
Operating System	Windows 95	It's relatively easy to setup, and works faster and better than Windows 3.1 when connecting to the Internet.

Remember, these are just guidelines. Plug-ins don't require any specific brand or make of hardware in order to run. And for the most part, they require relatively low bandwidth, which means you don't need a high-speed data link; your old 28.8Kbps modem will work just fine. Although the more memory you have the better everything will function.

One caveat though, more plug-ins are now being produced for the Windows 95 platform than any other platform.

HELPER APPLICATIONS? WHAT ABOUT THEM?

The Difference between a Helper Application and a Plug-In

If you've been browsing for any length of time, you probably have heard or read about helper applications. You might have even seen a reference to them when you initially configured your Netscape browser. So what exactly are helper applications?

I guess you could say helper applications are the precursor to plug-ins. A helper application is simply a program that can understand and interpret files which Communicator cannot handle itself. Almost any program can be configured to act as a helper application for Communicator. When Communicator is presented with an unknown file type, it passes it to the appropriate plug-in. If one isn't found, it then passes it to the appropriate helper application, assuming that one is configured for that file type.

Helper applications, much like plug-ins, can act almost as if they were an extension of Communicator itself. However, a helper application is different in that it is started and runs as a separate application, in its own window, and using its own memory space.

If you're interested in a more technical discussion of helper applications, check out what Netscape has to say at http://home.netscape.com/assist/helper_apps/index.html.

When Web browsers didn't do much more than just display very simple text and graphics, the idea of having your browser be able to point to another application in order to open files the browser couldn't understand was a great thing. That meant someone could place a spreadsheet file on his Web site, and if you had your Web browser properly configured, when it ran across this file, it would know to invoke Microsoft Excel and open the file. The only problem was most people didn't understand how to configure their browser to invoke the proper helper application at the proper time.

That's where plug-ins come in handy. They automatically install within your browser. You don't have to do much more than click an install button and automatically your browser knows what to do to handle a particular file type. By following certain standards set by browser manufacturers, plug-ins can also do all sorts of things external applications can't, such as display the file directly in the browser or bring up only those controls necessary for viewing the file, leaving other editing-type controls out of the picture. And from a software developer's perspective, since millions of people use Netscape Navigator, you have millions of potential customers to sell your plug-in to.

What Are the Advantages of Helper Applications?

It's a good thing Netscape hasn't abandoned the idea of helper applications altogether. When you think about it, any computer program on your hard drive can be configured to be a helper application. That means you can set up your Web browser in such a way that there won't be a single file it can't open or understand. This is an especially important concept if your company is using an Intranet, because it means you can configure your browser to not only be a window to the World Wide Web, but also a window into your own desktop. You'll never have to click the **Start** button again to launch a program. Instead, when your browser runs across a file, it will know to open the appropriate application, giving you the option to edit the information in the file.

The next "Zipped" file you run across will automatically open with WinZip. Or the next link to an Excel spreadsheet will automatically open into Excel. And the same will hold true for the next PageMaker document, the next Access database file, the next Adobe Freehand file, and so on. You have full control over editing and updating the information.

What Are the Disadvantages of Helper Applications Compared to Plug-Ins?

Since it's all about displaying files on your computer, from a user's perspective, the difference isn't that noticeable until you really start to delve deeper into helper applications and plug-ins. Some of the more apparent differences are listed in Table 1.5.

Table 1.5: *Differences between plug-ins and helper applications.*

Difference	Pro	Con
If you want to open a file with a plug-in, you must have a helper application instead of the application installed.	You have full editing control and use of all the features of the actual program.	You must purchase the application. Most plug-in viewers are free. The helper application would usually occupy more memory than the plug-in.
A plug-in can't be used as a stand-alone application.	It doesn't consume as much memory, cost as much, and it doesn't require as much hard disk space.	In order to use a plug-in you must be using a browser capable of using that plug-in. Not all plug-ins are compatible with all browsers.
You can configure your browser to use any helper application you want to open any file you want.	If you'd rather use a different application to view a file, you have full control. Plug-ins don't offer you that kind of control and usually only work within a range of file types.	You have to know a little bit more about how to configure your browser so it recognizes different file types and opens them with the intended application. Plug-ins don't require much more knowledge other than simply clicking an install button.
With a helper application you can multitask between the browser and the Helper Application.	If you wanted to copy and paste information between a working document and a Web page you could easily do that.	Running multiple applications takes up more RAM memory and oftentimes can be slower than simply using two windows within the same application.
Files read by helper applications can be downloaded then viewed within their own window after you've quit your browser.	You can retain the data, saving it for later manipulation when you aren't on the Internet. You aren't tied to the Internet and can travel with your data, easily editing it as you see fit.	This takes up more space on your hard drive and requires you to know how to work within the helper application.
Helper applications don't display the context of the file within the context of a Web page.	You can concentrate just on the file itself.	If it's a graphic, you won't see the graphic in the context of the Web page.
Your browser has no control over the helper application.	You don't have to worry about the browser taking over control of the helper application or file.	You loose the navigational controls and features of your browser.

Which One Should You Use?

Well, actually it does seem a little redundant when you think about it, but there's room for you to use both. Here's a quick rule of thumb I use when considering whether to configure my browser to use a plug-in or a helper application:

- If all I want to do is view a particular file format, I use a **plug-in.**
- If I want to edit the file, and a plug-in doesn't offer editing features, I use a **helper application.**
- If I'm low on memory, I use a **plug-in.**
- If I don't want to worry about how to configure the right file types, I use a **plug-in.**
- If I want to use my own viewer for a particular file type, I use a **helper application.**
- If I want to stay in my browser almost exclusively, I use a plug-in.

WHAT MAKES A GOOD PLUG-IN?

What makes a good plug-in? For me, it's anything that makes my life easier. It doesn't matter if the plug-in only does one thing or several things, as long as it does it well, does it reliably, and doesn't require me to jump through hoops to install it. I'd say those are hallmarks of a good plug-in. But let's take a closer look at what helps you determine whether a plug-in is worthy enough to be installed into your computer.

IT SHOULD WORK

No matter what, the plug-in should work as advertised. I know this sounds strange, but amazingly enough, many plug-ins I've tried simply don't work, work erratically, or end up corrupting my system to the point I have to uninstall the plug-in and in some cases uninstall my browser.

How do you know whether a plug-in works before you install it? Check around. Ask your friends if they've tried it. Contact your Internet service provider to see if they recommend any particular plug-ins. Post a message on newsgroups like *comp.infosystems.www.browsers.ms-windows* or *microsoft.public.inetexplorer.ie4* to find out if anyone has used the particular plug-in. Do a little research yourself first before you venture into installing a new plug-in. And use this book as a guide. I'll let you know exactly which ones work and which ones don't.

It Should Be Easy to Download and Install

Ideally, installing a plug-in should be as simple as downloading, running an installation program, restarting your computer, getting back on the Web, and then using that plug-in immediately. The plug-in should be smart enough not to interfere with other plug-ins you have installed or other start-up applications your system might use.

In my first book, *The Internet Phone Connection*, I reviewed a whole slew of programs that let you transmit your voice over the Internet in real time, much like you do with a telephone. Although I knew how to install and use a majority of these programs, none of them got high ratings unless my Dad was able to easily download, install, and then use them. Dad is no technical whiz. He's just an average everyday user who uses the Internet to help him with his search for long lost relatives, correspond with his three daughters, or sometimes entertain himself when there's nothing to watch on television.

So I've used the same measuring stick in this book. If Dad can't download and install the plug-in, the plug-in doesn't get a high mark. Computers should make your life easier, not befuddle you. The same goes with plug-ins. Plug-ins are meant to make the Web browsing experience not only more expansive, but also easier. I won't steer you in the wrong direction just because I think a plug-in is nifty to use. It must also be simple to install and simple to use, otherwise I don't consider it a worthy plug-in.

NOTE

If the process of downloading and installing doesn't seem easy, you can bet the plug-in itself probably won't be easy to use, or work as advertised.

It Should Add Substantial Value to Your Browsing Experience

I would never download or recommend a plug-in that displayed GIF or JPG files. All browsers already do this and do it quite well. If a plug-in is worth using, it must add value to your browser, not do something the browser already does—unless it can do it one hundred times better.

You'd be surprised how many plug-ins actually do almost exactly the same things your browser is capable of doing. A plug-in that reinvents the wheel is not a plug-in worthy of your hard disk space. Sure, there are twenty or thirty different graphic viewer plug-ins, but very few offer any features over and above what Netscape Navigator or Internet Explorer already offer. You have to look hard when evaluating exactly which plug-in you should install. Read as much information on the plug-in as you can to see if you can get the gist of what the plug-in offers. Oftentimes if you can't make out what substantial value the plug-in will bring to your browsing world, most likely it won't bring any.

IT SHOULDN'T REQUIRE LOTS OF COMPUTING RESOURCES

My motto is, only upgrade your computer if some new fangled feature is going to save you time, money, or headaches, or in some way enhance your life. Such is the case with Real Audio. I upgraded my computer specifically so I could use Real Audio. Why? Because I love listening to the radio and I love listening to several talk shows which radio stations in Alaska don't carry. With my new multimedia PC, booming speakers, and crystal-clear sound card, I can now listen to these shows without having to move to another town. And better yet, many of the shows are archived, meaning I can listen to them at any time. I don't have to rearrange my personal life around the shows I want to listen to. The cost to upgrade meant I could enrich my life, save time, and listen when I wanted.

If the plug-in helps you do your job better, lets you communicate with your clients better, or saves you time, and the plug-in requires you to update your hardware, weigh the benefits against the costs and I'm sure you'll find it will be worth upgrading. But make sure it's a plug-in you can use frequently enough to offset the cost for upgrading. A nifty three-dimensional plug-in that requires you to buy expensive 3-D viewing glasses, but only a few sites use, isn't a worthwhile plug-in to use, nor a reason to buy expensive hardware.

IT SHOULD FOLLOW STANDARDS

For a plug-in to be worth downloading, it should follow industry standards. Following industry standards means working according to the development guidelines, set forth by Netscape or Microsoft, which allow your plug-ins to work properly with your browser. You shouldn't have to tweak your Registry file or change any special settings in your browser.

SUMMARY

By now you should have a good grasp of what a plug-in is, how they work, where you get them, and what you need to use them. You should also be able to spot a good plug-in from a bad one. The plug-in concept is relatively easy to understand, and for the most part installation and implementation is no big technological feat either. Now you should be ready to tackle the toughest part of the plug-in technology—installation. If you're ready, simply turn the page and you'll start on a fantastic journey that will probably save you money, make your browsing experience easier, and maybe even entertain you.

CHAPTER

2

A Quick Tour of Plug-Ins

Ask most Internet-savvy users what plug-ins are good for, and most likely you'll hear that they're mainly used for viewing graphics and different types of multimedia or for viewing virtual three-dimensional worlds on your computer screen. But plug-ins offer more than just the ability to view graphics your browser doesn't recognize. There are plug-ins that offer a myriad useful functions your browser didn't come with, and a large majority of them are available free for the asking.

What's In This Chapter

In this chapter I'll introduce you to how plug-ins work and what they are really doing when you use them. This isn't a technical introduction; that comes later in Chapter 4. Instead, I'll show you a wide variety of plug-ins in action and show you how they work up close. You'll learn what plug-ins come automatically installed with your browser and how you can keep tabs on them all. You'll also learn what kinds of file types can be viewed, and you'll see your share of multimedia plug-ins. Finally, you'll see what happens when you don't have the proper plug-in installed. By the end of this chapter you should have a good idea of how plug-ins work and what features you should look for when picking out a plug-in to supercharge your browser.

If you think you've never used a plug-in, think again. You probably have and didn't even know it. Since new versions of Web browsers now come with a variety of plug-ins already installed, and since the whole idea behind plug-ins is to make the technology work effortlessly with the browser, spotting when a plug-in is in play is sometimes difficult for the untrained eye. From this point on you'll start to realize exactly how valuable plug-ins are, and how simple they are to use.

Checking to See What Plug-Ins You Have Installed

First let's determine exactly what plug-ins you already have installed to work in conjunction with your Web browser. Then we'll move on and check out how some of these plug-ins work. You probably have no clue what plug-ins you already have installed. Unless you knew specifically what you were looking for or stumbled on this menu item or opened up this file folder, you probably never had cause for listing the plug-ins installed to work with your browser.

Netscape and Microsoft could not have programmed into their browsers every possible file format known, so they added plug-in technology. You plug it in and go. Since plug-ins are not exactly part of the browser program you are using, and since they are only called into action when you run across a certain file type the plug-in can read, they are given their own unique folder with both Internet Explorer and Netscape Navigator. The currently installed plug-ins reside in this folder and when new plug-ins are installed they too are usually placed in this same folder.

If you open up your **Program Files\Communicator\Program** folder or your **\Program Files\Microsoft Internet** folder, you will see a folder labeled "Plugins." Open that folder and inside it you may see several files or folders. These files or folders are the plug-ins you currently have installed. When you first launch your browser, the browser looks in this folder to see what plug-ins are installed as well as checking the **Windows Registry** file. Figure 2.1 gives you a sneak peek at what my **Communicator Plug-ins** folder contains. Again, you may have more or less, or maybe none at all, listed in your plug-ins folder.

But there's also a simpler way to find out what plug-ins you currently have installed in Netscape Navigator. Simply select the **About Plug-ins** option from the **Help** menu or type "about:plugins" in the **Location** field of any browser window. From there the current browser window will change to display the list of plug-ins installed to work with your

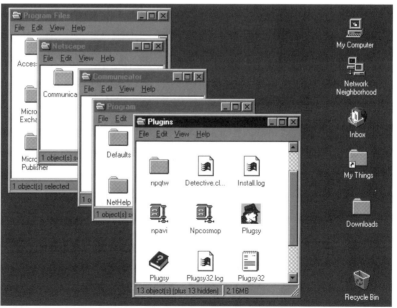

FIGURE *A look at what's in my Netscape Plug-ins folder.*
2.1

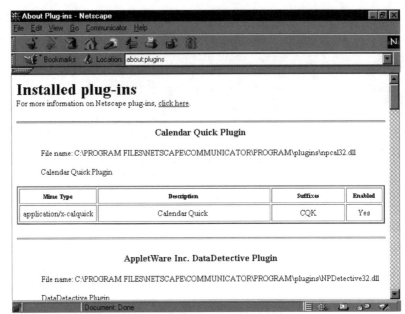

FIGURE *A look at what you get when you choose About Plug-ins from the Help menu.*
2.2

browser. Figure 2.2 is an example of what this browser window might
look like. Yours will be different depending on what plug-ins you currently have installed.

Let's take a quick look at what this page is telling you. The first entry
on my list of plug-ins starts with *AppletWare's DataDetective* Plug-in, a
plug-in that lets me search my hard drive using any keyword I wish. First
my plug-in page lists the name of the plug-in, followed by the location
of the actual plug-in itself. From there it lists the name of the plug-in.
Underneath the name, you have a table listing four categories: Mime
Type, Description, Suffixes, and Enabled. Table 2.1 lists what each means:

TABLE 2.1: *What the "About Plug-Ins" page tells you.*

Column	Explanation
Mime Type	MIME stands for Multipurpose Internet Mail Extensions. This column of information tells you what type of software or file type is used to view the particular file format. The first section, called the Mime or content type is followed by the subtype, listed to the right of the slash. The subtype tells you specifically what format the file is in, such as in the form of a sound file or video file.

(Table 2.1 continued)

Description	Gives you a brief description of the installed plug-in.
Suffixes	Tells you what file extensions this particular plug-in can read, interpret, play, or display.
Enabled	Tells you whether the plug-in is currently active; it will be automatically initiated when your browser runs across this file type.

TIP

Through the use of MIME, computers can send a wide variety of data to each other, not just text, GIF, or JPEG images. Here's how it works. Someone places a file on a server. The server is configured to know how to handle the file through the server's MIME configuration file. When someone using a Web browser runs across this file, through the use of MIME, the Web server sends this file to the browser along with it information about this kind of data. The browser receives this data and the accompanying information about this file, the MIME information; and if the browser is configured to interpret this type of file, it displays the information properly. If not, the browser asks to save the data or pick an application that can interpret the information.

As you scroll down through this list, you'll notice there are numerous plug-ins already installed in your system. Each new upgrade to your Web browser software includes more plug-ins. That's one reason why browser software like Netscape Navigator has grown from occupying a single disk to now occupying over 11MB of space once installed. You should familiarize yourself with the plug-ins you already have installed and the types of files and file extensions they understand and display.

There are numerous plug-ins that display, play, or interpret the same types of files. There are a ton of sound player plug-ins and an abundant list of video players, all that play the same file types. If you don't want to change your current configuration, don't install plug-ins that offer the same capabilities as your existing plug-ins. If you install multiple plug-ins that read the same file type, you can run into problems and conflicts. So before you run off installing all sorts of plug-ins, keep in mind which plug-ins are currently installed in your system. The **About Plug-ins** menu option is a quick and easy resource to remind you of what you have, and a reference point you should use before you install any plug-in.

A SIMPLE PLUG-IN IN ACTION

Now that you know what plug-ins you have installed and a bit about those plug-ins, let's get down to business. First let's take a look at a few simple plug-ins in action. Don't worry about how to download or install these plug-ins, just concentrate on what they offer and how relatively easy it is to use and interact with a wide variety of them. In this chapter I'll introduce you to some plug-ins that are probably already installed in your browser, and show you a few that most definitely are not. Remember, plug-in technology is really all about letting you see files you wouldn't normally be able to see with an ordinary Web browser, and more importantly it's about supercharging your browser with functionality it doesn't already have.

YOUR FIRST LOOK—A COUPLE OF MULTIMEDIA PLUG-INS IN ACTION

You probably didn't know your browser was capable of displaying inline movies, or playing a wide variety of sound files. Yet through the use of plug-in technology, what was once a rather mute application is now a full-featured multimedia tool. If you have the latest version of Netscape Navigator or Internet Explorer, your browser now comes with plug-ins that allow you to hear a wide variety of sound files including:

- **WAV**—Wave files, a standard Windows sound file format, which could be music or voice sound files
- **AIFF**—Apple Computer's creation for playing not only sound files, but also musical instrument information
- **AU**—Created originally for Unix computers, this offers music and voice sound files
- **MIDI**—Musical Instrument Digital Interface, the software that lets you play digital music sound files
- **AVI**—The video format used with Windows where the sound and picture frames are stored together
- **RA**—Real Audio files, that is, if you are using Internet Explorer

TIP

Confused by all the different acronyms and abbreviations that seem to abound on the Internet? Check out C\Net Central's glossary of computer terms. You can find it at http://www.cnet.com. Click on the link for the glossary that is listed in the lefthand column and just about any acronym you were ever curious about is listed alphabetically.

THE DEFAULT PLUG-INS ALREADY INSTALLED

Actually your browser, Netscape Navigator in particular, comes with a whole host of different plug-ins installed. These plug-ins let you play a wide variety of sound and video files. Specifically, these pre-installed plug-ins include

- **LiveVideo**—This plug-in displays and plays AVI video clips, the movie format for Windows-based computers. LiveVideo is automatically installed with the latest version of Netscape Navigator. When you run across an AVI movie file, once loaded, the movie should play or display in a Web browser window. All controls for playing the movie are available by right-clicking on the movie frame itself.
- **LiveAudio**—LiveAudio plays the wide variety of sound files available on the Internet, including AIFF, AU, MIDI, and WAV. Regardless of whether the sound file format is specific to a particular platform, such as AIFF being specific to Macintosh computers, the use of LiveAudio the sound file will play through a Web browser window when your browser comes across such a file. Like LiveVideo, the controls for various sound files are either available by right-clicking on the frame that depicts the sound file, or directly within the frame, depending upon the type of sound file embedded within the page.
- **Live3D**—Live3D is the Virtual World plug-in which lets you view three-dimensional worlds within your browser's window. As long as the virtual world you want to view complies with the Virtual Reality Markup Language, or VRML, the Live3D plug-in can show you the file or page. 3D text and graphics can be viewed and streaming audio files can be played through the use of this plug-in.
- **QuickTime**—Originally created for viewing video files on the Macintosh, QuickTime has quickly picked up steam on the Internet because of its capabilities and cross-platform compatibility. The QuickTime plug-in lets you play QuickTime movies directly in your Web browser screen, offering the controls by right-clicking the QuickTime movie frame.

By now you should have a good idea of the capabilities available in your browser, and that means you're ready to get going. First let's check out a few sites that offer these types of files so you can see and hear them in action. In order to do that, you'll need a computer with a sound card and speakers. It really doesn't matter what brand or type of speakers you have, just as long as you have something that will allow you to play sounds, other than the standard PC beep.

TIP

If you don't have a sound card and speakers, you should get them. If you don't you will miss out on some of the best the Internet has to offer. More importantly, you will miss out on a wide range of plug-ins if you are sound challenged. Plus, the cost of sound cards and speakers has dramatically dropped over the last few years. You should be able to buy a sound card and speaker combination for $100-$500 depending upon the features you want in your sound card.

A simple sound card that can play 8-bit sound should be sufficient. (However, sound cards offering various features such as wave tables, polyphony, full duplex, and 16-bit CD quality stereo let you hear music, MIDI files, and voice over Internet telephony in crisper, clearer quality.) Of course the more features offered on a sound card, the more likely it will have a higher price. If all you plan to listen to is talk radio using Real Audio, you really don't need fancy music options. But if you want to listen to music, or maybe even create your own MIDI music, you might consider buying a sound card and speakers that offer more than just a few features. Table 2.2 provides a list of several sound card and speaker manufacturers you might want to check out if you need to buy or upgrade your existing system:

Table 2.2: *Various sound card manufacturer sites.*

Manufacturer	Web Site
MediaVision	http://www.svtus.com
Ensoniq	http://www.ensoniq.com
Creative Labs	http://www.creativelabs.com
Gravis	http://www.gravis.com

Taking A Plug-In for a Spin

The first stop on our plug-in tour will be a noisy site called MIDI.COM, the ultimate guide to MIDI tesources on the Internet. It's a place that houses tons of MIDI sound files, and is an excellent site to check out how one of the major plug-ins, Live Audio, works with Netscape Navigator. It's also a great place to grab some MIDI files to include in your Web pages. If you plan on adding inline plug-in MIDI files to your Web page, this is a great source for those types of files.

To check out this site, type *"www.MIDI.com"* in the **Location** field of a browser window. In a few minutes the site should load and a MIDI file should start playing in the background. If you have the volume control on your speakers turned up, you should also hear the sound file playing. You may or may not see the embedded MIDI controls as well. Figure 2.3 is an example of what an embedded MIDI file will look like in a Web page. You can also control the MIDI file by right-clicking on it, and selecting what option you want from the pop-up menu.

If you want to change the volume, simply move the slider to the left or right. If you want to pause the sound file from playing, click the **Pause** button, the third from the left. To stop the file from playing altogether, click the **Stop** button, the third button from the left. Or again, you can right-click and select any of those options from the pop-up menu.

TIP

Most embedded plug-ins, regardless of the type, offer right-clickable pop-up options. If you can't find controls within the embedded file itself, try right-clicking on the embedded file's frame.

FIGURE *The embedded MIDI file as it looks in a Web page (see embedded file in the*
2.3 *upper-right of screen).*

Notice when you do right-click on the embedded MIDI file you can also save the sound file directly to your hard disk. Figure 2.4 is an example of how you could save this file; however, not all file types displayed through plug-ins can be saved. In the case of streaming files, streaming audio or video files cannot be saved because instead of downloading the file, it is actually streamed to your computer in parts. More about streaming audio and video in Chapter 5.

Amazing, but true. You just viewed, played, and manipulated your first plug-in file. There wasn't much to it, was there? It all worked without much intervention from you, and it worked as if MIDI were a file type your Web browser was capable of handling. In case you missed it, here's what really happened:

- The MIDI file was stored on the MIDI.COM server.
- The Webmaster configured the server to recognize the file and let the browser requesting that file know it was a MIDI file.
- When you requested the page, your browser recognized it as a MIDI file. Knowing it wasn't an HTML, GIF, or JPEG, file type, it then looked for a plug-in associated with MIDI files.

FIGURE *With some plug-ins you can actually save the file directly to your hard drive.*
2.4

- Your browser then found the LiveAudio plug-in, which it then loaded and handed control of to the plug-in.
- The plug-in took control of the file, and based on the instructions provided in the Web page displayed, played the file accordingly.

Had a plug-in not been available, the browser would have looked through the list of helper applications associated with the browser, and if one were associated with the MIDI file type, the helper application would have been launched and control of the file handed over to it.

Whew! You never knew so much was going on behind the scenes, did you? The plug-in concept is relatively simple and works pretty much the same across all sorts of file types. As long as the plug-in is installed properly and there are no other plug-ins that could potentially conflict with another, you should have no problem using a wide variety of plug-ins.

That's what makes this technology so appealing. Unlike Java, which oftentimes can send a computer crashing, plug-in technology usually works the first time. Of the hundreds of plug-ins I've installed, used, and evaluated, only a handful have given me problems, unlike Java which crashes my browser on a regular basis.

The one problem you may encounter when using plug-in technology is not having enough memory. 16MB is enough if you plan on using just a few plug-ins. But you really should have at least 32MB or more if you want to avoid any glitches. And since memory is relatively cheap these days, you may want to consider upgrading your system with as much memory as you can afford.

TEST DRIVING SOME OTHER PLUG-INS

Next we'll try a few more plug-ins that once again are part of the standard Netscape Navigator installation. Don't worry whether you will use these plug-ins on a regular basis or not. The key point here is to take notice of how the plug-in works with your browser to display the data file, and what controls different plug-ins offer. In the next chapter you'll be introduced to more plug-ins you probably will want to use on a daily basis.

The next two plug-ins we'll look at are the QuickTime plug-in and the Live3D plug-in. The QuickTime plug-in lets you view QuickTime movies, whereas the Live3D plug-in lets you traverse through three-dimensional worlds. Admittedly, these are not things you would do on a regular basis. The speed of the Internet may prohibit you from downloading large QuickTime movies; and although gliding through three-dimensional worlds is fun, and there are some useful things you can do with VRML. These plug-ins are more for entertainment than anything else.

Don't get me wrong. QuickTime movies could be used for training, and VRML or three-dimensional worlds could be used as a better way to browse the Internet. But technology, specifically the speed of the Internet, will have to increase greatly before these technologies become mainstream. Currently a 1MB QuickTime movie can take anywhere from five minutes to an hour to download, depending upon your connection. Remember this when you run across a plug-in that seems to take forever to load. Usually it's neither the plug-in's fault, nor a problem with your computer; rather it probably has something to do with a slow Internet provider, clogged network lines, or overcrowded servers.

THE QUICKTIME PLUG-IN

Now that you know you need memory, patience, and a fast Internet provider, it's time to check out a few QuickTime plug-in movies. QuickTime can play video, music, sound, animation, and MIDI files. It can also show you virtual reality photographs in the form of QuickTime Virtual Reality movies, which are basically a series of pictures strung together that either step you through or around a place, such as a room, an interior of a car, or a deserted field in Africa.

If you want to see QuickTime VR movies, you must install the QuickTimeVR plug-in. The standard version of the QuickTime player installed with Netscape Navigator does not include the QuickTime VR option.

According to Apple's QuickTime site, QuickTime is "a multi-platform standard used by multimedia software tool vendors and content creators to store, edit and play synchronized graphics, sound, video, text and music." Having the QuickTime plug-in installed in your browser, means it is capable of displaying all sorts of content, including animation, movies, music, and sound files. QuickTime is not streaming, which means in essence you have to wait for the entire file to download before you can view or hear the QuickTime movie in its entirety. However, if the download of a QuickTime movie is interrupted, you can still see or hear the movie up until the point where the download was halted.

A great place to see all sorts of QuickTime plug-in movies is Apple's QuickTime Plug-In Sample Web site located at *http://quicktime.*

apple.com/qt-city/. Type this address in your browser, and let's experience some of the samples on the sites. Remember, this site is always subject to change, so the samples I'll outline here may or may not be available when you connect to the site. However, there should always be a wealth of QuickTime movies to choose from here, so if you can, go with the flow, look around, and experiment to your heart's content.

What you should see is a Web site greeting you and a list of links you can click on to see QuickTime movies. If the **Samples** link is showing, click on it. You'll notice a list of QuickTime samples to choose from. The five different QuickTime plug-in movie types you can view or hear include:

- **Audio files**—This could be voice or music. Unlike MIDI which is more akin to electronic music, QuickTime Audio files could be just about anything that can be recorded.
- **MIDI**—These are the same types of files you heard before when you checked out MIDI.COM. If you click to play one of these files, Netscape knows, because the file type ends in .MOV instead of .MID, QuickTime is the plug-in it will choose to play this file. Although QuickTime MIDI files sound the same as MIDI files played through LiveAudio, the file itself was actually recorded using QuickTime instead of another recording option, and then saved in the .MOV file format.
- **Video**—These files contain moving pictures, just like a real movie, along with sound synchronized with the pictures.
- **QuickTime VR**—QuickTime VR is like a big picture you can move through either in a circular motion or a picture you can actually move through. A good example of a QuickTime VR movie is a movie of a hotel room you can move around in, that allows you to navigate through the bathroom, entryway, back to the bed, and around the room. Again, this type of file requires you to have the QuickTime VR plug-in installed, which is not part of the QuickTime default package installed within Netscape Navigator.
- **Animation**—QuickTime Animation files are just like little cartoons. They don't include real photos, but can include sound, and are an awful lot like those flip cards you used to have as a kid. You know, the ones that showed the stick figure diving off the diving board or running across the bottom of a page.

Try out one of the QuickTime movies by clicking a link to one of the files listed at the bottom of the screen as shown in Figure 2.5. The first

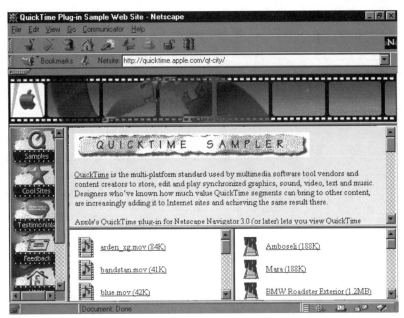

FIGURE *There are plenty of QuickTime movies to choose from at the bottom of this page.*
2.5

screen of the movie should display, with the Netscape Navigator status bar showing you the amount of time it will take to download the remaining parts of the QuickTime movie. Again, the amount of time it takes to download the file is dependent upon your Internet connection and the speed of your modem. Once the file has fully downloaded, the QuickTime plug-in will automatically kick in gear and start to play the file. You may hear sound or you may simply see a video.

You may see controls or you may not. It depends on whether the movie is an animation, a MIDI file, or a QuickTime movie. You usually don't see controls with animations or MIDI files, but you usually do with videos or sound files. If you want to stop the play of the movie and there are no controls visible, right-click anywhere in the middle of the movie and choose **Pause** from the pop-up menu as shown in Figure 2.6.

In order to get MIDI files to stop playing, you may have to move back to the previous page or frame. MIDI files that have been embedded to hide the controls do not allow the user to control any aspect of the file. The person who created the Web site has full control over whether a plug-in displays a file type as hidden, full-screen, or embedded. You as the user have to put up with whatever style they chose. In

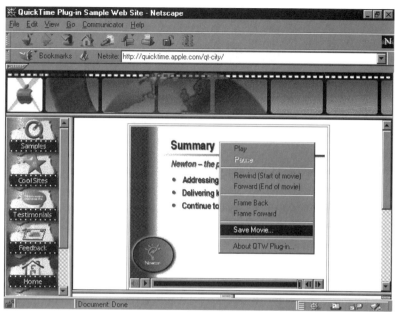

FIGURE *Just right-click to the control the movie or save it to your hard drive.*

2.6

Chapter 8 you'll learn how to set up sites using a wide variety of plug-ins.

If you spend some time at this site, you'll start to understand the vast amount of potential plug-ins have. As you might have noticed, QuickTime movies can sit side by side with text, static graphics, or even other plug-ins. They can play on demand or automatically, and they can enhance any Web site with additional information that entertains, amuses, and informs whomever happens upon the site. So instead of having just boring graphics or text, or using cheesy animated GIF files, you can use full-featured movies on your site with relative ease. And since QuickTime is now included with Netscape Navigator, just about anyone with a Web browser can experience feature-rich sites.

Just think, if you owned a bed and breakfast, you could actually record a movie stepping your potential guests through your humble abode, instead of having a static list of pages with boring pictures. Each room could have a separate Web page which would include a QuickTime movie and the price list next to it. Your potential clients wouldn't have to download a thing. You could greet them virtually, then let them pick and choose which room suits their tastes.

Or maybe you work in a large company and on your Intranet site you'd like to include a videotape of the latest TV commercial your company is running for all the employees to see. Next to the commercial you could include a schedule of the times and channels the commercial can be seen.

Or perhaps your family is spread out all over the world and you just recently had a baby. You could make movies, encode them into QuickTime movie formats, place them on a Web site, and have all your relatives join in on the wonders of your new little bundle. Each week you could keep them informed of the child's progress via real movies that let them see and hear about the child's development, with pertinent static information on the same page such as height and weight. These are just a few examples of what you could do with QuickTime plug-ins.

A QUICK LOOK AT 3-D WORLDS USING THE LIVE 3D PLUG-IN

By now you're probably getting the idea that plug-ins are not difficult to use. And if you're like most people, you probably never knew when you were using plug-in technology like QuickTime or MIDI. Things just worked without any intervention on your part. Maybe you never even ventured to sites that offered anything more than just text and graphics.

Up until now, the plug-ins you've seen are relatively tame. They have a few controls, mostly to regulate sound and display videos or music. But now you're about to embark on another world, a foreign world you've probably never ventured into. You're going to go where few people have gone before. That's right, you're going to the world of virtual reality. By the virtue of the Live3D plug-in, which accompanies all new installations of Netscape Navigator, you can now explore worlds you may never have thought of exploring.

TIP

I'm not a big fan of virtual reality for one simple reason—it's just not there yet. Still encased in a clunky wire-frame type animation, most virtual reality sites offer little more than a glimpse of what the technology could be. Most books dedicated to plug-ins gush about virtual reality. This isn't one of those books. In order for the technology to get high marks in my book, it has to serve a somewhat useful purpose and be relatively easy to use the first time out. Not all virtual worlds measure up to these criteria. As a matter of fact, most of them are relatively boring, don't really make you feel you're in a virtual world, and offer little or no real value. But I'm not discounting the technology altogether, or writing off its potential uses even today. Virtual reality has its uses in training, medicine, entertainment, and potentially in the way in which we travel through the maze we call the Internet. Just realize that this technology is evolving and so is the hardware that will make it easier and faster to fly through virtual worlds.

The best place to get a good look at some interesting virtual worlds is through the Netscape Live3D site. At present you can find this site at *http://home.netscape.com/eng/live3d/live3d_coolworlds.html*. If you can't find it at this location, simply use the **Netscape Search** option to search for the **Cool Worlds Live3D** page. At this site you'll find a list of all sorts of virtual worlds you can cruise through. There's one thing you should keep in mind during your journey—always right-click through your virtual world to see what options might lurk below the surface. And remember, help is just a click away, available at any time by clicking the **?** icon on the dashboard of your 3-D viewer.

The idea of virtual 3-D worlds is relatively simple. You have an object you can view three-dimensionally. That object may also have links to other sites, sounds, or files connected to it. The premise is that you are walking around, examining, and looking at objects in your 3-D viewer. The closer you get to those objects, possibly the more detail you will see. The further away, the more overall perspective you'll get. In some cases you'll even hear sounds, some in stereo three-dimensional sound. That is to say, the further away you get from them, the softer they sound. The closer you get, the louder they sound.

My favorite 3-D world to venture into is one that was created in 1996 for the SIGGRAPH conference. Called Musical Earth, it's a world that offers not only a view of different locations on a globe, but also plays different music as you fly over certain spots on the globe. When you first locate the Cool Worlds demo site, this should be one of the first links listed on the left-hand side of the page in the left frame. Figure 2.7 is an example of this.

Click the link for this demo and in a few minutes the plug-in will load, and the globe should appear in the right-hand frame. Notice when a plug-in is loading, the status bar at the bottom of the page will notify you of its progress. Wait until the plug-in has fully loaded before venturing into the 3-D world. While you're waiting, notice the right-hand frame offers a panel of buttons you can use to fly through your virtual world. This is called your **Dashboard**. It offers you the functions to fly through your virtual world. Almost every virtual world that uses the Live3D plug-in will come with this standard dashboard.

The **Gravity** button holds you down, preventing you from flying freely through the world. The **Walk** button lets you walk around the

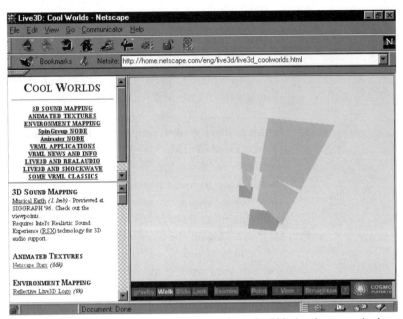

FIGURE *The Musical Earth 3D Sound Mapping demo should be listed amongst the demos*
2.7 *available.*

object by holding down the left mouse button and moving your pointer in the direction you want to go. Before you can try out these features, you must first click the right arrow next to the **View** button. This will bring you into full view of the globe. Experiment with using the **Walk** option. Click it first, then hold down your mouse button as you slide left or right, up or down. Notice the globe moving around the axis point of your mouse pointer?

After you have experimented a bit, right-click anywhere on the globe. This will bring up a pop-up menu listing a variety of options, many found on the dashboard itself. You should definitely try the option entitled **Viewpoints**. When you select **Viewpoints**, you should see a list of different viewpoints associated to this virtual world. Select **Scotland**, and in a few seconds the globe will rotate showing you where Scotland is on the map, and if everything is working right, will also play Scottish music. Right-click again, select another viewpoint, and the globe spins around to that location, playing that country's music. If at any time you are confused as to how to navigate around your virtual world, simply click the **?** on the **Dashboard**. A Web page will display listing all the options available, along with links to keystroke shortcuts you can use to navigate through your worlds even faster.

This is a very interesting demo in that it uses both three-dimensional graphics and three-dimensional sound. As you move from one location to another, you hear that music fade away and the new sounds move through your stereo speakers. Such an example shows you how 3-D worlds could really help children learn about geography, mechanics learn about engines, or travelers learn about new sites around the globe. Eventually this technology may even change the way you browse the Internet or view your city or town's local Web site.

TIP

If you're having problems playing or navigating through virtual worlds, make sure you aren't running any other applications and that you have enough memory. Virtual worlds can take up a lot of memory while they're playing, and are prone to crash or freeze occasionally.

*If your system does crash, don't worry. Just reboot, and try again. If the site continues to crash, empty your browser's cache by selecting **Edit | Preferences**, then click the **Advanced** tab. Expand the **Advanced** tab, then click **Cache** to select this option. Click the **Clear Memory Cache** and **Clear Disk Cache** buttons, then try reloading the site again. If it still crashes, something may be wrong with the site itself.*

QUICK PLUG-IN QUESTIONS AND ANSWERS

By now you probably have plenty of questions about plug-ins. Although I promised you I wouldn't get too technical, now is the time to answer some of those questions. That way, when you get to Chapter 4, you'll already know how most of this technology works and you'll understand how to avoid some common problems. Here's a list of questions most plug-in users have after test-driving plug-ins for the first time.

How do I know when a plug-in isn't installed?

You will see a puzzle piece on the Web page where the plug-in should be. Figure 2.8 is an example of what this puzzle piece looks like. If the Web page has been developed properly you don't have the required plug-in, you will be prompted to get it.

How can I tell which files are displayed by plug-ins and which are displayed by helper applications?

You can view which file types are displayed with which helper or plug-in applications by following these steps:

1. Select **Edit | Preferences**.

2. Click the **Navigator** tab to expand this category.

3. Click the **Applications** option.

4. Click the file type you are curious about. In the **File Type Details** box below the **Description** listing, the **Extension**, **MIME** type, and **Handled By** information will be listed. If a plug-in handles this particular file type, the word "Plugin" will be listed next to the **Handled By** field.

When I click a link for a QuickTime movie, it asks if I want to save the file instead of playing the movie. What's wrong?

You may not have the proper version of QuickTime installed. Remember, if it's a QuickTime VR movie, you have to download a separate QuickTime VR plug-in extension to play those types of QuickTime movies.

When I try to access a page, I get a message saying "Helper Application Not Found." What's wrong?

Most likely you don't have the plug-in the page is requesting installed in the plug-ins folder. Make sure you install your plug-ins in this folder or they may not work properly.

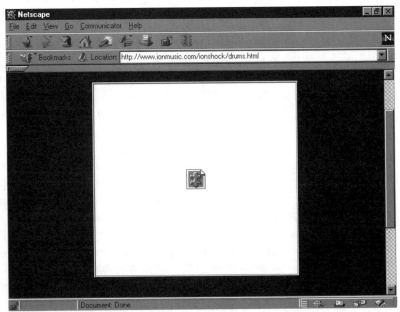

FIGURE   *If a plug-in isn't installed, a plug-in puzzle piece is displayed in its place.*
2.8

When I click a link for a particular file type, I get the error message "You've started to download a file of type XX/XX. Click More Info to learn how to extend Navigator's capabilities." What should I do?

You should definitely click the **More Info** button. This will take you to the Netscape plug-ins page and show you what type of plug-ins you can use to view the particular file type you initially clicked on. This is the easiest way to figure out what types of plug-ins you need. Let Netscape direct you to those plug-ins and their manufacturers.

Is there a place I can go that lists all different types of file formats so I can test my browser to see which ones are installed already?

An excellent test site is the **WWW Viewer Test** page, located at *http://www-dsed.llnl.gov/documents/WWWtest.html.* Just about every different type of file format is listed here. Simply click the link for the file format you want to test. If the appropriate plug-in or helper application is installed you will see the contents of the file in a separate window. If not, you will be prompted to click the **More Info** button. If you do you will be taken directly to a page listing what plug-ins are capable of displaying that particular file format.

When I try to play one of those 3D worlds, my machine crashes. I've cleared the cache and have plenty of memory. What else could be the problem?

Your video card may require a different software configuration. Check your WIN.INI file by selecting **RUN** from the **Start** menu and typing WIN.INI in the **Open** field. Search for an entry called **DeviceBitmaps**. If you find one in your WIN.INI file remove it, save the WIN.INI file, reboot your browser and try again.

SUMMARY

By now you should have a good grasp of how plug-ins work and what plug-ins are included with your browser, and how to solve some common problems should they arise. In the next chapter you'll learn first hand how people are really using plug-ins in everyday situations. I'll take you beyond the simple plug-ins, introducing you to some wild, wacky, and very useful ones. Once installed, you'll never know how you lived without them. In Chapter 4 you'll learn exactly how to install your plug-ins of choice.

3 What People Are Doing with Plug-Ins

If you asked someone what they use their spreadsheet program for, you'd probably hear a myriad things, from keeping track of their finances, to creating forms, drawing organizational charts, or even creating name tags. I doubt the boys who created Visicalc, the first popular spreadsheet program for desktop computers, ever envisioned spreadsheets would end up having the capabilities they have today. Nor did they probably envision people using spreadsheets for so many things.

The same holds true for the Web browser. When it first started out, the Web browser was little more than something that could read text embedded with hyperlinks. It was little more than a piece of software that helped those in higher education share information across networks using a variety of computer systems. Now Web browsers are almost entire home entertainment centers, offering streaming video, the ability to listen to radio stations around the world, and the option to send voice mail messages directly from Web pages. Better still, today's browsers are almost capable of doing just about everything else all those other programs stuffed in your hard drive can do, from fiddling with spreadsheet figures to reading the latest company report saved in Microsoft Word format.

Close your eyes for a minute and envision the perfect program. Imagine how this program would pretty much do it all for you. It would help you get your work done; would entertain and inform you, and help you communicate worldwide; and it would be as simple as clicking a button. I'm here to tell you you can have that perfect program. Regardless of whether you're using Internet Explorer or Netscape Navigator, you have the tools to add whatever features you want to your browser.

When I was researching this book, I went to the bookstore looking for books on plug-ins. There were plenty to choose from, and most provided enough information on how to install and use plug-ins, along with long rambling lists of the where, what, and when of plug-ins. But none showed me real-life examples of why I'd want the latest virtual reality plug-in, or what applicable uses Adobe Acrobat really has in a business setting. None showed me how different plug-ins helped people overcome problems. Most gave very terse explanations of what plug-ins did, but few showed me how they really work in the real world.

But not this book; no sir. Sure, I could take the easy route, telling you what this plug-in does, and showing you how to install that plug-in. But if you don't have a clue as to the potential of a certain plug-in, you'll probably do what I did for so long—give most plug-ins just a passing glance. In some cases that would be just the right thing to do, but not with the plug-ins I've outlined here. These are the plug-ins you should pay special attention to if you want to supercharge your browser, make your life easier, or do things you never envisioned your browser could do.

This chapter is aimed at turning on the light bulb in your head, showing you real applicable uses for a wide variety of plug-ins. I'm using real-world examples; although, as they say on TV, the names have been changed to protect the innocent and circumvent those legal hassles. And alright, I admit it; I've embellished a little with some of the examples to help you see more clearly the potential uses for many of the plug-ins today. Chapter 4 will delve deeper into specific plug-ins that help you tackle specific tasks. But for now, let's get started rocking your world.

NOTE

A lot of nay-sayers are constantly preaching that plug-ins are a dying technology and that no one uses them. When you consider that they offer building block features to your browser, you'll soon see why plug-ins are here to stay, in one form or another.

In this chapter you'll see how different people's needs can be met by a variety of plug-ins which are now available. However, to come up with a browser that offers all the features these users need would overwhelm anyone's hard drive.

Plug-in technology is probably one of the most exciting, yet most misunderstood technologies on the market today. The more you work with it, the more you realize that it has limitless possibilities.

A DAY IN THE LIFE...

...OF A DOCUMENT SPECIALIST

In the world of oil tanker escorting, training is everything. Every day escort vessels help ensure safe passage through Prince William Sound, one of the most majestic wilderness areas in all the world, and the site of America's largest oil spill. And every day the crew of these vessels must practice, practice, practice to prevent another oil spill. Every day crew members review training materials to refresh their memory on the proper use of boom, oil spill dispersants, safety, and heavy equipment.

The Problem

It doesn't take a genius to figure out that too many cooks in the kitchen make for some very funny tasting stew. And that's just the way Jane Tongen felt when the training manuals she so laboriously slaved over, were now going to be circulated electronically on her company's Intranet. The original idea was to install PageMaker, a popular desktop publishing program, on every manager's computer so each could read, then markup, the file with suggestions and changes.

> *"I don't want these guys going in there and mucking up what I've done. That's hard work getting things just so. I'm afraid if I let people fool with things, everything will get out of hand, and I'll end up with a mess I'll never get out of. I need some way to let everybody see the manuals, but not let them change them. These guys aren't computer geniuses you know, Jane said in her Minnesota accent. It's got to be easy. It would help if they could just send in their changes through e-mail so I had a paper trail and didn't have to show them how to work a new program. I'm afraid if PageMaker is installed on every-body's computer, it'll take twice as long to teach them just how to bring up the file."*

The Solution

Jane's dilemma was not unique. Thousands of corporations are now learning that yes, indeed, the twentieth century is the century in which we will all have paperless offices. And with the advent of the Web, and specifically Intranets, companies with large and small networks can take advantage of plug-in technology to distribute information electronically.

Less than a year or so ago, becoming a paperless office meant making sure everyone had the same program, even the same version of the program, installed on each computer within the company network. It also meant installing all the same fonts, so documents would look much the same from one computer to the next. This usually worked fine if the document was created in something relatively simple like Microsoft Word or Word Perfect, since such software was likely to be used on every computer. But when a department used a specialized program to create more elaborate documents, that meant spending hundreds of dollars purchasing a single program most users probably wouldn't use more than 50 percent of the time. Moreover, each user involved needed some instruction just so they could do simple things such as print, save, or view the file. And in some cases each computer would have to be upgraded just so the software was capable of running. Worse yet, if the file was stored on a network and the application was not network aware, oftentimes you'd end up with multiple copies of the same file, all with varying changes that needed to be implemented.

The solution is simple. Create a PDF file using Adobe Distiller, then place that file out on the network so anyone can view, print, or search it. Make sure everyone has a Web browser, equipped with a plug-in such as Adobe Acrobat, or create a page with an embedded link that takes the user to the location where the plug-in can be downloaded. Store the file in a public directory so everyone can have access to it, then request everyone offering additions or changes to submit them via e-mail back to the document specialist, Jane.

By using a Web browser and a plug-in that can easily be installed by any user, you accomplish several things:

- You don't have to spend any money purchasing additional software; plug-ins are usually free.
- You don't have to train users on how to use plug-ins; they're as simple to use as a Web browser.
- You don't have to worry about multiple versions of files. You place one file out there for anyone to view. The plug-in restricts them from making any changes.
- You don't have to worry about what fonts are installed since Adobe Acrobat embeds them within the file.

If you've browsed around the Internet for any length of time, you may have run across special document collaboration software that could afford Jane's managers more collaborative freedom than what the Acrobat/e-mail option offers. Why not recommend using such software and plug-in technology instead? Mainly because of the simplicity factor. By having everyone e-mail Jane with their changes, you first create a verifiable audit trail, something Jane can refer to again and again as she institutes the changes. You also make it simple for the manager. He doesn't have to worry about learning some elaborate collaboration program.

Moreover, you make it simple for the overworked computer people, who would most likely have to install some sort of specialized software or server in order for such collaborative options to work properly. In a few minutes Jane can create a Web page that embeds the file directly in it, and include a link to the location to download the plug-in. The managers download the software, run the installation program, and view the file all, hopefully, without any assistance on the part of the computing department. Jane saves the company money, the managers save time, and no one has to learn anything new. Better yet, both Mac and PC platforms can view the file since the plug-in is available in both flavors.

The Potential Plug-Ins You Could Use

Table 3.1 gives you an idea of the plug-ins Jane could use in her quest to share information with her co-workers. Although there are other plug-ins that could help Jane in her day-to-day work, these are probably the ones that she and her co-workers will find most useful.

TABLE 3.1: *The potential plug-ins you could use.*

Plug-In	Location	Pros	Cons
Adobe Acrobat	www.adobe.com	Relatively easy to use. Offers a search feature. Includes the fonts so the document looks the same on screen as it would on paper. You can add hypertext links to the file so the reader can jump to outside Web sites or pages.	Somewhat of a memory hog. If pages aren't optimized when created, users could have problems viewing them. Some features, such as printing, require you to use Acrobat's options instead of Netscape or Explorer options. Requires Adobe Distiller to create PDF files.
KeyView plug-in	www.ftp.com	Lets you view up to 200 different file formats, giving you access to just about any file created, and those files can retain their native formats.	It is a pay-for product; so if the entire network needs this capability, there will be costs involved.
LaserGo Script	www.lasergo.com	Lets you view, convert, and print postscript files on screen and on Web pages. Lets you print postscript files to non-postscript printers, and lets you fax postscript documents to any fax machine. Company offers fixed-time licensing on its products. Can also view color postscript files.	Like Key-View LaserGo, is a pay-for product that requires each workstation to purchase a copy of the plug-in. This can be costly, but you can use the fixed-time licensing if it's for a special need.

...OF AN ARCHITECT

Jeff Blume never imagined the architectural world would be so fast paced. But with the recent building boom in North Carolina, the second Silicon Valley as they call it, he is busier than ever. With the advent of the Internet, it's much easier for him to communicate with clients spread out all over the world. No more voice-mail hell. No more telephone tag. E-mail has made his life much easier—until now.

The Problem

Jeff has a problem. The office building he is helping design for a client will be like no other office building he's ever designed. Skywalks, outside elevators, atriums, and indoor fountains make this one unique. But that's not so much the problem as is the fact that his clients are thousands of miles away in California. He's been printing out his drafting plans, rolling them up in a big tube mailer, then sending them via FedEx. That's worked OK until now. It's getting expensive, is very time consuming, and oftentimes frustrating when he has to wait days for approvals of his plans, not to mention having to wrangle with the drafting plotter he uses to print out his plans. Time is of the essence, and with only a few more weeks left in the design phase, he's beginning to get behind schedule. If he had a way to transmit electronically his plans to the client, a high-tech firm capable of handling such a task, he'd be in hog heaven. But the client, advanced as he may be, doesn't have AutoCad or the other complimentary drafting programs Jeff uses to create his plans. And they aren't about to waste time installing a product they'll never use once this project is done. Plus, their time is valuable too. Up against a deadline themselves, they have no more computing gurus to spare.

The Solution

If Jeff could make his plans available via the Internet, so his client could view them, then comment on any changes, he could shave weeks off the entire approval process. And better still, he wouldn't have to waste money on FedEx packages or waste time fiddling with an already temperamental plotter. While searching for a solution one night, Jeff came across a product called *SwiftView*. Swiftview lets Jeff publish any of his drawings on the Internet through a Web page and the use of the SwiftView plug-in.

Although computer literate, Jeff is no guru himself. He was looking for something that was not only easy for his client to use, but also easy for him to use. He knew he had to prepare his drawings for viewing on the Internet, then create a Web page that would let them see it, but he didn't know how difficult the preparation part would be. With SwiftView all he had to know was how to install the program, then how to print his file.

And if SwiftView didn't work, he also could choose from a handful of other plug-ins that allowed users to see, zoom, markup, and print the drawings he created. AutoCad has their *AutoCad Whip!* Plug-in; *Dr. DWG NetView* is widely used throughout the manufacturing industry, with big name companies such as Boeing taking advantage of the features that Dr. DWG NetView offers.

By using a Web browser and a plug-in that can easily be installed by any user to view AutoCad and other related files, you accomplish several things.

- You don't have to tell the client to purchase AutoCad, just the appropriate plug-in.
- You don't have to train users on how to use plug-ins; they're as simple to use as a Web browser.
- You don't have to worry about multiple versions of files. You place one file out there for anyone to view. The users can't make changes to the files, but they can view, zoom, pan, and print them, and they can make comments.
- You don't have to waste time and money printing out big drafting documents, spending money on FedExing.
- The client has immediate access to your drawings, making turnaround time for changes almost immediate.

Jeff may also consider using a three-dimensional photographic plug-in to help the client step through the site as if he were actually there. With a simple video or still camera, Jeff can make a panoramic scene of the actual house, building, or location, then create an image his clients can experience from the comfort of their computer chair. With such a viewer, Jeff could accomplish several things.

- He could record the progress of the construction in photos.
- He could allow remote clients to view the actual project as if they were walking around the project themselves.
- He could provide small photo files with quick download times that allow his clients to zoom in and out in particular areas to get a closer look at the project.

- He could link sections of his AutoCad drawings to Web pages that offer panoramic views of the portions of the building he is creating, thereby giving perspective to the overall project. When the client wants to see what the drawing really looks like, he simply clicks that section of the drawing and is immediately shown the 3-D photograph of the area.

The Potential Plug-Ins You Could Use

Table 3.2 outlines the plug-ins most useful in Jeff's situation. The world of vector drawing and AutoCad viewing plug-ins is relatively crowded, so in Jeff's case he may decide to try out several before deciding on the exact AutoCad or drawing plug-in to use. Jeff might also benefit from trying out some of the VRML plug-ins that offer his clients the ability to see things in three dimensions. *Cosmo*, one of the plug-ins which now comes with Netscape Communicator, and is available from Silicon Graphics as a separate plug-in, is one to consider. Another to consider is *JutVision*, a plug-in that allows the viewer to experience three-dimensional photographs, moving through these photographs as if he were actually there.

TABLE 3.2: *Plug-ins that could be used in an architectural firm*

Plug-In	Location	Pros	Cons
AutoDesk Whip!	www.autodesk.com	Lets users view and share 2-D vector data, and uses the same rendering technology as release 14. You can also view GIF, JPG, and CGM files, and embed links to Web pages directly in the file. Assuming that AutoDesk maintains the plug-in technology within Whip!, you'll never need to worry about whether this product is capable of reading the latest versions of AutoCad 2-D-rendered vector graphics.	Doesn't offer as many features as some of its competitor products.
Vdraft	www.softsource.com	Available currently as a public-domain viewer. With it, you can view simple vector-formatted files, and magnify, zoom, and pan them. You can also add hyperlinks to Web pages.	The public domain version allows you to view SVF files, but you have to buy the commercial version to get the AutoCad DXF file format viewing capabilities.

Table 3.2 (continued)

Dr. DWG Netview	www.drdwg.com	Lets you view release 12 and 13 drawings quickly, and add hyperlinks within the file itself. The user can zoom, pan, show layers of the drawing, change viewpoints, measure distance, and print from within the browser.	Like most of the Auto-Cad viewers, this is a pay-for plug-in. Before purchasing the plug-in, the user should try similar plug-ins to see if all features match his needs.
Apple's QuickTime VR	http://quicktime.apple.com	Lets you view real panoramic three-dimensional photos, moving around up to 36 degrees and zooming in on anything seen in the picture	Requires time to develop the panoramic pictures, and the developer software can be somewhat costly.

...OF A TROPICAL GUESTHOUSE

Eden House, located in Florida's beautiful Key West is a paradise like no other. Offering as much Hemingway-esque charm as you can stomach, it's a tropical hideaway that will help you lose yourself in the warmth of the tropics. It's the location where Goldie Hawn filmed her movie *Criss Cross*, and an excellent place to just relax and unwind.

The Problem

The only problem is letting potential guests experience how relaxing the Eden House can be and how beautifully appointed all the rooms and common areas are. Most people like to get a feel for the accommodations before they plunk down their cash. And for those who have never visited Eden House, let alone Key West, it's hard to describe in words and simple pictures exactly what they are missing. Having a way to tour the place virtually in a three-dimensional way is really the only way you can get a feel for all that Eden House has to offer, save from just going there in person.

You could shoot movies, turn them into QuickTime videos, and place them on the site; but a QuickTime movie takes up a great deal of space, and simply doesn't give you the true feeling you are really there. If there were some way to give the visitor this feeling that would be the ticket. And more specifically, if it were easy for the visitor to do, something that didn't take a lot of computer knowledge to complete, that would be the perfect solution.

The Solution

The solution is quite simple. Just create 360-degree movies which anyone can experience online through the use of a plug-in or ActiveX control. Let them spin around the room, explore nooks and crannies, and get a feeling of really being there. With a plug-in/ActiveX control called *Surround Video*, that can easily be done.

I've never been there, but I've experienced the pool, the lobby, their spacious, delightfully appointed rooms, and the relaxing hammock area. After having visited their Web page, I actually feel like I've been there. The Eden House uses a plug-in called Surround Video, which lets you move around in a picture some 360 degrees. I can virtually stand in a room, and get a feel for the place without getting out of my jammies.

You'll find more and more Web sites popping up with the ability to show you their worlds from a three-dimensional perspective. Anyone with a camera, some video editing software, and a little time on their hands can create interactive, panoramic movies that show others their worlds through a Web browser enabled with a photographic virtual reality viewer such as Surround Video or QuickTimeVR. Just last week my friend, Bobby, created a QuickTimeVR movie of his newly built cabin in the Alaskan wilderness, embedded a link to it on his Web page, then let everyone know it was available. With a click of a button, I was there, cruising through the kitchen, looking closely at the fireplace and out the window. And since I had the QuickTimeVR plug-in installed, I was flying through his cabin in one frame of his Web page while chatting with him in real time about what I was seeing in another frame.

With a photographic virtual reality plug-in or ActiveX control viewer, you can accomplish several things on your Web site:

- Let people see for themselves what you have to offer
- Use it as a training aid to help people understand where things are located
- Offer more detailed information than your competitor does, something that entertains and draws people back to your site
- Lets you create hotspots in the picture so the viewer can go directly to a Web page
- Some plug-ins also provide support for sound as well as a 3-D picture

Eden House has made it simple, for anyone who knows enough, to click a link on a Web page to install the plug-in. They've made it even easier by offering an ActiveX control as well. With ActiveX the visitor simply clicks the link and that's it. No need to download a thing. In a few minutes the page loads, complete with 360-degree virtual reality capabilities. Eden House could have chosen another plug-in or ActiveX control to use, but Surround Video works just fine since it's a relatively small plug-in and ActiveX control. It really doesn't matter which one they use, although it's more likely people will have already installed QuickTimeVR capabilities. The point is they've made it accessible, easy to download, and have provided plenty of instructions and examples to create a buzz about their site. I definitely will recommend it to my friends. And I'm certainly more inclined to consider Eden House as a vacation destination since, well, I feel like I've already been there and am familiar with the place.

Although you can't really experience the 3-D-ness of the page, Figure 3.1 is an example of how Eden House invites you into its lobby, where you can quickly and easily view the entire lobby as if you were standing in the middle of it. Other rooms for your three-dimensional viewing pleasure are also available, regardless of whether you are using a plug-in or an ActiveX control.

TIP

When developing a page with any type of plug-in, consider whether the plug-in is available on the platforms your users have. For example, not all plug-ins are available on the Mac.

The Potential Plug-Ins You Could Use

Table 3.3 gives you an idea of what plug-ins you could use if you wanted to give the visitors to your Web site an idea of exactly what your place looks like. There are several three-dimensional viewers that let you experience firsthand how things look. Since almost all of them require pay-for creation tools, there really aren't too many differences between the various plug-ins. You should simply experiment to find the one you like best. Apple's *QuickTimeVR* format is the most widely used at the moment, but on the Internet anything can change quickly. Watch for QuickTimeVR to become a standard part of the QuickTime plug-in and part of the popular browsers.

But don't count out the others. Watch for the *BubbleViewer* to pick up speed since it's partnering with Kodak, and because you can have an IPIX photographer develop and create the film for you. The *JutVision Java viewer* may also take a lead in the near future, because it is now offering a Java version of its 3-D viewer; and since Java is installed in almost all major browsers, the JutVision viewer may become very pop-

FIGURE
3.1

ular. Figure 3.2 shows what the IPIX Bubbleviwer offers. In this example you're sitting in the latest car model from Honda, cruising down the
road and listening to music. The little bull's-eyes depict hotspots, or
places you can click to get more information about something you see
in the picture. These hotspots will take you to specific Web pages or
other photos.

TABLE 3.3: *Some three-dimensional plug-ins*

Plug-In	Location	Description
Apple QuickTimeVR	http://quicktime.apple.com	Lets you create QuickTime VR files.
BubbleViewer by IPIX	www.ipix.com	Lets you view 360-degree environments, offering very good quality 3-D photographs. There are lots of excellent examples of how this type of plug-in could be used. This site also offers the SmartUpdate feature to take you directly to the plug-in, if you don't have it already installed.

Table 3.3 (continued)

JutVision by Visdyn Software	www.visdyn.com	Lets you view 3-D photo-realistic files within your browser. You can look up and down, pan and zoom. The new version only requires Java, although you may experience some problems with the Java version if you don't have enough RAM memory in your computer.
Black Diamond's Surround Video	www.bdiamond.com	Lets you create hotspots that link to Web pages. It also offers sound capabilities and can link to Javascript and Vbscript files. It's an amazing product with great clarity, and even provides clean printed images of the 3-D files as well. Some of the demos are simply amazing.

Figure *The IPIX Bubbleviewer is a site to see.*
3.2

...OF A NETWORK ADMINISTRATOR

Ten different servers and hundreds of users. That's what Linda Sullivan has control of. There's the Lotus Notes server, the FTP server, and the five Web servers in her company. She's constantly running around fixing user problems, installing software, and reconfiguring servers. It's a daunting task. And with the servers located all over the place due to wiring problems, Linda never seems to be in one place for any length of time, thus she never seems to find the time to work on long-range projects like user training, network reconfiguration, or lunch.

The Problem

If they could clone Linda and not have to pay the clone a salary, everything would be just fine. But for Linda her biggest problem is distance. Offices are spread out all over the place. Because of the leasing arrangements, that problem isn't going away anytime soon. And with servers stuffed in telephone closets here and there, just going up and down, back and forth is time consuming. In addition, with the latest hiring explosion she has problems accommodating all the users. Those that budgeted for computers get them, but those that didn't have to settle for the leftovers, and thus many of the users are left out when it comes to running some of the necessary software.

Linda needs more than just a clone of herself; she needs the right set of plug-ins. And there are plenty of plug-ins that could take the load off Linda, freeing up time for loftier pursuits. First, Linda needs to find a way to install software quickly across her network, and to make it easy for her clients to install software themselves.

Next she needs to find some way to offer those users who are utilizing older technology the ability to run advanced applications. It would also be nice if she could cut down on costs by not having to install all the applications on all the machines. Since some people only use certain applications like Excel or Lotus Notes occasionally, if she could just install what's absolutely necessary on all machines, then offer additional programs remotely, she could save the company a ton of money. Plus, by allowing certain traveling users to download applications as they need them, she would free up a lot of time by not having to configure laptop after laptop.

Moreover, with the recent merger she has a conglomeration of loyal Netscape and Internet Explorer users. That makes it even more difficult in terms of deploying solutions across the network, and training users to do particular tasks. If she could provide users with access to products, and could quickly train them, she would be the hero of the day.

The Solution

Linda simply needs the right plug-ins, and she needs the time to set up the associated servers that many of these plug-ins work from. Let's summarize what Linda actually needs.

- A plug-in that automatically installs software when a user clicks the link to it
- A plug-in that lets any user use any application that Linda may place on the network server
- A plug-in that lets Netscape users use ActiveX controls
- A plug-in that helps manage all the plug-ins she might install
- A plug-in that helps her provide on-screen support and training
- A plug-in that lets her control another user's computer remotely
- A plug-in that lets users see her schedule so they know if she is in or out of the office
- A plug-in that lets her chat with users who might be traveling or in remote offices
- A plug-in that offers the ability to view any type of data file on the network

No doubt Linda needs a lot of plug-ins and could really benefit from installing a few. First let's take a look at her remote sharing, remote control, and remote application needs. If Linda installed either *Look@Me* or *CarbonCopy*, two of several remote control plug-in applications on each user's system, anytime a user had a problem, all she would have to do is log in to their computer from her computer using one of the plug-ins, and then she would have full control. Without leaving her office, she could watch what the user was doing, text chat in real time, and even take control of the user's machine to show him exactly how things are done. She could also remotely install, change, or reconfigure a user's system without having to be at the user's workstation. Anywhere there was a network connection and a Web browser with the proper plug-in installed, she would have access to any machine across the network, provided that she installed the software on all machines on her network.

Her next mission would be to offer access to a wide variety of programs that not all users may have access to. This is actually a twofold need. There are those workstations that may have the capability of running particular applications but, because of a cost-saving need, simply don't need the software installed full-time. And then there are those users who have the need, but may not have the horsepower to run various applications on a casual basis. First, she needs a plug-in like *Epicon's ALTiS* or *Net-Install's* plug-in which allows users on a network to run applications stored on a remote server. Instead of having to install expensive applications for one-time or even casual use, these plug-ins let users remotely install applications over the network without having to know of anything more than how to point and click. As long as the computer is capable and has enough RAM, hard disk space, and processing power, the user can quickly and easily install and run whatever application the network administrator provides on the server. With plug-ins like *Net-Install* and *Net-Zip*, users could gain quick access to programs stored remotely on another server, and could quickly add them when needed without any knowledge of how to install software programs.

TIP

If you develop a lot of in-house software, you need to look into NobleNet's line of Web-based software distribution tools. With NobleNet you can quickly and easily distribute applications across a network. And when you decide to update or upgrade that application and want everyone on the Network to use the latest version, you can do that easily with NobleNet's line of Web distribution tools. These plug-in and server tools let you distribute applications to users through a browser, and have those applications decompress, then install securely and automatically on the user's machine. You'll find NobleNet at http://www.noblenet.com.

But in the case of many users who use old technology, they need to run the application, but simply may not have the necessary processing power. In that case, *Cytrix's WinFrame* or *Epicon's ALTiS* could do the trick. The user could view, work with, and print from an application that is stored and run off a remote server. In the case of WinFrame, the way it works is relatively simple. The application is summoned and loaded on the remote server. The user uses a Web browser to view the screen of the running application, using his mouse and keyboard to provide input to the application. The application, however, needs only the processing power of the server, sending the results to the user with the WinFrame-enabled Web browser. Therefore high-powered applications can be run on low-powered computers with just a Web browser. And you don't have to go around to each workstation and install all the applications a company uses, if half of them are not needed. Instead all the applications would be available to anyone, and no computing support would be needed to install them.

Finally, Linda needs a whole bunch of plug-ins installed both on her computer and on the rest of the network computers to help her and others keep track of things, read files created in virtually every type of program, run ActiveX controls with Netscape Navigator, and help train users.

If half of her installed base wants to use Internet Explorer and utilize many of the ActiveX controls available, yet the other half wants to stick with Netscape Navigator, she doesn't have to force any of the users to use one product over the other. Instead, she can install Ncompass Lab's

ScriptActive plug-in, so that Netscape Navigator users can use ActiveX controls should they be programmed within Web sites.

And with a little help from MacroMedia's *ShockWave* and several PowerPoint viewer plug-ins, Linda can create amazing online presentations and training materials that she can use not only in a stand-up seminar presentation format, but also on the Web by simply dropping her presentation files on the server.

TABLE 3.4: *The potential plug-ins you could use.*

Plugin	Location	Pros	Cons
Ncompass's ScriptActive	www.ncompasslabs.com	Lets Netscape users run ActiveX controls as if the browser had that capability built in.	Not all ActiveX controls work 100%, and the software does require a decent amount of memory, at least 32MB to work without major problems. If Netscape were smart, they would license the technology and this would be part of all Navigator browsers.
WinFrame	www.cytrix.com	Lets a user run an application on a remote server without having to have the horsepower or application installed. This opens up all sorts of possibilities for actually creating virtual workstations that only have the browser and plug-in installed, with the application and data files stored remotely.	Somewhat slow if you are using it over the the Internet to connect to a remote server. It also requires a server with a hefty chunk of RAM memory allocated for each remote machine to use. The company is owned in part by Microsoft, and you just never know what Microsoft will decide to do with the product.
InstallFromTheWeb	www.installsheild.com	Lets you install software directly from Web pages. You can create the software packages that are then automatically decompressed and installed once a link is clicked.	Some applications may not install without a little intervention from an actual human being. Temporary installation files may also be left on the user's hard drive once the software has been installed, causing the user to loose valuable hard disk space.

Table 3.4 (continued)

Plugsy	www.digigami.com	Lets you resolve conflicts between plug-ins, and helps you assign specific MIME types to a variety of data files you might encounter. Excellent if you have a lot of plug-ins and want to quickly pick and choose which one is used for a specific data type or which one should be used in a one-time situation. You can also quickly disable a plug-in without having to drag the DLL file out of the plug-ins folder manually.	A lot of what this plug-in offers could be done manually, although such reconfigurations can be time consuming.
ALTiS	www.epicon.com	With ALTiS you can quickly and easily deploy applications over the Internet or your Intranet by creating ALTiS-enabled files that allow the user to click any link and begin executing an application almost immediately.	Can be slow over a slow dial-up line and does require additional knowledge to set up the server applications.

...OF A VIDEO COMPANY

Biff Horton and his brother-in-law, Bob Gould, are wheeling, dealing entrepreneurs. Their last venture had them selling videos of Alaskan wildlife scenes to shoppers on the QVC channel. But even the QVC world is not enough. They want to market their videos to the world, letting everyone know how their photographers, story lines, scenes, and production set their videos apart from the rest of the market. But they don't know if the Internet will do their videos justice. Plus, they aren't too certain about the buying habits of online users. They want to set up a Web site that will showcase their videos properly, yet they want the site to be easy enough for the potential consumer to use, without having to have a lot of hardware or software capabilities.

The Problem

They want to let people see the superior quality of their videos, and have the potential buyers call them directly to place orders for videos via a Web form, a fax form, or the telephone. And, since they aren't computer geniuses by any stretch of the imagination, they want to be able to set up a Web site with minimal programming efforts. They also want to offer users not only immediate access to ordering videos, but all the options available, so regardless of the potential buyer's technology, he can easily order their video products. They have little knowledge of technology and have only recently set up a Web page, so whatever they decide to add to their site, it needs to be relatively simple to add and not too taxing on them or their server.

Another problem is that while Biff is in Seattle, Bob is hobnobbing around London, working on more schemes to make more money not only with video but also with all sorts of Alaskan-type trinkets and candies. They are constantly talking on the phone or faxing each other the latest plan or the latest contract with their vendors, or exchanging the latest pictures of their kids. They need some way to send information over the Internet, communicate with each other without spending thousands of dollars on overseas calls, and still be able to view faxes as if they were actually faxed to a fax machine.

The Solution

First these video jockeys need to encode some of the video clips of their best videos into *RealPlayer* format, or into some other streaming video format. By placing video clips on their site, the potential buyer can try before he buys. They could select from a variety of different streaming video plug-in technology, but they'll find that more people have the RealPlayer capabilities than any other streaming video plug-in. And since the RealPlayer is available for virtually every platform, they should be able to offer video demos to just about anyone.

In addition, they don't have to worry about buying, installing, and maintaining a RealServer. Because of the way in which RealPlayer can stream files over the standard HTTP or Web server protocol, there is no need for a special video server. Better still, *RealVideo* encoders, such as *RealPublisher*, can compress the video to very small files. An hour-long video file can be compressed to as small as 6.6 Megabytes or less, depending upon the compression technology used. Since they are only going to be providing a few clips of less than ten minutes in length, their clips will be less than a megabyte of space.

TIP

They may also consider using a non-plug-in, plug-in-type technology called Emblaze! Emblaze! which lets you put high-quality images, such as photos, on your Web page, but does so by compressing the files first. A JPEG photo that might have taken 300K and minutes to view with a 28.8 modem and a slow Internet connection can be reduced to under 50K and less than a few seconds to view. If you are placing large numbers of photos on your site, you should consider checking out Emblaze!, located at www.emblaze.com. They also offer streaming video and audio options that are pretty astounding when you consider that you don't even need a plug-in to view the video files.

With a streaming video plug-in, you can accomplish several things within a standard Web site:

- Offer clips of videos so people can see what they are purchasing
- Include sound with each video so they can hear what each video offers
- Offer the ability to save the clips or sound so they can be e-mailed across a network
- Offer links within the video to other Web sites
- Synchronize video and audio with Web pages

By hooking up a VCR to a video capture card or to a multimedia-enabled PC or Macintosh, Bob and Biff can select the frames or clips they want to encode into RealPlayer format. Then with either the help of some free RealPlayer publishing tools, or the RealPublisher commercial encoder itself, they can create simple clips that show off the wonderful photography and excellent narration that their videos offer. Instead of potential customers wondering if the video really offers some spectacular shots, they can see it for themselves, as if they were watching the actual video. Since the RealPlayer files don't require a specialized server or huge amounts of space for the files they encode, they can still use their current service provider to browse the Internet and get their e-mail.

Better still for the user, the file is streamed instead of downloaded to his computer. Thus the user can quickly gauge whether the file is something he wants to view, without having to waste hours waiting to see exactly what the file has to offer. And since no data is stored permanently on the user's computer, he doesn't have to worry about having large amounts of video files occupying his hard drive.

They also want to offer quick and easy access for ordering over the Internet. If they used a variety of products that linked customers to their phone ordering and fax system, they could quickly fill orders. With *PhoneFree*, a technology that connects browsers to phone systems, and the *PaperPort Viewer*, they can communicate with their customers and each other without ever picking up a phone to make an overseas call. PhoneFree allows a Web site to link to the phone system or to Internet telephones, so when a person clicks a link on a Web page, he is automatically connected to a live person on the other end of a phone or Internet telephone program. This allows the customer to order right away, with the click of a button, and also to speak directly to someone taking their order. No longer does the consumer have to disconnect from the Internet, then pick up a phone to make a call to their company or place an order. Bob and Biff can also use *CyberCash* wallet to verify the consumer's credit card information input on a Web form instantly.

And with Bob's PaperPort, and with Biff having the appropriate plug-in installed, when Bob needs to fax something to Biff, he simply pops it in his PaperPort scanner, which then scans the document into the computer. Bob uploads his file automatically to the Internet and then e-mails Biff regarding the location of the file. He could even e-mail the file to Biff, and as long as the plug-in is installed in his browser, Biff could click a link and instantly see the fax. He could then print it out, save it, or in certain cases, change it, then send it back to Bob. Both Biff and Bob can also use the PhoneFree option to call each other over the Internet, and speak in real time. While connected, they could also transfer files, simultaneously view Web pages, or text chat with each other. Thousands of dollars could be saved with a few plug-ins, a little time, and some patience.

TABLE 3.5: *The potential plug-ins you could use.*

Plug-In	Location	Pros	Cons
RealPlayer	http://www.real.com	It's the most widely used video and audio player on the Internet and offers superior sound and amazing compression options without having to have a specialized server to serve the files.	Video still only offers from 3 to 10 frames per second, not exactly TV quality, but getting there. If the viewer has a slow-speed modem, however, he may not be able to see the video but he could possibly hear the audio. For RealPlayer to work, the user must have a relatively fast computer, like a Pentium, and must have a fast connection.
Vivo	http://www.vivo.com	Like the RealPlayer, Vivo offers streaming audio, but does so with the plug-in embedded directly in the browser. With the RealPlayer, the separate helper application is most commonly used. Vivo offers some incredible sound and streaming quality.	Not as popular on the Internet as the RealPlayer, and the video quality is somewhat poorer than the RealPlayer. In addition, compression and encoding tools are more expensive than the RealPlayer's.

Table 3.5 (continued)

Com One plug-in	http://www.com1.fr	Several videos can be displayed on a single page. This offers the ability to have them playing all at one time if the user so decides.	This product has a strong following in France, but is not as prevalent in the U.S.
PhoneFree	http://www.phonefree.com	Lets the user connect directly to a live operator with the click of a button. From there, the user can place an order without having to disconnect from his Internet connection.	The user has to install the plug-in and he must have a multimedia-enabled computer with a microphone plugged in. Most end users are still not multimedia aware, or may not have all the hardware necessary for this option to work properly.
Cybercash Wallet	http://www.cybercash.com	Now you can use your major credit card over the Internet without having to worry about security. Credit card information is verified in seconds.	People are still reluctant to pass along information, especially credit card information, over the Internet even if it's using a secure transaction.
PaperPort Viewer	http://www.visioneer.com	Lets you scan, then send or upload fax or scan documents online.	Must have sufficient hard disk space to accommodate files and some files can be slow to load.

...OF A BUSY EXECUTIVE & HIS SECRETARY

Larry Makinson is criss-crossing the country, spouting out the latest political campaign finance data he has uncovered to the press, politicians, and the people. He's in such hot demand that his secretary is caught in a kind of scheduling nightmare, constantly updating, changing, and rearranging his calendar. Keeping him in synch and keeping her in synch with his travels and commitments, plus keeping up with him, is a constant battle. Oftentimes she needs his signature on paperwork, but he's off in some faraway time zone talking about how politicians are bought and sold with big corporate bucks. They need to communicate with each other more effectively. And she needs a way for him to be in the office, if only virtually.

The Problem

Larry carries a laptop and a personal digital assistant, so he can always be reached by e-mail. But if he had a better way to manage his time, his calendar, and even his personal finances while he travels, he would have half the battle won. He needs some way to share his calendar with his secretary, updating her as he adds and changes his schedule. And he needs some way to share with the rest of the world the speeches he gives on campaign finance reform. And finally, he needs help keeping track of the time zone he's in and the money he has spent on all his travels, as well as his own investments that seem to need constant monitoring.

The Solution

To make everyone's life easier, he should put everything on the Web, including his investment information, calendar, presentations, and signature. Yes, that's right, his signature. Plug-ins like *WebPublisher* from NowSoftware allow him to upload his ever-changing calendar to the Web. His assistant can then view his schedule and let those who want to meet with Larry know when there's an opening. With plug-ins like *PenOp*, Larry can also securely put his signature on digital documents. With Microsoft *Investor*, an ActiveX-enabled Web site, he can interface his Quicken data with this Web site, and quickly upload and have access to his financial information regardless of whether he's at home or a million miles away.

With the PenOp plug-in, he can scan in his signature, create a digital certificate to assure those who install the PenOp plug-in viewer that his digital signature is authentic, and use it to sign legal documents. By signing legal documents electronically, he saves time and money by not having to FedEx documents back and forth between his office, his clients, and wherever he might be at the time.

TABLE 3.6: *The potential plug-ins you could use.*

Plugin	Location	Pros	Cons
Web Publisher	www.nowsoftware.com	Interfaces with personal digital assistants so you can upload your calendar to your laptop, then to the Web.	Really none, except that you have to keep updating the calendar in order for those who share your calendar to know exactly what your schedule is.
Microsoft Investor	www.investor.com	Will keep track of your investments, your taxable income, and more.	Requires an ActiveX-enabled browser. You should be aware of security. Make sure you password protect whatever information you keep, and don't keep important information such as social security numbers online.

Table 3.6 (continued)

Point Plus	www.net-scene.com	Allows you to view Power-Point presentations complete with Real Audio and Video embedded in the files. This lets anyone see and hear what you've presented without having to be at the seminar, trade-show, or wherever you've presented the information.	Requires a fair amount of RAM memory to display and play presentations with audio and video embedded in them. Also requires the user download the RealPlayer plug-in. Also some color schemes may not translate from Power-Point presentation to the Web.
EarthTime	www.starfish.com	Shows you time zones, currency, and more information about the particular part of the world you are visiting or living in.	The software plug-in is now bundled with a complete set of personal information management software, which actually is worth the price, even though the plug-in offers something that a relatively complete day-timer offers.
PenOp	www.penop.com	Lets you digitally record your signature, and creates a secure digital certificate so that your signature cannot be copied or used without your authorization.	The technology is a little confusing at first. The potential of theft is always around, although the security is relatively high. Really no worse than sending your signature through a fax machine.

...OF A TRAVELING SALESMAN

Don Diggins is a traveling concrete salesman who understands the importance of technology. He carries so many gadgets with him when he travels that it takes an hour and a half for him to clear security. From voice recorders to CD players, from personal digital assistants to tiny VCRs that help him while away the monotony of travel, he's the poster boy for Sharper Images. He loves to stay in touch with what's going on back in his hometown of Anchorage while he travels. Plus, he wants to leave a lasting impression with his customers after giving them his sales presentations. When a sale does come through, he wants instant access to his company's online PC-based ordering system, a somewhat antiquated system that has been tied into his company's Intranet. And he wants to let his secretary and clients leave detailed voicemail messages without having to call long distance.

The Problem

Don needs to cut down on the amount of hardware he lugs with him, yet he needs to still be able to stay in touch with his home office and entertain himself while he travels. He needs easy access to all sorts of data and applications stored on his firm's computers. He needs to be able to read reports quickly, and get in contact with his home office without spending a bundle on calling cards.

The Solution

If he could replace all the electronic gadgets he carries with a laptop and a few handy plug-ins his life would be so much simpler and so would the airport security guards'. First, he should save all his presentations on the Web so others can view them, and they can be available for him regardless of where he might be. With the *Digital Voice* plug-in, people can leave him voicemail messages without ever having to pick up a phone. They simply record their message using the Digital Voice plug-in, and Don can pick up the messages using his laptop and Web browser.

Speaking of listening, with the *RealAudio* Tuner, he can listen to his favorite hockey games even if he's on the road. While he's listening if his home office leaves the server computer running he can access his inventory system, his proposal-based creation system, or use it to remotely run any Windows-based application he might have forgotten to load on his laptop.

If clients provide him with electronic specs in Word format, he can use the *Word Viewer* plug-in to view these files without having to have Word installed. And the *PhoneFree* plug-in helps him save on costs, because he can use the Internet, rather than the telephone to call his home office.

Table 3.7: *The potential plug-ins you could use.*

Plug-In	Location	Pros	Cons
RealAudio Tuner	www.davecentral.com	Offers over 150 different preprogrammable radio stations in an easy to use interface.	Requires the RealAudio player, so it really isn't a stand-alone plug-in.
PowerPoint Viewer	www.logicpulse.com	Lets you view PowerPoint presentations that also offer RealAudio-enabled audio options so you can hear as well as see the presentation.	Excellent plug-in, but requires their maker application in order for you to transform the PowerPoint presentation into an Internet-ready application.

Table 3.7 (continued)

PhoneFree	www.phonefree.com	Lets you call people over the Internet using Internet telephony. You can create links within Web pages to automatically access those people whom you call most frequently.	Sound quality isn't always that great especially during peak hours of the Internet. Requires a sound card and decent microphone, plus some patience in getting the sound just right.
Word Viewer	www.microsoft.com	Lets you view Word documents without having to have Word installed.	Although it does let you print, view, and search documents, it doesn't offer editing capabilities.
WinFrame or ALTiS	www.cytrix.com or www.epicon.com	Lets the remote user run real Windows applications through a Web browser.	May be very very slow over a dialup network.
Digital Voice	www.digital.com	Lets you leave voicemail messages from a Web page.	Doesn't work with newer versions of Netscape and Internet Explorer browsers. It's a free plug-in that's in constant development, so support can be hit or miss. Don't count on the author to update or add features quickly.

...OF A SMALL BUSINESS WOMAN

Nancy Littlepage is a small businesswoman with a mission. She's just starting out as a consultant to hospital gift shops, providing them with valuable information on how to merchandise their products, recruit volunteers, design displays, create easy to make handmade crafts, and increase profits. She started her career by boosting the sales of several small hospital gift shops. Now she wants to spread her message to gift shops everywhere that you can make tens, and sometimes hundreds, of thousands of dollars in profits that can then be turned over to the hospitals to buy much needed medical equipment.

The Problem

Being a sole proprietor, Nancy only has so much time. She's chief cook and bottle washer, not to mention purchasing agent, receptionist, marketing manager, editor, publisher, designer, idea person, and janitor. She needs quick and cheap ways to get her message out, and to run her business. Anything that could help her save time is worth the price.

She works with a lot of different gift shops across the country, commenting and making recommendations on how policy and procedure manuals can be updated and streamlined. What's she's found in working with all sorts of clients is that just about every word processor imaginable is used, and reading files from other computers can sometimes be a nightmare. In addition, although most gift stores use some form of spreadsheet to balance their books, she would like to give her customers a quick and easy way to see how she recommends tracking inventory, reconciling bank statements, and keeping track of sales. Not all of her customers use Excel as she does, so having some way for her customers to see her spreadsheet creations is a must-have feature.

She also has a limited amount of time for reading the volumes and volumes of e-mail she gets every day. If she had a way to have that e-mail scanned and read for her, it could save her a great deal of time. It would also be great if she could have a personal shopper to shop for the best online values. She even would love to have an electronic travel agent to seek out the best travel deals so she wouldn't have to go shopping for travel specials herself. Plus, like all small business people, she needs a quick and easy way to put her PowerPoint presentations online so other people can see them. Finally, because she is no computer wizard, if she had something that helped her locate the files she has scattered about on her hard drive, she could save a lot of time.

The Solution

While she travels around she needs to quickly and easily be able to read the memos, documents, and spreadsheets the gift shops give her in order for her to analyze their sales and procedures. The *KeyView Plus* and *Formula One Spreadsheet* viewer plug-ins can help her do just that. With the help of her trusted KeyView plug-in, Nancy can read any file. It reads hundreds of different document formats, so she can easily and quickly view various hospital gift shop records and information online without having to have the application that created the file. This saves her a tremendous amount of time, and she doesn't have to be a computer expert or learn how to convert files to the Microsoft Word format she is so familiar with. In addition, the gift shops don't have to jump through hoops to cater to her just so she can see their digital documents. And in the competitive world of hospital gift shops, this is what helps Nancy stand out from the crowd.

With all the information she needs to keep current about, including the latest trends with Beanie Babies, baby bows, teddy bears, and chocolate cigars, Nancy is swamped just trying to keep up with the latest trends which seem to pop up on the Internet almost daily. With the help of the *ReadToMe* plug-in, she can actually work on other documents as the plug-in reads her the Web pages she uses to keep up on gift trends. This saves her time, as she can have the computer read a page to her while she prepares a baby bow or overheads for her next gift shop seminar.

And when she wants to find out the best values on the Internet, not only for gift shop supplies but also for travel, groceries, computers, and everything else she needs to buy for her family, she simply puts *RoboShopper* to work. RoboShopper will go out and scan Web sites, then bring back the information to her electronically in the form of a Web page. She no longer has to scout out the best buys, just as the traveling executive put *IntelliTrip* to use when he wanted to scout out the very best airline deals.

When Nancy wants to gather information from her clients, instead of faxing or mailing out questionnaires or spreadsheets with information about what's currently selling well in gift shops, she creates a Web page form using her spreadsheet program. She then uploads the form to a Web site. With the help of the *Formula One/Net plug-in*, her clients can then enter information interactively into the spreadsheet file. Nancy doesn't have to know a thing about making Web page forms. All she has to do is put in the <EMBED> command in her Web page, then point it to the spreadsheet she's uploaded, and with the help of the FormulaOne/Net plug-in, her clients can easily and painlessly interact with the data she's presented.

Finally, with all those files floating around on her computer, she needs a little help just finding them. But since she lives her life on the Internet, she would like to be able to use a Web browser to search her hard drive for the files she needs. With *Data Detective* she can not only search for the important files using keywords, but she can also use her Web browser to open, find, and save files any place she likes. Data Detective makes it easy for her, since she sometimes loses files because of her scattered filing system. With a single interface, she can use her computer like an expert.

Table 3.8: *The potential plug-ins you could use.*

Plug-In	Location	Pros	Cons
ReadToMe	http://www.davecentral. com/2021.html	Will read Web pages to you provided you have a sound card and speakers. Works well if you are sight impaired or don't like reading long Web pages.	The voice can be a little difficult to understand, and not all Web pages were made to be read. With the exception of news-related sites, many Web pages may not sound as if they are making sense when read to you.
KeyView Plus	http://www.verity.com	Can display hundreds of files saved in different file formats from spreadsheets to word processing documents. Doesn't require you to own the program that created the file in order to see it.	The plug-in is relatively large and requires a fair bit of memory to operate well. You also need to check the Web site periodically for new features and updates to the product as new software file formats become more and more popular.
Formula One Spreadsheet viewer	http://www.visualcomp. com	Allows you to view spreadsheet information and use spreadsheets as interactive forms.	Requires a fair amount of RAM memory in order to view larger spreadsheets. Requires an understanding of how to create security options in spreadsheets in order to produce customized forms. Also, problems with Excel spreadsheet calculation bugs, anyone offering interactive live calculation spread sheets should examine their results before putting them on the Web. Some calculation bugs in Excel cause inaccurate results.
Data Detective	http://www.appletsite. com	Lets you search and find files easily and quickly, regardless of whether you are looking for them by name, date, content, or just about anything else. Better yet, you can find them directly in a Web browser.	Takes a fair amount of space on your hard drive and uses a fair bit of RAM memory, so your machine must be relatively hefty in order to use this plug-in without crashing your browser.
RoboShopper	www.roboshopper.com	Lets you create a profile that will go out on the Internet and find the items you want for the best prices.	Can't always do the shopping for you if you don't know what you want. Can also take some time setting up and may not check all the sites you are familiar with.

BUILDING THE PERFECT BROWSER

Now that you've seen how different people are using different plug-ins to accomplish a wide variety of things, it's time to mentally construct your own perfect browser. As you've seen, the perfect browser is a combination of different plug-ins that accomplishes different tasks for different people. And that's the beauty of Netscape Navigator and plug-ins. Your computer doesn't have to be overloaded with superfluous plug-ins. And when you need something, you don't have to buy a whole new program; you simply install the plug-in that meets your needs. My perfect browser looks something like this:

Adobe Acrobat—I need this for reading licensing agreements and manuals, and for viewing illustrations for books that I write. I would say on average I use this plug-in at least four times a month on documents that clients and editors send me or place on Web pages. And I frequently run across the need for this plug-in when I'm trying out new software, since most computer software manuals are becoming less and less available on paper and more and more available digitally.

QuickTime and the QuickTimeVR Player—Although the recent versions of the browsers I use now come with QuickTime, I need this plug-in for my laptop that has an older version of Navigator. My friend, Bobby, is constantly taking videos of the progress of his cabin as it's being built, and putting them up on a Web page for all his friends and family to see. And more recently I've been using this plug-in to view training videos on software products and technical concepts. When I can make it to a computer trade show, I often find that the presentations are available on QuickTime format. With the QuickTimeVR plug-in, I can explore places I've never been, like inside the cockpit of a fighter or the Sahara desert. This is strictly for entertainment value, but I also find that I learn more about worlds I may never visit by using this three-dimensional viewer than if I simply looked at static one-dimensional Web pages. On average, I run across pages that require this plug-in at least twice a week.

RealPlayer—Every day I tune in to listen to my favorite radio talk show personality. But I don't have to fix my schedule around the airing of her show. Nor do I need to be within a certain distance in order to hear her broadcast. Instead, I use the RealPlayer plug-in (and helper application) to listen to archives of her shows wherever and whenever I want. When the radio station that carried her locally moved her to the afternoon, when I'm the most busy with work, I didn't despair. I simply tuned her in when it was convenient for me. Sites such as AudioNet

(*www.audionet.com*) and TimeCast (*www.timecast.com*) also have links
to special live and recorded broadcasts of TV programs, rock concerts,
speeches, and even books on tape. I haven't purchased a music CD in
over a year. I get most of my music off the Internet. And I don't gripe
any more about the lack of decent music stations up here in Alaska.
Instead, with the RealPlayer, there is a world of radio stations just waiting for me to tune in.

KeyView—I deal with all sorts of clients who do all sorts of things
with their computers. It's amazing how many different software programs
they use. From AutoCad to WinZip and everything in between, if it's a
computer software program, most likely my clients have it. But that causes problems for me. I can't possibly afford to purchase and install all the
programs my clients may have. But I do have to have the ability to use
their data when they send it to me. And I have to be able to sometimes
view and manipulate information within that same data. With KeyView
it doesn't matter what word processor, spreadsheet, drawing program, or
database I have installed on my computer. Almost any file a user might
throw my way, I can easily read, view, print, and sometimes manipulate
without having to have the application that created that file installed on
my computer. No longer do clients have to convert documents into formats my computer programs can understand. And with some of the
more advanced features of KeyView I can save and convert the files
myself into formats I can use to edit the documents. Plus, when I travel
I can save space on my laptop's hard drive by not installing every possible application I might need. Instead I install KeyView in my browser
and I'm able to read virtually any file sent to me.

WinTerm and WebTerm—Periodically I do work for a company that
uses Lotus Notes. I've worked with Notes extensively, but since mine is
a relatively small network, I don't use it as my e-mail application and
therefore I don't have it installed on my network. But I can use my Web
browser, loaded with the WinTerm plug-in, to access the Lotus Notes
application demo stored on a distant computer. I can also use the product when I'm traveling and don't want to transfer a bunch of different
applications to my tiny laptop. Instead, if I leave my computer running
at the office, and connected to the Internet, I can quickly use my Web
browser to connect to, then run applications from my desktop computer or the server I've set up that stores all my more computing-intensive
applications.

Sir Browse-A-Lot and ScriptActive—I love Navigator, but ever since
Internet Explorer hit the scene, more sites are employing ActiveX, Active

server pages, and more Microsoft-specific technologies on their pages. I don't want to be left out, but I don't want to switch either. So I use two different plug-ins. Sir Browse-A-Lot lets me view Active server pages, and ScriptActive lets me view ActiveX-enabled sites. With such technology, I am never left out, regardless of whether a site is formatted for Netscape or Internet Explorer. These are must-have plug-ins for us diehard Netscape fans.

InstallFromTheWeb—I have lots of computer consulting clients, and one thing I've learned is that it's very difficult to help keep them organized and up to date, especially as I travel around the state and the lower 48 states. When a client needs an upgrade, I usually try to point him in the right direction, but sometimes the software installations can be confusing. A plug-in like InstallFromTheWeb can help alleviate installation problems and allow me to do my consulting remotely. I create driver updates, software patches, and online training materials, then place them on my Web server. I notify my clients via e-mail, the updates are available. Since I've configured the update package using the InstallFromTheWeb software, my clients simply double-click a Web page link, and instantly they are updated. No more trying to find the right FTP site, and no more fuddling with installation instructions. One click does it all.

CarbonCopy and Look@Me—When I do travel, invariably my clients will have a problem that I can oftentimes fix over the phone. But sometimes it would be helpful if I could see what they are seeing and possibly guide them through whatever problem they are having. With plug-ins like CarbonCopy and Look@Me, I can do just that. I can look at their computers and see what they are seeing, and I can do it all through a Web-based interface. For a consultant like me or for anyone who wants to do collaborative computing, such products are godsends.

NetZip—NetZip is a plug-in that quickly and easily allows you to unzip zipped (compressed) files from the Internet. For clients who don't want to be bothered with learning the steps to uncompressing files, NetZip does wonders. Moving data back and forth is so much easier when all you have to do is click a button, and immediately your files are not only downloaded, but uncompressed.

PointPlus—I do lots of PowerPoint presentations, and oftentimes I'm asked to send copies of these presentations via e-mail to clients and customers who have attended one of my seminars. The only problem is that my presentations often balloon to tens of megabytes. Instead, I use the PointPlus presentation software package to create, upload, then view

PowerPoint presentations. It even lets me narrate using Real Audio and Video, so even though people might have missed my live presentation, they can still see my virtual presentation many months later.

A Few Words About My Perfect Browser

Notice I don't have a whole lot of other plug-ins. I'm not loaded down with a lot of MIDI players, and I don't have a ton of MPEG viewers. Nor do I have a large number of virtual world-oriented plug-ins. I mainly have utilitarian plug-ins, leaving the weird, wacky, and wild plug-ins for someone else. I only add a plug-in when I absolutely need one, and I don't overburden my computer with plug-ins I hardly ever use. And even though I am a computer consultant by trade, and encourage my clients to venture into the wonderful world of plug-ins, something most know absolutely nothing about, I don't make them download and install plug-ins for one-time use only. I make sure there is a need.

I also make sure the plug-in works as advertised, the cost for the software that creates the data file will be recouped over a short period of time, and it works within their network, on their computer, or is easy enough for their users to understand. Too many computer geeks are enamored by new software and nifty bells and whistles, but don't spend the time to find out if new software will save time and money. If you plan on investing in this type of technology, make sure you do your homework, and make sure the products you choose do what you want them to do. Many don't. Many crash. Many plug-ins mimic features already available in the most recent versions of your Web browser. Check first to see if that capability is part of your browser. And make sure the time and effort it takes to download, test, and install the plug-ins you want to use. In writing this book, I spent over 80 hours downloading, installing, testing, and uninstalling, to determine whether the plug-ins listed here were worth it.

Summary

Now that you have an idea of what plug-ins can actually do for real people like yourself, you're probably itching to get started. In the next chapter, I'll introduce you to the installation procedure of a simple plug-in and show you how you can download, uncompress, install, and then try out your new software option.

CHAPTER

4 Getting Down to Installing Plug-Ins

You've seen how plug-ins work and you've seen a glimpse of real people using them in real-life situations. Now it's your turn to install your own plug-ins, then put them to the test in real-world situations. And in this chapter you'll learn what you need to know to install a plug-in, along with learning about some of the pitfalls to avoid during the installation process. Just be forewarned—not all plug-ins offer the same installation process and not all plug-ins work as advertised. In addition, if your system isn't already in good shape, you can bet you'll have problems. But even if it is, don't assume everything will work flawlessly. Plug-in technology, like any other technology, is still evolving and there are times things just won't work as advertised. If you know this in advance and realize that supercharging your browser takes time, you'll be much better equipped to deal with problems if and when they arise.

BEFORE YOU START

You'll need to do a little preparatory work before you venture into the world of plug-in installations. That means cleaning up your computer, making sure your browser is properly configured, and understanding what plug-ins you already have installed so you don't waste time reinstalling things you don't need to. If you think your system is ready and you don't need to read through this section, think again. Most likely it's been months since you last backed up your system. Or maybe you've never defragmented your hard drive. Possibly you've been living that carefree life and have no virus protection installed on your computer. Or maybe you've never even tried backing up your Registry file. If this is you, save yourself headaches by following some of the preventative measures you can take before you install anything. I can't guarantee all the steps outlined here will prevent your system from crashing after installing that nifty personal information manager plug-in, or the latest Real Audio plug-in. But by doing these few steps you may avoid some of the common problems.

TIP

Important! Don't sweat it. None of these steps require a degree in computer science. As a matter of fact, most are simple processes which, if followed closely, are relatively easy to do. And these are things you should perform on a regular basis. Just remember, if my Dad can do it, so can you.

STEP 1—BACKING UP YOUR SYSTEM

Let's start at the beginning—backing up the important files on your system. Let me take a few minutes here to talk about backup options, before we delve into the actual backup process. If you want to back up your system, you can use floppy diskettes, but you better have time on your hands, and I mean LOTS of time. With the technology changing so quickly and the demand for backup options forcing the prices down, I strongly recommend, if you don't have any other backup option than diskettes, you invest in one of several different backup options outlined here:

- **A Streaming Tape Cartridge Drive**
- **A Removable Cartridge Drive Like a Zip or SyQuest**
- **A Recordable CD-ROM Writer**

Which one is the best for you? It depends on how much you want to spend and how much you want to back up in any one sitting. Let's take a look at each option in a little more detail.

Streaming Tape Cartridge Drives—the Least Desirable Choice

Streaming tape cartridge drives are a relatively old technology that has been around for years providing reliable backup to millions of computer users. But with the advent of newer technology that provides for faster, longer-lasting backup options offering more features, a streaming tape backup drive is the one option I wouldn't recommend you run out and buy. If you already have a tape cartridge drive installed in your unit, great. Use it. And if you don't know how to use it, either dig up the documentation for it and get it working, or visit one of the many manufacturers of tape backup drives on the Internet for more information on how to backup your entire drive on to tape.

What are the inherent disadvantages to streaming tape cartridge drives? In Table 4.1 I list a few problems and what they mean to you as the consumer.

Table 4.1: *Problems with tape drives.*

Option/Problem	What That Means to You
The information is written on the tape sequentially which means in order to restore a portion of your hard drive, you have to first find the spot on the tape where that information starts, then restore from that point.	Lots of time waiting in front of the computer for the tape software to find exactly what you're looking for.
The tape doesn't allow for you randomly to write to or use the information on it.	You can't use the cartridge as you would normally use a hard disk or a removable cartridge. All you can do is back up data, and not use the drive as a secondary storage unit for saving files, running programs, or quickly backing up information.
You usually have to use the special tape software in order to back up.	You can't use the Windows 95 interface and simply drag and drop your files to the tape. Note, however, some software now allows you to do that with some tape drives. Check the manufacturer's Web page to see if your drive has this capability.
Tape media has a definitive shelf life and is susceptible to the environment and to magnetic fields.	If you live in a hot climate, the tape could melt if left exposed to high temperatures. If you live in a cold climate, the tape could freeze and break. If you place the tape close to a magnet, the information could be entirely erased.
Tapes usually cost from $5–30.	Using tapes is much cheaper than using boxes and boxes of diskettes.

By now you can see tape cartridges are really not the best solution for your backup needs. They used to be the only solution, but that's no longer the case. You now have choices that don't break your bank.

Zip or Removable Cartridge Drives—Recommended

Just think of having an unlimited hard drive. Never having to worry about having enough space for that next plug-in you download or that video file you want to store so you can play it back later. Just think how easy it would be to organize sections of your hard drive into data, programs, plug-ins, games, and so on. Well, cartridge drives like the Zip and the SyQuest offer that capability. I know it sounds like a sales pitch, but since I use both brands of drives I can vouch for their usability and reliability.

A cartridge drive, unlike a streaming tape drive, works much like a hard disk. As a matter of fact, if you take a close look at the cartridge itself, you'll notice it resembles a platter from a hard disk. What are the inherent advantages or disadvantages to Zip or removable cartridge drives? Table 4.2 lists a few.

TABLE 4.2: *Problems with removable cartridge drives.*

Option/Problem	What That Means to You
Some cartridge drives usually allow for less than 400MB worth of data to be written on a single cartridge. *Note: Iomega JAZ to one gigabyte of data on a single cartridge.*	It usually means you can't make an entire backup of your system. Instead you have to back up your system in pieces This also allows you, however, to segment out your backups by putting your data on a single cartridge, your programs on another, and your operating system on yet another.
Usually can't be booted from the cartridge drive even if a system is copied to the cartridge.	This prevents you from "running" directly from your cartridge drive, avoiding problems your computer's system files themselves may have.
Cartridges are susceptible to the elements.	Their shelf life is longer usually than tape, but less than other media. If you stick the cartridge in a hot, steamy car, you can bet you'll have problems reading from that cartridge later on.
You can use a cartridge drive much like a hard drive.	This allows for unlimited space, so to speak. You never run out of room. You simply buy more cartridges.
Price for extra cartridges runs about $10-30.	A relatively low cost method for adding unlimited storage to your setup.

Writable CD-ROM Drives—the Best Choice for Backup

Removable cartridge drives are an excellent choice if you frequently back up, then erase, data. But if you want a long-term reliable backup solution, you can't beat writable CD-ROM drives. Writable CD-ROMs offer a full 600MB of data per CD, relatively long shelf life, and the ability to run programs or open data files directly from the CD. It's an excellent choice for backing up because a single CD holds so much information, can easily be accessed, much like a second hard disk drive, and in some cases, with some computers, can be used as a boot drive.

The major disadvantage of writable CD-ROM drives in the past has been the cost. But now you can get a CD-ROM drive for under $500, including software. If you plan on buying a SCSI-based CD-ROM writer, however, you may have problems initially setting up the unit because of potential hardware conflicts with the SCSI interface card.

Also, you do have to have a fair amount of RAM memory in order to write large chunks of data to the CD all at one time. Aside from those shortcomings, I would highly recommend investing in a writable CD-ROM drive. I purchased one of the original Pinnacle Microsystems CD-ROM writers, and although the speed is relatively slow, I must have burned over 100 CDs with little or no problem since buying it. I've backed up my system, created interactive multimedia presentations, and even burned a few CD-ROMs for the books I've written. This technology allows me to back a bunch of data into a single portable CD I can take with me anywhere and if I created the CD this way, it allows me to open it on either Mac or PC platforms. The next section covers the steps you'll need to take before you install your plug-ins. No matter which technology you use, the first step should start with is backing up your system. Each one of the backup technologies mentioned usually comes with its own backup software. It would be impossible to outline here the exact procedures for all available backup software, but what I can show you is how to use the backup software provided by Windows 95, and how to back up the important files, including your Windows 95 Registry file.

STEP 1—BACKING UP

The backup software provided by Windows 95 allows you to back up an individual file, a folder, or a collection of folders or files to any disk drive, removable cartridge drive, or other external storage source, such as a network drive.

It's actually just a simple five-step process that can be run at any time. These steps are:

- Launching the backup software
- Selecting the files or folders to back up
- Selecting the location where you want the files to be stored
- Starting the backup process
- Double-checking the integrity of the backup

What You'll Need and How Long It Will Take
- *Your Windows 95 computer*
- *Either diskettes or a cartridge drive and tapes (either tape or removable)*
- *Time: 1-3 hours depending on backup method used*

TIP

Let's start by backing up your current Netscape or Internet Explorer application folder. That way if, during the installation of any particular plug-in, something goes wrong and damages your current browser, you can easily reinstall the software from back up. To backup your Netscape or Internet Explorer, follow these steps:

1. Launch the backup software by opening **My Computer**, clicking once to select your hard drive.
2. Right-click your hard drive, then select **Properties** from the pop-up menu. This will open the **Properties** window for your hard drive.
3. Click the **Tools** tab as shown in Figure 4.1. This will display the list of disk management tools installed on your system.
4. Click the **Backup** button to start the backup process. *Note: If you don't see a backup button, the **Windows 95 Backup** utility has not been installed on your system. Use the **Control Panel | Add New Software** option to install the backup software.*
5. If this is the first time you've backed up your system, a dialog window will appear informing you of the steps required to back up your system. Follow these steps to complete the backup process.

STEP 2—CLEANING UP YOUR SYSTEM

Once you've backed up and verified your backups, you're ready to start cleaning up your system. This means cleaning out old temporary files you don't need, removing Read Me files you probably will never read, and defragmenting your hard drive so all the files are lined up in a neat little package. It also means running the ScanDisk program to check the integrity of your system.

Like the backup software, the ScanDisk and defragmenting software are just one part of the overall disk management tools installed on your computer's hard drive. And like the backup software, they are relatively easy to use, and require little configuration in order to work properly. Let's start first with the ScanDisk software. This software examines your hard drive for problems with the Windows 95 filing system, and will automatically repair any problems it can. You should always run ScanDisk before you install any software, since any problems your Windows 95 filing or directory system structure have could prevent the new software from being installed properly.

Checking Your Computer System for Errors

To start and run ScanDisk, follow these steps:

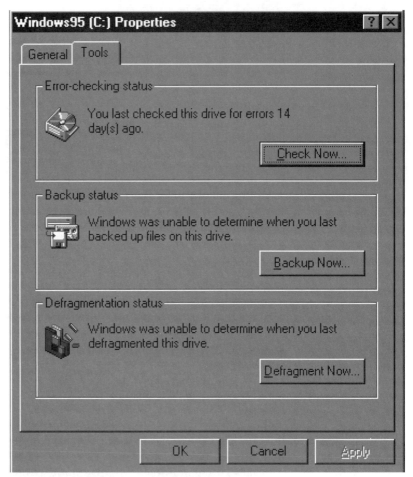

FIGURE *The list of available disk management tools.*
4.1

1. Launch the **ScanDisk** software by opening **My Computer**, clicking once to select your hard drive.
2. Right-click your hard drive, then select **Properties** from the pop-up menu. This will open the **Properties** window for your hard drive.
3. Click the **Tools** tab as shown in Figure 4.2. This will display the list of disk management tools installed on your system.
4. Click the **Check Now** button to start the error checking/scanning process. Click the **Thorough** option to have ScanDisk thoroughly check your hard drive for errors.

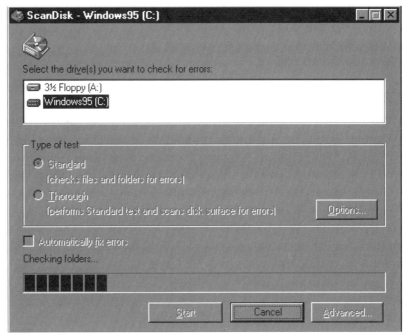

FIGURE   *Error-checking your hard drive with ScanDisk.*
4.2

5. Click the **Start** button when you're ready. Make sure you do not have any other applications running at the time you run ScanDisk. Also make sure you have the **Automatically Fix Error** option checked so any problems will be fixed during the scanning process.

After the ScanDisk process is complete, it's wise to reboot your computer. If a large number of errors were detected, however, you may consider reinstalling your operating system software after you have backed up your data. Multiple errors could be a signal that big problems lie in your Windows 95 Registry file or within the file structure of your hard disk. If you do get lots of ScanDisk errors, and you've reinstalled your operating system software, and maybe you've even tried reformatting your hard drive—you may have hardware problems. In that case it's wise to have a computer technician check your system.

Defragmenting Your Hard Drive

The process of defragmenting your hard drive is about as complex as running ScanDisk. Defragmenting simply arranges the files in order so that files can be accessed faster. If you use the Internet a great deal, you will need to defragment your hard drive regularly simply because temporary files are stored then erased on your drive at regular intervals. This means files are scattered electronically all over your hard drive in a somewhat random fashion. By cleaning things up and putting them in order, your software will respond faster since your drive won't have to hunt all over the place to find the pieces of the files it needs.

To defragment your hard drive follow these steps:

1. Launch the deframenting software by opening **My Computer**, clicking once to select your hard drive.
2. Right-click your hard drive, then select **Properties** from the pop-up menu. This will open the **Properties** window for your hard drive.
3. Click the **Tools** tab as shown in Figure 4.3. This will display the list of disk management tools installed on your system.
4. Click the **Defragment Now** button to start the cleanup process. Click the **Advanced** button and select **Full Defragmentation** to give your drive a full cleanup. Click **OK** to continue.
5. Click the **Start** button when you're ready. Make sure you do not have any other applications running at the time you run the defragmenter. When the process is finished, click **Exit**, then **OK** to close out this dialog window.

TIP

What You'll Need and How Long It Will Take
- *The Windows 95 CD-ROM disk*
- *Defragmentation software if you don't want to use the Windows software*
- *A boot disk in case things go wrong or can't be fixed from your hard drive*
- *Time: 10-60 minutes*

Step 3—Doing Some Preventative Maintenance

The next step is to prepare your system by doing some preventative maintenance. The first thing we'll do is clean out any temporary files that may be clogging up your system. Then we'll run a virus-scanning program to make sure the system is in good working order and not infected with any viruses.

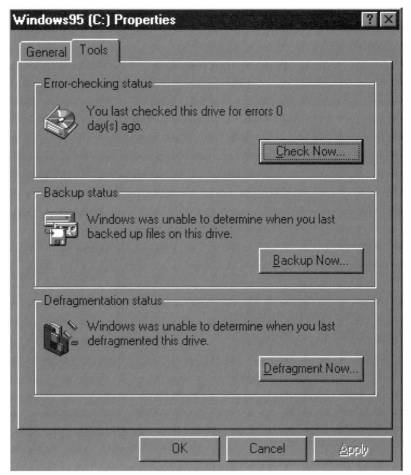

FIGURE *The list of available disk management tools.*
4.3

   There are two locations where temporary files can clog up your system. One is in the **Windows\Temp** folder and another is in your browser's **Temporary cache** folder. To clean out your **Windows\Temp** folder,
first close all applications you currently have open, then open the **My
Computer** icon on your desktop. Inside of **My Computer** open the
icon for your hard drive, then open the **Windows** folder. Inside this
folder you should find a **Temp** folder. Open that folder up, then select
Edit | Select All. Once all the temporary files are selected, hit the **Delete**
key on your keyboard. A dialog box will appear asking you if you really
want to send the items to the **Recycle Bin**. Click the **Yes** button, and

these files will be removed from your **Temporary** folder. Make sure to empty the **Recycle Bin** to ensure they are lost and gone forever.

Emptying Temporary Files from Your Browser's Cache

Next, follow these steps to clear out your browser's cache:

1. Launch your Web browser, then select **Edit | Preferences** in Netscape Navigator or **View | Options** in Internet Explorer.
2. Click the **Advanced** category in Netscape Navigator or click the **Advanced** tab in Internet Explorer.
3. Click the **Cache** subcategory in Netscape Navigator or click the **Settings** button in the **Temporary Internet Files** section in Internet Explorer.
4. Click the **Clear Disk Cache** button in Netscape Navigator or click the **Empty** folder in Internet Explorer.
5. Once you've done this, all your temporary Internet files will be deleted. You should then be ready to install any plug-in you wish. Click the **OK** button to continue.

Checking Your System for Viruses

You should have some form of virus checking installed in your system. Later in this chapter you'll learn how to install a plug-in that also checks every download you select for potential viruses before the file is saved to your hard drive. But in the meantime, to prevent any problems installing plug-ins, it's a good idea to run a thorough check of your system for viruses.

There are numerous virus-checking software programs available for download or purchase. Two of the best companies offering virus protection software are Symantec (*http://www.symantec.com*) and McAffee (*http://www.mcaffee.com*). If you don't already have virus-checking software installed, you should investigate one of these companies for a complete virus-checking package.

It's always best to run your virus checks from a bootable floppy so the virus software will be able to also check your boot and system software. Check with the manufacturer of the virus software to learn how to configure a bootable disk to accomplish such a task.

Also be sure you update your virus-checking software regularly. Visit the Web site of the manufacturer at least once a month, or more if you suspect your system is highly susceptible to frequent virus attacks. No virus software is any good if you don't keep updated on the latest and greatest viruses that those evil programmers create.

After you've run a thorough check of your system, you're ready to start downloading system upgrades, then actual plug-ins themselves.

What You'll Need and How Long It Will Take
- *A virus scanning program*
- *An Internet connection*
- *Time: 10-60 minutes depending upon your Internet connection*

STEP 4—UPGRADING IF NECESSARY

When was the last time you installed an upgrade to your Windows 95 computer? If the answer is never, I strongly urge you to upgrade. "Upgrade?" you're probably thinking. "I didn't know there was an upgrade to Windows 95."

Windows 95 is not a bug-free system by any stretch of the imagination. The original version of Windows 95 had hundreds of bugs, so many that a book was written entitled *Windows 95 Bug Collection*, by Bruce Brown, editor and publisher of *BugNet*. By the way, you should periodically check out *BugNet* for a list of the latest Windows 95 bugs. You can find *BugNet* at *http://www.bugnet.com*. You can also subscribe to his *Bug of the Day* e-mail newsletter directly from his site.

Windows 98 should be available by the time you read this. But that doesn't mean it will fix all the problems Windows 95 has. Always check Microsoft's Web site at www.microsoft.com for the latest bug fixes.

With this many bugs, you can bet Microsoft engineers are constantly improving and updating this operating system software. In addition, hardware manufacturers as well as many software manufacturers are constantly updating their products to work better with Windows 95. You should probably visit the Web sites of your computer, monitor, modem, and printer manufacturers regularly to see if new drivers or software updates are available. Oftentimes these updates will fix many common and more esoteric problems you might encounter. No computer software program is error free, and not every combination of hardware and software can be tested before a product is shipped. But you can prevent a lot of headaches if you update your software regularly. Let's take a look at one important update—the Windows 95 System Pack Upgrade—which can be found on the Microsoft Web site.

What You'll Need and How Long It Will Take
  - *An Internet connection*
  - *At least 100MB of free hard disk space*
  - *A backup of your existing Web browser*
  - *Time: 1-3 hours depending on your Internet connection and what you need to install*

Launch your browser, and enter *"www.microsoft.com"* in the **Location** field. In a few minutes you should see the Microsoft Web site appear in your browser window. Click the link for **Support**, then look for the link for the **Service Pack Upgrades**. There you should find a list of Service Pack updates along with updates for modem, printer, and video drivers. If you haven't already updated your system, you should follow the steps to upgrade your Windows 95 software. By the time you read this book, undoubtedly Microsoft will have yet another Service Pack upgrade (a.k.a. bug fix) for the problems inherent in Windows 95.

Also, if you spot your modem, printer, or monitor manufacturer's name listed on the long list of driver updates, check into what make and model new drivers are available for, especially if you have a newer modem. Many bugs are being worked out of the newer modem technology and, believe it or not, Microsoft's Web site is one of the best places to keep tabs on the new upgrades to a wide variety of hardware manufacturers.

Downloading and installing these upgrades is relatively simple and quick. You simply follow the instructions, which usually include downloading the upgrade to your hard drive. Exit all applications, then run the upgrade installation program, which usually will restart your computer for you once the installation process is complete. If you're uncertain about installing any Service Pack upgrade, refer to the **ReadMe** files or documentation that usually comes with the upgrade. Almost all bugfix upgrades are available free of charge if you download them from the Microsoft Web site. Requesting upgrades on CD-ROM, however, may cost you a few dollars.

THE COST OF A PLUG-IN

Most plug-ins are free, so why the discussion on cost?

TIME IS MONEY

First of all, your time is money. And any time you spend supercharging your browser better be worth the effort. Before you decide to install a plug-in, make sure it's something that can save you time, and offers your browser capabilities it doesn't already have with another plug-in or helper application. Make sure you read the documentation for the plug-in before you install it. If it offers the same functions or reads the same file formats as other plug-ins you currently have installed, it may in fact override other plug-ins. So make sure you really want and need the feature it offers.

A PLUG-IN MAY NEED MORE HARDWARE

Second, a plug-in may force you to upgrade your system or buy additional hardware. You have to weigh the costs with the benefits. Unless the additional hardware the plug-in requires is additional memory or a sound card and speakers, you may want to consider finding another plug-in that can read the same file format without the additional hardware requirements. You can't go wrong if a plug-in requires additional memory or a sound card and speakers—hardware you don't already have. More memory will always help you with other software applications, and if you don't already have a sound card and speakers, you simply don't know what you're missing. Streaming audio and video on the Internet are two of the most exciting things on the Internet today. With a sound card and speakers, you can hear the latest CD from your favorite musical group, you can listen to live radio broadcasts from half a world away, or, if you have a fast enough connection, you can watch the *Fox News Network* broadcast live audio and video.

YOU NEVER KNOW WHEN THINGS WILL CRASH

Third, a plug-in may crash your system. You must proceed with caution when installing any plug-in. It may be a conflict with another plug-in, or a plug-in that hogs all the computer's memory, or a poorly written one that doesn't work well with Windows 95. Whatever the problem may be, the cost of installing an unstable plug-in can mean many hours of reconstructing your system if you have not fully backed up. You should only download and install plug-ins from reputable sources. Although there are plenty of talented freeware authors-programmer hobbyists that offer their latest software inventions free to the world— it's best to stick with plug-ins programmed by companies that can offer support if something goes wrong. Remember also to read the ReadMe and preinstallation documentation before installing any plug-in, so you'll know if there are any potential conflicts, known bugs, or problems.

As you can see, the hidden or real cost behind any plug-in is your time and frustration. Keep in mind the whole concept of plug-ins is to make your life easier. If a plug-in doesn't install properly, causes conflicts, or doesn't work as advertised, it can be expensive.

ONE MORE THING BEFORE YOU INSTALL YOUR FIRST PLUG-IN

OK, you've backed up your system; you've done a little preventative maintenance; you understand the cost a plug-in may require of you; and you figure you must be ready to install your first plug-in. But wait. Before you do, make sure you have all the pertinent information on hand. That way you won't be stopped cold in your tracks, scrounging around for the information you need before you can continue the installation.

THE PREINSTALLATION CHECKLIST

What do you need to have at the ready before you install a plug-in? Here's a quick checklist of some things you should know about your system:

- What version of Windows you have and the latest service pack you have installed
- The total amount of RAM installed in your computer
- The type of computer you're using
- The total amount of hard disk space you have and the amount of available (free) hard disk space
- The current version of Netscape or Internet Explorer you're using
- Your e-mail address
- The plug-ins you currently have installed
- The speed of your modem
- Your name

Why do you need this information? A plug-in may want you to register online and will require this information. Or the plug-in may require you to have a certain amount of memory, a certain version of Netscape or Internet Explorer, or it may want to know your e-mail address during the installation process so the company can automatically register you, then send you notices of updates and bug fixes.

If you already know some but not all of this information, let me briefly show you where you can get all of it in case you're clueless. Most of this is relatively easy to find so if you don't know for sure, make sure. When you install some plug-ins, you will need to provide some if not all of this information, and if you provide the wrong information the plug-in may not work right. Once you've found this information, either write it down on a piece of paper and tack it up next to your computer, or save it in a text file using something like NotePad or WordPad. Either way, you want to keep the information handy.

A CLOSER LOOK AT THE INFORMATION YOU NEED

The Amount of RAM, Type of Computer, and Version of Windows 95 Installed

To find out what version you have and how much RAM memory you have installed, follow these steps:

1. Click the **Start** button from the **Windows 95** taskbar.
2. Click, **Settings | Control Panels** folder.
3. Once the **Control Panels** folder opens, locate, then double-click on, the **System** icon.
4. The **System Properties** dialog should display much like that shown in Figure 4.4.

Under the word "System" the version of Windows 95 should be displayed. Under the word "Computer" you should see the type of computer microprocessor you're using (in my case a Pentium) and the amount of RAM installed (in my case 32MB).

The Total Hard Disk Capacity and Free Space

Next let's find out how big your hard drive is and how much free space is available. To find this out follow these steps:

1. Double-click the **My Computer** icon on your **Windows** desktop.
2. Right-click on the icon for your hard drive and select **Properties** from the pop-up menu.
3. Click the **General** tab if it's not already selected.
4. You should see the used space, free space, and overall capacity in the **General** tab dialog which should look much like Figure 4.5.

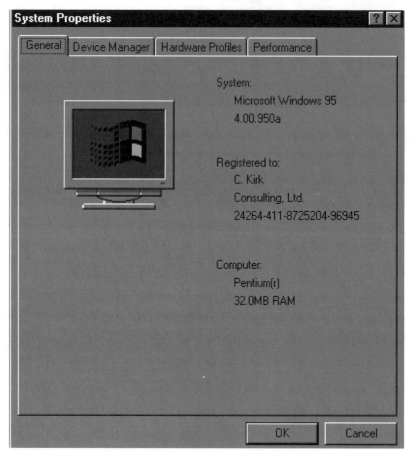

FIGURE   *The System Properties dialog shows you not only the version of Windows 95*
4.4   *you're using but also the amount of RAM installed in your computer.*

The Version of Netscape or Internet Explorer Installed, Plus Your E-Mail Address

To find out the version of your browser software check the **Help** menu's **About** option. This usually tells you the version of the software you are using regardless of the browser you use.

If you want to find out your e-mail address, either double-check with your Internet Service Provider or check the **Option** or **Preferences** settings in your browser software. Check the mail server settings. This should tell you what your return e-mail address is.

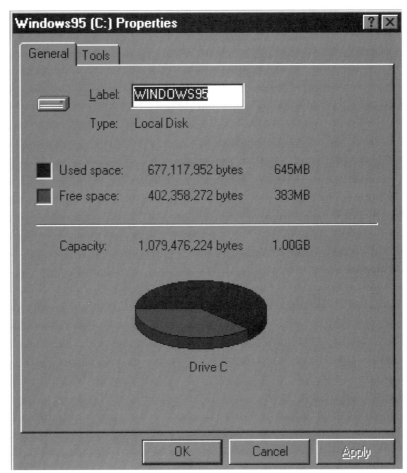

FIGURE *See how much space you have left?*
4.5

The Speed of Your Modem

The speed of your modem should be displayed every time you log on to the Internet. However, those numbers can be bogus. The best way to check for the speed of your modem is to either locate the speed on the modem itself or check the system configuration information in your Windows 95 computer. To do that, follow these steps:

1. Click the **Start** button from the **Windows 95** taskbar.
2. Click the **Settings | Control Panels** folder.

3. Once the **Control Panels** folder opens, locate, then double-click on, the **System** icon.
4. The **System Properties** dialog opens, then click the **Device Manager** tab.
5. Locate the **Modem** icon, and click to expand it.
6. Your modem should be listed, hopefully with a model number and speed.

The First Real Step—Finding Plug-Ins to Download

Of course the best place to find a plug-in is on the CD-ROM accompanying this book. But there are plenty of great places on the Internet that offer links to the most up-to-date plug-ins available on the Internet, with Netscape's NetCenter being the best place to find plug-ins specifically for any version of the Netscape browser. *BrowserWatch* and *Plug-In Plaza* are also great places for finding comprehensive lists of plug-ins. Table 4.3 offers you a list of the most popular plug-in-oriented Web sites currently available.

But unfortunately there isn't one definitive place that offers a listing of every single plug-in. Why is this? Although companies such as Netscape and Microsoft encourage developers to provide them with links to their plug-ins, plenty of companies develop plug-ins without notifying either Microsoft or Netscape.

Good Starting Points

However, there are plenty of sites dedicated to browser plug-ins. Some are listed below. We'll use several of these sites throughout the example of downloading and installing plug-ins, and will continue to go back to them to find the plug-ins we need quickly.

Table 4.3: *Great places to get plug-ins.*

Site Name	Site Location	Comments
Browsers.com	http://www.browsers.com	C|Net Central's list of browser plug-ins and browser tips, tricks, and techniques for using both Internet Explorer and Netscape Communicator.
BrowserWatch	http://www.browserwatch.com	A whole host of information about both types of browsers, along with links to plug-ins and add-ons.

Table 4.3 (continued)

Microsoft's Web Site	http://www.microsoft.com/ie/	Microsoft's Web site for Internet Explorer. Click the link for the **Explorer Add-Ons** for information on Active X and plug-in controls.
Netscape's Plug-Ins List	http://home.netscape.com/comprod/ products/navigator/version_2.0/plugins/ index.html	Over 176 plug-ins are listed here, almost all major plug-ins from most major manufacturers.
Plug-In Plaza	http://browserwatch.com/plug-in.html	Just about every platform is catered to here. From Mac to Unix, there are plenty of plug-ins listed by categories.
The Latest Browser Plug-Ins	http://www.phoenixat.com/scott/ plugins.html	A long list of plug-in descriptions and links.
TuCows Plug-Ins for Windows 95	http://home.texoma.com/mirror/ tucows/plug95.html	A great place for shareware software, and a great place for finding the most popular plug-ins. A search facility is also available.
Windows 95.com Web Browser Plug-Ins	http://www.windows95.com/ apps/plugins.html	Tons of plug-ins listed by category, all specifically for Windows 95.
Yahoo's List of Plug-In Resources	http://www.yahoo.com	Click the link for **Computers** and **Internet, Software, Internet, World Wide Web Browsers,** then **plug-ins.** You'll then see a list of browser plug-ins and resources.
ActiveX.com	http://www.activex.com	If you're looking for ActiveX controls for Internet Explorer, this is a great place to go. It has plenty of links to all sorts of ActiveX controls and development options.

THE SECOND STEP—PREPARING TO DOWNLOAD

Now that you know where to get plug-ins, you're almost ready to install your own. But before you do, there are a couple more things you should do to prepare your system. The first thing to do is to check to see what plug-ins you already have installed. That way you won't spend time downloading plug-ins you don't need. Although Netscape Navigator and Internet Explorer are both smart enough to know what plug-ins are installed and will not redownload any of them, many shareware sites compress files, making it impossible for your browser to know if the compressed file is actually a plug-in.

Checking for Installed Plug-Ins

To check for installed plug-ins with Netscape Navigator, follow these steps:

1. Open a **Navigator** window.
2. Select **About Plug-ins** from the **Help** menu.
3. The list of plug-ins will be displayed in the active **Navigator** window.
4. Scroll down to see the list of all plug-ins installed.

*The C:\program files\netscape\communicator\program\plugsins directory is where all the Netscape plug-ins are installed. You can also type "about:plugin" in the **Location** field of your **Navigator** window.*

To check for installed plug-ins with Internet Explorer, follow these steps:

1. Open the **My Computer** icon on your desktop.
2. Open the icon for your hard drive, then open the **Programs Files** folder.
3. Locate the **Microsoft Internet** folder and open it.
4. Inside this folder is the **Plug-in** folder. Inside this folder are all the plug-ins currently installed.

Internet Explorer can use plug-ins installed for Netscape Navigator. That's right; Internet Explorer can understand and use any plug-in installed in Netscape's plug-in folder as any installed in its own plug-in folder.

Now that you have an idea of what's installed in your system, the next thing to do is create a temporary folder just in case some of the plug-ins you plan to install are compressed. The best place to put this temporary folder is on your desktop. Just right-click anywhere on your desktop, then select **New | Folder** from the pop-up menu. Label this folder "downloads." If any of the plug-ins you download are compressed, this will be the place you should put them. This folder can also serve for other files you choose to download. That way you can keep all the compressed files in one place, periodically deleting them once you've completed installing whatever files were contained in the compressed file.

THE THIRD STEP—DOWNLOADING, UNCOMPRESSING, AND INSTALLING THE PLUG-IN

By now you should be champing at the bit to download a plug-in or two. So let's get to it. The first one we'll download is the one you'll need before you download any others. It's a plug-in product called *ViruSafe Web*. Although you may already have a virus-checking program installed on your hard drive, you still need ViruSafe Web. Unlike your standard virus-checking software that scans diskettes and applications as they are launched, ViruSafe Web automatically scans files as you download them, even before you download it to your computer. ViruSafe Web will also scan executable files, compressed or zipped files, and Word documents that could contain macro viruses.

STARTING THE INSTALLATION PROCESS

ViruSafe Web works in the background as a plug-in in tandem with your browser. When you click a link to download a file, ViruSafe Web jumps into action, checking the file before it hits your hard drive. You can find ViruSafe Web in a number of locations including the ViruSafe manufacturer's home page at *http://www.eliashim.com.* Or you can search *Download.com's* archives. In the following example, we'll use the Download.com site instead of the manufacturer's site just to show you how to search and use the features of Download.com, a great site to use in the future when you need to download more plug-ins.

Let's get started. First launch your Web browser. In the **Location** field of your browser's window, type *"www.download.com"* and hit **Enter**. In a few seconds or minutes, depending upon the speed of your connection, the main **Download** page will display. It should look something like that shown in Figure 4.6. Remember, these sites are often redesigned so your screen may look somewhat different.

In the **Quick Search** option type in "virusafe," then click the **Search** button. The next screen will display all the files that match your search criteria. One of them will be ViruSafe Web as shown in Figure 4.7. The link for this file will take you to a page listing the features of ViruSafe along with a link to download the file. The **Click Here to Download** link will display sites where you can download the file. Click one of the links listed, preferably one that is geographically closest to you. When

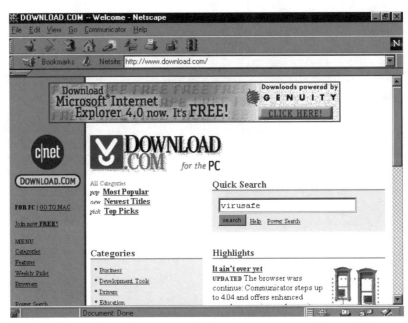

FIGURE   *The main Download.com screen is shown once you summon it in your Web*
4.6   *browser window.*

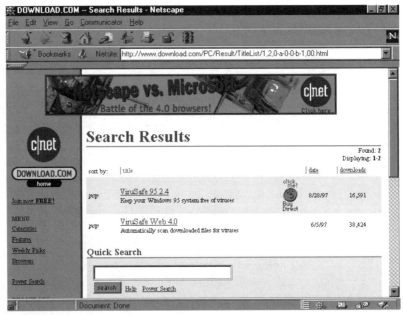

FIGURE   *The list of files matching your search criteria will be listed.*
4.7

you click the link, the **Save As** dialog window will display. Remember the download folder you created? Make sure you store the **ViruSafe Web** file in this folder, then click the **Save** button.

In a few minutes the download process will complete, and the **Saving Location** progress window, shown in Figure 4.8, will go away displaying the last Web page you displayed. At this point it's a good idea to quit your Web browser to ensure the installation process goes smoothly and the plug-in is properly installed in your Web browser software. Also make sure no other programs are running at the time you install a plug-in. You never know when a plug-in could bomb your system, taking with it any unsaved information you might have been working on.

*If you're using Netscape Communicator 4.0 or above and your download is interrupted, just go back to the link to download the file again, click the link, then click **Yes** to replace the file. Communicator will automatically pick up where the download left off. This is an excellent feature not implemented in previous versions of Navigator, and another reason to use Navigator as your main browser.*

Once you've closed your browser and any other applications, open the **Download** folder stored on your desktop. Inside this folder should be an icon that looks much like that in Figure 4.9. Double-click this icon and the ViruSafe Web installation program will open.

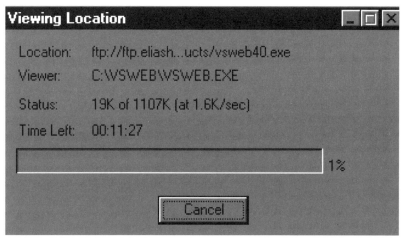

FIGURE *The Viewing Location progress window.*
4.8

FIGURE *The ViruSafe Web icon.*
4.9

After reading the main **Welcome** splash screen, click the **Next** button to continue the installation process. Select the directory where you want to store the uncompressed ViruSafe Web installation software, then click the **Next** button. The next step is for ViruSafe to find the Web browsers currently installed on your system. You can pick and choose which browsers you want the plug-in installed into. Select or deselect which browser you want the plug-in installed into, then click the **Next** button.

After a few seconds, that's it. You will be notified the plug-in was successful installed. Click the **Finish** button and you'll be returned to the Windows 95 desktop. Amazingly simple, isn't it? You can restart your browser, try downloading a file, and ViruSafe Web will automatically check for any viruses. You won't see any indication the plug-in is working. After the file has been checked, and is verified clean, but before the file is saved to your drive, you will see a dialog window like that one displayed in Figure 4.10, notifying you the file is indeed clean. If the file isn't clean, you will also be notified. At that point ViruSafe Web will alert you the file is infected and warn you not to download it.

SUMMARIZING THE INSTALLATION PROCESS

That's all there is to installing a plug-in. It's about as easy as browsing a Web page, and most plug-ins require you know no more than just where you want to place the compressed plug-in file. But just so you know you aren't missing anything, Table 4.4 reviews the steps involved in installing just about any plug-in.

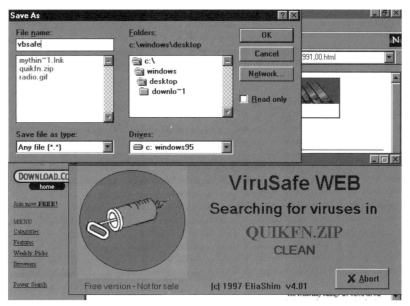

FIGURE   *If the file you are downloading is free of viruses, you'll be notified.*
4.10

TABLE 4.4: *The installation process summarized.*

Step	What It Does
1. Create a **Download** folder on your Windows 95 Desktop.	This keeps your computer clean. Once you've installed the plug-in, you can delete this folder without having to worry about whether you're deleting the wrong files.
2. Locate the plug-in to download.	Remember, you can use Download.com to locate just about any shareware or freeware plug-in available. Either type the name of the file in the **Quick Search** field, or click the link for the list of plug-ins available.
3. Click the link to download the file.	This will bring up the **Save As** dialog window asking you where to save the file. Make sure you save it in your download folder just to make it easier to find and easier to clean up later.
4. Once the compressed plug-in has downloaded, quit the browser application.	This will ensure the plug-in is installed properly.

Table 4.4 (continued)

5. Double-click the icon for the compressed plug-in you've just downloaded.	This will start the plug-in installation process, usually bringing up either WinZip or an installation Wizard to guide you.
6. Once you've gone through the entire installation process click the **Finish** button.	By this time your plug-in should be installed into the proper location and attached to your browser.
7. Launch your browser application.	This will help you test the plug-in.
8. Try using the plug-in by either accessing a file type or by performing the function the plug-in is used for.	This will tell you whether the plug-in is properly installed.

UNDERSTANDING THE DIFFERENCE BETWEEN PLUG-INS AND HELPER APPLICATIONS

If you've read Chapter 1, you should have a good idea of the difference between plug-ins and helper applications. But now that you've downloaded your first plug-in, it's a good idea to also acquaint yourself with helper applications. Helper applications are separate applications that your browser knows about. When you click a link to open a file your browser doesn't understand, and there is no plug-in, but there is a helper application associated with the file, the helper application will launch and display the file.

A helper application can be anything you choose. It can be your word processor. It can be your spreadsheet. And it can also be a mix of plug-ins and helper applications. Real Audio, one of the plug-ins/helper applications you should definitely download and install on your computer is a prime example of such a piece of software. Real Audio, a piece of software that plays audio and video files, can do so either as a plug-in playing that video or audio file directly in a Web page, or it can play the file using the Real Audio player, a separate application that works independently of the browser.

What's the difference? And why would you install a separate application instead of just installing the plug-in option? It all depends on your computer, how you want to set it up, and whether you want more features that a helper application offers over a plug-in. Table 4.5 offers a quick rundown of the differences between a helper application and a plug-in:

TABLE 4.5: *The difference between helper applications and plug-ins.*

	Helper Application	**Plug-In**
RAM Memory	Uses additional memory while the helper application is in use, and afterwards, until the helper application is exited.	Only uses memory when called into action.Once the plug-in is no longer needed, the memory is freed for use by other applications.
Hard Disk Space	Helper applications are usually larger than plug-ins, so they will most likely require more hard disk space.	Plug-ins are relatively small, and usually require much less space on your hard disk than helper applications.
Installation	Helper applications may require you configure your browser manually, and know exactly what file types they should interpret.	Plug-ins are usually installed automatically.
Usage	Helper applications can be used separate from Web browsers. As a matter of fact, you don't need to launch the browser in order to display the files helper applications can display.	Plug-ins require the use of the browser in order to work.
Controls	Helper applications usually offer full controls and features.	Plug-ins may offer more limited controls than helper applications, usually just enough controls to play, rewind, control volume, or adjust the view options.
Saving or Printing	Helper applications usually offer the ability to print or save files directly to the hard disk.	Plug-ins usually have the option to save the file if applicable, but may not have full controls for printing.

INSTALLING HELPER APPLICATIONS

The actual process of installing a helper application is almost identical to installing a plug-in, with one special exception. If the helper application did not also install as a plug-in, you will have to configure your browser so it knows to launch the helper application when it runs across the file type the helper application can display. This is not a difficult process, but one that requires you know a little more about your computer than installing a plug-in requires.

First you must know where the helper application is installed on your computer. Second, you have to know what kinds of files the helper application can understand and display. Third, you must know how to configure your browser to summon the helper application at the proper time. In Chapter 2 you learned how to view helper applications. Now you'll learn a little more about configuring files to work them. What you'll learn here is actually what the installation programs of most plug-ins do for you automatically—tell the browser which MIME types work with which applications.

Let's take a look at assigning WordPad to read WRI files. Although your browser may already have this application configured, and although you probably won't encounter too many WordPad files on the Internet, the process should give you some insight into how helper applications are configured to your browser. Since most new installations of helper applications and plug-ins do this messy work for you, this may be the only time you ever venture into the dark world of configuring MIME types.

First, open the preferences of your Web browser, then locate the **Helper Applications** option. In Netscape Navigator you do this by clicking the **Navigator** category, then clicking the **Applications** subcategory. Scroll through the list of helper applications and their file types and you'll see a wide assortment of helper applications have already been assigned for you automatically when you first installed Netscape Navigator.

Click the **New Type** button. The **New Type** dialog box will appear as shown in Figure 4.11. There are only four fields to fill in. The first is the description. If you run across information on configuring a particular helper application to a particular file type and the instructions mention which description to include, you would fill that information in here. For our example simply type "WordPad." Since WordPad files end in .DOC, enter ".DOC" in the **File Extension** field. Leave the **MIME Type** field blank. Since this isn't a file format native to the Internet, you can leave this option blank. When you get to the **Application to Use** field, click the **Browse** button and locate the **WordPad** application.

That's all there is to it. If you were to save this information, the next time Netscape Navigator comes across a file ending in .DOC, if there were no plug-in to view the information found in the file, Navigator

New Type   ☒

Description of type: │Document   │

File extension: │doc   │

MIME Type: │   │

Application to use: │"C:\Program Files\Accessories\Wordpad.│

                                              [Browse...]

                              [OK   ]   [Cancel]

FIGURE *Creating a new helper application type.*
4.11

would launch WordPad instead and display the contents of that file in a separate WordPad window.

In this example click the **Cancel** button. I wanted to step you through the process, but at this point you don't want to mess up any configuration already instituted to read DOC files.

*Both Internet Explorer and Netscape Navigator offer the ability to assign helper applications to various file types through their **Options** menu.*

NOTE

Once you've installed your plug-ins and/or helper applications, if you have any problems check Chapters 11 and 12 for a list of tips, tricks, and traps you might encounter with the general helper application and plug-in installation processes. Most likely you won't have a single problem installing plug-ins. Most problems surface when you start using them. However, Chapters 11 and 12 will help you troubleshoot through any problem.

SUMMARY

Sometimes things will not go right, no matter how many preventative measures you take. But with a few simple preventative measures, the first plug-in you've installed should install without a hitch. The next step is figuring out how to configure your browser so that it provides you with exactly what you want and the plug-ins work as advertised. The next chapter shows you exactly how to do that, and then some.

5 All about ActiveX Controls

What exactly is ActiveX? Well it isn't a technology used by agents Scully and Mulder of *X-Files* fame to track down aliens. And no, X doesn't exactly mark the spot, although I guess it could. ActiveX is actually Microsoft's name for new technology (*i.e.*, software programming that extends Internet Explorer). It's part of both versions 3.0 and 4.0 and is a capability that's built into the Internet Explorer browser. It can best be described as a cross between Java applets and plug-ins, coupled with the ability to link to and interact with just about any Windows-based program. It's a technology that really lets the browser reach beyond the Internet and become a fully interactive application, no longer tied to just interacting with Web pages.

I've devoted an entire chapter to ActiveX mainly because, like plug-ins, ActiveX controls do indeed supercharge any Internet Explorer 3.0 or 4.0 browser. And they work in much the same fashion as plug-ins. But to say ActiveX controls are merely plug-ins for Internet Explorer, wouldn't be giving them the justice they deserve. ActiveX controls are more than plug-ins, although they may accomplish many of the same things plug-ins accomplish and a few of the things Java applets do. But because they can interact with more than just Web pages, ActiveX controls are much more robust in the features they offer. This chapter will serve to give you an overview of what ActiveX is, how it works, and how you install it to work with your system. There's a great deal more about ActiveX than this tiny chapter can cover, so I'll also give you a list of resources you can browse on your own if you want to go further in terms of understanding and developing ActiveX-enhanced sites. At times this chapter will get somewhat technical, but hang on, it evens out in the end.

A Look at ActiveX

I'm an administrator of my company's Intranet, and I want people to be able to install the latest update to their browser, word processor, or network applications even if they aren't very computer literate. And more importantly, I want them to be able to do that just by clicking a link on a Web page. With a little help from the ActiveX technology, I could place an ActiveX control on a Web page. Since Internet Explorer is ActiveX enabled, when an employee of the company needs to update his software, all he has to do is go to the page I've created and click a link. With the ActiveX controls programmed into the Web page, the updating process happens right on his computer. The ActiveX control takes over, runs the installation process, maybe even restarts his computer, reconnects him to the Intranet, and alerts him that the update process is complete. He didn't have to know anything more than how to click a link, and better yet, I as the administrator didn't have to visit every single computer, running the installation process myself. I simply send out an e-mail to everyone in the company, encouraging them to visit the page at their leisure and update their software themselves, even though most of them are not technical wizards.

Here's another scenario. Maybe I want to take the information stored in my Access database and make it available to anyone on the Web. I could easily do that with ActiveX, since it could go out to my Access database and grab the information a visitor might request through an interactive Web page form. ActiveX can do this because it is a function of the Windows operating system, like the ability to copy and paste between applications. This sharing of data and interacting with applications is key to all the advantages, and some of the disadvantages, ActiveX offers. Not only can ActiveX controls provide such Web page form elements as pop-up lists and pull down menus within the page itself, but they are also available to query, then report back information from a database like Access or even a spreadsheet like Excel.

WHERE ACTIVEX CAME FROM

Initially based on Object Linking and Embedding technology, a part of such desktop applications as Microsoft Word and Excel, and an integral part of Windows 3.1, Windows for Workgroups, Windows 95, and Windows NT, ActiveX is actually a slimmed down version of OLE. ActiveX is intended to provide more connectivity between a desktop computer and the Internet and Intranet worlds, and in some cases, let the client do some of the work instead of the server. Whereas Web servers used to be responsible for offering a certain level of interactivity, with Web pages being relatively static; now ActiveX controls can take over, going to work on the client's PC, freeing up servers, and more importantly, freeing up bandwidth, thus making response times faster for certain functions.

If you've been using a PC for any length of time with a recent flavor of Windows loaded on it, you might have run across the term OLE, although maybe not have understood what it offered. OLE is the technology that lets you transfer or embed data from one application into another. For example, when you copy a range of cells in an Excel spreadsheet, it's OLE that lets you take those cells and the data stored in them and place them in a Microsoft Word document. Although this sounds like simple copy and paste, OLE actually takes it one step further. When you embed an OLE object, like cells from a spreadsheet into another application, like Word, then change information in the spreadsheet, that same information is automatically updated in the Word document. This means you can enter the information once, and know that all documents that have the spreadsheet cells embedded in them will automatically have the new information displayed in the documents. Moreover, when you click on the cells you've embedded in your word processing document, the controls for the spreadsheet appear right in your word processing application, allowing you to edit the information just as if you were in the spreadsheet application.

ActiveX is simply a slimmed down version of OLE, intended to work within the parameters of the Web. In Microsoft lingo, Internet Explorer is the container for the ActiveX controls, providing a link between the Web and the Windows computer. As the name implies, ActiveX can also control various features of a Web page or even your Windows 95 operating system. These controls can run the gamut, from offering connections to databases or spreadsheets, to controlling simple things like Web page animations, or adding pop-up menu controls like those you see on Microsoft's Internet Explorer site. And in the case of Internet Explorer, they can even help a Web site, such as Microsoft's, determine what add-ons are installed within a visitor's browser.

To bring all this technology mumbo jumbo into perspective, ActiveX can basically do the same things OLE can do, but it can do them within the context of a Web browser. Therefore, if I create a Web page, and embed a word processing file into that page, anyone with an ActiveX-enabled browser like Internet Explorer could click that embedded item and start editing the file without the need of additional plug-ins. All the Word editing tools would appear and become available for use right within the browser. That's the power of ActiveX.

How Does ActiveX Differ from Plug-Ins?

How does an ActiveX control differ from a plug-in? Plug-ins let you view, manipulate, and edit file formats your browser doesn't natively recognize; ActiveX controls also offer you features your browser may not have, and that's where the differences become apparent. As a matter of fact, there are several big differences between the two. These differences are outlined in Table 5.1.

If you are planning on developing plug-ins or ActiveX controls, the differences are even more apparent. But this book won't delve much deeper into the development world, other than to show you how to include ActiveX controls or plug-ins on a Web page. For more detailed ActiveX development information, consider picking up a copy of Microsoft Press' "ActiveX Controls Inside Out" or "Understanding ActiveX and OLE." Both are excellent resources for developers. Or check out the Microsoft ActiveX development Web site at http://www.microsoft.com/activex/, a part of Microsoft's Site Builder's network.

TABLE 5.1: *The difference between plug-ins and ActiveX controls.*

Plug-Ins	ActiveX Controls
Mainly deal with handling different types of data the browser can't handle.	Handle different data types the browser can't handle, but also provide Web pages with more functionality such as drop-down menu items, scrolling animations, and so on, elements more akin to Java applets than programs. Also can interface with other desktop programs.
Requires a separate installation program.	Automatically installed when the control is encountered and the user authorizes the installation.
Installation usually requires stopping, then starting, the browser once the plug-in is installed.	There is no stopping or starting when you want to install an ActiveX control.
Plug-ins are relatively self-contained and only interact between browser, data, and plug-in.	ActiveX controls can interact with a wide variety of applications that are ActiveX aware.
Plug-ins are developed to work only with a Web browser.	ActiveX controls can work with other applications such as Visual Basic.
Development of plug-in technology is not limited to the operating system platform.	ActiveX controls are built primarily for use on Windows-based computers and are a subset of the Windows operating system environment. Although other companies are developing software that links ActiveX to other platforms, such as Unix or Mac OS 8, it is primarily for use on Windows-based computers.

WHAT'S THE DIFFERENCE BETWEEN ACTIVEX AND JAVA?

From the user's perspective, Java and ActiveX are more akin to each other than plug-ins are akin to ActiveX. This is due mainly to the fact that ActiveX is more of a programming environment, whereas plug-ins are mini-applications you simply attach to a browser. Java, a programming language based on C++, is not machine specific, and therefore does not contain parameters to interact with any one particular operating system. And although ActiveX can offer nonspecific functions, it's heart and soul is its ability to interact directly with the operating system and the desktop application software.

Table 5.2 outlines some differences between Java and ActiveX. Again, a good percentage of differences appear more on the programming or development level, than on the user level; but here are those a user should pay attention to:

TABLE 5.2: *The difference between Java and ActiveX.*

Java	ActiveX
Is not meant to be machine or operating-system-specific.	Is tied directly to the Windows environment.
Works only within the confines of a Java-enabled piece of software such as a browser.	Controls can be made to work not only with a browser but also with other applications that share the Windows environment.
Applets have no direct access to the user's computer operating system or file structure.	Can be tied directly to the user's operating system and file structure, allowing for direct access and manipulation.
Java is an interpreted language, meaning the computer has to read, then interpret, the instructions on the user's machine. This means things can take a few minutes to process. *Note: Explorer 4.0 offers what is called a Java Just-In-Time (JIT) compiler for making Java applets run faster.*	ActiveX controls are compiled and, therefore can run faster than most Java applets.
Java has a tendency to crash computers.	ActiveX has a tendency to open up security holes to outsiders.

The Four Main Pieces of the ActiveX Architecture

ActiveX actually comes in a variety of technologies aimed at offering both the programmer and Web page designer technologies they can use. Each serves a purpose for communicating and controlling Web pages, non-Web documents, and controls that work within a Web page. It's useful to familiarize yourself with the nomenclature so that if you want to use ActiveX technology on your own Web pages, and even if you don't, you'll still run across various dialog boxes, installation procedures, and ReadMe files that allude to a variety of ActiveX geekspeak. If you have a good idea what they are talking about, you'll be better able to answer questions, properly install software, and maybe even deploy ActiveX controls with greater understanding of what's going on.

And believe me, most of this seems like jargon aimed at further confusing the unassuming user about the technology. So I'll try to cut out the geekspeak chatter and explain the various components of ActiveX in a way that's understandable.

There are four main elements to ActiveX that are called into service when ActiveX is encountered. Those three elements are:

- The ActiveX container
- The ActiveX document
- The ActiveX control
- The ActiveX script

The ActiveX Container

An ActiveX container is just a fancy name for the program that has the ActiveX capability included in it. Simply put, a container is a program, like Word, Excel, or Internet Explorer, that can contain ActiveX elements and, more importantly, understand what to do with those elements once they are activated. In essence, it is the controlling application in which all the nifty ActiveX things happen.

The ActiveX Document

As the name implies, the ActiveX document is the document containing ActiveX controls. It can be viewed, browsed, or edited within the container (*i.e.*, the browser). As in the previous example, a Word document can be embedded in a Web page. When your container, Internet Explorer, runs across an ActiveX document, a Web page, it can then let you browse or edit the ActiveX document.

The ActiveX Control

The ActiveX control is the piece of programming code embedded in the ActiveX container, like the browser, the word processor, or the spreadsheet. It's the piece of programming that jumps into place when you run across an ActiveX document. So you have the controls that work within the container, that jump into place when the container encounters a document.

The ActiveX Script

An ActiveX script is a set of instructions that activates the controls. You can place an ActiveX script within a Web page to activate an ActiveX control. And if you are a Web page developer, you can use the Visual Basic scripting language to write your own controls and documents.

WHAT'S USED TO WRITE ACTIVEX CONTROLS?

To create an ActiveX control, you need to use some type of programming language. To place that ActiveX control on a Web page, you simply need to use a little HTML—more about that in Chapter 9. ActiveX developers can use a wide variety of tools, including Visual Basic Script, JavaScript, or any other ActiveX script technology available to create ActiveX controls. It's entirely up to the developer which scripting language is used, but you'll find a large majority of controls scripted with VBScript. As a matter of fact, type "ActiveX" in any search engine and you'll find more information about programming controls than about using them.

BUT WHAT DOES ACTIVEX REALLY MEAN TO YOU THE USER?

Web pages by themselves are relatively boring. Just text and graphics, maybe a few animated graphics, but that's about it. Plug-ins let you read and interact with different file formats. So what do ActiveX controls offer you? Obviously more interactivity, but also more control within Web forms, more interactions with databases, and more integration with the Windows operating system. ActiveX is an interactive electronic set of building blocks that lets you assemble a wide range of interaction between the user, the browser, the application, and the operating system.

Let's take a look at some ActiveX controls, documents, and scripts in action so you can see firsthand how these things work. If you're champing at the bit for a list of ActiveX controls you can install, check out *ActiveX.com*. Many ActiveX enhancements are available through C|Net

Central's ActiveX.Com Web site, found at *www.activex.com.* If you're interested in trying out some of them firsthand, check the **Control Library** link off the main page or the **Browser Enhancement** link. Remember, you must be using Internet Explorer 3.0 or above in order for these controls to work; but if you aren't so antsy to get started, I'll show you exactly how the whole installation process works, and give you more links for more ActiveX sites.

TIP

For more case studies, check out Microsoft's Component Object Model case study site at www.microsoft.com/workshop/prog/com/cstudy/cstudy. There are plenty of case studies listed here, although some are somewhat technical in nature.

THE INFOSEEK SEARCH CONTROL

First let's start with something you do practically every time you jump on the Internet—search. If you're like me, one of your favorite search directories is InfoSeek. Maybe you've bookmarked the site, or maybe you have it installed as your default search option, but you want a better way to use the search site to your advantage. The answer is the Infoseek ActiveX control. This control gives you instant access to the Infoseek Search directory within Internet Explorer. You don't have to juggle multiple windows trying to keep the results of your search query listed in one while the actual site is displayed in another. It also helps you eliminate the need to plow through links for the information you need.

This ActiveX control is activated when you encounter the ActiveX-enabled home page, located at *www.infoseek.com/Home?pg= activex.html.* If you have the ActiveX control installed, you'll see a page much like that shown in Figure 5.1. Notice on the left-hand side you have a familiar folder orientation to the overall Infoseek site. Looking for something? Just click to open the folder and you'll find more information nested within. The right-hand side of the screen shows the results of the folder you selected. Need to search the entire Web or maybe search for an e-mail address? No problem. Simply click the **Search** tab, then type the keyword or individual's name. The results will display once again in the right-hand frame.

If you have a chance to download this control, one advantage you'll notice over Java applets that offer the same functionality is that this control is faster. Much faster. Why? Because unlike Java, which is not a compiled language, this control is compiled, and once installed within your

FIGURE   *The Infoseek ActiveX control gives you greater control over your Infoseek searches.*
5.1

browser it is available at the click of a button. There is no need for you to download the application, wait for it to compile, then hope it responds to your requests without bombing out.

Now let's take a look at an ActiveX-enabled site, one that incorporates a fair amount of ActiveX components to help you learn, manage, and understand all about investing.

MICROSOFT INVESTOR—AN ENTIRE WEB SITE WITH ACTIVEX CONTROLS

The sad thing about ActiveX controls is that if you are using another browser that does not offer the capability to use ActiveX technology, you almost never know what you are missing when you come upon a Web site that uses it. Such is the case with Microsoft's Investor.com, located at *http://www.investor.com.*

Can Netscape Navigator use ActiveX controls if this technology has primarily been developed for Internet Explorer? Yes, with a product called ScriptActive from a company called Ncompass. ScriptActive is a Netscape ActiveX plug-in module available for free from Ncompass labs, located at http://www.ncompasslabs.com/. This plug-in installs into your Netscape browser and provides a connection to ActiveX controls that you wouldn't normally get with the standard installation of Netscape. This, by the way, is a "must-have" plug-in if you plan to visit many of the Microsoft related Web sites, such as Investor.com or Expedia.

It's amazing what this site offers in terms of fully utilizing ActiveX technology, things you simply wouldn't see or be able to interact with if you didn't have an ActiveX-enabled browser. For example, in the Portfolio Manager, browsing visitors using an ActiveX container—Internet Explorer—would have the following options available to them, all ActiveX controls programmed specifically for this site, and downloaded the minute they connect to the site with Internet Explorer:

- A constantly rolling stock ticker with clickable links to business-related stories
- Historical charts that let you chart out investments and play "what if" analyses
- The ability to buy and sell investments that you've stored in your Portfolio Manager
- The ability to import data directly from Microsoft Money or Quicken into the Portfolio Manager, so you can view your investments
- Automatic notifications of stock splits and dividends to your Portfolio Manager

These are just some of the many features you would miss if you didn't have an ActiveX-enabled browser. Or if available in plug-in form, would require you have an ActiveX-enabled browser, download numerous plug-ins to give you all these interactive features. Notice the option to bring data from other applications directly into, of all things, a Web site! Amazing. Such options open up a whole new way to do business within an Intranet, not to mention on the Internet. Figure 5.2 gives you a glimpse of what you can expect to see on the Investor's main site page. Many of these elements are ActiveX controls that are being fed data from a server, or waiting to retrieve data stored on your hard drive for display in some chart or graph.

FIGURE   *The main Investor screen complete with scrolling ticker and business news symbol.*
5.2

Figure 5.3 is an example of an ActiveX control in action, a control that pops up the minute you enter the Portfolio Manager for the first time. Notice how the Portfolio Wizard appears as if it were just installing any other Windows application. But in this instance, the Web site is the application. By now you should start to see how ActiveX controls can actually bridge the gap between Web site and your desktop.

Once you do set up your Portfolio, your list of accounts is displayed in the browser window. From there you can select to work with your data much like you would if it were in your favorite spreadsheet application. The buttons listed at the top, **File**, **Edit**, **View**, **Analysis** are all ActiveX controls that let you interact with the information displayed on the page. Figure 5.4 is an example of one of these buttons that offers drop-down menu options. In this particular example, I've selected to import data from my Quicken program. Amazing, wouldn't you say? You're interacting with a Web site, using features normally found within Windows applications, not Web pages.

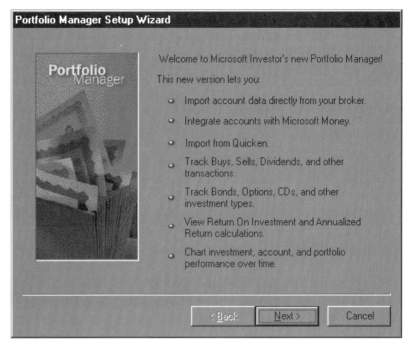

FIGURE
5.3 *When you set up the Portfolio Manager for the first time, it's like installing a Windows application.*

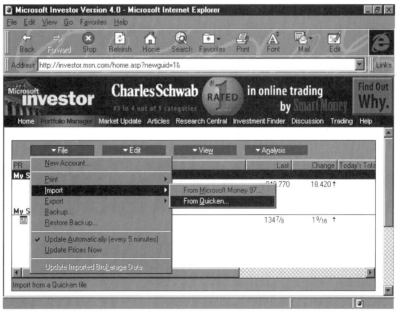

FIGURE
5.4 *These drop-down menus are ActiveX controls that let you interact with other programs on your computer, such as Quicken.*

Are There Any Standard Controls I Can Use or Should Download?

Actually the answer to this is yes and no. Because each site can be programmed with whatever ActiveX functionality you please, there are no standard controls to rush out and install on your system, like there are with plug-ins.

If you enjoy interactive animation, then by all means you should check out the Shockwave ActiveX control by visiting MacroMedia's site, which we'll do when I introduce you to the steps of installing ActiveX controls.

What you'll start to realize is that the Web sites are the must-have "containers." They have built-in ActiveX controls, so you don't need to seek out controls. In essence, when you run across a site, the control seeks you out, installing, then working almost without you knowing the control has been installed. That's why at first glance there just doesn't seem to be a big repository of "must-have" ActiveX controls. Remember previously when I said to type "ActiveX" into any search engine and you'll get more information about developing controls than you will about using or downloading them? That's simply because the technology was made in such a way that you, as the user, simply don't have to think about what to do when you encounter a control, other than to ensure it's coming from a source you trust.

When I first started out on my quest for ActiveX controls, I was baffled by the fact that there wasn't a single place that listed every single control available. Why? Because each developer creates his own set of controls based upon what he needs for his site. So even though there are some great controls out there, and even though sites like ActiveX.com (*www.activex.com*) offer plenty of links to many of the major commercial sites offering their own ActiveX controls, there is no single source that shows you every single control in action. However, BrowserWatch's ActiveX area (*www.browserwatch.com*) does come close.

If you are a developer, or simply a Web page designer, you're in luck. There are a ton of resources that offer the developer and designer controls you can examine, manipulate, and add to your site. Chapter 9 lists most of these resources.

What About Security?

With all this talk about ActiveX, I'm sure you're wondering what could possibly be the downfall of such a technology? That's a simple question to answer—security. All you have to do is look at what you open up when you institute such a technology on your computer. You potentially open up your entire computer to the rest of the world, which isn't a good thing. Plenty of hackers could easily write ActiveX controls that literally could delve through the data on your computer, or control the applications on your hard drive. That may not be a problem if you store nothing personal on your computer. But if you have last year's taxes, plus all those love letters to the cast of *Baywatch* you've written, tucked away on your PC, someone could create a control, embed it on a Web page, then, when you visit that page, suck your system dry of all its secrets.

So how does Microsoft handle this potential security threat without crippling some of ActiveX's best features? By offering what is called **Authenticode**, a kind of software labeling that ensures the information you are receiving is from a reputable source. Microsoft calls this technology "digital shrink-wrap for Internet software," and in essence that's exactly what it is.

How It Works

Authenticode is a relatively easy technology to understand and one that applies not only to ActiveX controls, but also to plug-ins, dynamic link libraries, and Java applets. It's a way to protect anything coming into your computer through your Internet Explorer browser. And basically it's a technology that identifies what company is sending you this information, and whether they have proven to be legitimate.

This is how it works. After you download the ActiveX component, the browser will call into action the Windows CryptoAPI, a piece of software code/program designed to verify the signature assigned to the ActiveX component. The Windows CryptoAPI checks to see if the ActiveX control has a digital signature, a special identifier that has been verified by a third party as having come from that particular company. If the ActiveX component does not have a signature, it will notify you, assuming you have the proper safety checks in place. This would be the first sign an ActiveX control may not be coming from a reputable place or is simply something an individual, not a company, programmed.

Next, the CryptoAPI checks to see if the signature is invalid or has been revoked by the authorizing company. If so, this means you probably should not download this ActiveX component. The authorization may have been revoked for security reasons, or may be invalid because someone is trying to forge the information. If, on the other hand, the

CryptoAPI finds everything in order with the digital signature, it passes along the ActiveX component to your computer and alerts you to the name of the developer and the certifying authority.

So basically all Authenticode does is vouch for the company sending you the ActiveX component. It does not check to see if the component was sent through secure channels, nor does it check whether the component has ominous code in it that could cause problems with your computer or even suck the data out of your drive. You're assuming that if the component went through the security check and has been programmed by a reputable company, then things should work. But it also doesn't check to see if the component has viruses, bugs, or other problems with it. And herein lies the big security flaw that makes many people nervous about using ActiveX. Since the downloading and installation of ActiveX controls is relatively easy if programmed for malicious actions, ActiveX controls, because they can communicate with the operating system, have the potential of destroying or damaging the data on your hard drive. Therefore never accept a control from an unsigned organization, and be very careful where you get your controls. Also check *www.news.com* on a regular basis for news about security flaws that seem to creep up daily with just about every browser.

How ActiveX Components Are Installed

Now that you know a little bit about what's available, let's take a look at how an ActiveX component is installed. Believe me, this will be a real quick look, since you do almost absolutely nothing aside from clicking the link for the control or component you want to install.

First, we'll be using the old standby version of Internet Explorer, version 3.02, since it is more persnickety than Internet Explorer 4.0. If things are going to go wrong, they are more likely to go wrong in this version than in IE4.0. If you are still using the venerable version 3.0, I strongly urge you to upgrade to version 3.02, like I'll be using in the following examples, or version 4.0, which offers even more advanced features. Otherwise, you may find that many ActiveX controls will not work due to serious security flaws in the previous versions of Internet Explorer. You can find all updated versions on Microsoft's Web site at *http://www.microsoft.com/explorer/* or at Browser.com, located at *http://www.browsers.com*.

Second, if you have version 3.02 or above, let's check to make sure you have ActiveX turned on and enabled. To do this, select **Options** from the **View** menu, click the **Security** tab. Your screen should look something like the one shown in Figure 5.5. Notice the section labeled **Active Content**? The following options should be checked in order for you to experience full ActiveX features:

- Allow downloading of active content
- Enable ActiveX controls and plug-ins
- Run ActiveX scripts

These three options combined together give you the full ActiveX functionality. If you do not allow for downloading, or do not enable the

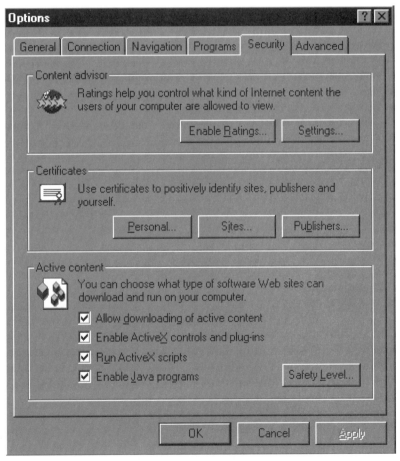

FIGURE   *The Security tab will display the options necessary for ActiveX technology to work.*
5.5

controls or ActiveX scripts to initiate, you may not reap the full benefits of ActiveX controls.

Now click the **Safety Level** button in the **Active Content** area. This option lets you control exactly what kind of content you'll allow and won't allow, using the **Authenticode** technology we talked about earlier. Depending upon the safety level you choose, when you encounter an ActiveX component, you will be alerted either when an application is being downloaded, or when there is a potential security risk, or simply none at all. You choose the level of safety to incorporate in your Web browser. I would recommend you leave the setting activated for at least the medium level, or high if you are visiting numerous ActiveX-enabled sites and are uncertain as to the security risk you may be exposing yourself to.

Internet Explorer 4.0 handles ActiveX notification a little differently than version 3.02. With IE4.0 you can actually set up a variety of different zones which allows you to pick the sites or collection of sites you should trust or shouldn't trust. You can create your own zone for those ActiveX sites if you wish. The amount of security you employ is entirely up to you.

Once you have the security levels set, the ActiveX options enabled, and have a good connection to the Internet, you're ready to try your first ActiveX control. The best place to see how quickly ActiveX controls can be installed is MacroMedia's Shockwave site. Macromedia's Shockwave plug-in or ActiveX technology is probably some of the loudest. Simply type "*www.macromedia.com*" in the **Address** field of your **Explorer** browser. In a few minutes or seconds, depending upon your connection, you should see the main MacroMedia page. This main page offers Shockwave files that can only be displayed with either a Shockwave plug-in or a shockwave ActiveX control.

Assuming everything is in proper working order, when you first encounter the site, you may or may not be notified that an ActiveX component is about to be installed within your browser. If your safety levels are set to alert you, you may see a dialog box resembling the one shown in Figure 5.6.

If you don't have any safety/security activated within the Internet Explorer browser, the ActiveX control will automatically start to install. You should see an indication of this in the status bar of the browser. Figure 5.7 is an example of what you might see. Also take notice that the area in which the control will be placed resembles a little building block. This type of icon signals an ActiveX control is embedded in the Web

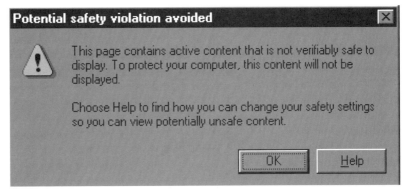

FIGURE   *When you have your safety levels set high enough, you're always notified when a*
5.6   *control is being installed into your system.*

page, and is either in the process of being installed or is not installed to
display the information properly.

Once the control has been installed, that's it. The object embedded
within the Web page will display, allowing you to interact with it. In the
case of Shockwave ActiveX controls, you should see animation, hear
sounds, even be able to interact with the elements. The control actually
allows you to see Shockwave movies, so to speak; yet these are not like
ordinary movies. These movies can interact with the user, taking input
from him, Web pages, and returning the results. Be sure to check out the
library of Shockwave examples which MacroMedia offers on its site.

Amazing, isn't it? That's all there is to installing an ActiveX control.
There is no need to stop your browser, unzip files, run setups, or reboot
your computer. The control simply installs while you wait, or even while
you read or browse through other Web sites. You don't have to worry
about where to put the control; that's done for you. And you don't have

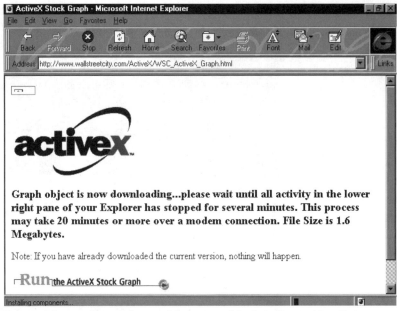

to worry about activating the control. It automatically activates the minute you run across a site with data or ActiveX scripts destined to be displayed within the control.

Unlike installing plug-ins, there isn't much to installing ActiveX controls. But once again, remember there are controls for the user and controls for the developer. You should not have to download or unzip any control worth its weight. If a control does require you to download a compressed file, that's a good indication it's a control you would place or embed within a Web page itself, and not something you would install as a browsing user.

WHAT PROBLEMS MIGHT I RUN INTO WITH ACTIVEX CONTROLS?

Although it depends on what version of the Internet Explorer browser you use, you can run into all sorts of strange problems. ActiveX is not without its own problems, although at this moment I find it a more stable technology than Java. With the way things change in the computer business, that could change at any time. But here are a few things I've encountered with ActiveX controls. I've included questions and answers about some potential problems you'll run into in the next section.

Be sure to check Microsoft's Knowledge Base for more information on other problems that you might encounter. (Don't bother calling; you'll be put on hold or in voice-mail hell.) You can find the Knowledge Base at *http://www.microsoft.com/support/*.

The Control Won't Install—Says Something about Authenticode.

Oftentimes this has to do with your browser having an older version of Authenticode installed in it. Although your browser will normally tell you when this happens and take you directly to the Microsoft Web site to update your software, you should periodically check the Microsoft Web site to see if there are updates to the browser itself, particularly security updates like Authenticode.

The Control Won't Install—Nothing Happens.

This could happen because you have a problem with your Internet connection, or the control has been installed halfway. Check your connections to the **Internet**. Then quit **Explorer**, empty out the **Windows\ Temporary Internet Files** folder, and restart your system. If you're still having problems with the installation, the site offering the control may be having problems itself.

Once Installed, Explorer Takes Me to Sites I Didn't Ask For.

Most likely you simply need to restart your browser. Possibly the memory cache has become corrupted. Restarting your browser will help, so will emptying out your temporary and history files through the **View | Options** menu option.

All I Get Is a Little Building Block Icon. What Does That Mean?

This means the control is still loading or has not been able to load. Try restarting the browser, then reloading the control. You might also try lowering your security options if you know the control offered is through a site you can trust. Only turn off your safety options in individual circumstances, and then turn them back on again, immediately afterwards.

How Many ActiveX Controls Are There and Where Do I Get Them?

There are literally thousands of ActiveX controls and there are plenty of sites that cater to ActiveX. But there are two kinds of ActiveX gadgets you'll run across—those controls for public consumption and those for developers' consumption. Definitely read the information accompanying the control before you attempt to download any software to your computer.

Remember, if you run across a site using ActiveX technology, you literally have to do nothing in order for that technology to come to you, besides clicking the **OK** button when you are notified of the site's attempt to load information into your system. So finding ActiveX controls is somewhat different than finding plug-ins, since most ActiveX controls are simply an extension of a Web site. There are, however, several places that offer links to companies offering specific user-oriented plug-ins. One of the best places is BrowserWatch, which will give you a complete listing of all the ActiveX controls available to both user and developer. You can find BrowserWatch at *www.browserwatch.com*. Table 5.3 lists other sites that offer links to controls.

Table 5.3: *Sites that offer links to ActiveX controls.*

Site Name	Location
DaveCentral—a shareware repository	www.davecentral.com
Shareware.com—search for links to sites containing shareware	www.shareware.com
Download.com—links to demo and pay-for products	www.download.com
ActiveX.com—more for developers, but does have a list of browser enhancements for the user to peruse	www.activex.com
TuCows—a repository for shareware applications	www.tucows.com
Browsers.com—a place for all sorts of things relating to browsers in general	www.browsers.com
BrowserWars—a site for all sorts of interesting information related to both Netscape and Microsoft browsers	www.browserwars.com

There are plenty of resources available for developers. Some of the best resources are other developers. Check various search engines using the keyword **ActiveX** for a list of sites created with ActiveX in mind. You'll be surprised at what you'll run across. Also check the venerable Activex.com site and sites shown in Table 5.4.

TABLE 5.4: *Sites for developers developing ActiveX controls.*

Site Name	Location
ActiveX.org—the organizing body for implementing ActiveX as a network standard	www.activex.org
Microsoft's Developer's Network	www.microsoft.com/msdn/
Microsoft's Site Builder's Network	www.microsoft.com/activex/

MAILING LISTS AND NEWSGROUPS

There are probably at least 40 newsgroups that deal with certain aspects of ActiveX technology. You can find a complete list of newsgroups at the Microsoft Technical support site, located at *http://support.microsoft. com/support/news/default.asp.* Click the link for **Internet Explorer Newsgroups** and you'll see a complete list of newsgroups available. The development tools link provides you with direct access to development-oriented newsgroups, many dealing specifically with the Visual Basic scripting language.

Microsoft is constantly changing its Web site locations. If you don't find what you are looking for based upon the locations I've supplied here, simply use the **Search** *button from the main* **Microsoft Web page***, www.microsoft.com, to find what you are looking for.*

There are plenty of mailing lists devoted to ActiveX as well. Like the newsgroups, Microsoft runs most of them itself. At the time of this writing, many are currently closed, but others are still open to the general public to subscribe to. You can find a complete listing at *www. microsoft.com/sitebuilder/resource/mail.asp*, or through the Information Desk link on *www.activex.com.*

SUMMARY

By now you should have a feel for what ActiveX offers you and how it differs from the plug-in technology now employed in Netscape Navigator. Although each technology has its pluses and minuses, when you get right down to it, it's all about supercharging your browser to give you features and controls you never thought possible. Now you're ready to see more closely how you can let your browser take over the world, and let your computer provide you with almost every function imagineable.

6 Using Plug-Ins and ActiveX on an Intranet

Up until now, just about everything you've read in this book pertains to using ActiveX and plug-ins on the Internet, the global network of computers. But what if you want to use plug-ins or ActiveX controls on your company's own internal network? Are there any plug-ins or ActiveX controls that work specifically well on internal networks? Do you have to configure internal servers differently? Does an internal network offer more capabilities for plug-ins or ActiveX controls than the Internet? And what exactly is an Intranet?

In this chapter you'll learn just enough to be dangerous. Dangerous enough, that is, to possibly motivate your company to move towards Intranet technology if it hasn't done so already. And more dangerous still to those computing folks who may not be fully aware of all the various plug-ins and ActiveX controls that could make your life as a user easier, and their life as system administrator simple. This chapter is mainly meant to inform you of what an Intranet really is, which plug-ins and ActiveX controls you might consider deploying on your own Intranet, and how these options work. This chapter is not intended as a how-to guide for setting up Intranets. Instead this chapter is meant to give you the information and resources to help you consider venturing into Intranet technology and to teach you how plug-ins and ActiveX controls can help you further that technology.

NOTE

*This section couldn't possibly cover all there is to know about setting up, converting to, or implementing an Intranet. If you're one of those computing systems administrators who need to know how to do just that, check out **The Intranet Bible** (published by IDG), **PC Week Intranet** and **Internet Firewalls Strategies** (published by Ziff-Davis), or **Building the Corporate Intranet** (published by John Wiley). If those books don't do it for you, check **Amazon.com** at http://www.amazon.com or **Computer Books** at www.cbooks.com. You'll find over 70 different Intranet titles available on the electronic shelves. If that sounds overwhelming, the best way to find the right one is to read reviews and comments about such books at **Amazon.com**. At the end of this chapter I've also included a list of resources available on the Internet that offers tons of information relating to setting up, maintaining, and running Intranets.*

INTRANETS, INTERNETS, AND EVERYTHING ELSE

First let me explain exactly what I mean when I say Intranet. Hopefully this will help you understand the difference between a standard network and an Intranet. It's important you understand the difference if you plan to use plug-ins within your internal network. Plug-ins and ActiveX controls will not work on just any network, and to understand whether your network is capable of using plug-ins you must first understand the difference between a standard network and an Intranet network.

WHAT IS AN INTRANET?

An Intranet is simply a network of computers that employs certain technology, like that used on the Internet. But instead of offering access to Web servers, file servers, or other types of Internet-oriented servers to the world, access to these servers is offered internally within a company, university, government agency, or even within your house. Only the people within your organization who are authorized to use your company's Intranet would have access to these resources. Your company's network may or may not be an Intranet. Your network may use a different protocol than what is employed on the Internet. For example, your company may be using a Novell network running the IPX protocol. Or your company's network may be a Macintosh network using the AppleTalk protocol. And instead of using a Web server, your company may be using a file server—a central computer where everyone shares files and applications. Table 6.1 gives you a better idea of the exact differences between an internal network and an Intranet.

TABLE 6.1: *The differences between an Intranet and an internal network.*

An Intranet...	An Internal Network...
Uses the TCP/IP networking protocol to communicate with all the other computers on the Intranet.	Can use whatever network protocol or way to communicate with other computers on the network. This sometimes means some systems cannot communicate with other systems, or require specialized hardware or software to interact.
Uses a Web server or other type of Internet server as a kind of central server for exchanging information.	Usually uses a file server to transfer information back and forth.
Uses what is called client/server applications where the client requests information, then is sent the response from the server.	An internal network oftentimes relies on a direct connection to a database or other file on the file server.

Table 6.1 (continued)

Can easily be linked to the Internet because of the underlying technology.	Since an internal network operates on its own networking protocol, connecting to the Internet usually takes a lot more hardware and software.
Intranets can be protected from outside intruders and unauthorized access of Internet content through the use of a firewall, a computing device that filters information in and out of the network.	Internal networks don't need firewalls because they are not a part of the Internet.
Intranets can easily use Internet-based applications and server programs for access to e-mail, Web pages, file servers, and group discussions.	Internal networks rely on specific networking software and usually cannot use Internet-type software.
Doesn't require every user to use an application to view data on a Web page, but can use plug-ins, thus reducing the overall costs of the computers employed on the network.	Usually requires each computer to have a copy of the applications used to create files so information can be shared and viewed on the Internet.
Requires little or no training since the point-and-click analogy circumvents users from having to learn complex instructions.	Usually requires substantial training on how to connect to, work with, and exchange information from sources on the network.
Can have forms set up for specific database queries. This can be done relatively quickly with simple Web page making tools. Those queries can easily use Web browsers to query, then return that information.	May require advanced queries programmed to meet the needs of the users, or it may require that users be trained in how to query systems
Gives a fair amount or appearance of control to the user in terms of what they can access and the way in which that information can be accessed.	Seems restrictive to the user and may require the user to go through many different requests, databases, or applications to get what he wants.
Can use standard Internet e-mail and newsgroup applications for one-on-one, company-wide, and worldwide communications.	Oftentimes uses e-mail systems that don't offer connections to the outside world.
Can easily be connected to the Internet, and when used with security features, can offer easy remote access without complex software or hardware procedures.	Requires additional dial-in hardware and software products for remote access. Such access is relatively limited and difficult to implement and use.

As you can see, Intranets offer a better way to distribute information across a company network because Intranets can use a simple, standard interface such as a Web browser. And Intranets can, with a little programming, connect to existing databases easily through a Web browser interface, reducing the cost of specialized programming and training. Now let's look at some of the advantages Intranet technology has over standard internal network technology.

THE ADVANTAGES OF AN INTRANET

If you've worked within a corporate network, you either love it or hate it. Things either work or they're breaking all the time. Most likely things don't always work right. The printers go down and you can't access the databases. Asking for new ways to view data is like pulling teeth. Forget about connecting remotely; it's an elaborate process that takes a degree in computing science to understand. And worse yet, every time you try to access data created by a co-worker it's a major production. You either don't have the right version, the right software program, or enough memory or hard disk space to view the file. Sometimes it takes additional software or macros you may not have installed. Maybe your co-worker has created an elaborate file requiring detailed instructions on how to view the data, none of which makes sense to you. Or maybe they've created it and have it on their Mac but your PC simply can't view the data because it doesn't have the right software.

Just for a minute forget all those network problems you're having at work and think about how relatively easy it is to view Web documents on the Internet. At the least all you have to know is how to point and click. At most you have to know the address of where the document you want to view is stored. But think for a minute where those documents might be stored. They could be stored on Unix computers, on a Macintosh, on a Windows 95 computer, or even on a Windows NT server. You never know, nor do you really care. There isn't a single indicator as to what kind of computer those documents are stored on. When you click a hypertext link, little thought goes into the "hows" or "whys" of where the document you want is stored. You simply click the link and hope the information you want displays on your computer screen in a relatively quick amount of time. Most of the time the document does display with a simple click of a button.

Most likely you never gave it a second thought as to what kind of computer created the document. And why should you? As long as it displays in your browser window, what does it matter what type of computer created the Web page? Regardless of the computer used—from PageMaker to Microsoft Word running on a Windows 95 computer, from text editors to FrameMaker running on a Mac—the Web page still displays on your computer screen, as you would expect. Sometimes that display contains graphics; sometimes sound. Sometimes you may even hear live audio or watch video. You may even get to fly through three-dimensional worlds.

Now think for a minute about your internal network. Is it as simple to view data on your network as it is to view it on the Internet? Can you easily move from reading information about your 401K plan to viewing your department's budget in an Excel spreadsheet, to electronically conversing with your co-worker miles away, to requesting additional safety glasses from the safety department? Can you call someone up on your Intranet phone application and leave him a voicemail message that he can later retrieve through his e-mail application? Can you sit at your desk and watch a training video that helps you learn more about your job?

Most likely, if you don't have an Intranet deployed, all of these things require separate applications, different networks, and maybe some options aren't even accessible electronically. An Intranet can give you, the worker, instant access to all sorts of data regardless of where that data is stored or what kind of computer or application created it. An Intranet can also utilize video, audio, multimedia, and virtual reality over the network, allowing for more feature-rich data to be transferred from one worker to another. Since Web servers and Web browsers can be configured to play, display, or work with whatever kind of data is available, an Intranet doesn't require additional programming when a worker wants to deploy information on the Intranet. Better still, the computing support department doesn't have to train end users how to access data on the network, since most data can easily be gotten at with the click of a mouse button.

Finally, since most applications such as Microsoft Office are now coming with built-in HTML/Web page making functions, creating data that can be shared with others is relatively easy to do. Most of the time it's simply saving or printing the file in HTML format, then uploading the file to the Web server. And because the data can't easily be altered, sharing data through Web pages means better control, with little or no fear of having that information altered when it shouldn't be.

Intranets offer a wealth of capabilities that older internal style networks never could. To reiterate exactly what these advantages are, here's a quick rundown of the major points:

- Uses a standard Web browser interface for connection to all sorts of data, even that contained in existing databases and mainframe systems
- Allows use of all sorts of data types including video and audio
- Provides remote access relatively easily from almost all parts of the world
- Doesn't require installation of full-featured software
- Allows users to easily create data and place it on the Intranet

CONVERTING FROM THE OLD TO THE NEW

How does a company of any size go about converting from the old to the new, from an internal network to an Intranet? First your company should have a plan, then implement the technology in relatively slow fashion, and test, test, test before you turn over your entire network into an Intranet. Although I can't delve into the depth needed to actually help you convert your existing system to an Intranet in this book, outlined below are the major steps most internal network administrators follow when converting from a traditional network to an Intranet. You may not need to do all these steps since some pieces may already be in place with your existing network. But if yours is like most, you'll have to do these steps, in relative order, to transfer from an internal network to an Intranet.

- Change the wiring that connects the computers together, replacing it with Ethernet- enabled cabling
- Implement the TCP/IP networking protocol on all computers
- Replace existing file servers with Web server with file transfer capabilities
- Replace the existing electronic mail application with an Internet/Intranet e-mail-based application
- Convert existing networking access and data to HTML format for access through the Web server
- Update, upgrade, or implement access to existing databases so they can be accessed through Web page-based forms
- Create groupware options such as online text, video and/or audio conferencing, and data sharing

- Install Web browser and groupware access software on each client's workstation
- Implement firewall and security protection to protect network from outside intrusion
- Create remote access through secure means
- Teach users how to access the system locally and remotely

How Plug-Ins Enhance an Intranet

An Intranet is a perfect place for plug-ins. First there really isn't the worry about modem speed or bandwidth connections. That means you can offer up a wide variety of content that isn't constrained by how much data and at what speed your network can pump to the user. This content can be video, audio, or three-dimensional virtual reality worlds. It can be a ten-minute video or an hour-long training tape. It can be a page full of photos or an elaborate PowerPoint presentation. It can be a live audio broadcast of the company president's speech. It really doesn't matter since you don't have to worry about users who are using slow-speed modems.

NOTE

If your company has lots of documents to convert from Word, Excel, PowerPoint, AmiPro, FrameMaker, or other older applications, you may want to look into investing in a conversion tool called HTML Transit. This product allows you to quickly and easily convert not just text, but also the accompanying graphics and charts in legacy documents into Web pages with clickable links, table of contents, and links to pages within the document. You can find more information about HTML Transit at their Web site at www.infoaccess.com.

But the speed of the network and the amount of bandwidth aren't the only things that make Intranets and plug-ins an ideal match. Plug-ins make it easy for just about any data file to be placed on the Intranet server. Instead of having to install new software on every single workstation, varying file types can be viewed with a Web browser and the appropriate plug-in. If the user doesn't have this plug-in, all you have to do as a network administrator is create a link to the plug-in so the user can download it. This ease of use and simple installation procedure is a godsend for any overworked network administrator. You don't have to configure every single workstation or install software that may only be used once or twice, and you don't have to worry about software taking up users' valuable hard disk. Better still, since the plug-in is only loaded into memory when it's called into play to view the data file, workstations don't have to be fully loaded with lots of RAM memory to work properly with plug-ins.

Also plug-ins are relatively easy to install globally. Many browsers, including Netscape Navigator and Internet Explorer, offer network administrator kits, software that lets the network administrator deploy updates, enhancements, and new features. This means a network administrator can quickly update software as needed, especially when a new plug-in may need to be installed.

THE ADVANTAGES OF ACTIVEX CONTROLS ON AN INTRANET

I hate to say it, but Microsoft does "get it." Although their products are often buggy, one thing you must give Microsoft credit for is that, in many ways, it understands corporate computing, in particular network computing. And it's never been so obvious as in the past few years, when the company finally got on the Internet bandwagon. Ever since then, almost every corporate-oriented software program they've released has some sort of hook, link, or connection to Internet and Intranet technologies. This means that with little effort on your part as network administrator, and usually even less if you are an end user, you can now publish, collaborate with, query, or exchange information over your network relatively easily. Intranet/Internet using and publishing options now come standard in Office 97. And whether you want to keep the information you have stored in Microsoft-oriented databases, such as Access or FoxPro, private or offer it up for public consumption, you have to do very little in order to accomplish this task.

To install ActiveX controls, all the user has to do is visit the Web site. No specialized installation is required, no real directions to follow, other than to simply visit the page. More importantly, because ActiveX is based on the Windows Object Linking and Embedding technology, connecting Web pages to standard desktop applications such as Microsoft Office means more robust Web pages that can do amazing things such as transfer, save, update, and manipulate data between Web browser and desktop application.

TIP

OK, maybe I lied a little. If you know a simple line of code, after downloading a Netscape plug-in you can quickly activate the plug-in without having to restart your browser much like is available with ActiveX. Regardless of whether you're on the Internet or an Intranet, if you type in this line in your browser's location or address field, once you've installed the plug-in, it will immediately become active. The line of code is

javascript:navigator.plugins.refresh(true);parent.location.reload()

*Make sure you hit **"enter"** after you type this into your browser's **Location** or **Address** field. Once you do, the plug-in you've just installed will become active, much like ActiveX controls become active once they are downloaded to the browsing visitor's computer.*

IDEAL PLUG-INS FOR INTRANETS

You could say that just about any plug-in could increase a company's productivity. But there are some Intranet-oriented plug-ins that lend themselves better to use on Intranets than other plug-ins that work well over the Internet mainly due to bandwidth constraints. In the following list, I've outlined some of the more important ones you should consider adding to your Intranet. And I've included some ideas on how these plug-ins could be used on an Intranet. I'm sure you'll find more uses for them in your own unique situation.

This is by no means a complete list of all Intranet-oriented plug-ins, only a wide sampling of available mainstream plug-ins. This list is intended to give you some ideas on what you can do with plug-ins and what capabilities are available through your browser's desktop. For a more complete listing check Chapter 10. Throughout this listing I'll show you a few plug-ins and how they work with files. Each plug-in offers its own controls, features, and idiosyncrasies, so your best bet is to read through all the ReadMe files and documentation provided to learn exactly how to use the plug-in of choice.

To make this book last as long as it can on the shelves and to provide useful information to you, I've elected not to delve into the step-by-step instructions of installing or working with each plug-in since software vendors are constantly updating their products. Let's face it, most plug-ins offer very few controls or features, unlike their full-featured cousins, helper applications. To find out what those controls are, remember what you learned in previous chapters on how to control plug-ins. Simply right-click where the plug-in data file is located on the Web page and just about every control available to the plug-in will be listed in the pop-up menu. Full-screen plug-ins will offer more controls at the top, usually under the Web browser's own menu bar.

Remember too, there are new plug-ins being created almost monthly. Make sure you check Browsers.com, located at *www.browsers.com*, and Browserwatch, located at *www.browserwatch.com*, and Netscape's own home page. You'll find plenty of information about new plug-ins at both sites. In the meantime, make sure you check out the following plug-ins for use on your Intranet. I've segmented them out for you into different categories: plug-ins that share data, those that work to enhance online training and could provide extended multimedia options, those that help you and your co-workers communicate better, and those that may enhance your own desktop unit or help those who develop Web pages for your company.

I've tried to give you an idea of how some of these plug-ins can be used. In obvious cases, I've left out long, boring descriptions; and in other cases, I drone on and on about how you could use a plug-in or ActiveX control, as a way to motivate you to try it for yourself. That's usually because I've had great success with a particular plug-in or control in solving a need within the Intranets I manage, and I'm trying to encourage you to do the same. If none of the suggestions make sense, or if you are considering adding a plug-in but don't know whether you should, e-mail me with your plans and I'll offer up my opinion. You can always contact me at *ckirk@ptialaska.net* or *ckirk@alaska.net*.

Check Chapter 3 for more real-world examples of how plug-ins are used within company Intranets and on the Internet. Although I touch on how the plug-in can be used, Chapter 3 gives you more detailed information about how real people are using them as well.

TIP

SHARING DATA AND VIEWING FILES

Plug-ins that let you view other data files are probably the most abundant type of plug-ins available. With these types of plug-ins you can easily view data files of just about any type. On most Intranets these would be the most widely used plug-ins simply because they let anyone on your network access any type of information placed on your Intranet. Viewer plug-ins work relatively easily-they view files without you having to have the application that created the data file. For example, if you're preparing a manual in PageMaker and you want a group of people to use and view a draft of the manual, but those people don't have PageMaker installed, you could create an Adobe Acrobat Reader document, called a PDF file. Then that document could easily be viewed, searched, even printed with the help of the Adobe Acrobat Reader plug-in by anyone on your Intranet.

By now you should start seeing the advantage here simply because, if you are the creator of the data file, you don't have to worry about people changing the information stored in your file. They have read-only access without you having to do a thing, or know anything about how to setup directory permissions on your network. Since the plug-in does not let you edit the file, you don't have to worry about the information being inadvertently changed. You never have to worry about someone changing the font style, adding new graphics, or implementing their unique touch to your file. And if you purchase the right mix of viewer plug-ins, no one on your Intranet would ever be left out of viewing any type of data.

The plug-ins listed below run the gamut, from viewing simple Microsoft Word files to viewing complex AutoCad documents. These plug-ins let you accomplish the following:

- Help anyone on the Intranet view specific types of data files without having to convert them to HTML/Web page formats
- Reduce the amount of money needed, by not requiring a full installation of an application
- Retain the format of the file without needing specific fonts, graphics, or graphic viewers

If you're a network administrator, you might save yourself some grief and make it easier for your users to view files by implementing some of these plug-ins. And if you're a user, you may look into using some of these plug-ins to make it easier to view a wide variety of data other users may have stored on your Intranet. If you find yourself working with outside contracts, make sure you investigate many of these plug-ins. You'll save yourself a great deal of time and frustration trying to track down the right software to read files your outside contractors or sources may feed you.

I haven't included every image plug-in viewer for one simple reason: With the latest versions of Netscape Communicator and Internet Explorer, some of the viewers, such as those that view different graphic file types, are no longer necessary. If you're interested in more viewers that simply didn't make this book's cut, check out Netscape's plug-in page located at http://home.netscape.com/comprod/products/navigator/version_2.0/plugins/image_viewers.html, or select the **Help** *menu, then select* **About Plug-ins** *from the menu, and click the link to learn more about plug-ins.*

Here's the list of viewer plug-ins you might consider adding to your Intranet. Some are also available in ActiveX formats. And more and more plug-in publishers are creating not only ActiveX versions but also Java versions. Check the manufacturer's home page for more information on updates and enhancements and remember in the computer world everything is always being upgraded.

NAME OF PLUG-IN: ADOBE ACROBAT READER

Location for Plug-In: http://www.adobe.com

What This Plug-In Accomplishes

This plug-in lets you view Adobe Acrobat documents. When you create an Adobe Acrobat document, commonly referred to as a PDF (portable document format), you print it to an Adobe Acrobat file instead of printing the file to a piece of paper. That means all the fonts, graphics, formatting, and everything else but the kitchen sink is included with the file. You can create a beautiful full-color brochure, with all sorts of fonts, a ton of photographs, and even clickable Web page links, create an Acrobat PDF file, and all your work will be retained.

Even better, unlike applications that turn documents like PageMaker or FrameMaker, Word or Excel into Web pages, Acrobat documents include all the graphics inside the file. The graphics are not separate, converted files that have to be uploaded in addition to the Web page. Instead, all the graphics, all the fonts, and everything else is stuffed into a single file. Adobe Acrobat documents are probably the most widely used types of documents on the Internet aside from standard HTML files simply because the Adobe Acrobat Reader is simple to use and easily downloaded.

How You Could Use This Plug-In:

Got a company newsletter? How about company policy or training manuals? Does your sales force need brochures when they travel, but they don't want to lug around boxes and boxes of them? Does your legal department need to send documents back and forth between offices? Would you like to offer your company catalog online without spending the extra bucks to turn it into a Web page?

There isn't a company that doesn't have a manual, a legal document, a brochure, or some other printed form of communication that either its employees, sales staff, or customer base needs to read or see. And there isn't a company around that doesn't want to save a few bucks on printing costs or storage costs. With Adobe Acrobat and the Adobe Acrobat plug-in, instead of printing up thousands of training manuals, hundreds of policy and procedure manuals, you can make these manuals available online from a central source, at the click of a button. No need to print them; the employee does so when he or she needs to. No worrying about updating the manual; when you need to, you update one-the master copy stored on your Web server-not thousands scattered about people's offices. No more need to print out, waste paper, binders, and time on manuals that may only be referenced once.

With the use of the *Acrobat Reader* plug-in, the viewer of the document can read, zoom in, zoom out, rotate, print, search for, or even click links to different pages or even different Web sites. And best of all, since you prepare the document in whichever application you want, your company doesn't have to switch to different publishing methods or learn how to create elaborate Web sites. When a document is "distilled" or turned into an Acrobat Reader file, the Acrobat plug-in can view, all the fonts, all the graphics, all the color is retained. Therefore you can create sales brochures for your sales force and customers, available any time they need them. And if your company moves, changes its name, updates pricing options or adds a new product to its line, the company hasn't wasted thousands of dollars printing brochures that are now outdated. And your sales literature is available to your salesmen whether they're in the office or across the country.

Anything you can print, anything you can create, whether it's in PageMaker, FrameMaker, Word, Excel, PowerPoint, or Corel Draw, can be turned into a document that can be viewed online and easily printed exactly the way you wanted it printed. All it takes is the Adobe Acrobat Distiller which costs under $500 and the Acrobat plug-in which is free. You simply install the Distiller software, use it like you would a printer, then print to a file rather than a piece of paper. You then take that file and upload it to your Web server, then let everyone know where to go in order to view the document. When you want to update that file, you simply make your changes in the application you used to create the file, print the file again to an Adobe Acrobat file, and then send out an e-mail notice informing everyone of the changes. It's that simple.

TIP

How the Acrobat Reader works is relatively simple, but it's also a type of plug-in you don't see too often—a full-screen plug-in. When the reader loads, it occupies the entire Web browser window. The controls offered at the top, underneath Netscape's own menu controls, let you zoom in, zoom out, print, search, and control the view of the entire document through the use of a toolbar that lies underneath the standard Navigator menus. Instead of seeing a familiar Web page, you are actually viewing an Adobe PDF file within the Reader application that just happens to fit neatly in full-screen mode with Netscape Navigator. No HTML code wraps around this file, like you would see with an embedded plug-in. This is one of only a handful of full-screen plug-ins that replace a standard Web page, thereby offering customized toolbars that are incorporated under the browser's normal menu bar.

NAME OF PLUG-IN(S): WORD VIEW PLUG-IN AND QUICKVIEW PLUG-IN

Location for Plug-In(s): http://www.microsoft.com and http://www.quickview.com

What These Plug-Ins Accomplish

These plug-ins let the user view Microsoft Word documents without having to have Microsoft Word installed. This plug-in lets the viewer print, search, and view any Microsoft Word document. With the *Word Viewer*, the user can also view headers, footers, and annotations, and can zoom in and out and view the document in different layouts. If included, the viewer can also activate links to Web pages or to OLE objects such as spreadsheets, PowerPoint presentations, or other OLE-oriented objects embedded in the Word document.

How You Could Use These Plug-Ins

It may not sound like much, but if you use Microsoft Office on a network, it may be that some of your older PCs may not be able to handle a full installation of Microsoft Word. Yet your users may need to read company memos, print company policies, or view reports without the need to edit the documents. One option is to turn documents in to HTML format so they can be viewed as Web pages, but that means you'd loose the formatting and font control. Maybe instead of having Word come up as a default, you want all the computers on your network set up so the Word Viewer plug-in loads first, preventing the user from changing the document in any way.

For example, say the company you work for manufactures valves. The guys in the shop doing the dirty work-welding, shaping, and making the valves, need to read company memos, updates to policy, and procedure manuals, and maybe view detailed reports. But they may not have a need to edit any of these documents. Instead of loading up a powerful computer with the full compliment of Microsoft Office products, you could simply include the Netscape browser with the e-mail option and the Word Viewer plug-in on a less than desirable 486 unit you have lying around the office ready for the junk pile.

Here's another example. The state I live in is spread out in an area bigger than the state of Texas. Each major city has a legislative information office, where I can go to read the latest senate or house bill proposed. Since these documents are created and formatted in Word, instead of spending the extra time to convert them to Web pages, the state could simply place them in one Web server directory. Then each legislative office around that state could have a low-end computer, such as a 486, set up with a Netscape browser and the Word Viewer plug-in so anyone could view or print these documents. It would save on time and it would allow the state to extend the life of older equipment destined to hit the junk pile.

Viewers that let someone view documents created by more powerful software that requires faster machines don't have to run on fast machines themselves. That means you can fully configure a system that offers the ability to view information across a network, not just create or edit any of that information, without having to invest in lots of RAM, hard disk space, or processor power. If you start seeing the possibilities, you are probably now starting to view people on the network in two different categories—those who produce and those who need to view, but not produce or edit. When you start looking at your user base this way, you can easily start to see who really needs powerful computers and who can get by on less powerful, older units. And this makes it easier when considering where to shuffle old PCs and who to budget for newer models.

Although they aren't plug-ins, if you want the capability to view just about any Office document, check Microsoft's free download site for a whole cadre of document viewers, actually helper applications you can install to work in tandem with your viewer to view any Office 97 document. You can find these viewers at www.microsoft.com/msdownload/default.asp.

NAME OF PLUG-IN(S): AUTOCAD/DXF VIEWER AND THE WHIP! PLUG-IN, DWG/DXF BY SOFTSOURCE, DR. DWG NETVIEW, AND VISUALWEBMAP BY PROJECT DEVELOPMENT

Location(s) of Plug-In: http://www.autocad.com, http://www.soft-source.com, http://www.drdwg.com/netvw.htm, and http://hem.pas-sagen.se/project/

What These Plug-Ins Accomplish
These plug-ins let you view AutoCad and DXF files through a standard Web browser without needing expensive AutoCad software installed on each workstation. With these plug-ins, users can view or print AutoCad documents and drawings, plus use various views to zoom in and out of documents.

How You Could Use These Plug-Ins
Is your company an architectural firm that does work for people world-wide? Maybe your company has an engineering department that produces lots of engineering drawings. Maybe your department is constantly moving people from one location to another, and since you're coordinating the moves, you have to know where all the electrical outlets are located.

Regardless of whether your company is an architectural firm or simply a company constantly playing musical chairs with its employees, if you have AutoCad, DXF, or mechanical drawing files produced on AutoCad or Microstation workstations, deploying one of the above plug-ins makes sense. It especially makes sense when you consider that installing a complete working version of AutoCad on a single workstation, just so the user can view or print AutoCad files, takes up about 100 MB and about $1,500 dollars.

Here's a perfect example of how I would have used this plug-in on an Intranet had the technology been available at the time. I once worked at an oil field service company as a senior computer systems analyst. This particular company stored drawings of its facility and oil producing sites in AutoCad files. Oftentimes when engineers needed to add a new valve here, or maybe move equipment there, they needed to view these drawings. But that meant their computers had to have AutoCad installed. Since many of these systems didn't have the memory or hard disk space to accommodate such a powerful program, they were either relegated to view the documents from computers in the document library, or beg time from one of the assigned AutoCad technicians. Oftentimes when they did view the documents, accidental changes were made, causing problems for the engineers.

Since they didn't have any need to change or edit these documents, but simply needed to view or print them, the use of such AutoCad plug-in technology could have saved them tons of money, and time. And by adding this type of plug-in technology, a fair bit of frustration for the engineers could have been avoided.

Name of Plug-In(s): Formula One/Net

Location of Plug-In(s): http://www.visualcomp.com

What These Plug-Ins Accomplish

These plug-ins let you view Excel spreadsheets from within a Web page. The spreadsheet can be embedded in the page, which means the Web page itself could include additional comments, graphics, photos, or links to other types of information. The plug-in can display not only the spreadsheet but also any database elements included, as well as workbooks, and even graphics such as pie charts, line graphs, scatter graphs, or any other type of graph that can be created in Excel.

How You Could Use This Plug-In

This is probably one of the most useful plug-ins for most Intranets since so much company data is stored in spreadsheet format. From company telephone directories, to budgets, to profit and loss statements, to inventories, it's amazing exactly how much company information is input into spreadsheets. And with the *Formula One/Net* plug-in, you can easily view spreadsheet information right in your browser window.

But if your company is like most, almost every desktop computer has either Microsoft Office or some type of spreadsheet installed on its system. So why would you install a spreadsheet viewer on users' systems if there is already an application to view the spreadsheet documents? If you're involved in creating these worksheets and simply need to get reports and information to other users, you'll probably see the usefulness in having a plug-in display the information, instead of giving it the ability to change the data.

That's right. You don't have to worry about people changing the information in your documents. And you don't have to worry if someone has the old version of your budget. You place your files on your Web server, just like all other plug-in data files, and instead of having to e-mail everyone copies of your budget, report, or whatever, you simply fire up the e-mail program and mail the link to where the file is located. Then anyone on your network can view the file, print it, discuss it via e-mail or your discussion software, and you don't have to worry that the information will be changed. You have full control without having to worry about passwords, file-locking options, or any other security measures.

Another feature of a spreadsheet plug-in is that you can use a spreadsheet as an interactive form instead of having to script CGI programs. For example, say you are in the benefits department of your company. You want workers to be able to calculate their 401K plans or their individual retirement plan, but you don't know the first thing about CGI scripting. But you can create a mean spreadsheet with all the facts, figures, and formulas necessary. With the Formula One/Net plug-in, you can create an interactive form that takes input from users. They simply enter the information in the cells you designated and with the formulas you've provided the spreadsheet the user gets the information needed quickly and you don't have to do much more than create a simple spreadsheet file and place it on your Web server. The cells you don't want to change are protected and those that can be changed are left wide open.

The maker of Formula One/Net, Visual Components, has a variety of examples on its Web site of such interactive-type forms. All you need is the plug-in to view them. Simply point your browser to *www.visual-comp.com/f1net/live.htm.* On this site you'll find examples of how a loan agency quickly and easily helps customers decide which kind of loan package is right for them. You'll also see an example of how through the use of the Excel spreadsheet feature called Workbooks you can offer "live" ever-changing chart information based on what's input into a spreadsheet. One other nifty feature is that you can embed links directly into spreadsheets. If you need to provide additional data which can only be found on another Web site or Web page, you can add a link directly into a spreadsheet. If the viewer of the spreadsheet wants to view the site you've included, he simply clicks the link as he normally would in a regular Web page and his browser brings up the site.

NAME OF PLUG-IN: KEYVIEW PLUG-IN AND CSVIEW 150 PLUG-IN

Location for the Plug-In: http://www.ftp.com and http://csu-software-solutions.com

What These Plug-Ins Accomplish

Both of these products read and display data from over 150 to 200 different file formats. And thus these plug-ins can work with hundreds of different software packages. Virtually every file format any application creates, from Word Perfect to Corel Draw, from PageMaker to Paint, with these two plug-ins your Web browser can display virtually any type of file your computer can create. You don't have to have the application that was used to create the file. Instead, the plug-in will allow you to view, print, rotate, search, and zoom the file depending on whether the file is a graphic file or a text file.

How You Could Use These Plug-Ins

Without a doubt these are two of the best plug-ins to have because they can read almost every popular file format you'd ever encounter. If you have these plug-ins installed throughout your network, you will never again hear someone say they couldn't view a file. And if you have lots of visitors working within your Intranet, this makes it easier for those visitors to view the data placed there.

For example, say you have external auditors who visit your site yearly or maybe you have contractors who prepare reports or company reports for you. You could easily set up "visiting workstations" for these outside workers, fully loaded with either the CSView 150 or KeyView plug-in. Then any data file they need to view would be easily accessible through your network and could be viewed without any special configuration from the Web browser installed on the visitor's workstation. Since these plug-ins only allow for viewing and printing, not true editing, your data is safe from being accidentally changed, but is still available to anyone who happens to use the workstation. The users don't need to know anything more than how to save a file to your Web server and how to point and click.

NOTE

*What's the difference between this plug-in and say Adobe Acrobat? With the **KeyView** plug-in, for example, the creator of the file does not have to "distill" or print to a file using any special software. All he has to do is save the file as he normally would. He doesn't have to install any special software, or do anything different than he normally would, and as long as the KeyView plug-in is installed, neither does the viewer of the file. If KeyView is installed within every browser on your Intranet, no one ever has to worry if they have the application to view, search, or print the data. That's why this plug-in is not free, but the cost is definitely worth it.*

NAME OF PLUG-IN: FLASHPIX/IMAGING FOR THE INTERNET BY HEWLETT PACKARD

Location for Plug-In: http://www.hp.com and http://www.livepicture.com

What This Plug-In Accomplishes

The *FlashPix* digital image file format is a new way for storing photographic pictures on the Internet. With FlashPix the file can offer multiple resolutions of the photo in a single file. FlashPix lets you view higher quality images with better resolutions faster than standard GIF or JPEG formats. The viewer of the image can download a section of a picture, called a "tile," without having to download the entire image. The file is cached as it's transferred to the user's computer.

How You Could Use This Plug-In

Maybe your company handles a lot of photographs. Perhaps your company is a newspaper, magazine, or advertising agency. Maybe you work in a police department and exchanging photos between detectives and policemen is an important part of internal communications. Perhaps you work within a photo agency, or maybe your company simply needs access to view real photos over your company's Intranet without making users wait to see the image. With FlashPix you can add all sorts of photographs to your Intranet, without having to worry about lost resolution, slow viewing times, or need to reduce file images so they'll display quickly on a Web page.

FlashPix goes beyond JPEGs in allowing you to retain more colors and a higher resolution for the picture. The user can also zoom in to see finer details of the picture. As the Web page developer, you can also add hot-spots to the picture, where the viewer can click, and be transported to another Web page or location. Any time you need to share lots of photos over a network, you should consider using this compression technology and plug-in viewer.

NAME OF PLUG-IN: PNG LIVE VIEWER

Location of Plug-In: http://codelab.siegelgale.com/solutions/pnglive2.html

What This Plug-In Accomplishes

The *Portable Networks Graphics* file format is a relatively new file format being promoted on the Internet over and above standard GIF or JPEG file formats. With the PNG format, files can contain more colors and offer faster loading options than with other file formats. With PNG you get true-to-life color smaller files without having to remove color layers or reduce resolution. Without PNG, using the current Web-based file formats, graphics, and particularly the colors contained in them can appear different on different computers. One color on a Mac may actually look much different on a PC since, once you go over the first 16 colors, there really is no standard color table across different computers and monitors.

PNG files are also on average about 30 percent smaller than with GIF files. Thus the image is not only sharper, but also downloads faster. PNG is supported by a wide variety of applications including Photoshop and ShockWave.

If your graphics application does not currently have a .PNG file format available, check the software manufacturer's site to see if new patches, plugins, or file formats can be downloaded to add this functionality to your graphics software.

How You Could Use This Plug-In

If you're dealing with any pictures or photographs on an Intranet that is a combination of Macs and PCs, and you want your photos to retain their original color, plus you want them to download faster over your Intranet, this is an excellent plug-in to use. However, your software must be capable of saving graphics or photos to a .PNG format.

As with many plug-in viewers, such as the PNG viewer, the idea is not so much to offer new file formats, but to give the browsing visitor quicker access to information and graphics, plus provide for ultracompressed files. If you find your Intranet's server filling up because of huge files your users are putting on it, by all means check out some of these files compression plug-ins and programs. However, if you would rather stay with the standard GIF and JPEG file formats, but you want much smaller files with faster download times, with no need for any additional plug-ins, check out Emblaze's WebCharger picture compression utility located at http://www.emblaze.com.

NAME OF PLUG-IN: TIFF IMAGE VIEWER

Location of Plug-In: http://www.visionshape.com/freetiff.html

What This Plug-In Does
With the *TIFF Image Viewer* you can view TIFF files which may be created by various desktop publishing and graphics applications. With the TIFF Image Viewer you can view, print, rotate, zoom, and copy to the clipboard.

How You Could Use This Plug-In
TIFF files are pretty widely used across applications. For example, if you scan in images, most likely you've saved the files in a TIFF file format. Perhaps you're a real estate agent or real estate appraiser and you use your digital camera to take pictures of the properties you sell or appraise and want to share the pictures of the property with other agents or appraisers. With this plug-in you don't have to do any conversion. You simply save the image, place it on your server, and then share it with the rest of the people on your network. The big time-saver here is that you don't have to convert your TIFF files to JPEG or GIF and possibly loose the crisp quality of the TIFF file itself. This can save a great deal of time if you have a lot of TIFF files to transfer to your network's server.

NAME OF PLUG-IN: PENOP PLUG-IN

Location for the Plug-In: http://www.penop.com

What This Plug-In Accomplishes
With the *PenOp* plug-in and the PenOp application you can take handwritten signatures, certify the signature, then send that signature over the network or Internet. Using a low-cost digitizer and the PenOp software, you can capture the signature and create a legal electronic equivalent of a handwritten signature. Using specialized cryptography, a token is created which actually creates a record of who signed what, when, and why. The token is tamperproof and can be sent from system to system.

How You Could Use This Plug-In
At first I thought, "Hmmm...what could you use this plug-in for?" But soon I realized the amazing things you could do with this plug-in. No longer do you have to go to your boss' office for his signature. Just e-mail

him the need for a signature, then attach it to a document. In the human resources department you could easily have employees sign off on forms electronically, saving their signature and form for later retrieval. If you work in a law office, clients could electronically sign paperwork and other attorneys could view that same paperwork across your network. Any type of paperwork that requires a signature is fair game for this type of plug-in.

You do, however, need to buy the digital signature hardware or scan in a digital signature in order for clients or employees to be able to sign on the spot and have the signature saved, verified, and assigned a security certificate. This hardware, like you've seen in numerous large department stores, can be purchased for several hundred to several thousand dollars.

NAME OF PLUG-IN: RAOSOFT DATABASE GRID PLUG-IN

Location of Plug-In: http://www.raosoft.com/plugins/

What This Plug-In Does
This plug-in lets you view Dbase- or ASCII-delimited database files through a Web browser. You can view multiple records within a database and zoom in on those fields. You can double-click on any record and enter new information depending on how you want to configure your database. Within each field of data you can expand the columns, double-click to enter new data, print the information, or scroll through the entire database.

How You Could Use This Plug-In
If your company has databases stored on your network server, this is an excellent way to give those users who need only read-only access to database files. Instead of having to install the database application on each computer, you can install the plug-in and view the data. Simple and fast access makes this a great tool for any database information that might have been culled from other database applications and printed to ASCII-delimited files.

NAME OF PLUG-IN(S): JETFORM AND OMNIFORM INTERNET FILER

Location for the Plug-In: http://www.jetform.com and http://www.caere.com

What These Plug-In(s) Accomplish

With *OmniForm* and *JetForm* you can create electronic forms, or scan in existing paper forms and place them on your server. With the use of the plug-in you can view, interact, and fill out the forms and have the data saved into a database of your choosing.

How You Could Use These Plug-In(s)

Making interactive forms with HTML is sometimes an arduous task. In addition, unless you're using Javascript or some form of CGI scripting, HTML doesn't allow you to check the form for errors or create very interactive forms that help the user fill out the form completely.

But with products like JetForm and OmniForm, you can create interactive forms that check user input. In addition, you can also take paper forms and turn them into electronic forms. Thus all those FedEx forms, employee benefit forms, vendor forms, and legal documents your company might use on a regular basis can easily be scanned in, then turned into online forms that anyone in your office with a Web browser and the plug-in can fill out. Better still, since it isn't just the form that's being created but rules and help files, you can ensure the forms are filled out properly. The data can then either be sent via CGI scripts to remote databases or sent to form-specific database servers.

TRAINING AND MULTIMEDIA

In the past the idea of using computers to train workers was something that could only be undertaken by large corporations simply because of the cost that high-powered computers and specialized software involved. But with the use of a few simple Web pages and simple audio and video recording technology, now any size company can create interactive multimedia training applications with little or no programming experience. And since many companies now have upgraded to more powerful computers that include multimedia features such as sound cards and speakers, adding sights and sounds to an Intranet is an excellent way to make training, promotional campaigns, and sound and video options available to the workers.

Consider all the video training tapes your company has you watch, from safety videos to corporate briefings, from Word and Excel training videos to television commercials. Now, instead of gathering everyone in the conference room to view them, any employee can check them out electronically, watching or listening to them as they work on their own desktop computer. You can keep track of who watches the videos, quiz the workers on what they saw, and gather the results electronically; and you can simply make it easier for workers to get the information they need, regardless of the format the information might be stored in. With the RealPlayer, Shockwave, Flash, Asymetrix Neuron, or PointPlus plug-in, just to name a few, your corporate Intranet can deliver high-quality graphics, sound, and video over the Intranet with a minimal amount of effort. Here are some of the best video- and audio-oriented plug-ins. Again, this is by no means a complete list, just a list of some of the tested, tried and true plug-ins that are currently working in networks across the globe.

NAME OF PLUG-IN: REALPLAYER

Location of Plug-In: http://www.real.com

What This Plug-In Accomplishes
This plug-in allows you to view and/or hear Real files, sometimes called Real Audio or Real Video files. *RealPlayer* files can either stream "live" through a Real server, or can stream through a standard Web server. RealPlayer files can also link directly to Web sites.

How You Could Use This Plug-In
Adding video or audio to any Web page makes that page stand out. But adding Real Audio or Video files to your Intranet goes beyond simply the entertainment value. This plug-in could easily be used to create interactive training guides that work in conjunction with information stored on Web pages. Because you can link and time the changing of Web pages with Real Video or Real Audio files, you don't have to know much more than how to create a page, copy and paste a link, and record a Real Audio file. For anyone who has ever ventured into creating multimedia digital training programs, you know it can be a long and arduous task. By recording videos, adding audio, and placing links within the audio or video RealPlayer files, you can quickly and easily create interactive training and communication applications.

You can add audio of the latest shareholder's meeting, or place video from a particular training video on a Web page. Your Web pages can now come to life, offering more than just static tests to your co-workers.

NAME OF PLUG-IN: SHOCKWAVE/FLASH PLUG-IN

Location for the Plug-In: http://www.macromedia.com

What This Plug-In Accomplishes
With the *Shockwave/Flash* plug-in you can view graphics, movies animation, and interactive multimedia within a Web browser. Because Shockwave/Flash files can also include sound, the visitor can enjoy full-featured sites that offer not only rolling movies but also interaction between the visitor and the site. Many Shockwave/Flash-enabled sites offer interactive games, streaming music, and advanced sales presentations that you simply couldn't do with other programming options such as Javascript.

How You Could Use This Plug-In
The ShockWave/Flash plug-in could be used on a corporate Intranet in one of three ways:

- As a way to provide interactive training
- As a presentation tool
- To enhance corporate Web sites with interactive marketing materials

Unlike the RealPlayer, you can create animations, include video, and add audio to any storyboarded Shockwave file. Granted, creating Shockwave-enabled sites takes some artistic talent, yet Shockwave is an excellent application when you want to create feature-rich interactive training programs. Whereas RealPlayer files only allow for Hyperlinks, with Shockwave you can actually create full interactive programs.

NAME OF PLUG-IN: ASYMETRIX'S NEURON

Location of Plug-In: http://www.asymetrix.com/toolbook/neuron/

How This Plug-In Works
If your company uses the Asymetrix ToolBook to create multimedia training projects, the *Neuron* plug-in is the best solution to give Web-based access to all the projects produced with any of the Asymetrix ToolBook II authoring products. The Neuron plug-in lets the user view and play presentations, kiosks, courseware, and other multimedia applications produced in ToolBook.

How You Could Use This Plug-In
This is an excellent way to revamp the content your company might have created with the Asymetrix ToolBook II training and multimedia program. As a matter of fact, this is about the only way you can revamp existing content into Web based format. If you haven't checked out what Asymetrix ToolBook II can do in terms of online and interactive training, make sure you check out their Web site for more information. You can create and keep track of training records easily and create compelling training materials with the ToolBook II product.

COMMUNICATION AND COLLABORATION TOOLS

NAME OF PLUG-IN: WEBTERM BY WHITE PINE

Location of Plug-In: http://www.wpine.com/

How This Plug-In Works
This plug-in offers 3270, 5250, and VT420 terminal emulation within a browser. The plug-in also supports centrally administered emulation and connectivity remotely as well as automatic updates of the plug-in software with no user involvement required. You can also automate interactions between client and host, making it easier for nontechnical users to log on and access the information they need on mainframe and remote systems.

How You Could Use This Plug-In
If you have any need to connect to remote systems, whether they are within your own company's Intranet or remotely across the Internet, this is an excellent plug-in to accomplish such a task. You simply configure the plug-in according to the needs of the user, make it available to anyone who needs it, then update it remotely when new versions of the plug-in become available. You can also automate log-on tasks through the use of Javascript.

NAME OF PLUG-IN(S): OPSESSION PLUG-IN, WINFRAME, CARBON COPY/NET, LOOK@ME, ALTIS

Locations of Plug-In(s): http://www.netmanage.com/products/opsession/plugin.html, http://www.citrix.com, http://www.microcom.com, http://www.epicon.com

How These Plug-Ins Work

All of these applications offer access to remote computing resources, but in slightly different ways. *OpSession* and Citrix's *WinFrame* let you control applications remotely from within a browser window, whereas *Look@Me* and *CarbonCopy/Net* let you connect to remote PCs and fully control them and the applications, data files, and directories stored on these remote computers. All offer full security using password protection of files, access rights, and application-specific sharing so only those applications and data files you want shared can be shared across an Intranet or across the Internet. With OpSession, CarbonCopy/Net, and Look@Me, multiple users can work on the same document at the same time. And with OpSession multiple users can work on the same data files even if they are working on different computers.

With all of these products you can connect to your own PC over the Internet or through a corporate Intranet through a standard Web browser. Once connected you can use your PC to send and receive Intranet e-mail, copy files, organize your hard drive, or do anything else you normally would do if you were sitting in front of your PC.

How You Could Use This Plug-In

If your Intranet is spread across the country and you need to collaborate on files, this is the easiest way to do it. Better yet, if your network is comprised of both Macs and PCs, you can easily share applications even if the application doesn't exist on the other computer, by using either the Citrix WinFrame or OpSession plug-ins. With any of these plug-ins you can easily collaborate with other users, or connect to other computers and remotely control them. Thus, if you are working on a help desk, or need to support remote users, or travel a great deal and want easy connections to your computer through the Internet, these types of plug-ins are excellent ways to connect, collaborate, share data, or simply help others work better.

These plug-ins are also great if you need to send files across your Intranet, or need to offer information that others may not be able to get out because their systems are either not capable of running or don't have the software installed that helped you create the data file.

If every Intranet were left up to me, these plug-ins would be the first ones I'd install on every machine. I would not only reduce the need for me to get up and help other users, but I would offer any user on the network access to any application they needed without having to install and possibly later delete the application when they no longer needed it. Plus, if lots of my fellow workers traveled a lot, by putting in a gateway to the Internet, any of those travelling workers could easily connect to their computers without me having to install a bank of modems, specialized dialup software, or institute difficult to understand procedures. Access would be available at any time, anywhere. With the help of secure gateways, using logins and passwords both locally and remotely, any user would easily be able to connect to the local network through the Internet with a commercial service like CompuServe or America Online. All they would have to do is fire up a Web browser, and with a few clicks of a mouse, the user would have immediate access not only to his computer, but all the resources, such as printers, fax machines, or files servers on the network. With these options you also open up the world, offering workers on your network the option to telecommute either from home or the comfort of a beach in Hawaii.

Name of Plug-In: PaperPort Viewer

Location for Plug-In: http://www.visioneer.com

What This Plug-In Does
With the *PaperPort Viewer* a user can view PaperPort files that have been scanned in using the PaperPower scanners. The viewer allows for files to be viewed or printed regardless of whether the document was scanned on a Mac or PC.

How You Could Use This Plug-In
Any office worker knows there is no such thing as a paperless office. From printed documents, to brochures, to legal documents with signatures, office after office is buried under a mound of paperwork. With a PaperPort scanner and software you can scan in just about any piece of paper, then place it on your network for others to view directly from their browser with the help of the PaperPort viewer.

One example I can think of is my friend Bob, who has offices in London, Anchorage, and Seattle. His personal assistant Karen oftentimes will fax documents to Bob in London. Bob could save tons of money if Karen simply used her PaperPort scanner and Bob used his Web browser along with the PaperPort viewer to view documents stored online through their corporate Intranet. Any time you have to send scanned documents back and forth, this is one excellent way to do it.

NAME OF PLUG-IN: ABOUTPEOPLE AND THE ABOUTTIME PLUG-IN

Location for the Plug-In: http://www.nowsoft.com/plugins/

What This Plug-In Does

These are some of the first calendar and address plug-ins for Netscape, which allow you to view calendars and address books published by Now Up-To-Date Web Publisher, a product that can also interface with hand-held personal information managers such as the Newton and Philips Velo. You can also use the plug-in to view information uploaded from 3Com's Palm Pilot.

The *AboutTime* plug-in lets you view browseable calendars in a Web browser. The *AboutPeople* plug-in lets you view and search Now Address books, displaying their electronic business card.

How You Could Use This Plug-In

For any administrative assistant, these kinds of plug-ins are lifesavers. Now you can publish on your Intranet searchable calendars and address books and at the same time keep the information safe on your own desktop computer. You could arm everyone in your company with the innovative 3Com PalmPilot, a tiny hand-held digital assistant that interfaces easily with Now Software's AboutPeople and AboutTime plug-ins. Then you could simply instruct each user how to upload their own personal calendar files to the network, then create a Web page with a link to each employee's calendar file.

You might also look into CalendarQuick by Logic Pulse, located at http://www.logicpulse.com. CalendarQuick lets you publish schedules of events, calendars, appointment lists, timelines, and project schedules within a Web page. Events can be linked to other Web pages. With CalendarQuick you can also drag and drop your calendars to Web pages. Each of these three calendar programs offers different features. The best thing to do is check out the samples of each one to see which calendar format works best for you or your users on your network.

NAME OF PLUG-IN: ONLIVE TALKER!

Location for the Plug-In: http://www.onlive.com

What This Plug-In Does

The *Onlive! Talker* lets you communicate in real-time voice over the Internet or an Intranet in conference mode. You can talk to more than one person at a time and hear the other voices clearly. Used in conjunction with OnLive's LiveMeeting Suite and Studio and Audio Conferencing Server products, OnLive! Talker provides clear voice, a "raise hand" feature that lets you identify when you want to talk, and moderator capabilities, along with selective ignore features which allow you to moderate who can speak and can't. With the Audio Conferencing Server you can have up to 225 people at one time.

You will need a multimedia-enabled PC in order to use this plug-in.

How You Could Use This Plug-In

You can save thousands of dollars by holding online, across-the-globe conversations with other employees within your company, and also with your customers and suppliers. This plug-in beats having to use clunky Internet telephone software and lets multiple users within an Intranet or over the Internet communicate in real time, real voice.

You do have to purchase an Onlive! Talker Audio Conferencing Server in order to use this product.

Useful Utilities and Programming Options

NAME OF PLUG-IN: NET-INSTALL

Location for the Plug-In: http://www.twenty.com/pcie/

What This Plug-In Accomplishes

With this plug-in you can create software packages that can be easily downloaded, decompressed, and installed by simply clicking a link on a Web page. There is no need to exit your browser when you install the software, since everything happens right in your browser.

How You Could Use This Plug-In

If you are a computer support person or a network administrator and want to speed up the process of installing new software, software upgrades, or even plug-ins, this is the plug-in and application software you need. With *Net-Install* the user simply clicks a link and the entire download, decompression, and installation is handled all in one fell swoop. The user doesn't have to know where to save the file, how to unzip it, or even how to run installation or set up programs. Better yet, the user doesn't even have to exit his or her browser in order for the new application to become available. Plus, you decide to configure it this way. Net-Install will also back up your files prior to any installation. And if the download is interrupted in any way, the user can re-click the link and the download will start up where it left off. With this plug-in you can install upgrades, new fonts, new plug-ins, or just about anything you want to install. You don't have to teach users about ftping, nor do you have to create special ftp servers.

Why waste time going from computer to computer to upgrade users' computers? There's no reason to create elaborate installation instructions nobody ever reads anyway. Instead, you simply load up your network server, create a Web page with the links to the software, updates, or plug-ins you want to offer your users, then alert them to where the links are. Net-Install will do the rest for you, installing the software properly. You should look into this application if you want to automate the process of installing plug-ins on your network. Although I outline exactly how to create a poor man's easy install process with just simple Web pages, this product will handle three out of the four steps involved in installing any new piece of software. In other words, YOU NEED THIS PLUG-IN if you are a network administrator, computer support person, or programmer.

NOTE

If all you need is a plug-in that will automatically zip or unzip files, check into NetZip by Software Builders International. The plug-in is located at http://www.softwarebuilders.com. NetZip not only allows you to zip and unzip files within your browser, but it also contains virus protection, the ability to view Word documents, and the ability to uncompress some common file formats used on both Unix and Mac platforms. You could also try InstallfromtheWeb, created by InstallShield Software Corporation, located at http://www.installshield.com.

NAME OF PLUG-IN: NCOMPASS SCRIPTACTIVE PLUG-IN

Location for the Plug-In: http://www.ncompasslabs.com

What This Plug-In Accomplishes

This plug-in lets you run ActiveX controls within a Netscape browser, giving you all the functionality of ActiveX controls offered in Internet Explorer.

How You Could Use This Plug-In

Although I'm a big proponent of standardizing on one browser or another, this is the one main plug-in you should have installed if the users on your network would rather pick and choose the browser they want to use. It's also the plug-in to have if you want to use Netscape Communicator or Navigator and interface the browser with Windows-based software by utilizing ActiveX controls within Web pages you create. Take a look at the list of ActiveX controls at the end of this chapter and in Chapter 9. By looking at this list you'll realize this product is a must-have; it lets you take advantage of a number of controls that offer functionality that plug-ins may not offer.

Also, *ScriptActive* has support for DocActive which is a technology that integrates Microsoft Office 95 and 97 with your browser. With ScriptActive's DocActive feature you can open, view, edit, print, and save Office documents locally. This is a must-have plug-in if you want full integration between Office and your Netscape browser. Without it, you have to configure helper applications for each one of the file types created in Microsoft Office.

NAME OF PLUG-IN: EZ DOWNLOAD

Location for the Plug-In: http://www.primenet/~n314159

NOTE

Because this plug-in has been programmed by an individual instead of a huge corporation, this Web site address may have changed. If so, check www.davecentral.com or plugins.dyn.ml.org for more information. If neither of these sites work, send me an e-mail at ckirk@ptialaska.net.

What This Plug-In Accomplishes

With the *EZDownload* plug-in you can forget about the hassles of downloading software off the Internet or off an Intranet. You can configure this plug-in so the files are downloaded to the proper destination, along with configuring what to do with the file once it's downloaded. You can also choose to have the program scan the file for viruses before you actually install the application, and EZ Download will automatically unzip zipped files. This plug-in can be used with Internet Explorer, America Online's browser, and with all versions of Netscape Navigator.

How You Could Use This Plug-In

For most users the process of downloading files is often confusing and difficult, and sometimes ends in frustration. With EZDownload you can make it easy for any user by configuring the plug-in to save the file in a particular folder and to automatically unzip or self-extract the file.

A COUPLE INDUSTRY-SPECIFIC PLUG-INS

There are some industry-specific plug-ins you might consider if you are in various fields. I can't vouch for all of these simply because some require certain hardware or knowledge of the industry in order for you to use them or understand what features they provide. In this section I'll give you a quick rundown of what you might look out for if you are in need of a specific type of plug-in.

NAME OF PLUG-IN: LABTECH CONTROL PLUG-IN

Location of Plug-In: http://www.labtech.com

What the Plug-In Does

This plug-in interfaces with data acquisitions hardware so you can quickly and easily access data and view that information in graphical form. With the *LabTech* software you can connect remote data acquisitions hardware to a server or computer, save the data, and display the information graphically in a Web page.

NAME OF PLUG-IN: CHEMSCAPE CHIME

Location for the Plug-In: http://www.mdli.com

What This Plug-In Does

With this plug-in you can display chemical 2D and 3D structures within a Web page. You can easily embed chemical structures rendered from industry-standard input files from such programs as MDL's MolFile or the Brookhaven Protein Databank. Each data file is live, meaning you can use the mouse button to rotate, zoom in, or even modify the model.

You can even use it to represent chemical structures with their property or activity data listed in spreadsheet format.

Ideal ActiveX Controls for Intranets

Although this book is heavily oriented towards plug-ins, I must say ActiveX controls are fantastic options for Intranets because they require so little knowledge on the part of the user in order for the controls to be properly installed in the user's computer. And better still, they offer a great deal more interactivity between Windows- and Mac-based OLE-compatible programs such as Microsoft Office and Windows 95.

There are literally hundreds if not thousands of ActiveX controls available for both user and developer. However, you'll find many more development-oriented controls than consumer-oriented controls because of the nature of the beast. I've listed some of the more consumer-oriented plug-in's here, adding a few development controls at the end of this section. These are ActiveX controls that could easily work within any Intranet, regardless of what server you might be using. If you want to take full advantage of ActiveX controls in an Intranet environment, you should consider looking into FrontPage 98 or Microsoft's Internet Information Server, which incorporates what is called Active Server Pages (.asp). These applications help you further exploit the feature of ActiveX and add features other Web site management and creation tools simply don't offer, features particularly useful to Microsoft-oriented networks.

Even if you don't use FrontPage or Internet Information Servers, if you want more ideas on other controls worth implementing on your own Intranet make sure you check out ActiveX.com, located at *www.activex.com*, and BrowserWatch's ActiveX Arena, located at *www.browserwatch.com*. These are excellent sites for ActiveX controls and developer-oriented controls. You may also want to check the ActiveX Resource Center, located at *www.active-x.com*.

Some of these ActiveX controls are cousins to the plug-ins offered for Netscape Navigator. When this is the case, you'll notice the description is relatively brief. For more information about a control that has a plug-in cousin, check the previous section.

DOCUMENT VIEWERS

These controls offer you the ability to view documents saved in file formats that Web browsers can't understand and display. These controls let you view files, such as PowerPoint, Excel, PageMaker, Lotus 1-2-3, and AutoCad, directly in Internet Explorer 4.0. With the help of these viewers, all the existing information you might have on your network could easily be placed on your Web server and viewed without conversion of any kind. Every network administrator should consider purchasing at least one, if not more, of these controls to make viewing data over an Intranet easy for every user on the Internet.

NAME OF CONTROL: FULCRUM DOCUMENT VIEWER FOR ACTIVEX

Location of Site: http://www.fulcrum.com/activeX/activeX.htm

What the Control Does
The *Fulcrum Document Viewer* for ActiveX lets users view, navigate, and manipulate non-HTML-formatted documents without leaving their Web browser. Like Adobe Acrobat, the Fulcrum FulViewer lets you view files in their native formats with all fonts, graphics, and other features intact. You can place Word, Corel WordPerfect, Microsoft Excel, Lotus 1-2-3, and PowerPoint documents on a Web server and enable the users of the network to view all the features of these files without having to have the application that created the file. In addition, users can cut and paste information from retrieved files and copy it to other applications, or even run applications such as PowerPoint directly from their Web browser. There is no need to convert documents to HTML or launch helper applications to access information.

How You Could Use This Control
How could you not use this product is the question. This control should be able to display just about any document your users might create. Thus your users don't have to convert any files to HTML format, and you don't have to create a whole host of Web pages to link directly to the information stored on your server.

NAME OF CONTROL: AUTOCAD'S WHIP!

Location of Control: http://www.autodesk.com

How This Control Works

The *WHIP!* control allows AutoCad users to view, send, and share design content over an Intranet. Based on the same rendering technology as the high-performance WHIP! driver in AutoCAD Release 13, the WHIP! control offers you the ability to view AutoCad files without having to convert them into bitmaps, JPGs, or GIFs. With Whip! you can pan, zoom, and embed URL Web page links directly in files.

How You Could Use This Control

Any engineering or architectural company needs this control, as does any company that has any type of AutoCad drawings. If you need more information about using this control, look for the comparable plug-in description listed previously in this chapter. AutoCad makes a version for both plug-in and ActiveX technology.

NAME OF CONTROL: ACROBAT READER

Location of Control: www.adobe.com

How This Control Works

The Adobe Acrobat PDF control for ActiveX uses the *Adobe Acrobat Reader* to let anyone using Internet Explorer view and navigate Adobe Portable Document Format (PDF) files just like the Adobe Acrobat Reader plug-in does. You can create PDF files from virtually any application. And through the use of this control, you can search through various PDF document files for the text that meets your search criteria.

How You Could Use This Control

If you install Adobe Acrobat 3.0 on every machine in your Intranet, instead of printing to paper, users can print to PDF files, placing those files on your Web server. Then anyone who needs to print out these files, whether they be policy manuals, promotional brochures, forms, or even faxes, simply fires up their Explorer browser and uses the Acrobat PDF Control to view, then print, the files. With such a control you really can create an almost paperless office, giving people the control to print information only on demand. No more memos, no more thick manuals that nobody ever reads, no more forms stacked up in a closet gathering dust, or brochures that end up in the trash bin because the pricing information is no longer valid. Instead, the most up-to-date information is always available at the click of a button.

CONFERENCING, COLLABORATION, AND CONNECTIVITY

Want to get the whole company collaborating on things?

NAME OF CONTROL: ICHAT ACTIVEX CONTROLS

Location of Control: http://www.ichat.com

How This Control Works
The *ichat ActiveX* control allows users to communicate via real-time chat through a Web page. Web sites which are chat-enabled with ichat's ROOMS software offer anyone with the Internet Explorer browser the ability to communicate with others in real time in a text-based format. You can create public and private chat rooms, letting in only those who need to be in.

How You Could Use This Control
Is your company spread across the country? Do you want to offer better customer support? Are you looking for another way to collaborate on things without having face-to-face meetings? With ichat you can create text-based conferences. Ichat lets you conduct text chats. Administrators can control the flow of the conversation, and other users can talk to each other privately while a public conference is being held. Transcripts of the chats can be saved and links to Web sites, e-mail addresses, files, etc. can be included within the chats themselves.

Of course the best thing you could use this plug-in for is to replace face-to-face meetings,or to conduct electronic board meetings online. I volunteer for a nonprofit organization, and sometimes with the weather, people's schedules, and what not, having a face-to-face meeting is just not an option. So we decided a while back to conduct our meetings online. That way I can attend, regardless of where I might be. Our board president can attend while watching the kids, and other board members don't have to worry about being at a particular place. We simply schedule the meeting for a particular day and time, then all meet electronically. More board members attend and better still we have an instant transcript of who said what. No more need for the secretary to take notes, then transcribe them; and we can easily put up the notes online for those who may not be able to log in.

Name of Control: Farallon's Look@Me

Location of Control: http://www.farallon.com

How This Control Works
This control displays the screen of another computer that is running either *Look@Me* or Timbuktu Pro, from Farallon Communications. Look@Me is compatible with Windows 95 and Windows NT, but Windows NT computers cannot be observed.

How You Can Use This Control
Of course the best use of this control is to control another PC, and therefore this is an excellent way to provide technical support to users. If you need further ideas on how to use this control, check out the description earlier in this chapter in the plug-ins section. This control also comes in the form of a plug-in and the full description of what this control offers is listed there.

Name of Control: WinFrame Web Client

Location of Web Site: http://www.citrix.com

What This Control Does
For the first time, you can work with any 16- or 32-bit Windows application embedded in or linked to a standard HTML Web page. With *WinFrame* you can enrich your Internet/Intranet Web pages by seamlessly integrating any off-the-shelf Windows-based application with WinFrame application server software and WinFrame Web Client from Citrix.

How You Could Use This Control
You can open up all those Windows applications to users who may not have the hard disk space or computer processing power to run those applications. The server does all the processing, sending the information and screen back to the user. Citrix offers this control in the form of a plug-in. If you need other ideas on how to use this control, check out the description for its plug-in cousin.

MULTIMEDIA AND TRAINING CONTROLS

Multimedia and training controls help you deliver real online training direct from a Web page. Like their plug-in cousins, these controls offer access to sound, video, and animation or help you create interactive training Web pages. With some of these controls you can create slide shows, PowerPoint presentations, or simply add audio to your Web pages. Whatever feature they may offer, every company has a need to convert videos, stand-up and on disk training to their Intranet. If you are still wasting money and time trying to teach computing basics, safety information, or human resources, consider augmenting all types of training you do with interactive Web pages that utilize these controls. Not only can you replace some training, thereby saving you money, but also you can extend the training you do give by making it and additional supporting materials available on your Intranet.

You should also check out the multimedia and training plug-ins listed previously in this chapter. Many of those same plug-ins are available in ActiveX format.

NAME OF CONTROL: HTML SHOW ACTIVEX CONTROL

Location of Web Site: http://www.quiksoft.com/htmlshow/

What This Control Does
This control displays an HTML Web page in another Web page, creating a slide show effect out of multiple Web pages. Much like animated GIFs, instead of displaying GIFs, a Web page displays standard HTML pages.

How You Could Use This Control
Do you go to trade shows and want to show off your Web site with a rolling demo? This is the perfect tool for doing this. Do you want to create a simple timed presentation that anyone could view from any Web site? Again, this is the perfect tool. Each HTML file can be programmed to display for a certain amount of time, and can run at certain times of the day, making it possible for you to have updated information on your site at a particular time of day. You can also scramble the sequence each time the site is loaded, making sure that viewers of the site see a new page at the beginning of the presentation each time they view the site.

The things you could do are unlimited. You could have the stock price and news of your company scroll through your site. You could create a "Tip of the Day" page that rotates through multiple pages of tips for your users, essentially using it as an electronic ever-changing billboard.

Name of Control: Microsoft PowerPoint Animation Player for ActiveX

Location of Site: http://www.microsoft.com/mspowerpoint/internet/player/default.htm

What the Control Does
Coupled with the PowerPoint Publisher, the *Animation Player* is the quickest way to publish your PowerPoint presentations in Web pages. The PowerPoint Publisher compresses, then converts, your PowerPoint presentations into Web-accessible presentations via the PowerPoint Animation Player. You can also use the application to add Real Audio sound files so you can narrate or add music or sound to your presentation.

How You Could Use the Control
It's hard to find a conference, training session, or seminar where the presenters aren't using PowerPoint to present their ideas and information. Now anyone in your company can view and hear the PowerPoint presentations that other employees and vendors have created. But it doesn't stop at just marketing or sales presentations. With PowerPoint presentations virtually anyone could create interactive training materials with all sorts of animations, photos, graphics, sound, voice, and links to Web sites.

Want to teach people how to use your e-mail program? Struggling with teaching a whole bunch of users how to use Lotus Notes? Planning on teaching an auditorium full of people the ins and outs of Microsoft Office, but also want to make that presentation available to those who cannot attend? This is the way to do it. Create a PowerPoint presentation, then turn it into a Web-enabled presentation with the PowerPoint Publisher. As long as the people viewing your presentation are using the PowerPoint Animation Player for ActiveX, they can see and hear everything contained in your presentation.

NAME OF CONTROL: ASYMETRIX'S NEURON

Location of Control: http://www.asymetrix.com/toolbook/neuron/

How This Control Works

If your company uses the Asymetrix ToolBook to create multimedia training projects, the *Neuron* plug-in is the best solution to give Web-based access to all the projects produced with any of the Asymetrix ToolBook II authoring products. The Neuron plug-in lets the user view and play presentations, kiosks, courseware, and other multimedia applications produced in ToolBook.

How You Could Use This Control

This is an excellent way to revamp the content your company might have had created with the Asymetrix ToolBook II training and multimedia program. As a matter of fact, this is about the only way you can revamp existing content into Web-based format. If you haven't checked out what the Asymetrix ToolBook II can do in terms of online and interactive training, make sure you check out their Web site for more information. You can create and keep track of training records easily and create compelling training materials with the ToolBook II product.

Some other controls you should check out include the ShockWave ActiveX control, located at www.macromedia.com, and the VivoActiveX player, located at www.vivo.com. The ShockWave control, like it's cousin the ShockWave plug-in, lets you view ShockWave-enabled sites, which contain interactive multimedia. The VivoActiveX player lets you view Vivo video-enhanced sites. These sites offer streaming video through your Explorer browser. Both can provide great training tools online. You might also check out the Demo-X plug-in, which will play Demo-X files.

WEB PAGE DEVELOPMENT AND UTILITY CONTROLS

There are plenty of ActiveX controls that help you, the developer of Web pages, integrate Web technologies with your existing network, and that make gathering data from users easier. One of the best places to find ActiveX controls is ZDNet's Software Library. If you search the library with the keywords "activex controls," you'll find hundreds of ActiveX controls you can download for free. Here are some controls you might consider downloading for use on your Intranet. From controls that control users' computers to controls that connect to data acquisition equipment and display data from that equipment through a Web page, you'll find several listed on ZDNet's site. If you are thinking of incorporating ActiveX controls into your Intranet, you need to look here first so you don't reinvent the wheel.

Remember, most of these controls are not like plug-ins where you download the plug-in, create the file, then have the user view the Web site with the data file and plug-in embedded in the page. Instead, think of many of these controls not as end user programs, but building blocks for your Web site. You download the controls, embed the instructions into your Web site, place the controls on your server, then when the user runs across the page that contains the control, the control is sent to the user's system.

Name of Control: IntraLaunch

Location of Control: http://www.particle.net/IntraLaunch

What This Control Does
IntranetLaunch is an ActiveX control that lets you create an entire Web-oriented desktop. With IntraLaunch you can create links to executable programs through a Web page. As long as these executable programs reside on the user's computer or within a network drive, the user can access .EXE, .COM, .BAT, .LNK, .PIF, and other types of Windows 95/98-accessible files by clicking links on a Web page. You can also display default directories, password protect menu items, attach sound events, and pass along parameters to programs.

How You Could Use This Control
Run, don't walk, to Particle Software's site and download a demo of this amazing set of controls. This is probably one of the most valuable Intranet controls you could use since it turns your Intranet into one big clickable link. Anything that resides on the network servers or on individual users' computers can be turned into a clickable link, regardless of whether it's a Windows shortcut, a batch file, or a full-fledged application. All the computers and all the users' desktops are now accessible through a Web page, instead of through varying interfaces. If your network is comprised of different interfaces, such as Windows 3.1,

Windows 95, Windows for Workgroups, and Windows NT you can make the execution of programs as simple as clicking a link, which means no more specialized training is needed. Just think, you could pretty much throw away the user's desktop, replacing it entirely with Internet Explorer. Any application, any link, or any directory could easily be accessed through your Intranet. And better yet, you can password protect links so that only the appropriate people have access to certain applications.

NAME OF CONTROL: BLUE SKY SOFTWARE'S SMARTHELP

Location of Control: http://www.blue-sky.com

How This Control Works
The *SmartHelp* control allows Web authors to place a help button on their pages. When the user clicks on the button, a Windows help file is brought up, offering the user the help interface they are used to.

How You Could Use This Control
If you are developing sites for your Intranet, this is an excellent control to use to place help within a page. The help window that opens is formatted like any other Windows help screen. Therefore you can easily create online, automatic help options to help people understand how to use a particular Web site, function on the site, or controls within a plug-in or ActiveX control, without having to take the browsing user to another Web page for instructions. This allows the user to keep the help file open and use the Web application simultaneously.

Many ActiveX controls are actually building blocks per se for adding functionality to Web pages without the need for programming or scripting yourself. Not all the controls you find at sites such as ActiveX.com are like plug-ins where they are actually full-blown software applications. Instead, they may be controls or software pieces you add to your Web site for the particular functionality you are looking for. If you are simply a user, not a developer, make sure the control you download is for end users and not developers.

Name of Control: ScriptActive plug-in

Location of Control: http://www.ncompasslabs.com/scriptactive/ download.htm

What This Control/Plug-In Does

The *ScriptActive* plug-in lets anyone using Netscape Navigator 2.0 or above use ActiveX controls within Netscape Navigator. This is a standard plug-in that downloads and installs just like any other plug-in.

How You Could Use This Control/Plug-In

Can't convince some of your users to use Internet Explorer instead of Netscape Navigator? Would you like to implement ActiveX controls in your network, but are concerned about security problems regarding the Internet Explorer browser? If you've invested in both Netscape and Microsoft technologies and want to marry the two technologies, this is the plug-in you could use to do just that. You no longer have to isolate Netscape Navigator users simply because the browser they choose to use doesn't incorporate ActiveX technology. By installing this plug-in just about any control you've added to your site can be used by Navigator users.

Name of Plug-In: Net2000 ActiveX controls

Location of Control: http://www6.zdnet.com/cgi-bin/texis/swlib/hot-files/info.html?fcode=000H4R, or check Novell's Web site at http://www.novell.com

What This Control Does

Do you have a Novell network? Are you tired of getting up and going over to the server to do the network administration? Want to have quick access to those Novell tools from within a Web page? *Net2000 ActiveX* controls is a beta version of a suite of controls that lets you program into a Web page a host of Novell tools, including controls that will let you monitor servers, mount and dismount volumes, control user access, modify print queues, and load NLMs, among other options.

How You Could Use This Control

Do you want to access Novell network options from any computer on your network through a Web page? Just think, the next time you're paged, you can instantly jump to any computer and fix just about any minor Novell network problem you might run into, from clearing out print queues to changing user access options. But take that one step further. Say you're on call and you get the call in the middle of the night from a night worker who needs help clearing out a print queue. No need to drag yourself into the office. If your Intranet is connected to the Internet, or if you have dialup access, you can control just about any function on your Novell network. Net2000 gives you session, directory, and server control, which means you can do just about anything you'd ever need to do as a network administrator.

NAME OF CONTROL: ACTIVEX INTRANET SOLUTION

Location of Control: http://www.auscomp.com

What This Control Does
This turns your Intranet into an easy to navigate Web site based on a "tree structure" metaphor, much like that seen in the old Windows 3.1 File Manager. Each directory on your Web site is turned into an icon of a file folder, a folder that lets you click to expand or collapse the view. When you expand the view of a directory, you see all the subdirectories and files inside that directory. Inside each folder you see exactly what kind of files are stored in the folder.

How You Could Use This Control
Tired of setting up table of contents Web pages just so your Intranet site navigation is easier for all the users on your network? Want to use a simple expandable file folder metaphor? Do you have absolutely no programming experience but want to add such a feature? *Intranet 3.0* offers an easy to understand navigational tool through the use of ActiveX (and Java). All you have to do is change a few text files and you'll have this feature up and running in no time. Plus, this product is free. To fully understand what this control offers you, you have to experience it for yourself. Auscomp uses it throughout it's own Web site so you can experience it for yourself without having to download a thing.

TIP

Also check out SiteMapper, a similar ActiveX control available from Quiksoft, located at www.quicksoft.com. SiteMapper, like ActiveX Intranet Solution creates an easy to use nested listing of pages on your site. Quiksoft also has several other ActiveX controls for both Intranets and the Internet.

Name of Control: Disable Pro

Location of Control: http://www.infinet.com/~adkins/

What This Control Does

This control disables certain features of Windows 95 (and 98) just as disabling the Run option of the Start menu, or disabling the Shut Down option of Windows 95. It can also disable portions of the Control Panel, File Sharing, Printer Sharing, or the running of MS-DOS programs. These are controls you add to Web pages, that when viewed by the user, disable the options you include in the page itself.

How You Could Use This Control

Want to control a user's computer remotely and turn off certain features so you can troubleshoot or install certain software applications? This collection of controls lets you control a variety of Windows 95 features by simply viewing the Web page with the control embedded in it. Since these are kind of building block controls, the types of things you can do with them are entirely up to you. Say you want to turn off File Sharing over your network. Simply create a Web page, include the control, and then point your users to the site and File Sharing is immediately turned off.

My Ideal Intranet

I run my own little Intranet right here in my office, and have set up about a dozen Intranets for clients throughout the state. So I have a pretty good idea of what plug-ins I would use to create the ultimate Intranet. To me the ultimate Intranet would be a network that empowers users to do exactly what they need to do with minimal effort. I've worked with organizations, large and small, where the "computer guy," the person in charge of supporting all the computers, hardware, software, and networking, has hobbled the system. In doing so he has created a dependency on the support guru to fix all the problems inherent in the system. In my ideal Intranet there would be none of that. If a user needed to view a particular data file, he could easily do it. If a user needed a plug-in or ActiveX control, they would be readily available. No one would be left out of viewing any type of data, regardless of the application that created the data. And as a network administrator I would make it easy on myself by setting up my server the right way, and using the technology found in plug-ins to make my job of creating and updating Web pages even easier. Even if you have never administered a network before, implementing plug-ins is really not that difficult. I would make sure plug-ins enhanced my Intranet, and also cut down on the amount of work I'd have to perform. Here's my idea of what would make up an ideal Intranet.

STANDARDIZATION ON A PARTICULAR BROWSER

You would have to standardize on the type of browser, otherwise you might create a class of haves and another class of have-nots. I would strongly lean toward Internet Explorer for several reasons. First, the installation of ActiveX controls for the user is a no-brainer. You go to the site and let the software handle the rest. Plus, with the integration options between desktop software and the Internet Explorer browser, working with data regardless of where it's stored is much more integrated than with Netscape Navigator.

CAUTION

Because of some lingering security issues and the voluminous space the latest version of the Internet Explorer software requires, some almost 100MBs, if you install all the options including e-mail, some Intranet administrators may elect not to go with Explorer. In addition, using the e-mail portion of Internet Explorer means introducing a new application into the mix, which in turn means more training for the users.

Internet Explorer, however, isn't problem free. And those problems may sway you to stick with Netscape Communicator/Navigator since it does offer an all-in-one interface, with e-mail and discussion groups built right into the application. Although the installation of plug-ins is not as simplistic as ActiveX controls and although there are also security issues with Communicator/Navigator, overall it's a much more secure product and more commercially available plug-ins have been written to take advantage specifically of Netscape Navigator. Also, the product takes up far less room on a hard drive than Internet Explorer, something to consider if the computers on your network are not top of the line. Plus, you can automate the download and installation process for your users.

Either way, the idea is to standardize on a single browser, then beef up that browser so it's capable of doing just about anything anyone would want it to do. Too many times networks are a hodgepodge of different software and different versions, which makes it difficult not only for administrators, but also for users. With different versions installed, or allowing different browsers on your network, it's hard to know exactly what to do when you can't read someone else's file, or features that worked on your PC no longer work on the system you need to borrow down the hall. Standardization is key throughout any network. The more you can standardize, such as the browser, the plug-ins, and the structure on your Web server, the easier your job will be and the more productive your users will be.

Simplistic Web Server File Structures

This may sound simplistic, but I can't tell you how many times I've encountered the most bizarre, convoluted ways people have set up file servers. A server should make perfect sense to anyone not only inside the company but also outside the company, and a file structure should follow a certain order throughout. Nesting things too deep will confuse people. Having too many directories can also cause confusion. Here's how I would configure a simple Web server not only for users' data but also for plug-in options that should be made readily available to anyone on the network:

```
/Root Directory
        /Computing
                /FAQs
                /Newsletter
                /Requests for Service
                /Software
                        /Browsers
                        /Plug-ins
                                /Viewers
                                /Presentations
                                /Multimedia
                                /Others
                        /Other Software
        /Accounting
                /Internal (Within the Accounting Group)
                /External (Outside the Accounting Group)
                        /Presentations
                        /Payroll Information
                        /Newsletter
        /Human Resources
                /Internal
                /External
```

/Policy Manuals
/Benefits Information
/Newsletter
/Presentations

Get the idea? The configuration should be simple and logical, something anyone could understand. Of course you would restrict access through the server software to those directories that only users in a particular department should see. That's why you would have internal and external directories for each department, making it easy for people within a department to know where to post information and for those outside a department to know exactly where to go for the information.

The files placed in these directories could be anything from spreadsheets to PageMaker newsletter files, to just about anything you can think of. The idea is to have all the necessary plug-ins available in the Plug-ins directory so anyone can easily get what they need when they need it.

TIP

If you do administer a network, you should look into Netscape and Microsoft's network administration tools that let you automatically update and install plug-ins and browsers across your network with the click of a few buttons. If you aren't using this technology, you should-you'll save yourself tons of time. Check each company's Web site for more information on these tools.

SETTING UP A STANDARD INTERFACE FOR DOWNLOADING AND INSTALLING ALL PLUG-INS

Although you should be able to easily update and install new plug-ins on all the machines on your Intranet, there may be times when you aren't able to install new plug-ins on all users' machines. Maybe it's because of time constraints, or maybe it's because you don't think everybody needs a particular plug-in. But as always happens, there will be times when you'll want to offer a particular plug-in and make the installation easier.

NOTE

If you're using Internet Explorer, of course, you don't have to worry about setting up a particular standard interface for downloading and installing any plug-in.

The easiest way is to create a Web site that has links to all the plug-ins you want to offer, along with step-by-step instructions for installing those plug-ins. Those instructions should outline where to get the plug-ins, how to download that self-extracting or zipped plug-in into a desktop download folder, how to run the installation for that plug-in, then how to quickly update their browser, without having to exit the browser in order to activate the plug-in immediately.

In order for this scenario to work, you would have to ensure that all your users have a download folder located on their desktop. Otherwise the link would not work, since the link on this page could not necessarily be dynamic, but more absolute in nature. This folder is where the user would place the self-extracting or zipped plug-in file. You should also ensure that you've created or updated the helper applications in the user's browser preferences so that .exe and .zip files are allowed to run and open automatically. If you need to create a new MIME type, here's the information you need to place in each field:

Description of type: *Executable*
File extension: *exe*
MIME Type: *None*
Application to use: *"%1"% (This will automatically display when you type exe in the File extension field.)*

This page could contain several links that connect the user to his desktop download folder to give him easy access to where the downloaded plug-in was placed. When the user clicks this link, he would see the self-extracted or zipped plug-in. All he would have to do is click the link to the self-extracting file or zipped file. When he clicks on the self-extracting or zipped file, the plug-in would automatically install the plug-in, so long as the plug-in installs this way. Once installed, another link, when clicked, could automatically update the user's browser so the plug-in is activated immediately. A final link would give him access to see if in fact the plug-in is now activated on his browser.

One way to make access to a user's desktop easier is to create a shortcut. In the command line place the following:

c:\windows\explorer.exe /root,

Next place this shortcut in the Start menu so the user can access the Desktop at any time without having to minimize the Web browser windows.

This is the down and dirty way; remember you could always install *Net-Install* on all your users' machines. Or if you're interested in doing things a little bit more elaborate, check into implementing Java applets or scripts. Table 6.2 shows you what links you could add to a plug-in installation help page which you could place on your Intranet's server.

TABLE 6.2: *Some links to add to your plug-in help page.*

Description of the Link	HTML Code
Link to show the user what plug-ins are installed	about:plugins
Link to take them directly to Netscape's (or your Intranet) plug-in site	http://home.netscape.com/comprod/ products/navigator/version_2.0/ plugins/index.html
Link to the user's desktop download folder where all the plug-ins should be placed	File:///c:\windows\desktop\downloads\
Link to update the user's Web page automatically once the plug-in has been installed	Javascript:navigator.plugins.refresh (true);parent.location.reload()

When you access directories in this way, you may also want to include in your user's download directory a Web page that automatically takes the user back to the main link page. To do this you would put a META tag at the top of a simple blank page.

<META http-equiv="refresh" content="0; url=http://www.Webpage.html">

www.Webpage.html is the location of the main Web page created.

KEEPING IN TOUCH WITH ALL YOUR USERS

Intranet technology can help you support your users and make you appear like the wonderful techno-god or goddess you really are. Create a corporate e-mail newsletter, complete with links to Web pages, and send it out on a weekly basis. Let people know what plug-ins are available and what they can be used for. Give them examples of how other people on your Intranet are using these plug-ins, so they can have a point of reference to go to should they have specific questions.

Users on a network often say they only see the computer support people when something goes wrong and even then they slink in and slink out without being noticed. Get in front of your users so they know exactly what a wonderful thing an Intranet really is. And use technology such as e-mail, mailing lists, and newsgroup discussion servers to communicate with others.

The Plug-Ins to Use and the Way to Use Them

Here's what I would do if I owned the world; OK, at least a small Intranet world. This should give you an idea of how you can use plug-ins and which ones you should standardize on in order to share some common data across a network. Let's start with some basic stuff you find in just about any company. Outlined next are some of the plug-ins I would install on my perfect Intranet and the reasons why. This is intended to give you an idea of what you might be able to implement on yours.

All Policy and Procedure Manuals in Adobe Acrobat PDF Format

Why print big thick manuals when you don't need to? And why not get new workers online as soon as possible learning how to navigate around your Intranet by telling them to sit down and read your policy and procedure manuals online. Save thousands in printing costs by making the manuals available in electronic form. If a worker wants to print out all or just a part of any manual, he can. If you need to quickly determine if your policy manual covers a particular topic, that's easy. Just use the Find feature and in no time you'll find exactly what you need.

Add links to your policy manuals too. When you get to the place in the manual where it talks about benefits, link directly to your insurance carrier, your 401K company, or any other provider of benefits. Then any time a worker needs more information, he can quickly reference your manual, then click to the company he needs more information about.

All Training Videos Converted to RealPlayer Format

All you need is a computer with an Audio/Video interface card that lets you record directly into a PC. Then you can encode the video directly into *RealPlayer* format, making the video available on the Intranet. I can hear you shout and scream right now, "But wait, my server can't accommodate BIG video files!" Don't worry. RealPlayer files are extremely compressed, and depending upon the type of compression used, video files that once occupied hundreds of megabytes can be compressed into just a few megabytes. A full hour-long movie could occupy less than 12 MB of data, or only 3 MB of space if you record only the audio.

By making videos available at any time, without the need of a conference room with a television and VCR connection, workers could watch and listen in the privacy of their own cubicle or office. You may in fact find that they would actually watch those safety videos. And who knows, maybe they would even consider watching computer training videos. Moreover, consider how much money you could save the company by creating, then encoding, your own computer videos which anyone on the Internet could watch on their system. Better yet, you could also include links in the videos so they could click to learn more from a Web site or go directly to a particular site or link.

All Benefits Options, Insurance Tables, 401K Plans, Etc. Saved in Excel Format

Why not just put all this kind of information in an Adobe Acrobat document? For one simple reason-with the *Formula One/Net* plug-in any employee on your network could easily calculate and recalculate his benefits package based on a wide variety of variables, including length of employment and amount of deposits. All you would have to do is set up the spreadsheets, and create the fields that the employees could then fill out to see how their benefits packages change. Just imagine, no more calls to the human resources department by employees asking you what would happen if they retire early, add more to their 401K plan, or borrow from their benefits account.

Interactive Training (Not Computer Related, but Other) Created in Shockwave, Neuron or DemoX Format

Sure, you can encode the current videos you have into RealPlayer format, but what happens when you need more interactivity, or need to track the amount learned from computer-based training? The simple answer would be to create Shockwave or Asymetrix ToolBox II training projects, so not only could the user interact with the training program, but the training program could also track the sections accessed in the training program. And if created with the Asymetrix ToolBox II, the program could also quiz the user on the information presented and keep track of the user's score, location in the training presentation, and the name of the user.

All Presentations Saved in PowerPoint Format

Today's business world is almost nothing but meetings, presentations, and seminars. And what better way to make sure everyone has access to everything that's said than to have all these presentations online, available at the click of a button. If you required all presentations to be created and saved in PowerPoint file formats and uploaded to your Intranet server, then any employee in your network would be able to view any presentation and keep updated on the latest information parceled out in these endless meetings.

Additional Applications Accessible through WinFrame or OpSession

Some companies just don't have the money to update computer hardware as soon as the latest and greatest new processor hits the market. Therefore those who don't use computers as much as others are usually relegated to using older applications or are prevented from using various applications simply because their older machines don't have the necessary horsepower. In addition, many networks have a cross-section of Macs and PCs, making collaboration on files sometimes impossible because of the varying file formats and operating systems.

That's where *Citrix Winframe* and *OpSession* plug-ins can really come in handy. On those machines that don't have the horsepower to run applications like PowerPoint, Excel, Lotus Notes, or other extensive applications, you can use either the WinFrame or OpSessions plug-in and give those users access to these applications. Thus your company doesn't have to throw away old computers, and more people in your company can have access to applications without you having to go through elaborate installation processes.

Look@Me or Carbon/Copy and NetInstall Installed on All Systems to Help with Computing Support.

If you're involved in the computing support end of your network, you probably know firsthand how difficult it is to get anything done. You're always up and down, running here and there to fix all sorts of user problems. Most problems are easily fixable; maybe the user simply isn't inputting the right instructions or accessing the right menu option. Other problems may require a simple tweaking of an initialization file or adding something to the Windows Registry file. You probably also find yourself spending hour after hour installing software, something that is relatively easy to do even if you have little knowledge of how computers work.

A perfect Intranet should include easy access to any user's workstation and the ability to install software across a network. If the *Look@Me* or *Carbon/Copy Net* plug-ins and appropriate host software are installed on your network, you can easily control and view anyone's computer remotely. Whether you're at your desk or miles away accessing your network over the Internet, you can give immediate support to anyone on your network without having to get up out of your chair and walk to the user's location. And with NetInstall, the concept of installing software, upgrades, new browsers, and even plug-ins can be done with a few simple clicks, making software installation something anyone on your Intranet could do.

If You Need Terminal Emulation or Access to Remote Computers, I'd Install WebTerm.

If you have the need for 3270 emulation, the best way to offer that is in a Web browser. With *WebTerm* by White Pine you can offer access to mainframes through the standard browser interface. You won't have to train the user on a separate application or spend a lot of time installing software on systems that may or may not need access to the mainframe.

INTRANET RESOURCES ON THE INTERNET

There are numerous resources on the Internet containing not only articles about other companies employing Internet technology, but also sites offering FAQs, tips, and links to companies offering both consulting and products for Intranets. Table 6.3 shows some of the best Intranet-related sites available. If you are thinking of converting your existing company network into an Intranet, or simply want to be able to converse intelligently with your computing support department about your Intranet, these are some sites you should check out.

TABLE 6.3: *A list of Intranet sites.*

Site	Location	Notes
WebBusiness' IntraNet Case Studies	www.cio.com/WebMaster/ wm_cases.html	Although oriented toward large businesses, the case studies listed on the site offer plenty of valuable information on the approach, plan, and implementation of installing and converting to an Intranet.

Table 6.3 (continued)

The Intranet Research Center	www.cio.com/WebMaster/ wm_irc.html	This site offers an assortment of links to research papers, working examples, discussion sites, and products.
The Intranet Journal	www.intranetjournal.com	Although not as extensive as Developer. com, this site offers a good array of information on how to setup, maintain, and implement small to medium sized Intranets. Several site case studies are also listed that provide a good look into the trials and tribulations companies go through when moving from standard file server networks to client/server Intranets.
Developer.Com	www.developer.com	Make sure you check out their **Resources** link that offers the full text of many Intranet books for free. At last count there were about 5 to 10 books on Intranets and plug-ins.
Netscape's Virtual Intranet	http://vip.netscape.com/vip	If you want to see an Intranet in action, this is a place to go. Although it's really just a fictitious company, Netscape has created a full-functioning Intranet to show you how you can use Intranet and Internet technology to make your net work more user-friendly and productive.
Netscape's Intranet Solutions	http://home.netscape.com/ comprod/at_work/index.html	Case studies, detailed analysis of return-on-investment studies, and links to all sorts of Intranet products vendors.
Microsoft's Intranet Solutions Center	www.microsoft.com/intranet/ default.htm	If you plan to incorporate any ActiveX technology or if you use Microsoft Office on your existing network, this is a "must see" site. Besides giving you pointers on how to incorporate Microsoft technology in an Intranet, it also gives you some great ideas on how to use Internet technology on an Intranet. Included in this site are point ers to what products are available to do such things as track 401K employee investments, and connect to existing database systems, online company phones books, company newsletters, and more. Be forewarned, however, most of the information contained on this site is geared toward full "Microsoft shops," meaning you must use many of the Microsoft server technologies in order for the client-side options to work.

Table 6.3 (continued)

Building a Corporate Intranet Online Seminar	http://Webcom.com/wordmakr/ sem_1.html	If you want to know exactly what's involved in building a corporate Intranet, this is an excellent online seminar to take. It should take you about an hour to an hour and a half to complete.

THE QUICK INTRANET PLUG-IN FAQS

Do I need all these different viewers for different graphic file formats? I see a whole list of different plug-ins available that view TIFF, JPG, and GIF file formats. Isn't my browser capable of viewing these files?

You'll notice I haven't included many plug-ins that let you view different graphic file formats simply because browsers today are able to view a wide range of graphic file formats including JPG, GIF, AVI, QuickTime, and PNG. I would suggest that you only install specialized graphic viewer plug-ins if there is a particular graphic file format you must view and your browser isn't capable of displaying that file format, or if you need to use specialized compression formats that will make accessing large graphic file formats faster. Otherwise, adding plug-ins that already do what your browser does, doesn't make much sense.

Plug-ins are usually free or inexpensive. But how much does the software cost that converts files into a format that plug-ins can view?

It depends. Most software, such as Adobe Acrobat or Capture, costs less than $500. But unlike plug-ins, you must purchase either a single copy for each computer you plan to run the plug-in file-making software on, or you must purchase a site license for more than a single user license. Check the software vendor's site for more information on the cost of the specific software product you're interested in. Prices change often and you'll find mail-order houses like the PC Zone offering specials on such software.

Can I freely distribute plug-ins on my network without having to worry about buying a site license?

It depends on the software vendor and the license options the vendor provides. Each company offering plug-in technology has it's own way of handling distribution of multiple copies of the plug-in software. Most vendors allow you to freely distribute the software as long as you do not modify the software in any way, while others may require you to fill out paperwork or pay a fee to distribute more than a single copy of their plug-in on your internal network.

What about ActiveX Controls?

It depends on the control whether you can freely distribute it. As you know, some controls are developer oriented, some controls are user oriented, and some are components you add to other controls. You should check with the developer who created the control for the exact license afforded you.

Which Would You Use on an Intranet Plug-Ins or ActiveX Controls?

You should pick the technology that solves a need; but since you can use them both on an Intranet, it really doesn't matter. If you are using other Microsoft products, you should look seriously at ActiveX controls. Since ActiveX works not only within Web pages but within products such as Office 97, you could create a large number of integrated options between your Intranet technology and your co-workers' desktops.

However, if you are not a developer, and you want pre-made kinds of applications, look at plug-ins first, then venture to ActiveX controls. Plug-ins are ready-made, require little if any configuration, and usually work as advertised.

What's the easiest way to distribute plug-ins on my Intranet?

The easiest way is to create a link directly to the plug-in manufacturer's Web site and place that on the Web page where you plan to include the file that requires the plug-in. That way you never have to worry about installing the plug-in yourself, or scrambling to update the plug-in when a new version comes out. Nor do you have to worry about site license agreements or waste space on someone's computer, cluttering up their system with plug-ins they don't need.

If my Intranet isn't connected to the Internet yet, what should I do when I want to distribute a plug-in?

The best thing to do is set up a directory on your Web server where you can place all the plug-ins your company uses. When you need to update a plug-in, you'll know exactly where to go and you won't have to wade through different document directories. Again, check with the manufacturer of the plug-in to make sure you have the right authorization to store and distribute that plug-in. But before you do that, you should check with the software manufacturer to ensure it's legal to post the plug-in onto your Intranet.

Some plug-ins don't seem to work with our Intranet. What's the problem?

If you are using plug-ins that stream data from another network on the Internet to your Intranet, you may have to configure your firewall or proxy servers to allow for this particular data or site type to stream data through to your network. Check the software manufacturer's Web site for instructions on configuring your network to handle the kinds of data the plug-in is displaying.

If the plug-in needs to connect to a server, whether it's inside or outside your network, double-check that you have the server configured properly and have the plug-in configured to access the proper server. Oftentimes the problem lies in not being able to see a particular server the software requires in order to work properly.

Do all plug-ins work with all versions of the Netscape browser? Our network is planning to upgrade to version 4.0 or 5.0 of the Netscape browser. Can we be assured that all the plug-ins we've added will work?

No, not all plug-ins work with newer versions of the Netscape browser. Those that work with version 2.0 should work fine with 3.0. But not all that work with 3.0 will work with versions 4 or 5. Netscape Communicator incorporates new technology not found in previous versions of Navigator. If the plug-in says specifically that it works with version 4.0, most likely it will not work with 3.0. However, if the plug-in works with 3.0, try it with 4.0.

If I add lots of plug-ins, then decide to upgrade to Internet Explorer, will I be able to use all my investments in these plug-ins?

If you check with the manufacturer before you purchase the plug-in or accompanying server to see if they have an ActiveX version or to ensure they've tested it with Internet Explorer, you'll probably be OK. Most, but not all, plug-ins work with Internet Explorer. And some plug-ins have actually been programmed as ActiveX controls, which is what you should use if you have Internet Explorer. You have to be cautious, do your own homework, and test it out yourself in a variety of settings to ensure cross-browser compatibility.

Do I need special servers for some of the plug-ins or ActiveX controls mentioned?

Some plug-ins, such as the Netwriter, require a special server in order to share data across a network. Most plug-ins don't require any special servers, but do require that you configure your Web server so the server knows how to handle the file type you are planning to store on your network. Plug-ins like RealPlayer can work fine without a server, but work even better if you place your Real files on a Real Server. A Real Server will allow for more simultaneous connections and will stream audio and video with less drop-outs and congestion. Check with the vendor as to whether the plug-in you want to implement on your Intranet requires a special server, or if the files can be served through your existing Web server.

Do I really need to quit my browser once I install a plug-in?

No. With a Java command you can automatically invoke any plug-in you've just installed, without having to exit, then restart, your browser. Simply type the following into the Location field of your Netscape Navigator browser:

javascript:navigator.plugins.refresh(true);parent.location.reload()

Won't Java just replace the need for most of these plug-ins?

Although some software manufacturers are migrating their plug-in technology to Java, the need for plug-ins will remain strong for the next several years until Java becomes a more stable and more robust development environment. At this point, Java is still fraught with problems; it requires a great deal of memory to operate properly and has not been implemented consistently across the various browsers. Although I think Java is a perfect idea, Web pages with Java are very slow to load and consistently freeze my computer; and oftentimes I encounter all sorts of cryptic error messages that leave me wondering what went wrong. Even Netscape's own Web site is full of Java-related design errors.

Because of the way Netscape Navigator handles plug-ins, at least for now, I would use plug-in technology over Java technology on my Intranet. It's simple, relatively easy to install, and works consistently, whereas Java doesn't. My feeling is if it ain't broke, don't fix it. And if I have several plug-ins that work fine for me and my network, there's no use in trying to incorporate new technology.

SUMMARY

Whew! There are so many plug-ins you could use on your Intranet; I could just go on and on. But hopefully this chapter gave you a good overview of some of the more widely used plug-ins and how you could implement them on your Intranet. This list is by no means the be-all and end-all of Intranet-related plug-ins. As a matter of fact, if your company specializes in photography, architectural or engineering design, biology, or chemistry, there are several industry-specific plug-ins you should check out and implement on your Intranet. You'll find these plug-ins on Netscape's plug-ins page, located at *http://home.netscape.com/comprod/*.

Plug-ins and ActiveX controls are the missing links that can turn any standard Intranet into a full-featured network. Plug-ins and ActiveX controls make it easy for users to view, read, listen, and watch all sorts of data. And at the same time plug-ins and ActiveX controls can make it easy for network administrators to update, inform, and offer features to users which they were not capable of offering over standard non-Intranet-type networks. The options are virtually unlimited once plug-ins and ActiveX controls are implemented over an Intranet.

But what happens if you're not connected to an Intranet, but instead are using one of the nationwide networks like America Online or CompuServe? If that's the case, you need to read the next chapter. In Chapter 7 you'll learn how to supercharge your browser even if that browser is part of a commercial service's connection software.

CHAPTER

7

But Wait!
I Use AOL, CIS...

I f you're one of the millions of AOL or CompuServe users, by now you're probably wondering whether all this stuff will work with your connection software. You've probably heard that other specialized Internet software doesn't work, or doesn't work well. Maybe you're confused about where to save some of the plug-in and ActiveX options with your software, or maybe you just need a little help finding where Internet information can be found on your service. Maybe you are having problems finding out how to set preferences with the AOL connection software, or maybe you're not aware of the browser features available with CompuServe's Information Manager. This chapter will help guide you through the myriad options America Online and the CompuServe Information Manager software offer you.

FIRST THINGS FIRST

First let me say if you haven't upgraded to the latest version of the America Online or CompuServe Information Manager software, you need to. In order to take advantage of advanced features such as ActiveX controls, easy plug-in installations, and the numerous features new browsers have, you must upgrade to the latest version of the America Online or CompuServe software. One advantage you'll reap when you upgrade to the latest versions of either online service is that you can then pick and choose which browser you want to use. This gives you a certain amount of flexibility you didn't previously have. Also these new versions let you use other Internet-related applications such as Internet telephony or video conferencing.

TIP

*How do you know what version you're using? Simple. Regardless of whether you're using CompuServe or America Online, just look at the **Help** menu, then look for either **About America Online** or **About CompuServe**. Select this option and you'll see exactly what version you're using. Figure 7.1 is an example of doing this.*

In addition, if you're like me, and have not only an AOL and CIS account, but also a standard Internet account through an Internet service provider, with the new online software you can use just one browser. Regardless of whether you're connected to your service provider or connected to the Internet through America Online or CompuServe, the add-ins you install, be they plug-ins or ActiveX controls, only have to be installed into one browser. So when you check the Microsoft Investor

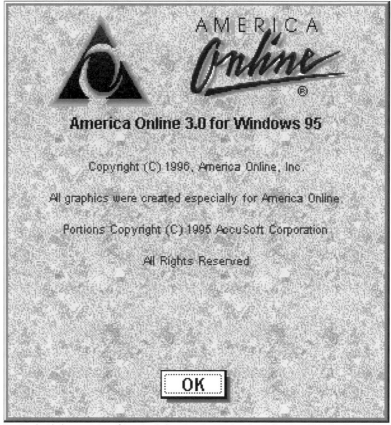

FIGURE *Finding out what version you're using.*
7.1

site, or add the Shockwave plug-in to your Netscape browser, those new features will be available, regardless of the service you use.

UPGRADING YOUR SOFTWARE

Although you can upgrade your software by downloading the new versions from the various companies' Web sites, either *www.aol.com* or *www.compuserve.com*, you're better off requesting a new CD-ROM disc from either company. Here's the contact information for upgrading either service:

CompuServe:
Web site: www.compuserve.com
Phone: 800-609-1674 or 800-848-8990
Outside of Canada dial 614-529-1340

Instructions for upgrading online—GO WINCIM, then click either the **Order Now** button or select the **Download Now** button. A list of different versions of CIM for either the Mac or PC will be listed. Select the version you need to download, then select the location to save the file.

America Online:
Web site: www.aol.com
Phone: 800-827-6364

Instructions for upgrading online—Use the keyword **Upgrade**. Double-click the **Order Upgrade CD** option from the list of choices. Select the version you would like to upgrade to by double-clicking that version. Next, enter your pertinent information in the fields supplied. Make sure you include your complete street address or post office box. Click the **Continue** button when you're finished. You should get the new software within one to two weeks.

You can also wrangle a free disc by checking out your local newsstand. Just about every other magazine is now shrink-wrapped with an offer for free connection time. If I were you, and I needed to upgrade, I'd check the newsstands first.

TIP

America Online recently purchased CompuServe. Although no major changes have happened just yet, you might find the two melding into one. This means the connection software may become one in the near future.

What Can You Expect When You Upgrade?
If you've been using previous versions of either America Online or CompuServe's software, you can expect a lot of changes when you upgrade. First you're going to get better Internet integration. But that also means the software will require more of your hardware. If you don't already have 16MB of RAM, you should upgrade to at least that much; but if you have the money, consider going even further, to 32MB or more, if possible. The more RAM you have, the better your online programs will perform.

Also expect that these new versions will take up substantially more space than previous versions. Because of the additional graphics and new features, these programs are naturally larger. Also realize if you have previous versions of Internet Explorer or Real Audio installed, the new software installations can and do override your previous installations. They can also change the default browser and this can be a problem if you have things customized. It's best to backup your hard drive, if possible, or move your Internet Explorer or Real Audio directories to another location. Here are some other issues you should be aware of when you upgrade:

AOL

- When you upgrade your software, just about all the important information such as screen names, preferences, and favorite places will be transferred over, but any items in your \AOL\Download directory will not be transferred. Make sure you copy over any files in this directory once you've upgraded
- A customized version of Winsock will be installed but will not replace any other existing Winsock files.
- The new version of AOL will allow you to run a wide variety of Winsock-compatible programs, but you need to be using the Windows 95, not Windows, version of the AOL program in order for these other Internet programs to work properly. Check Stroud's *Consumate Winsock Internet Applications List* for a wide assortment of Internet-related software you can use with AOL. You can find Stroud's at *http://cws.icorp.net/*.

TIP

Use the keyword **Upgrade** *to check out the differences and new features of this version. Just about any question you might have, in addition to a long list of troubleshooting tips, are listed in this area.*

CompuServe

- The Filing Cabinet in 2.01 and above is not compatible with the latest version, 3.0. In other words, you can't switch back and forth because 2.01 cannot read the documents stored in 3.0. In addition, you must convert the documents in your 2.01 file cabinet before those documents can be read in 3.0.
- The **Web** option now uses whatever browser you select. The software comes with Internet Explorer, but you can change the preferences to use Netscape Navigator.

- A large majority of commands have been changed, renamed, or removed, and many new commands have been added. Expect to spend about an hour learning where the old features are and what the new features do before you feel comfortable with the new version. The best way to learn the new features is to simply go through each menu and toolbar seeing what each option does, and what features each offers.
- The CB area has been renamed Chat.
- Almost everything is now Web based, or the interfaces for many new features use the integrated Web browser.
- You can now do more than one thing at a time (multitasking) without having to wait for one process to complete in order to go on to other processes.
- You can now customize many features, including the Toolbar and options such as your Web browser.

For more information on the new features found in CompuServe version 3.0 select the **Help** *menu's* **What's New in 3.0** *option.*

What Browser Options Can You Expect with These New Versions?

As mentioned before, you can expect all the same features any other standard Internet user has because you can pick and choose what browser you want to use. As a default, both AOL and CIS install Internet Explorer (currently version 3.X) when you install the upgrade. But again, either service lets you use whatever browser you want, although they do this slightly differently.

You can also expect to use whatever helper applications, ActiveX controls, or plug-ins you want. As a matter of fact, America Online offers a full multimedia showcase of applications and plug-ins you can download. Use the keyword **Multimedia Showcase** to access this list. If you plan to use Internet Explorer, don't worry about having to reload your ActiveX controls; they too will work without a hitch, provided you use the Internet Explorer browser.

What Problems Can You Expect?

There's no doubt online services such as America Online and CompuServe can be much slower than a direct connection to the Internet through a service provider. So expect some features such as ActiveX controls and standard downloading of files to possibly take longer. Moreover, other Internet options which double as plug-ins, like Real Audio, may not give you stellar performance. If you want to use network-intensive applications, you really have to temper your online usage so that you are not connected at peak hours. This usually means very early in the morning, very, very late in the evenings, or Mondays during *Monday Night Football*.

It also means that you are dealing with two levels of software—the connection software and the browser software. And you know what that means, don't you? More need for memory and system resources. So you should try limiting the number of other programs you are currently running and make sure you have not only enough horsepower, but also enough RAM memory.

TIP

America Online offers a wealth of information in their **Upgrade** *area, including a full list of error messages you might encounter when you upgrade. Use the keyword* **Upgrade** *to find this list.*

Finally, it means sometimes when you install plug-ins or helper applications, the browser software may not register the plug-in (commonly referred to as MIME type) properly. And this means when you run across a data file your browser doesn't recognize, you may be instructed to point out the plug-in or helper application to view the file. Therefore, you should read all installation and help files, paying particular attention to any instructions on how to configure your browser manually to use or read certain data types.

What Will Happen If I Don't Upgrade?

The skies will open up, lightning will strike you, and well, the floods will start. OK, maybe it won't be that bad, but you will have problems. Mainly you'll have problems because older versions of these online programs are not necessarily Internet aware. They don't handle true Internet-based applications properly and can give you fits, causing your system to crash or simply not display the information correctly.

Plus, the instructions that follow most likely won't work for you unless you're using either AOL 3.0 or CompuServe 3.0. If you want or need to continue using older versions of these online programs, the best solution I can give you is to point you to the **Help** files and online **Help** sections on these services. Using the keyword **Help** usually gets you where you need to go. One word of warning, however. Although both services still maintain support on older versions, the support may be somewhat lacking. Also realize you're probably missing out on a whole bunch of new options that could really save you time. And finally, if you continue to read through this chapter, and you don't have the latest software, none of the subsequent information will make much sense to you. At this point, if you haven't upgraded to the latest and greatest, I only have one word for you—UPGRADE!

Configuring Your Software

First you have to consider what browser you want to use. As I mentioned previously, both online services offer Internet Explorer as the default browser. But again, you don't have to settle for that if you're a Netscape fan. All you have to do is know where your browser is and how to launch it in order to use any browser of your choosing. With CompuServe it's a matter of simply setting your preferences. With AOL it's simply a matter of launching the browser you want to use.

Let's take a look at configuring each service so you'll know exactly where the controls are for the browser options. Think of this as a tour guide of where the configuration options are. We've covered many of these options already in previous chapters on ActiveX and Netscape Navigator, so I won't bore you with long, drawn-out details of each feature. The purpose of this section is simply to acquaint you with which options are the most important to configure when setting up your browser and online service software so that they work properly with helper applications, plug-ins, and ActiveX technologies.

Configuring and Using a Browser with AOL

Configuring AOL for browsing the Web is relatively easy. You don't even need to be online to configure your software. First select **Preferences** from the **Members** menu. You should see a screen resembling that shown in Figure 7.2. Click the **WWW** button to set the preferences for browsing the World Wide Web.

When you click the **WWW** button, a screen resembling the **Options** dialog window in Internet Explorer will display. This dialog window lets you set the general look of your browser, the security options, the start page the browser displays every time you go to the Internet portion of America Online, along with other advanced browsing options. It should look something like Figure 7.3. Briefly, Table 7.1 lists what each tab offers you.

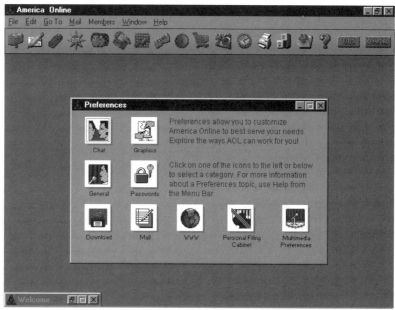

FIGURE   *These are the preference options available to any America Online user.*
7.2

TABLE 7.1   *The AOL Internet Preferences options.*

Tab	What it Offers	Things You Should Pay Attention To
General	Lets you set the overall look of the Web pages you view, including what fonts and colors you use for links and text.	This feature also lets you control whether plug-in features such as video and sound are displayed. Experiment with these settings if you want faster response in displaying Web pages.
Navigation	Lets you choose the Web page to display as your home page, search page, and QuickLinks pages 1-5. If you'd rather not use the AOL search page and would rather use AltaVista, Infoseek, or any other search site, you would change this option here. Make sure you have the full address of the site, however.	This feature also lets you clear out the history folder, which is a folder that stores pages and graphics you've seen and visited since a certain number of days. If you are running low on hard disk space, or if you keep having to reload pages, or the browser is crashing or freezing, empty this history folder often.

(Table 7.1 continued)

Programs	Lets you choose what Mail and News reader to use; currently, however, you must use AOL's online newsreader and e-mail client. This feature also allows you to set the helper applications and their associated MIME types manually.	This feature also lets you check the last option to ensure Internet Explorer is your default browser. Don't check this option if you plan on using Netscape instead of Internet Explorer. Otherwise, you'll constantly be asked if you want to set Explorer as the default browser every time you open up Navigator to browse Web pages.
Security	Lets you set the type of Web content suitable for browsing. If you have children, you need to explore this option since it will help block out some, but not all, of the more racy, sexually explicit sites from young eyes. Also lets you manage your digital certificates and view which sites you have authorized as being reliable sites for downloading or exchanging sensitive data.	The Active Content area is where you turn on or off ActiveX and the ability to download ActiveX components.Check Chapter 5 for more information on ActiveX and what it offers you. ActiveX is only natively available with Internet Explorer. If you want to use ActiveX with Netscape Navigator, you must first download, then install a plug-in that interprets ActiveX content.
Advanced	Lets you assign different levels of warnings for times when information is being passed back and forth from your computer to a Web server. Also lets you empty out or set the temporary files, which are stored on your system until deleted after so many days.	Try the smooth scrolling option and the friendly URLs. They are some of the best features of Internet Explorer.
Web Graphics	Lets you turn on or off compressed graphics so they display quicker on your screen.	Make sure this is checked. Otherwise, you'll be waiting for a long time.

NOTE

Remember, these options are for setting up Internet Explorer, and have nothing to do with Netscape Navigator.

The one special feature pertaining to plug-ins which you should take notice of is the **Programs** tab. This is where you set the helper applications to work with your browser. If you need to set these manually, you

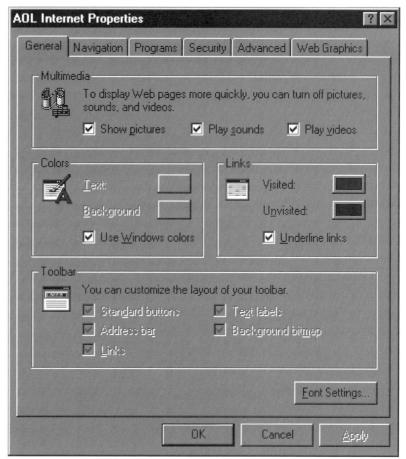

FIGURE   *The AOL Internet Preferences dialog window.*
7.3

will need to edit these just as you did in previous chapters using Netscape Navigator.

HOW TO CONFIGURE AOL TO USE NETSCAPE NAVIGATOR

Again, you can use any browser you choose with America Online 3.0 or above. All you have to know is where your browser of choice is located. There are really only two main steps in using your browser of choice. First, log on to America Online, and make sure you are connected.

When you hear that friendly voice say "welcome," you know you're online and ready to go to the next step.

Locate your **Netscape Navigator** browser and launch it. The **Start** menu is a good place to find your browser. If you have installed it properly, it should be a menu item listed somewhere within the other programs listed on your **Start** menu. Figure 7.4 is an example of my cluttered, yet easily accessible, **Start** menu, and the Navigator shortcut that was installed.

When you download or retrieve a plug-in or ActiveX control, you should follow the same procedures outlined in Chapters 2 and 5. Nothing else is different since you are simply using America Online to connect to the Internet, and your browser to connect to Web pages.

Amazingly simple, isn't it? The one question most people ask, however, is, "How do you make Netscape Navigator your browser of choice, replacing Internet Explorer?" At the time of this writing you can't, but in subsequent releases you should be able to. Check the **Preferences** option and the **Online Help** area regularly for any updates on when this feature might be implemented.

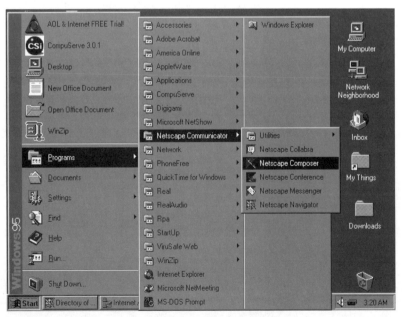

FIGURE *The Start menu is the place to find all your applications, assuming they were*
7.4 *installed properly.*

Always open AOL and connect to the service before you open up your Web browser; otherwise, you may encounter problems with the browser recognizing Web sites. Also, if you are having problems with your browser, double-check to make sure you are using the version specifically for Windows 95.

ENCOUNTERING THE NEED FOR A PLUG-IN WITH AOL

Hopefully you're already proactive about your plug-ins and are on the prowl nightly downloading a whole host of plug-ins for your browsing pleasure. But there are times when you might run across the dreaded error message that reads something like this:

"You do not have the plug-in needed to view the 'application/plug-in' type of information on this page. To get the plug-in now, click 'View Plug-In Directory'."

When this happens, don't panic. It simply means you need to summon up the plug-in and install it properly. With America Online you can do this by following these steps:

1. Click **View Plug-In Directory**. This will take you to the Multimedia Showcase, a repository of easily accessible, widely used plug-ins.
2. Locate the plug-in you need, ensuring that you are downloading a version of the plug-in specifically for Windows 95.
3. Next, click the button or link to initiate the downloading process. Make sure you remember where you are saving the plug-in since the file will probably have to be uncompressed and at least installed.
4. Once the file has been downloaded, exit the America Online software. If AOL automatically begins to uncompress the file you've downloaded, make a note of the new file name.
5. Double-click the file you downloaded or open the folder where the uncompressed file was stored.
6. Locate the setup or install program and double-click it to start the plug-in installation process.
7. Restart your computer, then restart AOL.
8. Sign on, then return to the page where you encountered the need for that particular plug-in. If all goes well, the plug-in should work properly.

It's a good idea to take note of the plug-in installation instructions. The installation process may be different for each plug-in. Consider printing out the installation instructions provided so you can have quick access to them even if you aren't online.

TIP

*Select **Preferences** from the **Member** menu, then click the **Download** button. Make sure you check **"Delete zip files after decompression."** This will ensure that after you download and unzip plug-ins, the compressed (zipped) file the plug-in originally came in will be eliminated. Once a plug-in is installed, you don't need the zipped file or the plug-in installation program hanging around your hard drive taking up space. By checking this option, you'll ensure AOL cleans up your hard drive after you've downloaded zipped files.*

CONFIGURING HELPER APPLICATIONS FOR USE WITH AOL

Even if you decide to use Internet Explorer, you may run across times when you need to configure a particular helper application for use with viewing a particular file type. Remember, you can configure any software program to act as a helper application to help your browser along when it encounters a file it doesn't understand.

If you get error messages saying "No Helper Application Defined," this means you are trying to view a data type that requires another program to open it up. At this point your browser will ask you if you want to set up a helper application to view the file. If you click yes to define a helper application for the type of file, then from that point forward, anytime your browser encounters that file type, it will launch the helper application using it to display the file. To define a helper application of your own, follow these steps:

1. Select **Preferences** from the **Members** menu, then click the **WWW** button.
2. Click the **Programs** tab, then click the **File Types** button.
3. Click the **New Type** button and enter a description for the file/MIME type.
4. Include the extension for the file type. For example, if you wanted to view bitmap files, type BMP.
5. Enter the correct content (MIME) type for this file. If you are unsure of the MIME type, check out *http://www.mindspring.com/ ~mgrand/url-content.html* for a list of MIME types.
6. Under **Action**, click the **New** button and enter a name for the action you want the helper application to perform. For example, if you want to open something, type **OPEN** for the action name.

7. Click the **Browse** button and locate the program you want to assign to this particular file type. For example, if you want to set up BMP files, use the MSPAINT program.
8. Click **OK**. The **New Action** window will close and you'll have to click **OK** again to close the next dialog window.
9. Click **OK** again to close the **WWW Preferences** window.

CONFIGURING COMPUSERVE

Configuring CompuServe is relatively easy, and requires even less configuration than America Online. There are only a few settings you have to select to ensure your browser works with the CompuServe software. Assuming you've already configured the browser itself and have set the options and preferences you want to use for fonts, start pages, and the like, follow these steps to assign that browser as your default browser:

1. Start the CompuServe software.
2. From the **Access** menu, select **Preferences**.
3. Click the **General** tab. Your screen should look like Figure 7.4.
4. Click the checkbox, **"Use external Internet browser."**
5. Click the **Select** button, and locate your browser program.

*For Internet Explorer, look either in your **Programs** folder or in the **Microsoft Internet** folder. For Netscape Navigator, check the **Programs** folder, then look inside the **Communicator** or **Navigator** folder. Inside this folder is another one labeled **Program**. Open that folder to find the actual **Navigator** application, and click to select it.*

6. Select the program you want to use by double-clicking it.
7. Click the **Define Browser Preferences** button if you want to modify any of the settings you previously chose when you initially set up your browser.
8. Click **OK**.

That's really about it. From that point on, the browser you selected will be used not only to view Web pages outside of CompuServe, but also many of the sections within CompuServe itself. All plug-ins, ActiveX controls, and helper applications assigned to your browser previously will carry over when you simply select it as the default browser for your CompuServe sessions. When you want to use the browser, simply select **Browser Desktop** from the **Window** menu and away you go, browsing the Internet through CompuServe.

Summary

There's no need to think that just because you use America Online or CompuServe you're left out of the picture when it comes to plug-ins. With the right software, you can easily install and use any plug-in, helper application, or ActiveX control of your choice. Now that you know exactly how and why, maybe the idea of setting up your own Web page complete with numerous plug-in options intrigues you. If so, read on, because in Chapter 9 you'll learn how to do that.

CHAPTER

8 Creating Web Pages Using Plug-Ins and ActiveX

By now you may be thinking to yourself, "Gee, maybe I should add some plug-in enhancements to my Web page." Perhaps you're thinking, "Plug-ins are just the thing for this project I want to do at work." If that's the case, you'll need to know a little bit about embedding HTML plug-in tags in your Web page. In this chapter you'll learn exactly that. But one word of caution before you start loading up your site with a ton of plug-ins—do so sparingly. Not all visitors to your site will have high-speed modems; and although your pages may load fine locally, don't assume they'll load as easily using a 28.8K, or even 14.4K modem—the most widely used speed on the Internet today.

Also remember if you plan to implement plug-ins on your Intranet, not all machines on your network may be capable of using multimedia-oriented plug-ins. And just because you can easily use and understand plug-in technology don't assume everyone else on your network can. This is a relatively new technology. If your co-workers have surfed your internal network but have never surfed the Net, the concept of plug-ins will be a relatively foreign concept for them.

Just remember, when you design your Web pages with plug-ins, make sure you also keep the potential viewers of your pages in mind. Assume they don't have the plug-in. Assume they don't know the first thing about plug-ins. Assume they are using very slow-speed modems. The one rule of thumb you should always remember is to create your Web pages with the lowest common denominator in mind. Assume your potential visitors and/or co-workers simply know how to point and click and that's about it. If you keep all of this in mind, you'll be ahead of the crowd, and you will have created some pretty useful sites that anyone can use with little or no assistance.

DISSECTING A WEB PAGE WITH A PLUG-IN

In order to understand how plug-ins are summoned through Web pages, let's first take a look at a plug-in in action, then we'll dissect the page from the back end. Even if you have little knowledge of the language that makes up Web pages, the HyperText Markup Language (HTML), don't worry. I'll keep this section relatively basic. At this point, the idea is to grasp the concepts, not worrying too much about understanding every line of code. In the latter part of this chapter, you'll actually create a data file, design a Web page, and place a reference to it in that page. That's when you'll really have to concentrate.

The example we'll look at is a QuickTime file that has been embedded in a Web page. This will give you a good idea of how a page is constructed to include a plug-in and how you can use the different options plug-ins offer when adding them to a Web page, such as embedding, hiding, or displaying them in full-page mode.

The QuickTime plug-in works with pretty much all existing QuickTime movies, particularly those movies that have been created to take advantage of the QuickTime "fast start" option. The "fast start" will show the first frame of the movie almost immediately upon the page loading and allows for the QuickTime movie to play almost automatically before the movie is downloaded. The QuickTime plug-in will also play MIDI and QuickTime VR files. You can download the QuickTime plug-in from http://quicktime.apple.com

A QUICK LOOK AT THE QUICKTIME PLUG-IN

If you haven't already downloaded the Apple QuickTime plug-in, download the proper version for your machine, then check out the Apple QuickTime Samples page located at *http://quicktime.apple.com/ sam/sam.html.* There you'll find plenty of QuickTime Plug-in-enhanced sites to choose from; or try the QuickTime Plug-in Sample Web site located at *http://quicktime.apple.com/qt-city/.*

If you clicked to these sites before downloading the QuickTime plug-in, you might have noticed the site prompts you, asking if you want to download the QuickTime plug-in, as shown in Figure 8.1. This is one option you can include in your Web page when adding plug-ins to your site. Such an option checks to see if the user has the plug-in. If he doesn't, it can prompt the user, then take him directly to the site where he can download the plug-in.

Click any of the sites, and soon you should see a QuickTime movie play within the Web page. Depending on how the page was constructed, the plug-in may or may not offer you controls to play, stop, fast forward, or rewind the movie. The movie actually appears as part of the page and does so because the designer of the page has elected to make this data file display through the Web page by using the QuickTime plug-in. The Web page designer has placed a QuickTime movie on his server and anyone with the QuickTime plug-in can play that movie. As you've seen before, that's about all you have to do to enjoy a plug-in. Download it, then check out a page that uses the plug-in to display a particular data type.

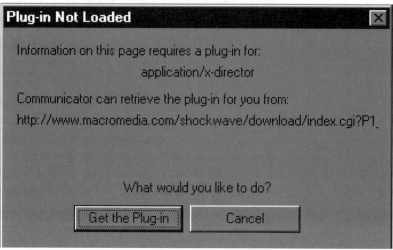

FIGURE *If the page was constructed correctly, you are prompted to download the plug-in,*
8.1 *if you don't have the plug-in installed in your browser.*

A QUICK TOUR OF HTML—THE INSTRUCTIONS BEHIND A WEB PAGE

Once the movie has stopped playing, let's take a look at how the page is constructed. To do that, select **Page Source** from the **View** or **Edit** menu. You'll see a screen like that shown in Figure 8.2.

Let's take a look at this page. First, you are looking at a plain text file. In other words, you are looking at a file that wasn't created and saved as a Microsoft Word file, or as an Aldus PageMaker file. Instead, it is a simple text file that just about any computer system could read. In this text file are special instructions. When your Web browser comes across them, it knows how to interpret, then display, the information accordingly. These special instructions, called HTML tags, tell the browser where an embedded QuickTime should appear on the Web page, along with where the actual QuickTime movie is located. This simple text file also outlines how text should be formatted, and which words or pictures will take you to other Web pages if you click your mouse button on these pieces of text or pictures.

In the example shown in Figure 8.2, you'll notice the first portion of the page starts by identifying this as a page containing HyperText Markup Language. Notice the <HTML> designator tag at the top. A tag, the special code a Web browser interprets, consists of a letter, word,

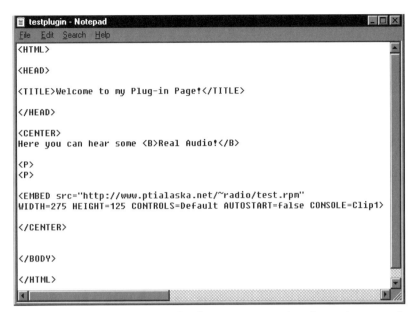

FIGURE   *By viewing the source or "code" of a page, you can see how the page is constructed.*
8.2

or words enclosed in brackets. A tag may contain a beginning and an ending tag, or it may be a single tag. For example, when you want to make a certain portion of text bold on a Web page, you would use the <B> tag in this fashion:

<B>This text is bold</B>

The above example contains an opening tag, the <B>, and a closing tag, the </B>. Anything between the beginning and ending tags will then be displayed bold in your Web browser.

But in the case of the <HR> tag, or the Horizontal Rule tag, there is no beginning or ending tag, only the tag itself. When you see the <HR> tag, your Web browser displays a simple horizontal rule across the page.

Some tags, however, go a little bit further than just formating text or displaying a horizontal rule. For example, the <BODY> tag lets you specify not only background image you might want to use, but also the color of the links or visited links, to name just a few attributes. Many tags, like the <BODY> tag have attributes that let you control a variety of options of the element the tag controls. In the following example the <BODY> tag sets up a page using different colors to designate links and visited links, and the background picture to be used.

<BODY VLINK="#100D4E" LINK="#330205" BACK-
GROUND="../images/background.gif">

In this example three attributes are used, one for the color of the visited links (vlink), one to set the color of the text signifying the links (link), and one for the picture used as a kind of background (background). Like the <BODY> tag, the tags you use to control plug-ins and data files all have attributes that pertain to the control of the data file and plug-in. We'll look at those attributes in more detail later. Now let's continue our short tour of the HyperText Markup Language.

Just as there are parts you can place in a word processing document, such as the header, footer, and body you can do the same with Web pages. For example, you can place <HEAD> elements, such as the title of the window, in the Head section. You can have the <BODY> section specify the default page color, text color, link color, and the text and pointers to graphic and plug-in files you want to display. You can also include a <TABLE> section that would display information in rows and columns like a spreadsheet. And you can even divide up a Web page window into different window <FRAMES> so information in one frame can scroll while another frame stays in place. Like word processing documents, such parts of a Web page follow a specific order. As you might have guessed, the <HEAD> tag comes before the <BODY> tag. Section-type tags such as <TABLE> and <FRAMES>, however, can be placed anywhere within the body of the Web page.

As you saw in Figure 8.2, most Web pages contain more tags than the few I've outlined here. Again, the idea is to give you an idea of how a Web page is constructed. If you really want to master the fine art of Web page creation you should familiarize yourself with the various HTML tags. Currently there are about 50 different tags you can use that will be recognized by most common browsers. Of those 50, about 20 to 30 are used often. More tags are introduced regularly to keep up with the demand of the browsing public.

The tags you will learn will mostly be formatting tags, which are pretty simple to understand and easy to use. Other more complex tags, such as the Frameset or Meta tags, take a little bit of study to understand. To get a simple plug-in to work on a page, you don't have to know more than a dozen tags at most. You should, however, spend some time learning what tag options a particular plug-in offers. Since each plug-in comes with it's own set of controls, you'll need to learn where and how to place those controls within your Web page in order for the data file to be displayed properly.

WHERE TO FIND OUT MORE ABOUT HTML

Once you get into creating Web pages, you'll probably want to learn some fancy tricks of the trade. A good place to start learning about HTML is right there on the Web. There are plenty of good HTML reference guides on the Internet. Most provide you with descriptions of the various tags, along with examples of how they work in the real world. Others offer special tips and trick sections that show you how to manipulate HTML tags to your specifications. Some of the better guides available for free on the Internet are listed in Table 8.1.

TABLE 8.1: *Some great resources for learning about HTML.*

Site	Comment	Location
BudgetWeb's List of Webmaster Links	Lots of links for both creating and running Web sites.	http://budgetWeb.com/ budgetWeb/links.shtml
The HTML Writers Guild WWW Resources	An excellent source for those serious about writing good HTML code.	http://www.hwg.org/ resources/index.html
The Webmaster's Reference Library	A ton of links, but definitely for those serious Webmasters.	http://www.Webreference.com
D.J. Quad's Ultimate HTML Site	Excellent site with lots of tutorials and just down-home good advice.	http://www.quadzilla.com (Lots of good tutorials)
The HTML Goodies Home Page	A great site for the beginner, with plenty of references to code, artwork, and tips.	http://www.htmlgoodies.com/
HTML Station	Can't beat this site-it shows you the code and how it should look as well.	http://www.december.com/html/

(Table 8.1 continued)

Bare Bones Guide to HTML	Just as the name implies, gives you the list of tags, their options, and some links to other sources.	http://werbach.com/barebones/
BigNoseBird.Com	Lots of tips, tricks, and resources for the beginning and advanced Webmaster.	http://bignosebird.com
HTML Help by The Web Design Group	Committed to helping just about anybody designing pages for just about any browser; this site has plenty of good tips and FAQs.	http://www.htmlhelp.com/
WebCom Publishing on the Web	Plenty of links for anything you might want to do with Web sites, from HTML tag lists to HTML validators.	http://www.Webcom.com/ ~Webcom/html/

Spend some time at these various sites studying the tips, FAQs, and how-tos. The more you know about this technology the easier it will be for you to figure out the best way to design sites, learn the tricks you can use if you are designing for various browsers, and learn how to troubleshoot problems. Plus, the more you know about the HyperText Markup Language, the easier it will be to add, delete, change, and supercharge those sites in which you want to add plug-in technology. Finally, you should definitely spend time reading about how to implement the plug-in on your Web site from the manufacturer's Web site. Almost everything you need to know will be available on the Internet either from the manufacturer's Web site or from other sources.

A Closer Look at a Plug-In Tag

Now that you have a rudimentary understanding that a Web browser reads a text file, interprets the tags listed in the file, then displays the information accordingly, let's take a look at the tags used to display plug-ins. The plug-in tags aren't that much different than, say, the <BODY> tag. Most plug-in tags offer not only the option to display the plug-in in embedded, hidden, or full-page mode, but also offer certain attributes for displaying and playing the plug-in-attributes the browsing visitor can control.

Let's take a look at how tag attributes work by first examining a simple plug-in tag used within one of the example QuickTime pages. In the example shown in Figure 8.3, notice the <EMBED> tag is followed by several other attributes:

<EMBED
SCR="ftp://video.terranint.com/video1/Obsidian/ObsidianCV10.mov"
WIDTH="200" HEIGHT="136" AUTOPLAY="TRUE" CON-
TROLLER="TRUE">

First let's dissect each piece of the tag. This is the only tag needed to summon the plug-in, then display the data file specified. Remember that a plug-in can take one of three forms-embedded, full-page, or hidden. In the preceding example, any QuickTime movie would certainly work better embedded into a page, than displaying full page. And it certainly wouldn't make much sense if the movie was hidden-no one would be able to see it. Since this is the case with most plug-ins you'll find you'll embed most of them into Web pages. The <EMBED> tag uses a variety of standard attributes to control the plug-in and data file. In this example, the attributes used are specific to the QuickTime plug-in. Table 8.2 outlines what each attribute does.

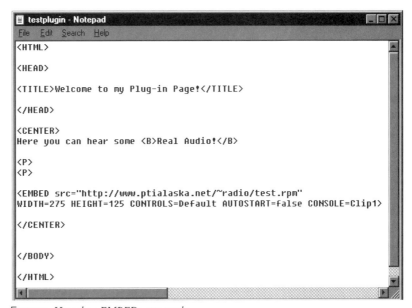

FIGURE *How the <EMBED> tag works.*
8.3

TABLE 8.2: *Dissection of the <EMBED> tag.*

Part of the Tag	Explanation
<EMBED SCR=	Embeds the plug-in into the page and tells the browser, yes, we're going to be using a plug-in.
ftp://video.terran-int.com/video1/ Obsidian/ObsidianCV10.mov is located, but also the name of	Tells the browser not only where the file the plug-in should display the file, ObsidianCV10.mov.
WIDTH=200	Tells the browser the exact width the embedded movie should display.
HEIGHT=136	As with width tells the browser the exact height the embedded movie should display.
AUTOPLAY=TRUE	Tells the browser and plug-in to automatically play the video after it's been loaded.
CONTROLLER=TRUE	Tells the browser and plug-in to display the QuickTime controller so the browsing visitor can control the playback of the QuickTime video.

You'll learn more about the global attributes used with the <EMBED> plug-in when you start creating your own Web page that displays a particular plug-in. But before we get too far ahead of ourselves, let's first take a look at what's involved in creating, adding, and testing out a plug-in-enabled site. Then, as we create a site, we'll cover each global attribute the <EMBED> tag uses, since this will be the tag you'll use the most when adding plug-ins to your site.

Just remember, although the <EMBED> tag offers certain global attributes that can be used with every plug-in, each individual plug-in comes with its own set of attributes. The QuickTime plug-in AUTOPLAY, for example, includes a control specific to the QuickTime plug-in. To fully understand how to implement the plug-in you want to use, you should visit the Web site of the software manufacturer that created it. The manufacturer's site will have a list of attributes that can be used with the plug-in.

NOTE

THE PIECES, PARTS, AND CONCEPTS

As mentioned previously, you should have a cursory knowledge of how to create a simple Web page or you should consider using some of the "What You See Is What You Get" Web page making programs such as Netscape Composer, Adobe PageMill, HotDog, Claris HomePage, Microsoft Publisher, or FrontPage Express. With the exception of PageMill, HomePage, and Publisher, the other software programs are available for free, downloadable from such places as Shareware.com (*www.shareware.com*) or Windows95.com (*www.windows95.com*).

You will also need the application to create the data file the plug-in will read, display, or play. For example, if you want to create QuickTime movies, you'll need to purchase or download a QuickTime movie making application. If you want to have your browsing visitors fly through three-dimensional worlds, you'll need an application that will let you create virtual reality files. If you simply want to create a Web page that displays your latest PowerPoint presentation, you'll need PowerPoint to create that presentation.

TIP

Up until now you probably wondered how these different software companies made money, especially if they gave away their plug-ins. Well, now you know. They make money by selling the application that creates the data file the plug-in reads. Although you can get many plug-in data making programs for free, many charge from $20 to several thousands of dollars for the plug-in data file making application. The software manufacturer's idea is that if lots of people have the plug-in, lots of Webmasters will want to create lots of data files that can be read by the plug-in.

Once you've created your data file, you'll need a place to store it. Your local service provider probably provides you with enough space to put up several files, assuming they aren't too large. My provider allows me three megabytes of space, which is just about enough for me to put up several pages, along with a couple short QuickTime movies. Besides just having the space to accommodate the file, my service provider's Web server also has to be configured to understand what to do when a browsing visitor encounters a QuickTime movie I've placed on my site. For example, if the Web server I'm storing my QuickTime movies on doesn't understand how to notify the visitor's Web browser what kind of file my QuickTime movie is, I wouldn't be able to put up my QuickTime movies and embed them in my Web pages.

TIP

Any time you add multimedia files such as video or audio to your site, you are going to need more space than the average Web site occupies. If you are shopping around for a server to store your site and plug-ins on, make sure you get at least 10MB of space, more if you have video. Also make sure that the server can accommodate the kinds of files you want to place on it. Ask the prospective Web server administrator if the Web server can handle and understand the types of files you want to place on your site.

Let's take a step-by-step look at this entire process of adding plug-ins. Although this may start to sound technical, just about anyone with a cursory knowledge of how to construct Web pages can quickly and easily add plug-ins to a page.

DETAILING THE PROCESS OF ADDING PLUG-INS

Now that you've seen how a plug-in works and some of the code behind the Web page that makes all these things work, the process of adding a plug-in is relatively simple. In this section I'll detailed the exact steps you need to follow in order to add a plug-in to your site. Assuming you are familiar with HTML, and feel comfortable enough creating Web pages, the process for implementing plug-ins into your site is as follows:

1. Decide on the plug-in that will best suit your needs.
2. Purchase or download the application that helps you create the data file the plug-in will read.
3. Create the data file.
4. Create the Web page that first points to the data file and at the same time tells the page an embedded plug-in will read/interpret the data file. Remember, you can choose from one of three page options—embedded, full page, and hidden—depending upon the plug-in.
5. Test the page locally if possible, making sure the current version of the plug-in works with no problems.
6. Make sure the server you will be uploading the file and Web page to is configured to interpret, then pass along, the information about the file to the browsing visitor. (This is called configuring your server for MIME types.)
7. Upload the Web page and the data file to the server.
8. Test the page on your network, making sure the plug-in and data files load properly.

9. If you are offering the site to the Internet world, test the page on a separate network and with varying modem speeds; or if you are offering the site on an Intranet, test it from a variety of machines across your network.

10. Let everyone know about your site and the plug-in(s) needed.

It's really not that difficult—only ten simple steps. Let's take a closer look at accomplishing each one of these steps. In the next section you'll learn how to add a Real Audio data file and embed the instructions for playing that file as a plug-in directly from your Web page. You can apply the lessons you learn here to just about any plug-in. Even though the data files will differ and the procedures may vary, the process is pretty much the same. You create the data file, then create the Web page with the reference to the plug-in and data file. Then you upload the file to your server and test it all out.

CAUTION

Just remember, along the way anything can, and most likely will, happen, so take things slow and remember that anything having to do with the Internet, especially these days, takes time and patience. If you get stuck, feel free to e-mail me at ckirk@alaska.net, or on AOL you can find me at KIRKCL. If you're a CompuServe user, you can find me at 76200.1660.

OUR PROJECT—ADDING REAL AUDIO TO A SITE

You've seen the steps involved. You've seen some of the code you'll need to add. Now you're ready to start creating, then adding your data file and Web page with a link for summoning up the plug-in and playing or displaying the data file. But which plug-in do you start with? If you add a PowerPoint presentation, you'll have to rush out and buy PowerPoint or have it installed as part of the Microsoft Office suite of applications. The same goes with many of the other plug-ins, such as Adobe Acrobat, Envoy, or Virtual World. So instead of rushing out and buying a plug-in data file making application, I'll show you how to create Real Audio files using the free Real Audio encoder available from Real Networks.

First let me tell you exactly why you would want to enhance your site with Real Audio, and the equipment you need to do just that. Real Audio offers an easy way to stream both video and audio to anyone with either the Real Player or the Real Player plug-in. Real Audio is the most widely used streaming audio and video format on the Internet today. Hundreds of radio stations worldwide are now broadcasting live over the Internet to anyone who wants to listen. And thousands upon thousands of sites offer Real Audio archives, which can range in content from keynote speeches from past Internet World trade shows to Christmas carols sung by the local church choir. Many corporate sites use Real Audio as a training tool, complementing information on Web pages. Other sites use Real Audio files to create virtual jukeboxes, and some offer daily stock or information updates, much like you hear on normal radio stations. The potential is unlimited. Just remember, whatever you add should complement or enhance your site.

What's so great about adding Real Audio or Real Video is that you don't have to have elaborate equipment to create the Real data files, nor do you need any specialized server software to stream the files to a limited number of listeners. Plus, Real Audio files are small compared to other types of digital sound and video files. With a simple multimedia computer you can easily record any sound from a microphone, CD player, television, or other sound source, then turn that recording into a Real data file with little or no experience in mixing, editing, or creating sound files. Better yet, most Web servers can be easily configured to stream Real data files, without the need of a special Real Audio server. If your service provider is relatively up on technology, he or she probably already has the Web server configured to transfer for Real Audio files properly to any browsing visitor.

If you plan to have a large number of visitors listen or view your Real data file, you should consider purchasing a Real Server. The Real Server allows you to broadcast audio and video live, and also streams data files to a larger number of simultaneous visitors. If you plan on doing a lot of Real Audio encoding, you should also consider purchasing the RealPublisher application. You can find out more about both of these applications by visiting Real's Web site at http://www.real.com.

The project I'm going to outline on the following pages regarding adding Real Audio to your site should take approximately an hour to complete. Maybe a little more if you are somewhat unfamiliar with creating Web pages or uploading files to a Web server. Maybe less if everything goes as planned. If you aren't already familiar with uploading files to the Web server you use, save yourself some time by checking with your system administrator to find out exactly how this is done. Not all Web servers are configured the same way for uploading files. Although you can test out your page and plug-in to your heart's content locally, if you plan on serving up the page to the viewing public, you'll need to know how to upload or transfer the page you create along with the audio file from your computer to your Web server.

My final recommendation to you is to take it slow. If something doesn't make sense to you, read that section again. If it still doesn't and you need help, feel free to e-mail me. Again, this is just an example. If you would prefer to create a page with a PowerPoint presentation or an Adobe Acrobat file embedded in a Web page, do that. You'll find that the steps outlined here are the same steps you'll go through whether you're creating a page that uses a RealPlayer plug-in, an Adobe Acrobat plug-in, a PowerPoint plug-in, or a MPEG plug-in.

WHAT YOU NEED

You really don't need too many things, especially if you already have a multimedia computer. Since this project will require you to first create an audio file, then encode it into a Real Audio file, your system needs to meet the minimum requirements for the Real Audio Encoder. These requirements are:

- At least a 486/66Mhz DX computer—A Pentium is preferred
- Windows 95 or Windows NT (you can also use a PowerMac if you prefer)
- At least 16MB of RAM memory
- A sound card with either a microphone or input jack (this is standard equipment with Macs)
- About 10MB of free hard disk space
- The Real Audio Encoder, available free from *www.real.com* or from *www.shareware.com*
- A sound source, such as a microphone, CD Player, camcorder, radio, tape recorder, or VCR
- A cable that connects your sound source to your sound card's microphone or input jack
- A Web page editing program or text editor such as Notepad or SimpleText

TIP

You should use Notepad instead of WordPad if you plan to use a text editor. Notepad saves the files you create automatically in a text file format. WordPad, on the other hand, as a default saves files as WordPad files.

- A file transfer program or such capability included as part of the Web page editing program
- Enough space on a Web server to accommodate your audio file

- A connection to the Internet and a Web browser
- The list of attributes that can be used with the Real Audio plug-in (I'll supply those later)
- A Web browser with the Real plug-in installed

Getting Started—Downloading the Plug-In Player

First let's make sure you have the latest version of the RealPlayer installed. You can download the latest version at *www.real.com*. Because Real's Web site changes frequently, instead of pointing you to a particular page, you should look around for the link for downloading the RealPlayer for your particular type of computer.

The RealPlayer Plus is the "pay for" player that offers you more features than just the standard RealPlayer. You don't need to buy the PlayerPlus to hear and see Real audio and video sites; the standard RealPlayer will work just fine.

After you have downloaded the RealPlayer installation program, exit your Web browser so the installation program can properly install the Real plug-in into your browser. Double-click the **Installation** icon to launch the installation program. Click past the License Agreement screen to accept the license agreement. Then enter your name, company information, and e-mail address. Click the **Next** button to continue the installation process. Select the speed of your modem connection, then select the directory where you want to install the **RealPlayer**. The next screen, shown in Figure 8.4, allows you to customize the browser options. Make sure you click the **Customize Browser Components** option, and make sure you select which browsers you want to install the plug-in into.

Click the **Next** button and make sure you select the **Install RealPlayer Plug-in?** option, as shown in Figure 8.5. Continue clicking the **Next** buttons through the rest of the installation options until you see the **Finish** button.

When the **Setup** option is complete, you should see a dialog box like that shown in Figure 8.6. This screen signals you have properly installed not only the plug-in but also the player. Next, you should restart your computer, then reconnect to the Internet and launch your Web browser. To ensure you've properly installed the plug-in and player and both work properly, make sure you check out some RealPlayer-enhanced

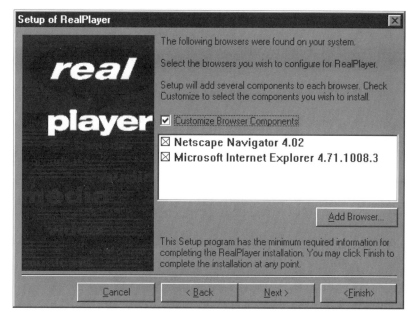

FIGURE *Make sure you click the option to customize your browser components.*
8.4

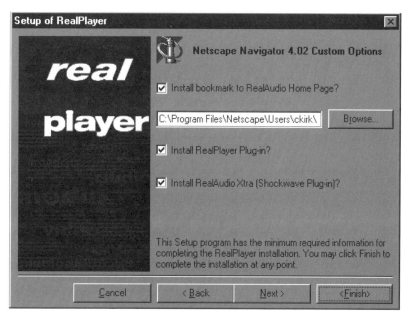

FIGURE *Make sure you select the option to install the RealPlayer plug-in.*
8.5

Figure *You're finished installing the plug-in. Congratulations.*

8.6

sites. You can find plenty at *www.timecast.com* or *www.audionet.com*. Make sure you can hear the RealPlayer files clearly and that all controls work, because if they don't, the rest won't matter. The player and plug-in must be working, otherwise you won't be able to hear the results of your own Real-enhanced Web site. Once you've used the plug-in and/or player, you're ready for the next step—downloading the Real Audio Encoder.

TIP

*If you're having problems listening to sites, first clear your browser's cache by going to either the **Edit | Preferences** menu and clicking to expand the **Advanced** tab, then selecting **Cache**; or by selecting **Option | Network Preferences** and clicking the **Cache** tab. If the problem persists, check out the support section of **Real Networks'** main site, located at www.real.com.*

DOWNLOADING THE ENCODER

The RealPlayer lets you hear Real files created by other people. But the Real Encoder lets you create Real audio files with relatively simplistic recording technology. Real Networks offers their basic encoder, a program that takes sounds and turns them into Real Audio files the RealPlayer plug-in can play, for free. The company also makes a product called RealPublisher, a more advanced encoder that does a lot of the dirty work for you, such as uploading your encoded file to your Web site. Although you don't have to purchase the RealPublisher application if you plan on adding a lot of RealPlayer files to your Web site, you may consider buying this application since it can cut down on the amount of time it takes to create, then add, Real files to your site.

Currently you can find the Real Encoder at *www.real.com/ encoder/index.html.* Or if you can't find it there, search the main site located at *www.real.com.* In this example, we'll use version 3.1 since we'll be creating a simple audio file. If your system is capable, you might try downloading version 5.0 since it offers other features not found in version 3.1, especially if you have plans for recording video files. In order to record sound files that any version of the Real plug-in can play, version 3.1 works just fine.

Once you connect to *www.real.com/encoder/index.html,* scroll down the page to find the link to the Real Encoder. Click that link, then type your name and e-mail address in the appropriate fields on the Web page, then select the right product, your operating system, processor and connection speed, as shown in Figure 8.7.

The process of downloading the Real Encoder may have changed by the time you read this. If so, follow the instructions for downloading the Encoder from Real Network's Web site.

Next click the **Go to download and instructions** page button. This will take you to another page where you should then click the location nearest you to download the file. In a few seconds, you will be prompted to save the file. Make sure you save the file in your Download folder or on your desktop so you can quickly find it. The file is about 825K and should take a few minutes to download. Once downloaded, you should see an icon on your desktop like the one shown in Figure 8.8. Double-click on this icon, and in a few seconds the installation program for the Real Encoder will start.

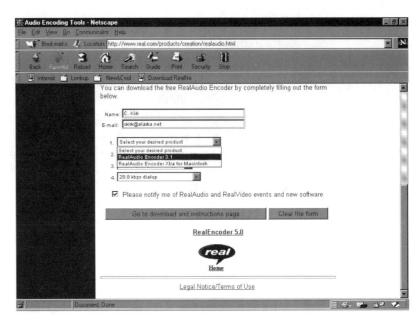

FIGURE
8.7
Make sure you select all the right options.

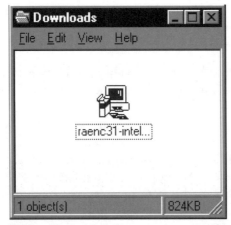

FIGURE
8.8
The Real Encoder setup program should be either on your desktop or in your download folder. If not, use the Start menu's Find option to find the file labeled "RAENC*.*"

This is the application that will create the Real Audio files you will embed in your Web page. If you were creating a Web page and embedding a PowerPoint presentation, you would be setting up PowerPoint and creating a PowerPoint presentation instead. The process is to first create the data file, then embed it in the Web page.

Click through the various screens asking you to accept the licensing agreement and the screen for adding your name and e-mail address. The next screen you should see is one asking where you want to place the Real Encoder, as shown in Figure 8.9. Either accept the default, C:\RAENCODE, or select another location.

Click the **Next** button to continue, then click the **Finish** button to complete the software installation. The Real Encoder will be installed on your system and the setup program will notify you with a dialog window alerting you of the components installed, much like that shown in Figure 8.10.

Once the installation is complete, you should see a folder open like the one shown in Figure 8.11. This folder contains all the Real Encoder components that were installed. Make sure you read the ReadMe file for any last minute additions, bug reports, or other information about the

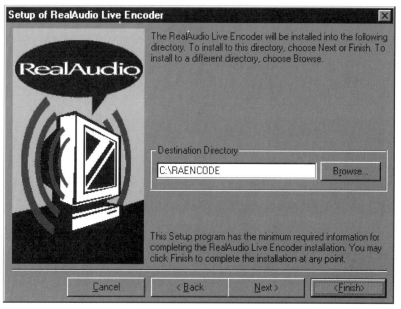

FIGURE   *Pick a folder to save your Real Encoder into.*
8.9

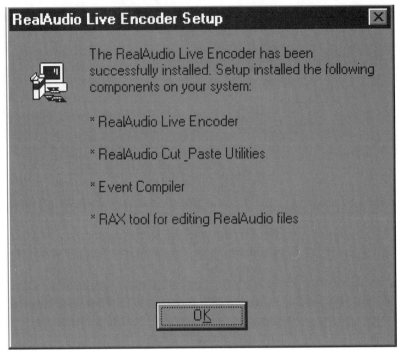

FIGURE 8.10 *If the installation was successful, you should see a dialog window like this one.*

FIGURE 8.11 *Once the Encoder is installed, you should see a folder open with all the Encoder components.*

Encoder. This file will tell you exactly what compression options are now included with this version. The ReadMe file will also outline what additional hardware or software you need to run the Encoder. Once you've finished reading the ReadMe file, close it, and restart your computer. The next step will be to set up your hardware so you can start recording a Real Audio file that you'll learn all about in the next section.

GETTING READY TO RECORD A SOUND FILE

Now that you have the plug-in to play your sound file and the encoder, the next two steps are to create the sound file, then create the page to embed the file into. To record a sound file you need a microphone, CD player, or other sound source, along with the appropriate cabling. If you have an internal CD player, you can use that. If you don't have a CD player, you can use your sound card's microphone plug or Line In input plug to get sound into your system. Your sound card most likely came with a microphone plug which allows you to plug in a microphone, external CD player, or even personal stereo, and record from these sources. All you need is an appropriate plug to connect the external sound source to the microphone plug located on the back of your sound card. You'll find the microphone or Line In input jack on the back of your sound card, which most likely is located on the back of your system close to where you plug in your printer or power cord in the same place you put expansion cards. If you're using a laptop, the microphone or sound input plugs might be on either the right- or left-hand side of your keyboard. If you're using a relatively new computer, the microphone or Line In input jack maybe be located in the front of your system. Read your hardware documentation to find exactly where your microphone or Line In input jack is located.

If you're going to use your microphone, plug it into the microphone plug. Refer to your hardware manual to find out which jack the microphone connects into. If you plan to use your CD drive, which you can record directly from, pop in the CD you want to record from. If you don't have either a microphone or CD drive, but you do have a separate CD player or radio or cassette player, connect these to your microphone or Line In input plug. You can find cables with the appropriate plugs at your local electronics store or in the video/audio department of your favorite variety store.

Once you've located the sound input source you want to use, make sure you have your computer set to pick up the sound from either the microphone, sound input jack, or CD drive. Right-click the Speaker icon in your **System** tray or double-click the **Multimedia** icon in the **Control Panel**. If you right-click the speaker icon in the **System Tray**, select **Audio Properties** or **Adjust Audio Properties** from the pop-up menu. The **Audio Properties** window should open. Figure 8.12 is an example of what you should see.

In the **Recording** section of the **Audio Properties** window, click the drop-down list for the **Preferred Recording Device** and select the input device you want to use. If you plan to use your internal CD player, select

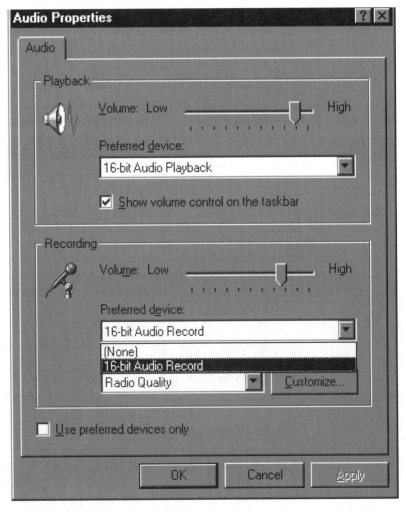

FIGURE *The Audio Properties window lets you decide the recording device to use.*
8.12

that as your recording device. Once you have your recording options set, you're ready to start recording the sound file. Remember, the idea is to keep the file relatively small, and that means we only want to record at most a few minutes of sound.

RECORDING THE SOUND FILE

In this example I'll be recording direct from the microphone. If you want the steps for recording from your CD player, check the file, "Creating RealAudio Files from Audio CDs," found at *www.real. com/devzone/tutorials/audiocds.html*. If you're planning to use the microphone, let's get started. First, open the Real Encoder you downloaded and installed previously. Let's take a look at the Encoder application to see what features it has to offer.

NOTE

Remember, the Encoder's interface may look different if you downloaded a different version.

The left-hand side of the **Encoder** window, as shown in Figure 8.13, is the source of your sound. It could be a file you've already recorded using the Windows 95 Sound Recorder application or sound coming from your microphone. Click the **File** tab if you want to take a WAV, MIDI, or other sound file you have stored on your computer and turn it into a Real Audio file. Click **Live Stream** if you want to pick up sound from a live source, such as your microphone, a radio connected to your Line Input source, or your CD player.

The big white box in the middle is where the sound displays. The slim box below that tells you the length of the clip. You fill in the title of the clip, along with the author's name and any copyright notices, in the field provided. This information shows up later when the file is embedded in the Web page, as shown in Figure 8.14.

The right-hand side provides information about the Real Audio-encoded file. Here you decide where you want to store the file, either locally as a file on your hard drive or remotely as a file on Real Audio. In the left-hand side of the window, the big white box shows the sound file as it looks while it is encoding and includes the time it will take to encode the file below the big white box. Aside from the **File** field, the other important field you should take note of in the right-hand frame is the **Compression** field. This essentially controls not only the size and type of the file, but also what version of the RealPlayer can play this file. For universal appeal, but low quality sound, select RealAudio 3.0-28.8 from the drop-down list, as shown in Figure 8.15. By selecting this

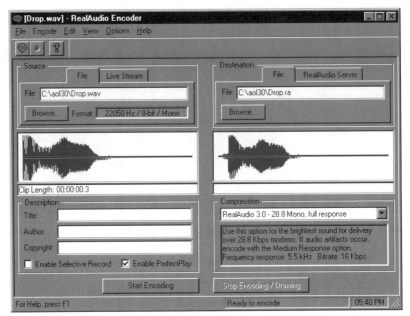

FIGURE *The Real Audio Encoder displays information about the file you are recording*
8.13 *and the attributes of the file as you save it.*

option, just about anybody with a RealPlayer and at least a 14.4Kpbs
modem can hear your file once you embed it in the Web page. If you'd
rather have higher sound quality, but realize listeners may need to
upgrade, select another format.

FIGURE *When you fill in the information during your recording session, it eventually*
8.14 *shows up when the plug-in displays the data file.*

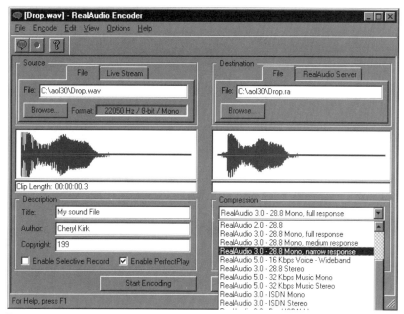

FIGURE   *Select the right compression code so everyone can hear your sound file.*
8.15

TIP

The idea is simply to record a sound file in Real Audio format. If you want to delve deeper into recording Real Audio files, make sure you check out the RealAudio Content Creation guide at www.real.com/create/ccguide. This online guide has tons of tips on how to maximize your recordings. Also, don't forget to explore the Help file by clicking on the ? icon. A complete reference guide for the Encoder is included in the Help guide.

By now you should be somewhat familiar with the Encoder. At this point you're ready to record your first sound file. Follow these steps and in a few minutes you should have a sound file that you will be able to upload, then play through a plug-in.

1. Click the **Live Stream** tab in the left-hand **Source** side of the **Encoder** screen.
2. Click in the **Title** field and enter the title of your recording.
3. Click in the **Author** field and enter the author of your sound file.
4. Click in the **Copyright** field and enter any copyright information.
5. Click the **File** tab in the right-hand **Destination** side of the **Encoder** screen.

6. Click the **Browse** button, locate the place where you want to store this file, then supply a name for the file in the **File** name field of the **Choose Destination** file field. Click the **Open** button after you've typed the name of the file. I recommend saving the file to your desktop so you can easily find it later.

7. Make sure your microphone or sound source is turned on and ready to go.

8. Click the **Start Encoding** button, or the first button on the **Toolbar** directly underneath the **File** menu.

9. Start speaking into the microphone or turn on your sound source and start playing the music, CD, or radio. You should see the big white box on both sides of the **Encoder** window fill with a graphic representation of the sound file being recorded.

10. After about 15 seconds, click the **Stop Encoding/Drawing** button.

11. Congratulations! You have your first sound recorded. Select **File | Exit** and you should see your file located in the folder. I've saved my file to my desktop, as shown in Figure 8.16.

Now That You Have Your Sound File...A Few Words about Tags

Now that you have a sound file encoded in the Real Audio format, you're ready to create the Web page that embeds the sound file into the page, then displays or automatically plays it with the help of the RealPlayer plug-in. Before you start creating your Web page, let me outline some specific information you'll need to know to embed a plug-in

FIGURE *Hopefully by now you have a file on your desktop like I do on mine. If so, you're*
8.16 *ready to move to the next step.*

into your page. First let's review the tags you can add to your Web page that will summon up the appropriate plug-in. You place these simple single-line HTML tags in a Web page; the browser and the server do the rest. A Web page can include three different plug-in tags.

The Embedded Plug-In Tag <EMBED>

The Embedded Plug-in tag is the most commonly used tag to specify a plug-in and its accompanying data file. Most Web page developers use the <EMBED> tag because not only can a browsing visitor see the plug-in, but he can also see the rest of the Web page. The embedded plug-in appears as a rectangular subpart of the Web page in which you place it. If the browsing visitor has the appropriate plug-in, he will see the data file through the rectangular portion of the Web page. If he doesn't have the right plug-in, he will see what looks like a puzzle piece where the plug-in data file should be.

These types of plug-ins appear as part of the Web page much like inline graphics. The major difference between an inline plug-in and an inline graphic is the fact that the plug-in can be live. It can be a live audio or video stream, or it can be a live connection to a database. Since the plug-in only occupies a certain amount of the Web page screen, you can add anything above or below the plug-in data file you embed.

You'll find most sites use embedded plug-ins simply because they are relatively easy to use, easy to create, and don't take a huge amount of time to load. Plus, they allow more than just the contents of the plug-in data file to display.

Here's an example of the <EMBED> plug-in tag:

<EMBED SRC="http://www.alaska.net/ckirk/sound.rpm"
HEIGHT=100% WIDTH=100%>

Full-Page Plug-In Tag <A HREF>

A full-page plug-in tag opens a new window, maintaining the browser toolbar features but usually adding its own toolbar or menu options as well. A full-page plug-in does not contain any parts of a Web page. Instead, with a full-page plug-in tag you don't see any other HTML code, Web page graphics, or links. You see only that information that's part of the plug-in data file. You'll most likely see full-page plug-in tags used when displaying Adobe Acrobat documents or using such full-screen plug-ins as WinFrame, JForms, or Look@Me plug-ins that need large screen landscapes.

Here's an example of the Full-Page plug-in tag:

<A HREF="filename.pdf> This is a PDF document that needs the Acrobat reader to display in full-page mode. </A>

Hidden Plug-In Tag <EMBED... HIDDEN or HEIGHT=0>

You won't see many hidden plug-in tags, because, well, they are hidden. You're more likely to hear hidden tags because most of them are used to play sounds or music in the background as the Web page loads. You create a hidden plug-in by using the <EMBED> tag and adding the HIDDEN attribute. You should use the hidden tag sparingly since you want to give the browsing visitor as much control as possible, especially if the system the visitor is using cannot play or read the data file because the plug-in isn't loaded or because the hardware is incapable of doing it.

With the RealAudio plug-in, if you want to play RealAudio files without having visible controls, essentially hiding the plug-in, you simply hide the control. You do this by setting the height and width of the plug-in rectangle that normally displays.

Here are two examples of how a hidden plug-in tag would look. The first sets the height of the rectangle, the plug-in would normally display to zero; the second uses the HIDDEN attribute.

<EMBED WIDTH=2 HEIGHT=0 SRC="filename.rpm">
or
<EMBED WIDTH=100% HEIGHT=100% SRC="filename.rpm" HIDDEN=TRUE>

Object Tag <OBJECT>

The object tag can be used to embed a plug-in or an ActiveX control and also lets you put Java components and applets, along with images, in a Web page. You'll most likely find the object tag used in pages that contain ActiveX controls, although you might also see some in Netscape pages, especially since the object tag offers more control than the <EMBED> tag.

Here is an example of how the <OBJECT> works:

<OBJECT ID=RA0CX CLASSID="clsid: CFCDAA03-8BE4-11cf-B84B-0020AFBBCCFA" HEIGHT=140 WIDTH=312>
<PARAM NAME="SRC"
VALUE=http://www.yourservername.com/file.rpm">
<PARAM NAME="CONTROLS" VALUE="all">
</OBJECT>

A CLOSER LOOK AT THE <EMBED> TAG AND ITS ATTRIBUTES

Since you'll most likely use the <EMBED> tag the most, let's take a look at how the tag works and some of its attributes. The basic <EMBED> tag, like the <IMG> tag you use to place picture pointers in a Web page, has certain attributes that let you control the display of the data file the plug-in displays. For example, this HTML code will embed a Real Audio file in the Web page stored on a Web server in a particular directory:

<EMBED SRC= "http://www.alaska.net/ckirk/hello.rpm" WIDTH=100% HEIGHT=100%>

There are three basic attributes you must include with each <EMBED> tag you add to a Web page. Table 8.3 lists these three attributes that are not only required but are considered global, regardless of whether you're using the Real Audio plug-in, the PowerPoint plug-in, or any other plug-in.

TABLE 8.3: *The List of Required Global <EMBED> Attributes.*

Attribute	What it Does	Example
SRC="file"	Specifies the data file the plug-in will access. The extension of the file must match those extensions the plug-in can understand, such as RPM for RealAudio files. You must include the full pathname of the file if the file is not stored in the same location as the Web page itself. You should also include the protocol used to get the file, whether it is from a Web server (HTTP://) or a File Transfer server (FTP://).	<EMBEDSCR="http://Webserver/mydirectory/file.rpm">

Table 8.3 (continued)

WIDTH=10	The WIDTH and HEIGHT attributes specify the size of the rectangle the embedded plug-in will occupy on the Web page. Unlike images you might include in a Web page, plug-ins don't size automatically as the window is resized. You can specify width and height in pixels or as a percentage of the Web browser window if you like. *Caution: If you don't specify the width and height of the plug-in, the rectangle may appear as a tiny box. Also make sure you don't include the size of either width or height in quotes.*	<EMBED SCR="file.rpm" WIDTH=100% HEIGHT=100%>
HEIGHT=30	Same as above	<EMBED SRC="file.rpm" WIDTH=300 HEIGHT=134> *Note: This creates a plug-in rectan gle 300-pixels wide by 134-pixels high.*

Don't place the <EMBED> tag within a table; it won't work properly. And always supply at least one setting either for the height or width, otherwise you may end up crashing the visiting browser's Web browser.

The attributes listed in Table 8.3 are required, no matter what. But there are also other optional global attributes that can be used with any plug-in. Table 8.4 lists these optional global attributes.

Table 8.4: *These attributes are optional and can be used with any plug-in.*

Attribute	What it Does	Example
Border	Creates a border around the rectangle that specifies where the plug-in and data file are located. It takes the size assigned by the width and height attributes. You specify the thickness of the border in pixels. If you don't specify a border or a border thickness, you'll end up with no border.	<EMBED SRC="file.rpm" WIDTH=100% HEIGHT=100% BORDER=2> This would give the plug-in rectangle a border of 2 pixels wide.
Hidden	Instructs the browser to hide the plug-in and any controls for the plug-in so none are visible in the Web page. The only two parameters for this attribute are true or false. As a default, hidden is set as false so you can see the plug-in and its accompanying data file. This attribute also overrides the height and width settings and with the EMBED option is the way to hide the plug-in. *Note: You should still specify at least something in either height and width so your browser and, more importantly, browsing visitors don't crash.*	<EMBED SRC="file.rpm" WIDTH=100% HEIGHT=100% HIDDEN=TRUE>

Table 8.4 (continued)

Align, VSPACE, HSPACE	These three attributes determine how the plug-in is positioned in the Web page. You use the ALIGN attribute to flow text around the plug-in much like you would the ALIGN attribute with the <IMG> tag. VSPACE and HSPACE set the vertical and horizontal spacing, basically creating a space around the plug-in rectangle. You use an integer to specify exactly how much vertical and horizontal space is left around the plug-in.	<EMBED SRC="file.rpm" WIDTH=100% HEIGHT=100% ALIGN=RIGHT HSPACE=5 VSPACE=10> Here are the parameters for the **ALIGN** option: **Left**: floats the plug-in to the left margin **Right**: floats the plug-in to the right margin **Top**: floats the plug-in to the top margin **Texttop:** aligns the plug-in to the top of the line **Middle:** aligns the plug-in to the middle of the line **Absmiddle:** aligns the plug-in to the absolute middle of the current line **Baseline:** aligns the plug-in to the base line of the line **Bottom:** aligns the bottom of the plug-in to the bottom of the line **Absbottom:** aligns the baseline of the plug-in with the baseline of the current line
Palette	This attribute sets the mode of the plug-in's color palette and works only on Windows-based computers. There are two parameters with the Palette attribute, foreground and background. If you use the foreground parameter, the plug-in will use the color palette associated with the foreground color. If you use the background parameter, the plug-in will use the color palette associated with the background color.	<EMBED SRC="filename.rpm" WIDTH=100% HEIGHT=100% PALETTE="background">
Type	With this attribute you can specify what MIME type to use. You use type when you want to specify a plug-in to load. For example, there are lots of plug-ins that can play MIDI files, but with Type you can specify what plug-in to use. Type replaces the SRC attribute and is oftentimes used with plug-ins that don't call data files, such as plug-ins that bring up clocks, stock tickers, or other types of dynamic data.	<EMBED TYPE="mimetype/subtype WIDTH=100% HEIGHT=100% >
Units	This attribute defines the unit of measure you want to use for the Height and Width attributes. The unit of measure is either by pixel or by half the point size specified. You don't have to include this attribute unless you want to set the units of measure to half the point size. As a default, the units of measure is in pixels.	<EMBED SRC="file.rpm" WIDTH=40 HEIGHT=60 UNITS="en">

Remember, even though the preceding examples specify a file named file.rpm, RPM is just the file extension for Real Audio files, not a default or standard for all files used with all plug-ins. Each plug-in data file will have a different three letter extension you need to specify along with the filename and full pathname where the file is located.

A CLOSER LOOK AT SOME OF THE REAL AUDIO PLUG-IN ATTRIBUTES

There are several attributes that are specific to the Real Audio plug-in, you might want to add to your Web site. Remember, these attributes may not work with other plug-ins and are specific to the Real Audio plug-in. So with each plug-in you use you should spend some time at the manufacturer's Web site learning what that particular plug-in's attributes are. Here are some you should be aware of:

The AutoStart Attribute

Adding an AUTOSTART=TRUE attribute tells the user's browser to automatically begin playing your audio when the page is visited. You can use this feature to begin narration or to play background music as the page loads. Remember to use this option only if you know the browsing visitor is expecting it and has the capabilities to load the Web page. An example of using the AutoStart attribute might look like this:

<EMBED SRC="file.rpm" WIDTH=100% HEIGHT=100% AUTOSTART=TRUE>

The Controls Attribute

The Controls attribute controls all the different control panel options normally found on the Real Audio player. If you set the Controls attribute to ALL, you will embed a full player in the Web page. Some of the other controls you can set include CONTROLS=PlayButton, which displays only the Play button; CONTROLS=InfoPanel, which embeds only the information you would have supplied, such as title, author, or copyright, when you created the file; and CONTROLS=VolumeSlider which embeds a Volume slider to control the volume. And example of how you would use the Controls attribute might look like this:

<EMBED SRC="file.rpm" WIDTH=100% HEIGHT=100% CONTROLS=all> or

<EMBED SRC="file.rpm" WIDTH=100% HEIGHT=100% CON-TROLS=InfoPanel CONTROLS=VolumeSlider>

These are just a few attributes you can add. To find other attributes you can use with the Real Audio plug-in, check out the Real Networks' content guide at *www.real.com/create/*. As you can see, each can be added to the <EMBED> tag regardless of the other global attributes that are required. You simply add them to the end of the <EMBED> tag, making sure they fit within the brackets of the <EMBED> tag. Just remember, some of the attributes you don't have to assign since the defaults set when an attribute isn't specified usually work just fine. The best thing to do is to try the plug-in without setting specific attributes, then add in those attributes you think might enhance your site or make it easier for the browsing visitor to view the data file.

WHAT DO YOU USE WHEN THE BROWSER DOESN'T HAVE THE PLUG-IN?

Some browsing visitors may not have the Real Audio plug-in, whereas other visitors may be using browsers that don't support plug-ins. So what do you do for those who don't have the technology to use plug-ins? Don't fear. The <NOEMBED> and <PLUGINSPAGE> attributes are here. The <NOEMBED> tag is used when the browser can't understand plug-ins. This tag includes HTML commands that point to other pages that explain what to do if a browser is incapable of using plug-ins. For those browsing visitors that have the capability of using plug-ins but simply don't have the plug-in installed, you use the <PLUGINSPAGE> attribute to specify where the browsing visitor can get the proper plug-in. Let's take a look at each option and some examples, so you know exactly what to do.

The <NOEMBED> Tag

You place the **<NOEMBED>** tag after the **<EMBED>** tag since you want to accommodate both those who can use plug-ins and those who can't. Browsers such as text-only browsers or older versions of Netscape or Internet Explorer browsers also fall into this category. So you need to include information on what to do if a Web browser is unable to understand plug-ins.

<EMBED SRC="sample.rpm" WIDTH=300 HEIGHT=134>

<NOEMBED><A HREF="sample.ram">If you're reading this, use the RealPlayer to listen to this file since your browser doesn't understand plug-ins.</A></NOEMBED>

　　Notice the <EMBED> tag is used by those browsers that can understand what a plug-in is. This line is ignored if the browser doesn't understand what the <EMBED> tag does. The second line, however, is recognized and instead of displaying the embedded plug-in, it will display a link to the file; so if the user clicks that link and has the appropriate helper application configured, it will launch and play the file. With this example this page would load normally with the plug-in and data file in place would show a page with the plug-in if your page were accessed by a browser supporting plug-ins, or would display the a linked message reading "If you're reading this use the RealPlayer to listen to this file...."

The PLUGINSPAGE or PLUGINURL Attributes

If your visitors don't have the plug-in, how can you tell them where to go to get it? Use the PLUGINSPAGE OR PLUGINURL attributes added to your <EMBED> tag. You place the PLUGINSPAGE attribute, which works with previous versions of Netscape Navigator, or PLUG-INURL, if your visitors are using Netscape Communicator, as an attribute to the <EMBED> tag to display a Web page from which the visitor can download the appropriate plug-in. The PLUGINSPAGE and PLUGINURL attribute's parameter is simply the location of the page where you want your browsing visitors to go if you they don't have the plug-in. Here's how it works:

<EMBED SRC="file.rpm" WIDTH=100% HEIGHT=100% PLUGINSPAGE="http://www.locationofWebsitecontainingpluginfordownload.com/"> or

<EMBED SRC="file.rpm" WIDTH=100% HEIGHT=100% PLUGINURL="http://www.locationofWebsitecontainingpluginfordownload.com/">

　　When the visitor using Netscape Navigator runs across your site, but doesn't have the plug-in, the PLUGINSPAGE OR PLUGINURL attribute automatically opens a window notifying the visitor where they can download the plug-in. Then the attribute allows the visitor to click the link to go to the site that contains a link to download the appropriate plug-in. You should always include this attribute to make it easier for those who don't have the appropriate plug-in to find it.

WHEW! NOW LET'S GET DOWN TO BUSINESS

Now that you know what tags to use to embed plug-ins in a Web page, you should be ready to create your own page using the tag attributes and their parameters as you see fit. It's time to create the Web page, embed the plug-in, add the attributes, test the page, and finally upload the file. I'll be using the Notepad application supplied with Windows 95 to create my Web page, but you can use whatever Web page editing program works best for you.

Once the Web page has been created, I'm going to use my Netscape Navigator application to not only test the page, but also upload the file to my file server. Believe me, this won't take that long, but you do need to know a few things before you get started.

- Where on your hard drive you placed the file you recorded and the Web page you created.

TIP

Create a separate folder on your Desktop, if you must, to keep track of these files.

- Your Web server and file transfer server's login name and password. These may or may not be the same name you use to connect to the Internet or your local network.
- The directory where your files are stored for global viewing on the Web.
- The URL for a file stored on your Web server .

If you don't know any of the last three options, check with your system administrator or Internet service provider. They will know the answers to these questions. If you have all the information you need handy, let's get started. The first thing we'll do is create a simple Web page. Fire up the Web page making application you are most familiar with or follow along as I use the simple Notepad program supplied with Windows 95. I'm going to start by creating the page, then creating what is called a META file, which allows me to stream the Real Audio file to the visitor without having to have a Real Audio server. Then I'm going to upload the Web page, the META file, and the Real Audio file onto my Web server and test the whole thing out. The parameters I use, such as the name of the server and the location of the file on the server will, be different than what you should use. If you include these parameters, you can bet you'll have problems, so make especially sure you replace such information as needed.

GETTING GOING

First, I open **Notepad** by selecting **Run** from the **Start** menu. I type **"Notepad"** in the **Open** field, then hit **Enter.** This opens the **Notepad** application, basically a blank canvas on which you'll paint your Web page picture. First I'll start by adding the following lines of HTML tags. I've segmented out the tags in Table 8.5 to explain what each means.

TABLE 8.5: *Here's what we're going to add and what it all means.*

<HTML>	This tells any browser that comes along that this is supposed to be a Web page and that this is where the HTML tags start.
<HEAD>	This tells the Web browser where the head elements such as the TITLE or META tags are located. By the way, META tags offer the ability, amongst other things, to specify keywords and phrases for search engine spiders or robots to pick up when they index your site.
<TITLE>Welcome to my Plug-in!</TITLE>	This sets the title of the Web page to say "Welcome to my Plug-in!" Notice the TITLE tag has an end tag that tells the browser where the title stopped. You have to close many tags like this so the browser knows where formatting or certain elements begin and end.
</HEAD>	This tells the browser that this is the end of the elements in the head section.
<BODY>	This signals to the browser the body of the page begins here.
<CENTER>	This starts centering anything between the <CENTER> tag and the </CENTER> end tag.
Here you can hear some <b> Real Audio!</b>	This displays "Here you can hear some" in plain text on the Web page, then displays "Real Audio" in bold format.
<P><P>	This adds two more paragraph returns.
<EMBED SRC="http://www. ptialaska.net/~radio/test.rpm" WIDTH=275 HEIGHT=125 CONTROLS=DEFAULT AUTOSTART=false Console=Clip1>	This embeds the plug-in data file called test.rpm which is located on my server (www.ptialaska.net) in my directory, radio, and into the Web page. It sets the size of the plug-in rectangle to 275x125, then makes sure the Real Audio controls are set to the default. Next it makes sure it doesn't start playing the sound once the page is loaded, leaving that up to the user; then sets the console to load the information about the clip into the plug-in display.

Table 8.5 (continued)

</CENTER>	This stops centering the information.
</BODY>	This tells the page that no more elements will appear in the body.
</HTML>	This tells the page that this is the end of the HTML tags.

TIP

Although capitalization is not a factor when you write your HTML tags, it makes it easier to read a Web page if your tags are capitalized and your text is in normal case. You should, however, pay attention to the capitalization used with the attributes and their parameters. These in many cases are case sensitive.

If you've typed all the information correctly, it should look like Figure 8.17. Next you need to save your page. You're almost there, but you have three more steps to go. Saving your page is one of those steps. Select **File | Save**, then type the filename, **"testplugin.html,"** in the **File Name** field. Make sure you save the file either on the desktop or in a folder you've created specifically for this project. Click the **Save** button when you know where the file is going to be saved.

FIGURE   *Your first Web page with an embedded plug-in.*
8.17

Next we're going to do something a little different than what you normally would do with most plug-ins. Normally at this point you would simply upload your Web page and your data file, test it out, then be done with it. But in this example we have to create a third file that interfaces between the Web page and the Real Audio file in an effort to stream the sound from the Web server to the visitor's computer. This third file is called a META file and contains only a single line of HTML code that points to the actual sound file itself. To be more succinct, here's how to works:

1. The visitor opens your Web page.
2. The <EMBED> command is read by the browser.
3. The <EMBED> command points to the META file.
4. The META file points to the Real Audio sound file.
5. The visitor presses the play button on the Real Audio plug-in controls.
6. This sends a signal to the META file to fetch the sound file.
7. The sound file is fetched and the sound is sent to the visitor through the Real Audio plug-in.

Why do you need these steps? Why do you need a META file? Basically, so both server and Web page can establish connections. As Real Networks puts it, "META files contain information needed to establish a connection between the server and your listener's Real Audio Player and to initiate the playback."

You create a META file and give it the three-letter extension RPM. This signifies to the browser itself that this Real Audio file should be played as a plug-in instead of through the use of the Real Audio stand-alone player application. Fire up your Notepad application or your Web page editing program and let's create this META file.

The only thing you have to put in this file is the location of the Real Audio file you want to play. For example, the Real Audio file I want to play is called *sound.ra* and it's located on my Web server in my directory. Therefore I would place this line followed by a carriage return in my test.rpm file:

http://www.ptialaska.net/~radio/sound.ra

This tells the plug-in I'll be using a Web server instead of a Real Audio server (pnm://), and that the Web server's name is *www.ptialaska.net*, my directory is ~radio, and the name of the file is sound.ra. I save this file as "test.rpm." Then when a visitor loads my page, testplugin.html, and the browser sees the <EMBED> tag pointing to the file, test.rpm, it reads the file, and grabs the sound file, then waits for the visitor to press the Play button.

If you would rather have the separate RealPlayer helper application launch, you would name your META file with a RAM extension instead of a RPM extension. RPM means Real Plug-in Meta file.

Now you have three files, the Real Audio sound file, the Web page, and the intermediary, the META file. If all went well, you're ready to upload these three files to your Web server and test them out. The next section will tell you how to do that provided you know what your Web server's login name and password are.

You could try loading the Web page locally, but since you aren't running a Web server, most likely all you would see is a broken puzzle piece, not the actual plug-in as it loads. This is because your computer isn't a server and doesn't know how to tell your browser what to do with the plug-in embedded into the Web page. The same holds true for your Web server. If it isn't configured for the correct MIME type which it would pass along to the browser, you would end up with the same results.

UPLOADING YOUR FILES

The next step is relatively easy and can be done with a variety of different software tools. In the following example I'll be using Netscape Communicator, but you can use the FTP program that comes with Windows 95 or other programs such as WS_FTP. Some Web development programs also have file upload options, so check around if you are using such programs.

I've collected the Web page, the Real Audio sound file, and the META file into one single folder so I can easily locate them and upload them to the Web server. I've placed them in a folder I've created on my Windows desktop. Now I open up my Netscape browser and type in the following into the Location field of my Web browser where I normally would type the location for locating a Web page:

ftp://radio:password@ptialaska.net

Let's take a look at this command and dissect each section. Table 8.6 outlines each section of this command.

Table 8.6: *The URL to connect to the FTP server.*

Command	What it Does
ftp://	The protocol used to connect to the server. FTP:// is the protocol to file transfer.
Radio	The login name I use to log in to the file or Web server.
Password	The password use to connect to the server.
Ptialaska.net	The name of the server I want to connect to.
: and the @	Delimiters used to separate the login name and password and the password from the server name.

You should replace the login name (radio), the password (password), and the server name (ptialaska.net) with your own login name, password, and server name. This logs me into my main directory on the Web server, as shown in Figure 8.14. The directory listed is where I should store all the documents and files I want the public to have access to. I click this link, and open the public HTML directory where I store all the files other people can access over the Internet. The directory you may use to place files for access over the Internet may be titled differently. Your directory may be called HOME/YOURNAME or ~YOUR-NAME. It depends on how your system administrator set up the Web server. Check with your administrator to find out exactly where you place Web pages for public consumption.

Once I've moved myself into my public HTML folder, I'm ready to upload my files. I do this by selecting **Upload File** from the **File** menu. When I select this option, the **File Upload** dialog box displays, asking me which file I want to upload. At this point I would select one of the three files I need to upload.

Figure 8.18 is an example of what you should see. I click the file I want to upload then click the **Open** button. The file should start to upload and you should see a dialog window similar to the one shown in Figure 8.19. Once the file has uploaded, you will see it listed in the directory window.

Continue to upload the other two files. Since the default is to upload only HTML-type files, you will need to change the **File Type** in the **File**

FIGURE   *When you upload a file, Netscape wants to know what file on your hard drive*
8.18   *you want to upload.*

Upload dialog window to **All Files** so you can see both the **META** file and the **Real Audio** sound file. Once you have all the files uploaded, you are ready to test them out. At this point you simply have to know what the Universal Resource Locator is (*i.e.*, the Web page address) for the Web page you uploaded. In my case it would be the following:

http://www.ptialaska.net/~radio/testplugin.html

Yours will be different based upon how your system administrator set up your Web server. This URL is indicating I am going to use the Web

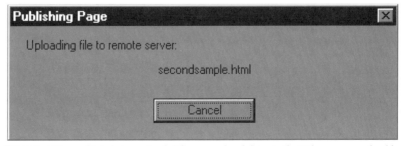

FIGURE   *When a file is being uploaded from your hard drive to the Web server, you should*
8.19   *see a dialog window indicating the process is in the works.*

protocol (http://) to see the testplugin.html file, which is located on the Web server located at *www.ptialaska.net,* in the user's (~radio) directory. Once I've uploaded all the files and know the actual Web page address of the Web page I created, I'm ready to test it out. If all goes well, I should see something like what's pictured in Figure 8.17. Once I click the Play button, I should start to see the file load and in a few minutes start to hear the file play. Figure 8.18 is an example of what I would see. I would see the title, the author, and the copyright information I supplied previously when I recorded the audio clip. Hopefully, you see something similar and, better yet, hear something as well. If not, check the next two sections for some tips on troubleshooting your page, server, or sound file. Otherwise, pat yourself on the back and bring out the champagne! You've created your first Web page, complete with an embedded Netscape plug-in.

A NOTE FOR WEBMASTERS

If you're Web server wasn't already configured to understand Real Audio files, you will need to enable these MIME types in your server. This usually involves editing the MIME.types file in your Web browser, but if you are not the person who would do that, you will need to tell the server administrator a few things. These include the following types of information as seen in Table 8.7.

TABLE 8.7: *Settings for configuring a Web server to offer Real Audio files.*

Data	Type	Subtype	File Extensions	Plug-Ins
Real Audio	Audio	x-pn-realaudio and x-pn-realaudio-plugin	.rpm .ram .ra .rm	Real Audio plug-in

If you are the server administrator and have never added new MIME types, to your server's configuration, check the server software documentation on how to do this. It's a relatively simple procedure but does vary from server to server.

If your server is not configured for the Real Audio MIME types you will have all sorts of problems and your plug-in simply won't work. Check with your system administrator before you start uploading files to your Web server to ensure these MIME types have been added.

TROUBLESHOOTING TIPS

Don't expect everything to go just perfect the first time. It didn't for me and although I hope it does for you, you may find yourself baffled at why things aren't working. If that's the case, here are several troubleshooting tips that might help you solve your problems. But feel free to e-mail me or check out the Real Web site for a wealth of troubleshooting tips.

SOUND PROBLEMS

I can't get any sound out of my microphone. Any suggestions?
Turn it on. Make sure you have the microphone turned on. Some microphones have on/off switches. Others may be controlled through software. Check the volume controls on your system software to ensure you don't have the microphone muted. Also make sure you have the microphone plugged into the microphone port. I can't tell you how many times I've plugged something into the wrong port!

The sound file is really distorted. What can I do about that?
Adjust your volume on your sound source and make sure the plug you are using has adequate shielding so it's not picking up interference from other sources such as a radio, television, or monitor. Also check out the Real Developer Zone at *www.real.com/devzone/* for more information on how to get the best sound quality out of your file.

When my friend visits the site, it tells him he doesn't have the capabilities or right player to play the embedded file. What's the problem? Most likely you've recorded and encoded the file in a Real Audio file compression that requires an updated version of the player. You can provide a link for downloading the right version or you can reencode the file as a lower compression type.

PLUG-IN PROBLEMS

My file doesn't appear as a plug-in. As a matter of fact, nothing shows up.
Most likely you either didn't save the file as text or you forgot to close off a tag or include the <HTML> tag at the top and the </HTML> tag at the bottom. Double-check the format you saved the file as, and check the code of your Web page.

The page displays fine, but nothing plays. What's wrong?
You must click on the **Play** button in order for the Real Audio file to play or set the **Autostart** attribute to equal **True.**

The page displays fine. The Real Audio file shows up as a plug-in, but I keep getting Errors 13 and 39. What's the problem?
Strange but true, nothing may be wrong. As a matter of fact, everything is probably set just right, but your browser's cache may need to be cleaned out. Empty both the **Memory** and **Disk** cache for your browser, then try reloading the page again. You'll find it probably works after you do this. It's a quirk I ran into when I first tried adding Real Audio files to my Web pages.

I'm getting an Error 50. What does that mean?
An Error 50 means the plug-in couldn't find your sound card. Make sure you have your system configured properly and that your sound card is in fine working order.

I keep trying to play the plug-in on my Mac but nothing seems to work. What's the problem?
At the time of this writing, the Real Audio plug-in does not work with the Mac. Keep checking the Real home page for more information on when this problem will be fixed.

I've placed my plug-in in a table. Now every time I try to load that page it crashes my computer.
Stop! Don't place your plug-in in a table. As a matter of fact, don't place any plug-ins in tables. The HTML code used to create tables conflicts with most plug-ins.

Every time I visit the page with the plug-in, it bombs my browser. What's the problem?
Most likely you have not specified the Width or Height option, or have set both to 0. You should set at least one of these attributes to something higher than 0, otherwise your browser may crash.

OK, I've added Height and Width options but things still aren't working right. It looks like some straggling HTML code is displayed now instead of the plug-in.

Most likely you've enclosed the Height and Width options in quotes. Although the other attributes require this, these options don't and will cause problems if you do include quotes around them.

ADDING ACTIVEX CONTROLS

If you would like to add an ActiveX Real Audio control instead of a plug-in, the following is what you would include in your Web page. You use the <OBJECT> instead of <EMBED> command to include the code for embedding a Real Audio ActiveX control in a page. Here are the commands for placing the <OBJECT> commands:

<OBJECT ID=RA0CX CLASSID="clsid: CFCDAA03-8BE4-11cf-B84B-0020AFBBCCFA" HEIGHT=140 WIDTH=312>
<PARAM NAME="SRC"
VALUE=http://www.yourservername.com/file.rpm">
<PARAM NAME="CONTROLS" VALUE="all">
</OBJECT>

The variables are HEIGHT, WIDTH, VALUES, and CONTROLS. You can change these variables and supply whatever values you select. For more information on changing the variables check the Real Audio Content Creation Guide, located at www.real.com/create/ccguide/config.html.

Remember ActiveX controls are for those visitors using Internet Explorer 3.0 or above or for those users who are using the ScriptActiveX plug-in with Netscape Navigator.

SUMMARY

Whew! That sure was a lot to take in, and hopefully it all worked. If not, well let me know by e-mailing me at *ckirk@alaska.net* on the Internet, or KIRKCL on AOL, or 76200,1660 on CompuServe. I'll be happy to help you out. Although there was a lot to take in, the actual process of creating a Web page and embedding a plug-in isn't rocket science. With a little patience and persistence you should be able to create tons of sites that are plug-in enabled. Now you're ready to find out what plug-ins you can add to your page, and to do this you need to have a list to choose from. The next chapter, gives you just that.

CHAPTER 9

The Big Netscape Plug-In List

This is it. The big chapter listing all the plug-ins you should take note of. At last count, a little under 200 plug-ins were available for both Netscape Navigator and Internet Explorer. The bulk of these can be found on the Netscape In-Line plug-in site, located at *http://home.netscape.com/comprod/pdocuts.navigator/version_2.0/plugins/index.html*. You can also find a number of plug-ins at BrowserWatch.com, located at *http://www.browserwatch.com*, and at DaveCentral, at *http://www.davecentral.com*. At these Web sites you'll find links to every single plug-in available. Some, however, are only available on specific platforms. If you check out the various plug-in-related Web sites, make sure you check that they have a version available for your particular computer platform.

TIP

Even if you are using the Internet Explorer browser, you can still take advantage of many of the plug-ins listed here by simply making sure you install them in the Internet Explorer plug-ins folder. Although most plug-ins will work with Internet Explorer, you may want to check the software vendor's Web page or the next chapter to see if an ActiveX version is available. Also remember, not all plug-ins work, or work well, with Internet Explorer; you may experience more crashes than usual if you install some of these plug-ins.

I'm not going to list every single plug-in here like they do on the Web. First of all, some plug-ins simply duplicate what is now available in Netscape Communicator, whereas others simply don't work or don't work well. And some duplicate what other plug-ins do, but not with any additional features that are worth mentioning. Instead, in this chapter I'll outline the best of the bunch, those plug-ins that include enough content to make the download worth the effort. About 112 plug-ins are listed here, and about 25 or so are available directly from the included CD-ROM.

NOTE

I'm also not big on virtual reality plug-ins since half of them don't work, and the other half don't work well, or don't work well over a dial-up line. I think the real thing is better than some wireframe representation. If you want three dimensions, consider looking at some of the photographic virtual reality plug-ins such as QuickTimeVR or Surround Video.

To make information easy to find, I've included the name of the plug-in, the location of the company that currently sells the plug-in, the level of user that can best utilize the plug-in, and a description of what the plug-in does. Those that are included with the accompanying CD are noted with a special CD-ROM icon. I strongly recommend you visit the

Web sites of each plug-in you want to download for the most up-to-date information about the plug-in, demo pages, instructions on how to add it to your own Web pages, and any costs involved. And don't forget to regularly check the Netscape plug-ins page. You can quickly get there by typing in the address listed previously, or by selecting **About Plug-ins** from the **Help** menu, then clicking the link to get more information. I'll also offer my own recommendations about why I think the plug-in is worth downloading.

TIP

I haven't included links to demo pages or instructions on how to install the plug-in, since this kind of information changes frequently. Instead, check the links from the software vendor's main page for the demo pages. Because the installation procedure for most plug-ins is pretty much the same, and sometimes the installation process can change, you should check the step-by-step instructions offered by most plug-in software vendors. For most plug-ins the installation process goes like this:

1. You **Click** the link for the download page.
2. You **Select** the file for your platform, be it Windows, Windows NT, or Macintosh.
3. Sometimes you'll supply your e-mail address and name.
4. **Click** the link to download the file into your download directory or onto your desktop.
5. You should then **Quit** your browser application; if you don't and the plug-in hasn't installed properly, you run the risk of having the browser crash.
6. Once the file has completed the download, you **Double-Click** the file and either have it self-extract or decompress into a designated directory on your hard drive. Most of the time the file will self-extract in a temporary location or in a separate directory it can create if one does not exist.
7. Next the installation process will ask you where your Navigator plug-ins directory is located. If you have more than one browser installed on your system, some plug-in installation programs will ask you if you want to install the plug-in in the Explorer or the Navigator directory. If this is the case, specify which plug-ins directory to save to it.
8. **Click** to install the plug-in. The installation process should alert you that the plug-in has been installed properly.

9. If you haven't quit Navigator, which is preferred, you can issue the JavaScript command: *javascript:navigator.plugins.refresh(true);parent.location.reload()*, in the **Location** field of your browser to activate the plug-in within your browser.

10. From there you should be able to view any documents that the plug-in recognizes, you should be ready to use the plug-in whenever and wherever you want.

You should also read through the other chapters on specific types of plug-ins, such as Chapter 6 which focuses on plug-ins for Intranets, and Chapter 11 which covers how to implement plug-ins within Web pages you might create.

Audio Plug-Ins

Audio plug-ins play sound files that your browser may not normally be able to play. They also may offer more features for playing sound files than your browser. I've tried to list only those plug-ins that have enough content available on the Internet to make it worth your time and effort downloading them. As with all multimedia-enabled plug-ins, you need to have a multimedia-enabled PC, which means you need a sound card and speakers. Most plug-ins are configured to work with Sound Blaster-compatible sound cards. If for some reason a particular audio plug-in doesn't work on your particular PC, check to make sure you know exactly what type of sound card you have installed and whether the plug-in you are using will work with your card.

Name of Plug-In: Beatnik by Headspace

Location of Plug-In: http://www.headspace.com

Description of Plug-In
Although Netscape Navigator offers the ability to play embedded sound files such as Musical Instrument Digital Interface (MIDI) files, and although the commercial versions of Netscape Communicator have this plug-in, for the non-commercial versions of Navigator or older versions of the browser, the *Beatnik* plug-in handles many more sound files than Navigator currently offers. Beatnik can play Rich Music Format (RMF) files, MIDI, MOD, WAV, AIFF, and AU files within the Web browser. With specialized sound compression software, the plug-in offers high-

fidelity sound quality comparable to high-end sound cards, even though it is entirely software based. And regardless of whether you are using it on a Mac or a PC, it provides clear sound across multiple platforms.

If you plan to develop content, Beatnik can also create interactive music files through the use of a comprehensive set of JavaScript functions. This means you can have the Beatnik plug-in play music not when a Web page opens, but when the user moves the mouse over the file, or even when he clicks the embedded link to the file. It is the only technology that currently combines security within MIDI files to protect the sound file from being illegally copied.

Recommendations

Don't bother downloading this plug-in if you have already purchased Netscape, since this plug-in is part of the commercial version of Netscape Communicator. It is not, however, part of the free version of Communicator, so if you downloaded version 4.0 or below off the Internet you'll find you still need to download the plug-in.

Since this plug-in plays such a wide variety of sound files that aren't just Beatnik specific, I would highly recommend you give it a spin. You'll be astounded at some of the RMF demos available from Headspace's demo page. Remember, however, that the files Beatnik plays are downloaded files, not streaming audio files, so there will still be some delay in downloading some larger files.

NAME OF PLUG-IN: CRESCENDO PLUG-IN BY LIVEUPDATE

Location: http://www.liveupdate.com

Description

With a new look that mimics a CD player, this plug-in offers a control panel, digital counter, and the option to control the playback of MIDI files in much the same fashion as normal music CDs. As with all MIDI files, even with the *Crescendo* plug-in you still have to download the MIDI music file. However, if you purchase the Crescendo Plus plug-in, you can use the real-streaming feature which requires no downloading.

Recommendation

If you download another plug-in that plays MIDI sound files, you may not want to download Crescendo. But if you are still using an older version of the Navigator browser, you may want to download Crescendo. Like Beatnik, the plug-in now offers Java scripting controls that help control the playback of the embedded MIDI files. Plus, you don't have to have your Web server configured for specific MIME types for the Crescendo plug-in to play. Although most Web servers these days are configured to send and in some cases stream MIDI files, for those users who are at the mercy of outdated Web servers, this may be a useful feature. Check the LiveUpdate page on embedding plug-ins for more information.

Overall, this would not be the first plug-in I'd download. You may find your browser already has all the capabilities Crescendo offers.

Name of Plug-In: Koan by Sseyo

Location: http://www.sseyo.com/

Description
Like all others in this category, this plug-in automatically plays music from within a Web browser. But with the *Koan* plug-in, the sound files are compressed, sometimes down to as small as one megabyte, yet still offer up to eight hours of MIDI files. These MIDI files can also contain multiple WAV file instruments.

The plug-in also offers synchronization with Web pages, so you can create an interactive sound-enabled presentation on the Internet. The Koan plug-in for Netscape Navigator loads Koan files and plays back Koan music—generated locally and in real time on a multimedia PC— and even plays Koan pieces that use SoundFonts which many sound cards now support. It can even play multiple WAV files.

Recommendation
You'll definitely hear a difference between Koan files and standard MIDI files. The sound quality is much richer, and oftentimes sounds like live music, rather than tinny computer-generated music. A fair number of sites offer enough Koan-enabled pages to make this plug-in worth downloading. However, Koan files are not streaming files, so you'll still have to wait for the file to downlaod before you can play it. But it will be well worth the wait.

NAME OF PLUG-IN: ONLIVE! TALKER BY ONLIVE!

Location: http://www.onlive.com

Description

The *OnLive! Talker* plug-in lets you use your Netscape browser (at least version 3.0 or above) to join live voice conferences through a Web page. Talker lets you speak in real time with other people from around the world. Instead of text chatting, you can audio chat, using your multimedia-enabled PC with sound card, speakers, and microphone. You can chat with up to 225 chatters within one chat room, depending on the capabilities of the server hosting the conference.

The sound is almost crystal clear, and the moderator of the chat room can control who speaks when and whether their voice is heard at all. Unlike point-to-point Internet telephony products, Onlive! lets you join in multiple voice chats. The server the Onlive Talker application runs on is based on software-only server products, so there is no specialized hardware to purchase. And the software can be used with other third-party products since it utilizes the Audio Conferencing SDK.

Recommendation

I love this company and the products they produce. They offer some of the most innovative products on the Internet. I strongly recommend you download the Onlive! plug-in. The only downfall is that the plug-in requires the use of a server, so you don't have the ability at present to create your own talk channels. And there may be limited public chat conferences available. At the time I wrote this book, only one site, Talk City, offered interactive voice chats; but I assume as chatting gets more and more popular, you'll see more and more Onlive! chat rooms opening up.

TIP

If you are interested in developing interactive chat rooms, you should consider looking at VoxChat, a development product created by VoxWare. You'll find VoxChat at www.voxware.com. It's another product worth looking into, but not one that could really be classified as a true consumer plug-in at this point.

Name of Plug-In: PhoneFree by Big Bits Software

Location: http://www.phonefree.com

Description

PhoneFree allows net surfers to engage in real-time, point-to-point phone-quality conversations over the Internet without using a telephone or incurring any long-distance phone charges. PhoneFree and its accompanying white page listings which are used to find other PhoneFree users are fully integrated with the Netscape Navigator browser. You can also place calls to VocalTec's Internet Phone users, opening up huge numbers of people to talk with. There is no need to learn a confusing new interface; just search the white pages for your party, click on the name, and you begin talking. Of course you do need a multimedia PC with a sound card, speakers, and micrphone.

PhoneFree also offers integrated voicemail. So if a user is unavailable, but has registered his e-mail address, you can leave him a voicemail message if he is not online. Better still, the recipient doesn't need any special software to hear your voicemail message. You can also include a photo or any other type of file with your voicemail. And if you are away from the computer, but still want to communicate with other PhoneFree users, you can leave an outgoing message, like an outgoing message on an answering machine.

Recommendation

Definitely download this product. It is fantastic. It's one of the best Internet telephony-based phone products around and by far the easiest to use. Even if you don't know anyone to talk to, there are a ton of people online who are also using PhoneFree. And that's half the fun. You can talk to people all over the world about anything you want, at any time, without the fear of running up a huge long-distance phone bill.

Sure, sometimes the sound quality isn't that great, but oftentimes it isn't bad, and usually it's audible enough to hear what the other person is saying. And you can quickly find all your friends and family with the click of a button. The only caveat is that if you find the product worthwhile, you will need to purchase it. But the cost is less than a month's worth of long-distance phone calls. You'll also need to have at least a Pentium computer to really use the product.

If you are interested in Internet telephony, make sure you pick up my other book, The Internet Telephone Connection. Everything you ever wanted to know about Internet telephony, including how to troubleshoot just about any problem, is listed there.

NAME OF PLUG-IN: REALPLAYER BY REAL NETWORKS

Location
http://www.real.com

Description
RealPlayer provides live and on-demand real-time RealAudio and RealVideo streaming content over the Internet through the use of an embedded plug-in or separate helper application. The sound is broadcast-quality stereo over 28.8 Kbps modem speeds or AM quality at 14.4 Kbps. You can also hear near CD-quality audio over ISDN, cable modems, or through Intranet connections. You can choose from thousands of sites that offer recorded and live information. Many radio stations broadcast live over the Internet, and many record companies are now offering clips from their most popular artists. Thousands of other sites offer Real content of a varying nature, from recorded clips of conferences to broadcasts of concerts. You can easily create content and deliver it to your users through a standard Web server. If you need to cater to large audiences, you will need a Real server, some of which are free.

*TimeCast and AudioNet list a whole bunch of sites that are RealPlayer enabled. TimeCast gives you up-to-the-minute information about live broadcasts as well as recorded content. You can find TimeCast at www.time-cast.com. AudioNet is another great source of live and recorded broadcasts. It also offers links to books on tape that have been encoded into the RealPlayer format. You can find AudioNet at **www.audionet.com**.*

Recommendation
Run, don't walk, to Real's Web site and download the latest version of the player that includes the plug-in option. This is by far the most amazing technology ever created for the Internet. And it extends out your Internet connection, bringing you news, information, live sports broad-

casts, radio broadcasts, music, books on tape, and technical conferences to your desktop. It's an amazing product offering amazing sound quality.

You may find your browser already has Real capabilities built in. This has been the case with Internet Explorer for a long time, and will soon be part of Netscape Navigator. But that shouldn't stop you from checking out the latest updates to the plug-in and helper application. These updates usually provide better sound compression and more features than previous versions. It will only get better and better, even though it's already pretty darn good to begin with.

NAME OF PLUG-IN: REALAUDIO TUNER

Location: http://www.Dragontek.com/RATuner/

Description
Working in conjunction with the RealPlayer, this plug-in lets you listen to thousands of different radio stations broadcasting in RealPlayer format from around the world. The tuner itself comes with 130 different stations preprogrammed, but you can add any station you want that broadcasts over the Internet. You can easily use the tuner to find radio stations, which you can add at the touch of a button, and you can remove those stations you may no longer listen to.

Although this is not a traditional plug-in, it works with the RealPlayer plug-in to give you immediate access to radio stations around the globe. It's actually more of a utility. I just thought it was worth including because it enhanced the RealPlayer plug-in and helper application.

Recommendation
Excellent if you are a radiohead like me. I love to listen to the radio over the Internet, and when one station starts to bore me, I simply tune to the next station. With over 130 stations preprogrammed, I don't have to spend time at sites like AudioNet finding stations that are currently broadcasting. I strongly recommend you download this plug-in even if you've never experienced live radio broadcasts over the Internet. It makes using the RealPlayer much more interesting.

NAME OF PLUG-IN: LIQUID AUDIO CD BY LIQUID

Location: http://www.liquidaudio.com

Description

The *Liquid Audio* plug-in works with the first commercial system to listen and purchase CD-quality music tracks and CDs over the Internet. Utilizing exclusive Dolby Digital technology, the CD player plug-in provides superior sound quality while allowing you to view album graphics, lyrics, and liner notes. Additional features include personal music library management, which lets you keep track of liner notes, tour dates, promotional materials about the artists, and the ability to record an actual audio CD from music purchased online. If you have a CD-ROM writer, you can use the CD player to create your own CD.

Recommendation

I see promise with this product, although I still don't see as much content as in RealPlayer. It is one of the most innovative audio software products available on the Internet, and it has enormous potential due to its amazing sound quality over low-speed networks. But the most unique features are tied more to protecting the content from theft and allowing the user to download and create his own music CD. If this type of technology takes off, and stays relatively easy to use, you will see the close of music stores everywhere, and the proliferation of online music stores on the Internet. Eventually, when you hear a song on the radio or on TV and want to instantly buy the CD, this software combination will allow you to do just that, day and night, every day of the year.

The only problem is that the files are still relatively large and the list of content providers relatively small. This may be due to the fact that you need a server in order to serve up the files. But you soon will see many record companies start to use this technology to actually sell audio over the Internet.

BUSINESS-ORIENTED PLUG-INS

Business-oriented plug-ins are ones that you, as a business person, can utilize in your day-to-day business life. From plug-ins that help you keep track of your electronic date book to plug-ins that help you find the best prices on travel, you'll find them listed under this classification. Some of them require you to have the software to create the file so that you can then upload to a Web server and view through the accompanying plug-in. For example, you need to purchase the *AboutTime* application in order to create the content that can be viewed with the accompanying AboutTime plug-in. So, if you want to share your calendar with everyone on the Internet, you will need the AboutTime application that creates the calendar file.

While other business-oriented plug-ins work within single Web sites to help you find the information you need, in the case of *IntelliTrip* or *RoboShopper*, these plug-ins work with more than one Web site to find you the information you need, whether it be the best airfares or the best price on office supplies. These plug-ins are like little robots that go searching for the best travel or office supply-oriented products that are currently being advertised on the Internet.

I surveyed hundreds of Web consultants and internal Webmasters on several e-mail mailing lists and newsgroups, asking which plug-ins they used the most. In order of popularity, Adobe Acrobat, MacroMedia's ShockWave, and RealNetworks RealPlayer were the most widely used, with several different Word viewers coming in a close fourth. From that point on, the plug-ins used were used to solve a pretty specific problem. If you're thinking of adding data files and the accompanying plug-in viewers, you might start by checking out these plug-ins since they are popular on both the Internet and on Intranets.

Name of Plug-In: AboutPeople by Now Software

Location: http://www.nowsoft.com

Description
AboutPeople works with the AboutPeople software program to allow you to share your address books and information with others on an Intranet or on the Internet. AboutPeople lets you browse and search dynamic address books on the Web from within your Navigator browser. The software also integrates seamlessly with *Now Up-to-Date* Web Publisher, letting you access employee lists, vendor contacts, hotel and restaurant listings, or anything else you might include in your databases. You can keep track of your business cards online, then search the list for names and addresses, and include e-mail addresses for quick links for sending messages to others. You can also drag and drop names listed in the Web

address file to your own Now Up-To-Date address book. You can even download the same content to your PalmPilot.

Recommendation

Although you have to purchase the Now-Up-To-Date software and Web Publisher to create the databases and lists, this is by far one of the best personal information managers that fully integrates with the Web. I would highly recommend that you download the plug-in and purchase the Now-Up-To-Date software, especially if you are on an Intranet, or want quick and easy access to all your personal information. This plug-in and the accompanying software would fix the big problem most companies have of keeping company address lists of employees and vendors.

NAME OF PLUG-IN: ABOUTTIME BY NOW SOFTWARE

Location: http://www.nowsoft.com

Description

AboutTime is a calendar plug-in that lets you view dynamic calendars on the Web from within your Navigator window. It works with the Now Up-to-Date Web Publisher, letting you access company meetings, training calendars, project schedules, and any type of event you've scheduled via the Web. You can search the calendars for specific events or times. You can drag and drop events from the Web calendar to the Now-Up-To-Date calendar, which is especially useful if you share calendars with others on the Internet.

Recommendation

The ability to update your calendar live and share it with anyone across the Internet makes this an excellent personal information manager. And the drag and drop features let you easily create and update calendars. Like AboutPeople, you need to purchase the actual Now-Up-To-Date software, but that shouldn't be a problem since that software integrates not only with the Internet and Intranets, but also with the Palm Pilot, to keep you on schedule no matter where you are.

NAME OF PLUG-IN: CALENDAR QUICK BY LOGIC PULSE

This plug-in is available directly from the enclosed CD-ROM.

NOTE

Location: http://www.logicpulse.com

Description

The *Calendar Quick* plug-in is the ideal tool for publishing schedules of events on the Web. You can use it to embed calendars, appointment lists, timelines, and project schedules in your Web page for easy viewing with Netscape Navigator. Events can be linked to other Web pages, and the unique user interface lets you browse schedules by using hyperlinks. Download the plug-in today and view some sample files to see just how easy it is to put your calendar on the Web.

Recommendation

I don't find the interface particularly pleasing, but the software does exactly what it says it does. And the plug-in displays the calendars relatively quickly. With the ability to link events to other Web pages and update information on the fly, it's a decent product to have if you want to share calendars and schedules with other people across an Intranet or through the Internet.

But the question that begs answering, when considering downloading and using this plug-in, is why? With HTML creation capabilities built into Microsoft's Schedule+ and other calendar programs, plus a full spectrum of HTML calendar creating shareware and freeware available, you may be better served by the traditional HTML/tables route if all you want to do is share a static list of events in calendar format. Clearly this product should be used only if you have a need to update, share, and organize calendars with other users, and if those calendars change considerably. Otherwise, if you make a user of your Web site download a special plug-in just to view a few events, you may find very few will do just that.

Name of Plug-In: Cybercash Wallet by Cybercash

Location: http://www.cybercash.com

Description

With *Cybercash Wallet* you can use your major credit cards to purchase goods and services online, without worrying about whether a site is secure or not. With Cybercash Wallet you create an account filled with whatever amount of funds you want to add to it. Then you can instantly pay for items with CyberCoin funds, even those priced as low as 25 cents. Your credit card information is never sent to the merchant, rather the payment to their account is credited from your Cybercash fund.

You can also use the PayNow service which lets you write secure electronic checks using your CyberCash Wallet. Though primarily used to make monthly electronic payments, you can also use the PayNow system just as you would for virtually any kind of payment regardless of whether it's recurring or not. Cybercash's main page contains a list of merchants that use this technology.

Recommendation

It's a great idea in that it leaps over the privacy and security issues that have plagued the Internet for years. The biggest problem is that people don't realize the difference between secure server transactions and CyberWallet-type transactions, and how much more secure CyberWallet transactions actually are. Thus too few vendors use the product even though it shows great promise and is relatively easy to use. Yet with Microsoft issuing support of the CyberWallet product through its Internet Explorer browser, you should see more and more vendors sign up. At last count less than 300 merchants used this technology, although some of them, like CDWorld, offer all the CDs you could ever want at relatively low costs.

NAME OF PLUG-IN: EARTHTIME BY STARFISH SOFTWARE

Location: http://www.starfishsoftware.com

Description

The *EarthTime* plug-in lets you tell time around the world at a glance, without having to leave your browser or to do the conversion yourself. The plug-in will display the local time and date for up to eight geographic locations from more than 400 world capitals. Its animated worldwide map also indicates whether the locations you choose are now in daylight or darkness. It even offers you quick information such as area codes, the local language, and the currency used.

In order to download this plug-in, you should check out the Web Surfing/Plug-ins section of DaveCentral. You won't find this plug-in, at least not easily, from the StarFish Software main site, although they are the creators of the product. You'll find DaveCentral at www.davecentral.com, and the last time I looked the plug-in was located at www.davecentral. com/671.html but that address could have changed by the time you read this. You can also purchase EarthTime as part of StarFish's Sidekick 98, a kind of personal information manager that integrates with the Internet.

Recommendation

Obviously this plug-in is best used by those who do business with and travel to foreign countries and need to know what date and time it is. But it's also an excellent reference tool for anyone who wants to chat with others worlds away, or simply wants to know what the area code is for Nigeria. You'll most likely have to pay for it as part of the SideKick '98 software package which StarFish is now selling. And since that's the case, I think its usefulness is limited since so much of the information available in EarthTime is available on the Internet or in the phone book for free.

NAME OF PLUG-IN: JC_ACTIVE DOC

Location: http://www.jcsoft.com/docobject/index.shmtl

Description

The technology called DocObject was first introduced by Microsoft in their Office Binder application. The Office Binder application lets you work with Word, Excel, and PowerPoint documents within a single binder window. When the more recent versions of Internet Explorer hit the market, Microsoft decided to add DocObject support within its browser so those users could easily view Office documents in Internet Explorer.

The problem with Netscape, however, is that it doesn't come with this same type of support. So if you use Navigator and want to view Office documents, you either have to get another plug-in or install something like ScriptActive from Ncompass Labs. With the use of *JC_ActiveDoc*, you can easily add this functionality to your Netscape browser. Unlike some Microsoft Office-oriented plug-ins, however, this plug-in does not allow you to save or print files, although the author of this plug-in indicates those features may become available in subsequent versions.

Recommendation

It works well, it's relatively small, and it doesn't seem to tax my computer system. It gives me more capabilities to interact with users who place Microsoft Office documents on my Intranet server, or offer these files out on the Internet. The biggest problem is that some of the features are limited, and restrain the user from printing the document. I would recommend you download this plug-in only if you need quick access to viewing Office documents and don't want to switch to Internet Explorer, or if you don't want to spend any money to get this capability in your Netscape browser.

NAME OF PLUG-IN: FORMULA ONE/NET BY VISUAL COMPONENTS

Location: http://www.visualcomp.com

Description

Formula One/NET lets you view Excel-compatible spreadsheets within a Web browser. You can also view accompanying charts and workbooks. Your live worksheets can include live charts, links to URLs, formatted text and numbers, calculations, and clickable buttons and controls. You can even update cells within worksheets. You pretty much do everything you can do in a regular spreadsheet, including entering data or formulas into cells, resizing columns and rows, and saving the spreadsheet to your own computer's hard drive.

You can even use the plug-in to create interactive forms that require no CGI scripting. Formula One/NET also supports embedded buttons connected to URLs. When the browsing visitor clicks the embedded button that is attached to a URL, he is instantly taken to the Web site specified in the link. The Embedded Charts feature lets you embed charts directly into a workbook, where they can be resized, modified, and printed.

Recommendation

This is definitely one of the best plug-ins, and one you should have it if you deal with or supply information to people using Excel-compatible spreadsheets. When you consider what you can do with spreadsheets—

almost anything from forms creation to simple lists—then this becomes a must-have plug-in. The fact that you don't have to script CGIs in order for information to be viewed is a fantastic option. Anyone with cursory knowledge of spreadsheets could provide some pretty interactive forms. If you work on an Intranet and want to share and view spreadsheets, this is an excellent application to install since, unlike sharing spreadsheets, you can pretty much control the type of information that browsing visitors can add, if any. You will have to purchase the Formula One spreadsheet component which works with Excel, but it's a small price to pay when you consider the Formula One component lets you create some pretty nifty interactive Web pages. Spend some time at their Web site to get some ideas on how you could use this plug-in with your business. The possibilities are endless.

NAME OF PLUG-IN: INTELLITRIP BY THETRIP.COM

Location: http://www.trip.com

Description
The *IntelliTrip* plug-in is an unbiased, honest electronic travel agent that resides on the user's computer. It queries the best travel sites on the Web for the lowest fares currently available for a given itinerary and enables the user to quickly and conveniently book a desired itinerary on the site with which the user chooses to do business. The plug-in manages the user's accounts on those sites, so he doesn't have to remember multiple logins for different travel sites.

Recommendation
Well, I downloaded alright, but when it went to search for the cheapest fares, it came back with some of the highest I've ever seen. When I visited Microsoft's travel site, Expedia.com, located at *http://www.expedia.com*, the fares listed for my destination were about $200 lower than what the IntelliTrip plug-in found. It's a great idea to have your own personal travel agent to search various travel and airline related Web sites and ferret out the best fares, but unfortunately I always came up with the wrong or inaccurate information, with no explanation why.

I'd take it for a spin if you have the time, but I'd still rely on finding fares the old-fashioned way visiting the actual airline's Web page, or relying on other travel-oriented sites such as Expedia or Travelocity, located at *Ewww.travelocity.com*.

NAME OF PLUG-IN: PAPERPORT VIEWER BY VISIONEER

Location: http://www.visioneer.com

Description
The *PaperPort* viewer works in conjunction with the PaperPort VX Scanner. You scan in documents first, then view them through your browser with the use of the PaperPort Viewer plug-in. First, to get the documents in the computer, you use the PaperPort VX scanner. It's the easiest way to send printed documents over the Internet. In just six seconds, the PaperPort VX scanner will take paper documents and scan them into your computer, and even enclose those scanned documents into e-mail messages. With the PaperPort Viewer plug-in for Netscape Navigator you can view those e-mail message attachments or view PaperPort scanned documents from within Web pages.

Recommendation
I can't say enough great things about the PaperPort scanner or the technology used to allow others to view faxes online. When you consider that the average businessman spends hundreds, if not thousands, of dollars on faxes and FedEx's, this is the perfect solution to save money on such inflated costs. A good example of how you could use this plug-in is a real-life example named Bob. Bob sends lots of faxes back and forth between his London and Anchorage office. Instead of spending money on long distance charges, he could easily scan in faxes and other documents into a Web site for others to view online. This product will pay for itself in just the first fiew faxes or packages the average businessman like Bob wouldn't have to send.

NAME OF PLUG-IN: PENOP PLUG-IN BY PENOP

Location: http://www.penop.com

Description
Approximately 2.3 million signatures are written in the United States every minute—each one on paper. The custom of signing won't go away anytime soon, but now the paper can. Using inexpensive digitizers, *PenOp* captures the dynamics of signatures as they are written, binding them to electronic documents to create a tamperproof evidential record of who signed what, when, why, and how. With the PenOp Netscape

plug-in, handwritten signatures can be captured by your Intranet applications onto HTML documents and verified over the Web. Eliminate the costs and delays of signatures on paper, while satisfying your business and legal objectives.

Recommendation

I understand what this technology is supposed to provide me, but I'm still kind of fuzzy on it. Sure, the idea of creating a tamperproof digital signature is a great idea, but I guess I would still prefer to submit my own John Hancock personally on any paperwork that requires it. Call me paranoid, but I think it will take a long time for this technology to catch on, simply because people still don't trust the privacy or security of the Internet entirely. But I do see a use for this type of plug-in within a corporate environment, where a business person, needs to sign all sorts of things. It would allow employees to submit paperwork electronically and have the appropriate person provide the sign-off also electronically, saving time, paperwork, and energy. So if you have such a need, I recommend you look into it. Otherwise, it's really not a consumer-oriented plug-in.

COMMUNICATION-ORIENTED PLUG-INS

Whether you want to chat by typing a few text messages to friends worlds away, or you simply want to leave a voicemail message, the plug-ins you need to communicate with others are listed right here. Some require sound cards, microphones, and speakers, others need only a browser, keyboard, and Internet connection.

NAME OF PLUG-IN: ICHAT PLUG-IN BY ICHAT

Location: http://www.ichat.com

Description

The *ichat* plug-in lets users access the full suite of functionality supported by ichat ROOMS servers, which are installed on more than a thousand of the most highly trafficked sites on the Web. Downloadable in just a few minutes, the ichat client opens up a whole new world of interactive experiences on the Web. You can join the more than eight million ichat users who enjoy communicating with people of similar interests on the Net.

Recommendation

It's a great idea, and it works well. But more and more Java-enabled clients are popping up, including one created by ichat itself, so the need for a plug-in to do text chatting is diminishing. The advantage of using this particular plug-in over Java is that the response is oftentimes much faster. As the browsers and Java are further refined, however, I suspect you'll find no need for this particular plug-in. But if you plan on doing a lot of chatting, you'll find the ichat plug-in worth the time it takes to download it.

NAME OF PLUG-IN: ONLIVE! TALKER BY ONLIVE!

This is the same plug-in reviewed in the Audio section of this chapter. I've included it here as well, just in case you were cruising through the book and were interested only in communication-oriented plug-ins.

Location: http://www.onlive.com

Description

The *OnLive! Talker* plug-in lets you use your Netscape browser (at least version 3.0 or above) to join live voice conferences through a Web page. Talker lets you speak in real time with other people from around the world. Instead of text chatting, you can audio chat, using your multimedia-enabled PC with sound card, speakers, and microphone. You can chat with up to 225 chatters within one chat room, depending on the capabilities of the server hosting the conference.

The sound is almost crystal clear, and the moderator of the chat room can control who speaks when and whether their voice is heard at all. Unlike point-to-point Internet telephony products, Onlive! lets you join in multiple voice chats. The server the Onlive Talker application runs on is based on software-only server products, meaning there is no specialized hardware to purchase. And the software can be used with other third-party products since it utilizes the Audio conferencing SDK.

Recommendation

I love this company and the products they produce. They offer some of the most innovative products on the Internet. I strongly recommend you download the Onlive! plug-in. The only downfall is that the plug-in requires the use of a server, so you don't have the ability at present to create your own talk channels. And there may be limited public chat conferences available. At the time I wrote this book, only one site, *Talk City*, offered interactive voice chats; but I assume as chatting gets more and more popular, you'll see more and more Onlive! chat rooms opening up.

NAME OF PLUG-IN: DIGITAL'S VOICE PLUG-IN BY DIGITAL

Location of Plug-In: http://interface.digital.com/voice/

Description

This is a free browser plug-in that lets users record and send voice e-mail directly from a Web page. The recipients of the message can listen to them with the most popular e-mail and audio applications. It functions as an element on a Web page, not as a separate helper application. The person who wants to leave the message simply clicks a button within the plug-in on the page. The person leaving the message can include their e-mail address as well as the voice message.

NOTE

Currently this plug-in only works with Netscape Navigator 3.0 and there are problems playing voicemail attachments in Netscape Mail client. Make sure you read the FAQs for information on work-arounds for some of the problems this free plug-in might still have.

Recommendation

At last look, this plug-in still only worked with Netscape version 3.0 or below, and it didn't work properly with Communicator. No other platforms were available at the time, although there are plans for the programmers to make different versions for Mac and Windows NT. But hey, what can you expect for free? This product has HUGE potential. It allows anyone to leave voicemail regardless of where they are located. And just think how easily you could use this plug-in in an Intranet. Remember, however, Netscape Communicator comes with a companion product, Conference, which allows you to talk live with other Conference users, and even leave voicemail. Because of this, and the inclusion of NetMeeting with Internet Explorer, you may not find this plug-in being updated past what's currently available.

NAME OF PLUG-IN: PHONEFREE BY BIG BITS SOFTWARE

Again, I'm not trying to repeat myself, I just want make sure you don't miss out on this plug-in in case you didn't read the Audio section.

Location: http://www.phonefree.com

Description

PhoneFree allows net surfers to engage in real-time, point-to-point, phone-quality conversations over the Internet without using a telephone or incurring any long-distance phone charges. PhoneFree and its accompanying white page listings which are used to find other PhoneFree users are fully integrated with the Netscape Navigator browser. You can also place calls to VocalTec's Internet Phone users, opening up huge numbers of people to talk with. There is no need to learn a confusing new interface; just search the white pages for your party, click on the name, and begin talking. Of course you do need a multimedia PC with a sound card, speakers, and microphone.

PhoneFree also offers integrated voicemail. So if a user is unavailable, but has registered his e-mail address, you can leave him a voicemail message if he is not online. Better still, the recipient doesn't need any special software to hear your voicemail message. You can also include a photo or any other type of file with your voicemail. And if you are away from the computer, but still want to communicate with other PhoneFree users, you can leave an outgoing message, like an outgoing message on an answering machine.

Recommendation

Definitely download this product. It is fantastic. It's one of the best Internet telephony-based phone products around and by far the easiest to use. Even if you don't know anyone to talk to, there are a ton of people online who are also using PhoneFree. And that's half the fun. You can talk to people all over the world about anything you want, at any time, without the fear of running up a huge long-distance phone bill.

Sure, sometimes the sound quality isn't that great, but oftentimes it isn't bad, and usually it's audible enough to hear what the other person is saying. And you can quickly find all your friends and family with the click of a button. The only caveat is that if you find the product worthwhile, you will need to purchase it. But the cost is less than a month's worth of long-distance phone calls. You'll also need to have at least a Pentium computer to really use the product.

If you are interested in Internet telephony, make sure you pick up my other book, The Internet Telephone Connection, or check out the accompanying Web site for the book at www.netphones.com. If you're interested in Internet telephony products for your business, check out Jeff Pulver's site at www.von.com.

NAME OF PLUG-IN: ECHOSPEECH BY ECHOSPEECH CORPORATION

Location: http://www.echospeech.com/plugin.htm

Description
With the use of the special *EchoSpeech* encoders, you can now add voice to your Web pages by embedding the files in your Web page and using the special EchoSpeech plug-in to play them back. With EchoSpeech you can listen in real time as the compressed EchoSpeech files stream from your Web server to the user's computer. Currently compression rates match 18.5 to 1, meaning 16-bit speech can be compressed so even 9600 baud modems.

Unlike many speech-oriented programs that require high-powered computers to decode the sound files, a 486-SX 33/MHZ can easily decode 11kHz speech file, depending on the compression used. In addition, the EchoSpeech plug-in itself is extremely small, requiring the user to spend only a few minutes at most downloading and installing it into their browser.

In order for EchoSpeech to download properly, you may need to tell your ISP to configure a new MIME type on its server. That MIME type would be audio/echospeech .es.

Recommendation
EchoSpeech started out by offering GamePhones, software that let game players converse with each other as they played electronic games over the Internet or through direct modem connections. So you can bet the sound quality of EchoSpeech is pretty darn good, and the compressed files relatively small. The big selling feature is that virtually any type of computer can easily play back the sound files. But the downfall is that it

competes with the RealPlayer in terms of what it can offer—speech coming from a Web page. However, the EchoSpeech plug-in, unlike the RealPlayer plug-in, works easily with Macintosh-based browsers.

I would definitely try this plug-in if only to entertain your friends and family. You may one day find this feature built-in to your browser along with other audio formats, since so many multimedia-enabled computers are now installed throughout the world.

DOCUMENT VIEWER PLUG-INS

This category contains by far the bulk of the plug-ins, simply because helping you view files your browser doesn't normally allow you to view is the heart and soul of plug-in technology. So if you've been having a hard time viewing files through your Web browser, or other people on your network simply can't get the hang of viewing e-mail attachments, you might consider adding one of these plug-ins. From viewing AutoCad files to Microsoft Office files, this section will point you to the perfect plug-in to suit your needs.

NAME OF PLUG-IN: ACROBAT READER BY ADOBE

Location: http://www.adobe.com

Description
Acrobat Reader 3.01 lets you view, navigate, and print Portable Document Format (PDF) files from within your Web browser. PDF files are compact and platform independent, and include all the graphics, fonts, and formatting that the file originally offered. Within the plug-in you can search, print, zoom, and save the PDF file. Hyperlinks can be added to the file for instant access to Web sites.

Regardless of the application, with the Adobe Acrobat option installed, you can print or create a PDF file, instead of printing a file. This means that virtually any application can create PDF files as long as you have the Adobe Acrobat software installed. Better still, the document retains the formatting without requiring the person viewing the file to download additional fonts or graphics. All graphics and fonts are contained within the PDF file.

Recommendation

You need this plug-in because so much information, from corporate reports to forms, is available on the Internet. This is by far the industry standard plug-in, allowing virtually anyone to view and interact with a wide variety of files created by other applications. If you plan on offering long documents, forms, brochures, or other documents that you want to retain the format of, you need to investigate using Adobe Acrobat to create PDF files. The plug-in itself requires about 3MB of hard disk space, and at least 16MB of RAM memory if it is to be used within the browser.

Unfortunately, Adobe Acrobat isn't without its problems. Check Adobe's Web site for troubleshooting tips and updates to the software. Large documents have a tendency to crash your browser, and sometimes certain fonts installed within the user's computer can cause conflicts with the Adobe Acrobat Reader plug-in. But this is certainly one plug-in you'll need when you travel across a wide variety of Web sites, particularly technology, and investment-oriented sites. Plus, if you plan on developing sites or administering internal networks, and want to give your viewers the ability to view, print, and search files, but not change anything, this is the right plug-in to use.

NAME OF PLUG-IN: AUTODESK MAPGUIDE BY AUTODESK

Location: http://www.autodesk.com

Description

Autodesk *MapGuide* is the first commercially available vector-based mapping solution that allows you to author, publish, and distribute richly detailed, layered maps. The viewer of the map can move through its layers, zoom in, rotate, and print the file. Autodesk MapGuide is actually a suite of products beyond just the plug-in. You'll also need the Autodesk MapGuide server and the authoring product. With the server you can deliver live maps with querying and reporting capabilities.

Recommendation

This is definitely a product worth looking into, although the costs for some may be prohibitive. It really caters to a specific market, which needs data charted in a map. Delivery drivers, salesmen, market researchers, newspaper circulation managers, and others could use this server-based product to keep track of customers by querying the database and having the requested data displayed within map form. In order to see exactly what capabilities this plug-in can offer you, you really have to see it. If you find yourself working with geographical data, this plug-in is worth investigating.

NAME OF PLUG-IN: KEYVIEW BY VERITY

This plug-in is available directly from the enclosed CD-ROM.

Location: http://www.verity.com

Not every plug-in available is listed here. Make sure you check the CD-ROM for links to virtually every plug-in available. You'll find the list of available plug-ins in the Webpages folder.

Description

View, zip, convert, or secure any file, anytime. *KeyView* provides cross-platform support for more than 200 file formats—word processing, spreadsheets, graphics, faxes, multimedia, and compressed and encrypted files—including HTML, ZIP, Microsoft Word, WordPerfect, Microsoft Excel, EPS, PCX, PGP, UUencode, and many more. Download the plug-in, and check out these cool samples.

Recommendation

Excellent. Worth every penny. A must-have product for Intranets and for any user who has to communicate with others. Just about every single file format you'd ever run into, from WordPerfect to Excel, is included with this plug-in. That means you can easily view any file anybody might place on their Web site, or any file available on your Intranet.

NAME OF PLUG-IN: OMNIFORM INTERNET FILLER BY CAERE

Location: http://www.caere.com

Description

The *OmniForm Internet Filler* plug-in extends the capabilities of Netscape Navigator by allowing you to view, fill out, print, and submit forms over the Internet or an Intranet. Unlike standard HTML forms, the OmniForm Internet plug-in and Publisher application can automatically convert forms from paper to electronic format and can program those forms so the user doesn't leave out pertinent information or fill out forms incorrectly. The information submitted via the form can then be directly placed in databases.

Recommendation

This product is probably best used in Intranets or within businesses that have large volumes of paper forms that need to be converted to electronic format. This plug-in would also be useful if you need to have the information filled out properly and then updated directly to a database. Without a whole lot of programming you can easily create interactive forms that can interface with other applications. I certainly would recommend any company that needs to work with forms to investigate this plug-in and publisher application. Caere is one of the premiere form-making programs, in addition to fax software, and their products are top-notch.

Name of Plug-In: QuickView Plus by Inso

Location: http://www.inso.com

Description

With this plug-in you can view, copy, print, or save almost any file within a Netscape Navigator window. *Quick View Plus* provides cross-platform support for more than 200 file formats including a wide range of word processing, spreadsheet, database, graphics, presentation, and compressed formats. You can also view PKZIP and UUE files. With QuickView you can view and use files just as if you have the original application that created them. All formatting, fonts, graphics, and embedded objects are left intact. You can try a fully functional version of QuickView for 30 days to see exactly what features it offers. Whether the files have been created on Macintosh or Windows-based computers, you can view them. You can also view e-mail documents stored in Exchange, Notes, Eudora, or any other e-mail application.

Recommendation

Like KeyView, QuickView is an excellent plug-in to have on an Intranet, or if you are a consultant and have to work with many clients and varying file formats. I recommend you download the plug-in then try uploading a whole bunch of documents saved in a variety of file formats to your Web server. When you use the plug-in to view those files, I think you'll find out exactly how useful this product is. No need to convert files to HTML format; no need to compress files; and even if you do compress files you can easily view them because QuickView also lets you view zipped files. All you have to do is use the Upload File menu option in Navigator to upload files, and the QuickView plug-in to view them. Anybody could then share and view data. I highly recommend this plug-in since it makes sharing data extremely easy.

NAME OF PLUG-IN: SWIFTVIEW BY NORTHERN DEVELOPMENT

Location: http://www.ndg.com

Description

Publish any document or drawing on a Web server by simply printing to a file using your HP Laserprinter drivers. The documents will display as if they have been printed to a printer. All the formatting, fonts, and graphics are displayed within the file through the Web browser. You can also use the *SwiftView* plug-in to view PCL and HPGL documents just as if they were printed on an HP LaserJet. The SwiftView plug-in lets you view PCL, HPGL, TIFF, JPEG, and other graphic file formats through a Web browser. The plug-in occupies less than 600K.

SwiftView is a commercial plug-in. Site licenses are available, allowing users on an Intranet to download the plug-in without worrying about licensing agreements. A single low price makes real documents and drawings available to your department, your entire company, or the entire world.

Recommendation

This plug-in moves the world closer to the possibility of paperless offices. If you use HP printers on your network, instead of wasting paper printing out reports, drawings, memos, or any other files, you can print the document to a file, then quickly upload it to your Web server for anyone with the SwiftView plug-in to view. Not every individual or corporation may fully understand this product until they start to use it in their network. When you want to produce information but don't want to waste paper, and you want people to see the document but not change it, this is the perfect product. You could even use this plug-in to view fax and scanned files, making it a product worth purchasing.

NAME OF PLUG-IN: CPC VIEW BY CARTESIAN PRODUCTS

Location: http://www.cartesian.com

Description
CPC View from Cartesian Products provides state-of-the-art viewing and navigation of black-and-white documents stored in a variety of document image formats, including TIFF, PBM, and Cartesian's own CPC format. CPC View supports document navigation, scaling, rotation, antialiased images, thumbnails, and much more. Cartesian's CPC file format uses Cartesian Perceptual Compression to provide the highest compression ratios for storing document images. Documents can end up ten times smaller for faster downloads and smaller storage requirements. With CPC compression and CPC View, it's now practical to make large-scale document image repositories available over the Internet and Intranets. Download the CPC View plug-in and try our demonstrations.

Recommendation
Like other TIFF viewers, this is a great plug-in to use if you need to view scanned images, faxes, or artwork files. Because of the compression this product offers, it's one that you may want to investigate if you need to not only share, but also store TIFF, PBM, or CPC file formats.

NAME OF PLUG-IN: CSVIEW 150 BY CSU SOFTWARE SOLUTIONS

Location: http://www.csu-software-solutions.com

Description
CSView 150 lets you view files from over 150 different file formats, including AutoCad, TIFF, Word, WordPerfect, HPGL, DXF, JPEG, Intergraph, CALS, CGM, IGES, BMP, WinFax, FileMagic, and others. The CSView 150 plug-in offers the ability to zoom, pan, and page-change across all file formats. You can also mark up documents and con-

vert files to other formats, as well as print and search files. And you can save the file to disk or ftp it to a remote server.

Recommendation

Much like other viewers such as QuickView, CSView 150 offers tons of file formats. But unlike other viewers, you can easily mark up documents with comments and on the fly file conversion. If you work on a network and want to share files, with the ability to annotate those files with specific comments, this is an excellent plug-in to use. You might want to compare this plug-in with Inso's QuickView plug-in to see which works best for you. Each offers a wide range of formats, but you may find one interface more user-friendly than the other.

The best feature about any of these multifile viewing plug-ins is that if you have a whole repository of information you want to turn into browse-able Web pages, you don't have to do any conversions of these files at all. CSU uses the following example: if you have 200 WordPerfect documents, 5,000 MicroStation documents, and 10,000 AutoCad documents and you want to make them all accessible on your Intranet, you don't have to worry about conversion, you simply install this plug-in.

NAME OF PLUG-IN: DR. DWG NETVIEW BY DR. DWG

Location: http://www.netview.com

Description

Dr. DWG NetView is the ideal way to view and share AutoCad drawings over the Web. NetView lets you view and redline R12 and R13 DWG/DXF files within a Web browser. You can view isolated drawings and add hyperlinks to the drawings. The hyperlinks let you quickly click to another Web page from within the AutoCad file. You can also zoom, pan, show, or hide layers or blocks, change viewpoints, measure distance, and print from within the browser.

Dr. DWG NetView is a small and compact AutoCad drawing viewer plug-in which can be easily installed from a single diskette. Dr. DWG NetView 2.0 is NetServ enabled. This means that NetView can communicate with the Dr. DWG NetServ service residing on Web servers. It can get redlining information from the server and can send your redlining back to the server if you have been granted permission at the server.

Recommendation

This plug-in is widely used throughout major corporations, such as Boeing and Ford. If it's good enough for them, well...Actually it's an excellent plug-in for anyone using AutoCad over an Intranet or sharing AutoCad files over the Internet. It works quickly to give you access to DWG/DXF files, and it gives you plenty of features such as panning, zooming, or measuring distance, which other AutoCad plug-ins don't offer. I highly recommend trying this plug-in first before you consider all the rest. Updates and technical information are available on NetView's Web.

NAME OF PLUG-IN: SVF VIEWER PLUG-IN BY SOFTSOURCE

NOTE

This plug-in is available directly from the enclosed CD-ROM.

Location: http://www.softsource.com

Description

The *SVF Viewer* plug-in for Netscape Navigator lets you dynamically view AutoCad (DWG) and DXF drawings over the Web. You can pan and zoom a drawing, and hide and display layers. You can also navigate to other Web pages through the hyperlinks embedded in the file.

Recommendation

This rates a close second to Dr. DWG, but offers a few less features. My personal opinion is that Dr. DWG is a better implementation of a DWG viewer than SVF, so I would recommend Dr. DWG first.

NAME OF PLUG-IN: PAGIS XIFF VIEWER BY SCANSOFT, INC., A XEROX COMPANY

Location: http://www.pagis.com or http://www.scansoft.com or http://www.xerox.com/scansoft.com

Description

With the *XIFF* plug-in, you can view Web pages that contain XIFF, an extended version of the Tagged Image File Format file. These files are created by applications such as Xerox Pagis Pro, and in comparison to standard TIFF files, can be dramatically smaller. For example, a full-color page scanned and saved in TIFF format can be around two megabytes in size. With the Pagis XIFF format, the file would be around 100K and would still retain all the color and clarity of the TIFF file.

Pagis Pro is a full-featured scanning application that lets you scan documents directly into your Windows desktop. These files can be color, gray scale, or binary. This allows you to view and post scanned documents on your Web page that contain text and color pictures and are both small in file size yet high quality.

Recommendation

If you do a lot of scanning and need some way to manage those documents, you should consider looking into purchasing the Xerox Pagis application, then using the accompanying viewer to view those files through a Web browser. The ability to compress what normally are huge files into very small files is the best selling feature of this product. You can also use Pagis to manage your scanned images. This plug-in offers relatively few options, but does allow you to view files very quickly. It would probably be best used on an Intranet, or with photographers, news agencies, or other companies that have to do photographic or picture-oriented business on the Internet.

NAME OF PLUG-IN: PNG LIVE BY SIEGEL & GALE

Location: http://www.siegelgale.com

Description
PNG Live 2.0 lets you view Portable Network Graphics, a new royalty-free image format designed to replace GIF images. PNG images can have trillions of colors in a single image; they are smaller than GIF files with the same number of colors; they include many levels of transparency; and they can contain searchable information in their content, history, and authorship properties.

Recommendation
This feature is now being implemented into Internet Explorer and will most likely be implemented soon into Netscape Navigator. The PNG file format has now been recommended by the World Wide Web Consortium, the Web governing body that recommends standards to be

used across all browsers. This plug-in will soon become a moot point. But if you haven't upgraded your browser recently, you may want to download the plug-in and see what you're missing. Eventually the slow GIFs will be replaced by the faster PNG files and those artists afraid of their artwork being stolen won't have to worry since authorship information is built into the actual PNG file itself.

Name of Plug-In: SmoothMove by Infinite Pictures

Location: http://www.smoothmove.com

Description
The *SmoothMove* panorama plug-in for Netscape 3.0 enables users to view and navigate high-quality computer graphic and photo-based panoramas in real time. Once installed, images embedded within Web sites come alive, allowing users to navigate them freely using the mouse or keypad, moving up and down, left and right, and all around the image. Images can include hotspots that can launch other Web pages, audio, video, or other image files directly from within the panoramic picture itself.

Recommendation
Nifty. I love these types of viewers and this one, like all the others listed here, offers you a truly interactive experience with real photos. You can move through a photo just as if you were there, viewing everything around you, zooming in on the picture, clicking on hotspots, and moving to new places. I think you'll be impressed with SmoothMove mainly because of it's clarity within the photos themselves. In terms of the clarity, it is one of the best I've seen among 3D panoramic viewers.

Name of Plug-In: Surround Video by Black Diamond

Location: http://www.blackdiamond.com

Description
The *Surround Video* plug-in lets you view 360-degree panoramic images in a photo realistic fashion. You can move up and down, left and right, and zoom in and out on the images. You can also display and click on

hotspots that can take you to other Web pages, images, videos, or other files stored on the Internet or on an Intranet.

Recommendation

Amazing, simply amazing. Those were my first thoughts when I saw the first 3-D pictures come through my browser. The quality of the 3-D files is excellent and the download time is relatively short, plus they start to display the moment you summon up the file, becoming more and more clear until the entire picture is loaded. Once the entire picture is loaded, it will start to swirl around until you click to position your point of view. These files download much quicker than any QuickTime VR movie I've seen. Check out the Eden House, located at *http://www.edenhouse.com* for a fine example of how you could incorporate this technology in your Web site.

NAME OF PLUG-IN: TRUDEF BY TRUDEF TECHNOLOGIES

Location: http://www.tmmgroup.com

Description

The *TruDef* plug-in lets you view up to twelve file formats including JPEG, TGA, BMP, PCX, and TDF. Also included are over 30 image manipulation and color conversion features available within the plug-in, offering online compression and image format conversion with TruDef's own 10-40:1 compression ratio.

Recommendation

This plug-in and the accompanying compression Codec software included in TruDef helps you create very small graphics files that require only a few kilobytes to a few hundred kilobytes, instead of multiple megabytes. Should you download this plug-in? It's one of those plug-ins I would put at the back of the list if you have no need for working with large file formats. If you're just a true consumer, this plug-in won't offer you much in the way of supercharging your Web browser. But if you are a producer of content and need a product that can easily and quickly compress image files, then I recommend you try this plug-in.

Name of Plug-In: ViewDirector Prizm by TmsSequoia

Location: http://www.tmsinc.com

Description

The *ViewDirector Prizm* plug-in provides high-performance display and manipulation of nonproprietary TIFF, JPEG, GIF, CALS, PCX/DCX, BMP, and other graphics file formats. The Prizm plug-in also supports very large raster engineering drawings up to "j" size. You can zoom, rotate, magnify, apply scale to gray and color smoothing, and even place annotations and hyperlinks on images, and save the annotations back through the server to be shared with others. This plug-in offers access to files within a multiplatform environment. The files being viewed through the plug-in can stream into the page before the entire file is loaded. You can also save the file as another type, annotate the file, copy it to the clipboard, and send the annotations to the server for later storage and retrieval.

Recommendation

If you work with large drawings, need to view a wide variety of images on multiple platforms, and are looking for a plug-in that can do all that, plus a few more things, you should try ViewDirector. Regardless of the image system you might use to create TIFF, JPEG, or other types of graphic file formats, this is an excellent plug-in to use.

Name of Plug-In: Visual WebMap by Project Development

Location: http://www.passagen.se/project

Description

Visual WebMap 2-D viewer is a plug-in that lets you view multiple CAD vector and raster file formats. You can handle information from databases and seamless maps for use in Geographic Information Systems (GIS) applications. You can use multiple embedded files at the same time. You can view, search, measure distance and area, print to files or printers, or copy to the clipboard, plus redline, and setup colors and levels information directly through the plug-in. Visual WebMap supports

IGDS/Microstation/MGE/FRAMME for DGN/RLE/CIT files from Intergraph Corporation or Bentley Systems.

Recommendation

If you work with any type of CAD system, you should investigate this plug-in, or if you work with GIS systems, this plug-in may work well for you. I'm no CAD jockey, so I can't say exactly whether all the capabilities will work for you, but the wide range of file formats this plug-in reads and works with make it one of the most comprehensive CAD-oriented plug-ins to use. With the ability to print, copy to the clipboard, and mark up files, I would say if you have to share documents over an Intranet or are still working with standard file servers, sending files back and forth, you may want to consider this plug-in. Those who create the files can easily keep control of any changes to the file, and those who simply need to view files and have a selective amount of interaction with CAD files may find this plug-in well worth the time, effort, and cost.

NAME OF PLUG-IN: WATERMARK WEBSERIES VIEWER BY FILENET

Location: http://www.filenet.com

Description

The *Watermark WebSeries* viewer lets you view industry-standard TIFF files for document imaging. The Watermark WebSeries plug-in lets you search, retrieve, view, and annotate images, and it offers high-volume document storage. The Watermark Enterprise Series is a Microsoft Windows- and Windows NT-based document imaging software system for organizing, storing, and managing scanned images, faxes, and other documents. You can also use the viewer to view Adobe PDF files, as well as 200 different file formats, without having to launch separate applications.

Recommendation

This really extends past the idea of a plug-in. It's actually a full-featured Intranet application that lets you work with and manage graphic files on an Intranet. It works in conjunction with the WebSeries server. To understand the true capabilities of this full-featured group of products, I recommend you check out their Web page. This is not a plug-in that the general consumer would use. Instead it's a product that would most likely be used in large corporate Intranets.

Remember, you can find many of these plug-ins at the shareware repositories around the Internet including www.windows95.com and www.davecentral.com.

Name of Plug-In: WHIP! By AutoDesk

Location: http://www.autodesk.com

Description
The *WHIP!* plug-in lets you view AutoCad Release 14 files in your Web browser. This plug-in is based on the same rendering technology as the high-performance WHIP! driver found in AutoCad Release 14. The WHIP! plug-in offers the ability to view bitmaps, GIF and JPEG files, and other vector standards such as CGM. You can pan, zoom, and embed URL links to Web pages, audio, video, or text files within your documents, and maneuver through multiple layers in documents.

Recommendation
If you need to view and work with AutoCad Release 14 files, this is the plug-in to use. Other plug-ins only allow viewing of AutoCad 12 and 13 files. If you are one of the many AutoCad 14 users and you want to share your files on the network, you need to download and purchase this plug-in.

Name of Plug-In: UnixLink87 by NetManager

Location: http://www.netmanage.com/products/unixlink/x.html

Description
UnixLink87 lets you view and interact with X applications within your Web browsers. You can click an HTML link to an X application, and then wait for the X client to appear within your Web page. Everything's automated so there's no need for users to learn X and UNIX connection commands.

Recommendation

This is a specific viewer that could be useful for those who use X applications and don't want to use bulky X emulators. If your network is comprised of Intranet technology connected to X servers and you need access to those X applications, you could benefit from this plug-in. Or if you want to make access to X applications easier for those who are not very computer literate, this is one way to offer such integration within your network.

NAME OF PLUG-IN: ARGUS MAP VIEWER BY ARGUS TECHNOLOGIES INC.

Location: http://www.argusmap.com/

Description

Argus Map Viewer is an intelligent client that enables users to interact with simple or complex maps. You can collapse or expand layers, make queries, create dynamic buffering zones, run custom reports based on selected objects, print to scale, and much more. Plus Argus Map Viewer is under two megabytes in size and allows you to view raster/vector-based graphics, multiline map tips, and attributes by scale; it lets you interact with legends and layer controls, set map widths and scale, and zoom in and out of maps. You can also copy your map to the clipboard, print the map with the scale bar, bookmark maps, display mouse positions, and cache maps for faster viewing.

Recommendation

You may already know about this plug-in if you use AutoDesk's MapGuide. And if you don't, you definitely need to check this plug-in out if you share your maps on a network. Without having to install the full AutoDesk MapGuide application, any user on your network can view maps stored on AutoDesk MapGuide servers with little or no knowledge of how to use the MapGuide application.

NAME OF PLUG-IN: DOCACTIVE BY NCOMPASS

Location: http://www.ncompasslabs.com/products/docactive.htm

Description
The *DocActive* plug-in offers the ability to view Office documents within a Web browser. This plug-in lets you view a wide variety of Office documents directly in a Web page without launching or configuring your browser to launch helper applications. Documents can be filed, edited, and viewed, text can be formatted, and tools can be used, all within the browser window. You can not only open, view, edit, and locally save, but you can also print Microsoft Office or other Document Object files.

Recommendation
Definitely look into getting this plug-in. It doesn't matter whether you are using Office on an Intranet or are just a single user of Microsoft Office. For example, if you are a traveling salesman, and want quick access to your Office documents, you could easily store them on a Web server, then with the use of the DocActive plug-in, you can view, print, and edit them. There's no need to lug around all your data. And if you are using Office on an Intranet, you should get this plug-in. No more need to convert documents to HTML format, or make it difficult for others to print or view the files you create. If you are a programmer, you can easily extend the capabilities of your browser through the use of this plug-in and the other NcompassLabs development tools, by providing access to other Document Object files.

NAME OF PLUG-IN: POINTPLUS BY NET-SCENE

Location: http://www.net-scene.com/

Description
PointPlus Plug-in Viewer supports full window and full screen displays of PowerPoint presentation files. You can interact with PowerPoint presentations, viewing automatic slide shows. You can fully interact with these presentations by pausing, resuming, muting, and restarting the presentation as you see fit. All commands are available by right-clicking on the presentation's slides. You can also hear Real Audio files, and view other graphic video files if embedded in the presentation.

Version 2.0 supports PowerPoint 7.0 presentations, RealAudio files, and RealAudio synchronization. There is also a Java version of the viewer that you may want to consider using if you don't want to spend time deploying plug-ins on your Intranet.

Recommendation

You will need the PointPlus Maker to convert your PowerPoint presentations into files that can be viewed with the plug-in player. So I recommend you check out the features of the PointPlus Maker first before you invest in converting all your files into this format. There are other PowerPoint viewers on the market, but with the RealAudio synchronization features, you may find this a worthwhile application to purchase. Despite the need to purchase the PointPlus Maker software, this is an excellent plug-in for viewing PowerPoint presentations over the Internet or through an Intranet, especially those integrated with Real Audio. If you or someone in your company does a lot of presentations, and you want to make these available over the Internet, this is the plug-in to have, and the one to recommend to your viewing visitors.

NAME OF PLUG-IN: GOSCRIPT GSPLUGIN BY LASERGO INC.

Location: http://www.lasergo.com

Description

With the LaserGo plug-in you can view PostScript documents on the Internet through your Web browser. You print PostScript documents to any Windows 95 graphics printer and then share those documents on the Internet. After *GSPlugIn* is installed, selecting a PostScript file within Navigator will automatically process and display the file in the browser. Just about any application using a PostScript-enabled printer can print PostScript documents to files, then have this plug-in view those files. These PostScript documents will retain the formatting, fonts, and graphics included within the documents.

Recommendation

This is an excellent product for any user on an Intranet; it can help you achieve an almost true paperless office. When you want to share a document with someone on your network, you can print the document to a file and let them browse it through their browser, instead of printing it out and walking over to the person and giving it to them, however, they won't be able to change or mark up the file. It is also a great plug-in to have if you are working with a print shop or bureau. With this plug-in you can send your PostScript files to your print shop, and if they need to change the file for some reason, they can change it, then allow you to see the changed file before it's printed.

Name of Plug-In: Formula One/NET by Visual Components

This plug-in was also highlighted in the business-oriented plug-ins. The information listed here is the same.

NOTE

Location: http://www.visualcomp.com

Description

Formula One/NET lets you view Excel-compatible spreadsheets within a Web browser. You can also view accompanying charts and workbooks. Your live worksheets can include live charts, links to URLs, formatted text and numbers, calculations, and clickable buttons and controls. You can even update cells within worksheets. You can pretty much do everything you can do in a regular spreadsheet, including entering data or formulas into cells, resizing columns and rows, and saving the spreadsheet to your own computer's hard drive.

You can even use the plug-in to create interactive forms that require no CGI scripting. Formula One/NET also supports embedded buttons connected to URLs. When the browsing visitor clicks the embedded button that is attached to a URL, he is instantly taken to the Web site specified in the link. The Embedded Charts feature lets you embed charts directly into a workbook. Charts can be updated by changes in the workbook, can be resized, modified, and printed.

Recommendation

This is definitely one of the best plug-ins, and one you should have if you deal with or supply information to people using Excel-compatible spreadsheets. When you consider what you can do with spreadsheets—almost anything from forms creation to simple lists—then this becomes a must-have plug-in. The fact that you don't have to script CGIs in order for information to be viewed is a fantastic option. Anyone with cursory knowledge of spreadsheets could provide some pretty interactive forms. If you work on an Intranet and want to share and view spreadsheets, this is an excellent application to install since, unlike sharing spreadsheets, you can pretty much control the type of information that browsing visitors can add, if any. You will have to purchase the Formula One spreadsheet component which works with Excel, but it's a small price to pay when you consider the Formula One component lets you create some pretty nifty interactive Web pages. Spend some time at their Web site to get some ideas on how you could use this plug-in with your business. The possibilities are endless.

GRAPHICS & MULTIMEDIA PLUG-INS

Sure you can view pictures on the Internet, but let's face it, those GIFs and JPEGs you've been viewing are pretty boring. With the installation of a few of these plug-ins, you'll find your Web browser coming to life like never before. From viewing panoramic images, to zooming in on maps, photos, and graphics, you'll find all the best graphics plug-ins listed in this category.

NAME OF PLUG-IN: BUBBLEVIEWER BY IPIX

This plug-in is available directly from the enclosed CD-ROM.

Location: http://www.ipix.com

Description

IPIX's *BubbleViewer* plug-in lets you experience location on demand by navigating within a totally immersive 360-degree environment. You can zoom in, pan, move up, down, left, and right, plus click links to hotspots stored within the photo. These hotspots will take you to different photos, Web pages, or any type of file stored on the Internet. The photo will automatically stream when you click the link to view the file, allowing you to see the file and decide if you want to wait for the entire photo to download.

Recommendation

Definitely download the viewer and take the sample photos for a spin. You'll feel like you're actually there, watching Shamu splashing through the water or you'll feel like you're there in the front seat of the latest

Honda. You can zoom in and view the dashboard, turn around and see what's in the back seat, or look at the window and see what the street sign says. It's a truly amazing plug-in and something you just have to experience.

Name of Plug-In: CMX Viewer and ShowIt! by Corel Corporation

Location: http://www.corel.com

Description
With the *CMX Viewer* you can view CMX vector graphic files through a Web browser. That means you can use your CorelDraw Gallery files and place them on the Web. You can zoom in and zoom out to view the details of the graphic files or rotate the graphic. With *ShowIt!* you can view Corel Presentation 8 files within a Web page. You can print the pages, move back and forth through the presentation, and play video, animation, and audio if those features are incorporated into the presentation.

Recommendation
If your company uses the Corel suite of products, you need to download this plug-in. That way any presentations or Corel Vector graphic files you place out on your Intranet can be viewed by anyone else. And better still, the people who are viewing your files cannot edit your files, protecting you from having information changed inadvertently. It's a must-have plug-in for any Corel Presentation 8 or Corel Draw user. Otherwise, from a consumer's standpoint you won't find many Corel files or presentations globally available out on the Internet, so downloading if you don't work with others using the Corel suite of products would be a waste of time. Although I must say that the Corel Gallery does have some pretty nifty pictures and presentations you might want to check out. You can even offer your presentations and files to be included in their gallery. One use that several of my clients have found is to produce their company newsletters online using Corel Draw files (and in one instance a client uses CorelDraw to do the entire newsletter), so anyone in the company can view the newsletter.

NAME OF PLUG-IN: INTERCAP CGM VIEWER BY INTERCAP GRAPHICS SYSTEM

Location: http://www.intercap.com

Description
InterCAP's CGM viewer lets you view Computer Graphics Metafiles (CGM) within your Web browser. You can view, pan, magnify, and view animations of these files, and you can include hyperlinks directly into the CGM graphic files. You can also use the Redline option to mark up the graphic adding entities to an overlay of the original file.

Recommendation
If you have a need to view CGM files, then you should consider this graphic; but CGM graphics are not widely used on the Internet. I would put this last on my list of plug-ins to download, unless I had a direct need to view CGM files.

NAME OF PLUG-IN: VITALIZE! BY EUROPRESS

Location: http://www.vitalize.co.uk/

Description
With the *Vitalize!* plug-in you can view interactive multimedia files on a Web page. This compact program which is less than 550K gives you instant access to any application, game, or multimedia package created using Corel Click & Create software. This plug-in also allows you to view applications developed using The Games Factory, Click & Create's software program. These applications are highly compressed so downloading over the Internet is very fast and the animation is very smooth.

Recommendation
There are several very clever games you can play with this plug-in, but you'll find it is more popular in Europe than in the U.S. And that's a shame because in comparison to MacroMedia's ShockWave, this is a much better implementation for interactive files because of the fast download times, and relatively smooth animations. If you have some free time on your hands, and want to check out some pretty awesome interactive game-related sites, start with this plug-in. You won't be disappointed.

NAME OF PLUG-IN: NETTOOB FROM DUPLEXX SOFTWARE

Location: http://www.duplexx.com

Description
NetToob offers high quality, real-time streaming audio and video using the MPEG standard. No special server software is necessary to offer or play real-time streaming files over the Internet or through an Intranet. NetToob can also play all the standard file formats such as AVI, MOV, MPG, FLC/FLI, WAV, and MIDI, regardless of whether you download them from the Web or play them directly from CD-ROMs. You can also embed links to NetToob files with most Internet HTML-enabled e-mail readers.

The player will automatically determine the available bandwidth and stream the best quality video. The plug-in also works with virtually all browsers including America Online's own Web browser and Internet Explorer. You can also use the videos you've downloaded as screen savers if you so choose.

Recommendation
This plug-in is the only one that plays virtually all digital video standards, making it a plug-in well worth downloading. It will even play QuickTime VR files. Plus, it operates using a standard VCR-like interface, making it very easy for just about any user to use.

TIP

Before you download other video players, download this one. It covers almost every video format, meaning you only need one plug-in to play virtually any video file you might run across.

INTRANET-ORIENTED PLUG-INS

Although Chapter 6 covers just about everything you'd ever want to know about Intranets, I've included the list of applicable plug-ins here as well, just for reference. To get a better idea of how you could use some of these plug-ins on your Intranet, make sure you read through Chapter 6. You'll be surprised at what your internal network is missing and what you can add to it to make your life as a user and as an administrator easier.

NAME OF PLUG-IN: INSTALLFROMTHEWEB BY INSTALLSHIELD SOFTWARE CORPORATION

Location: http://www.installshield.com/

Description
InstallFromTheWeb lets Webmasters, developers, and network administrators install applications with a click of a button.

Recommendation
If you're a network administrator, do you find yourself carrying around a ton of diskettes or CD-ROMs just so you can install software on your user's machines? Do you have a hard time convincing users that they can install their own software updates and software programs? Do you need a quick way to update lots of PCs with the latest version of a particular software program? If so, this is a plug-in you need to deploy on your network. I can't recommend it highly enough for anyone that has to support a network of computer users, or any developer that wants to entice more people to download and install your product. It works as advertised and helps you control exactly how an application should be installed.

NAME OF PLUG-IN: PC INSTALL WITH INTERNET EXTENSIONS

This plug-in is available directly from the enclosed CD-ROM.

Location: http://www.twenty.com

Description
PC Install is a full-featured installation plug-in designed specifically for distributing software from Web pages. The user clicks a link in the Web page and the files can then be automatically downloaded, decompressed, and installed in one simple step. There is no need to exit your browser, since once the file has been installed, you can use it immediately.

Recommendation
Like the InstallShield, this is a great tool for any network administrator. And the fact that you don't need to exit your browser in order to install

and use any application you download, makes these types of plug-ins extremely valuable to those who frequently download and update their applications from remote servers. I think it's a toss up in terms of which plug-in works best, so I recommend you download both and see which best suits your needs. Prices for the software to compress the files varies, so that's also something to consider.

Name of Plug-In: NetZip by Software Builders International

Location: http://www.softwarebuilders.com

Description
This plug-in lets you immediately unzip files from within a Web page. You no longer need to run a separate application to view, then unzip, files. You can also create, add to, and extract from ZIP and EXE compressed file formats from within a Web browser. The software also lets you view 18 other file formats including Word, ASCII, TIF, and BMP.

Recommendation
As *PC World* said in a recent review of this product, "if you spend any time online, you need this product." It is on my top ten list of plug-ins to download, and I highly recommend that every network adminstrator put it on his network.

Miscellaneous Plug-Ins

These plug-ins are really either industry specific or simply so bizarre that there's no other place to put them. If you're one of those people who could benefit from these plug-ins, I'm sure you'll understand exactly the features they offer. For more specific information, visit the vendor's Web site.

NAME OF PLUG-IN: MATHVIEW ON-LINE BY WATERLOO MAPLE

Location: http://www.cybermath.com

Description

With the *MathView* plug-in viewer you can view equations and display them realistically the way they should be within your Web browser to view MathView files and workbooks. You can also view graphs of the equations and work with them interactively by panning, zooming, or moving your mouse around, so you can interact with the equation. With the plug-in you can do limited math and save workbooks to your own hard drive.

Recommendation

If you deal with anything relating to math, you probably will find this plug-in worth the download just to see what it has to offer. The downfall of course is that in order to really get something out of this plug-in you should be using the MathView application to create mathematical equations and graphs. I flunked Algebra, so I simply have no use for this plug-in, and when I did use it, it brought back nightmares of struggling to understand what Mr. McGinnis, my high school Algebra teacher, was talking about.

NAME OF PLUG-IN: CHEMSCAPE CHIME BY MDL INFORMATION SYSTEMS

Location: http://www.mdli.com/chemscape/

Description

The *Chemscape Chime* plug-in lets scientists display chemically significant 2-D and 3-D structures within an HTML page or table.

Recommendation

If you're a chemistry type, you'll see the virtue of this plug-in. I know my Dad, the chemist, did. It helps him view molecular structures from within a Web page and share that same information with anyone else who has the plug-in installed. That means anyone within his company's network can easily see his latest chemistry creation without having to have any specialized software other than the plug-in.

NAME OF PLUG-IN: READ TO ME

Location: http://www.pixi.com/~reader1/intro.html

Description
That's right, this plug-in reads Web pages to you, and does so in either English or in Hawaiian language. You can customize the pronunciation of various words, or read text not only from Web pages, but also from the clipboard, Word, or text files. When the software is reading the text, the words and sentences are highlighted. You can customize the reading speed, pitch, and volume, and choose from five different graphical talking heads that display as the Web page is being read. This plug-in requires a sound card and speakers in order for you to hear the text spoken.

Recommendation
Nifty is about all I can say about this plug-in. And since it's free, it's well worth the download. The site listed previously also has links to hundreds of literature classics, so if you don't have anything great to read or listen to, you'll be able to find something there.

I can't say every word is pronounced correctly, or that listening to a computer drone on and on is the best way to view the Web, but what this plug-in does afford you is your own Web broadcast. Instead of having your eyes glued to a Web page, reading today's news, Read To Me can read the news to you as if it were your own Internet newscaster. Also, for any users who might be visually impaired, this is an excellent software product. Definitely try it out if you have the hardware to use it. You'll be delighted, surprised and impressed.

PROGRAMMING-ORIENTED PLUG-INS

If you program or if you develop prototypes of either hardware or software, you'll find some of these plug-ins will help you and your testers experiment with ideas by producing virtual prototypes that you can test within your browser. These plug-ins help you not only deploy but also simulate the projects you are working on.

NAME OF PLUG-IN: DEMONOW BY DEMOSHIELD

Location: http://www.demoshield.com

Description
DemoNow lets those visiting your site view your demo live, directly from within their browsers. DemoNow lets you Internet-enable your software demos and eliminate the unnecessary steps of downloading and installing your demo. This plug-in lets you view software without having to muck up your system, downloading demo and temporary files that eventually you may delete if you don't want to purchase the product.

Recommendation
If you create software and want people to get a real feel for how your product works, I recommend you purchase the software and place a link on your Web site to the plug-in. First, you don't have to have an ftp server to place your demos on, nor do you need to provide support to those who are just testing out your application. And you don't have to worry about updating remote ftp sites to ensure that they have the latest demo versions in their directories. Instead you simply Web-enable your demo, then place it on your Web server, and users can test it out to their hearts content.

NAME OF PLUG-IN: NOBLENET OPENER BY NOBLENET

Location: http://www.noblenet.com

Description
NobleNet Opener provides easy-to-use Web browser access to applications and data deployed using NobleNet Web. NobleNet Web lets programmers distribute existing client-server applications across the Internet, corporate intranets, and the Web in minutes, with no recoding and no new development. You can also use sophisticated security techniques to assure tamper distribution across your network. NobleNet makes sure users always have the virus-free versions of applications that you want to distribute over your network.

Recommendation

This is a tool that any large corporate Intranet could use. It's primarily designed for developing and deploying client-server applications, so as a consumer you may not find a use for this plug-in. Once you've created and are ready to deploy your applications, you create NobleNet-enabled files, then place them on a Web server. If you have a need to deploy files on a network, take a look at what this plug-in has to offer.

Name of Plug-In: Rapid Plug-In by EmulTek

Location: http://www.emultek.com

Description

The *Rapid* plug-in enables users to view simulations and prototypes of products developed in Rapid over the Internet and Intranets. Applications can be directly in Web pages, and they interact with these prototypes as if they are using the actual product. Users can view and operate virtual models of products or computer-based training courses can instead of simply looking at graphic representations.

Recommendation

Do you want to create a prototype for a product? Instead of spending tons of money to demonstrate exactly how the product will work, why not just create an electronic prototype instead? I invested in a company that creates a spinning-top toy that is placed on a drinking cup lid. My investment went toward helping the inventor get a prototype made so he could show this prototype to prospective cup manufacturers. Instead of spending about $10,000 in production costs, he could have easily had this prototype electronically created and saved about $8,000. If you are an inventor looking for investors, consider creating an electronic prototype first, before you have the real thing made.

Presentation & Training Oriented Plug-Ins

When you want to make a splash, these are the plug-ins to use to view those splashy presentations. They are also the plug-ins to use if you are creating online interactive training, be it computer training, human resources training, or industrial-type training. These plug-ins take your PowerPoint presentations and let the world view them, even if the person viewing the page doesn't have PowerPoint himself. They also let you view specific computer-based training documents created with specific interactive training software such as Asymetrix's ToolBook, through a Web page. Because the presentation or training file stays on the server, there's no special software or elaborate instructions needed when a user on your network wants to learn, interact, and use the training files you've created. If your company hasn't already considered implementing online, interactive computer-based training, complete with audio and video, it should. You can save not only a lot of money but could also save a great deal of time, and more improtantly get your point across more accurately. Such training options allow any user on your network the option to view and interact with your training information at the click of a button anytime he or she wants to. No longer do you have to have everyone gather in a conference room to watch a safety video. Instead you simply supply a link to your safety training file, complete with video, then everyone on your network can watch and interact with the information at their leisure.

NAME OF PLUG-IN: ASTOUND WEB PLAYER BY GOLD DISK, INC.

Location: http://www.golddisk.com

Description
The *Astound Web Player* is a Netscape plug-in that plays dynamic multimedia documents created with Gold Disk's award-winning Astound Studio or Studio M software. These documents can include sound, animation, graphics, video, and interactivity. The Astound Web Player features dynamic streaming: the next slide is downloaded in the background while you view the current slide. You can move through the presentation as if you were actually using the Astound Presentation Studio or Studio M software.

The Studio M software lets you create electronic interactive greeting cards, animated Web pages, and more. It's the consumer/home user software, whereas Astound Studio is for the professional presenter.

Recommendation
I love the Astound Studio presentation software. In many ways it's simply much better than PowerPoint, although PowerPoint 7 now does rival some of the features available in Astound Studio. You can add video,

audio, or animations to your presentation. Although PowerPoint is becoming an industry standard, if you're in the market for presentation software, I recommend you download the plug-in, take a look at the demo files found on Gold Disk's site, and see what you could do with the software. Then if you or your company hasn't decided to use PowerPoint, convince them that this is the way to go.

NAME OF PLUG-IN: LOTUS WEBSCREEN SHOW PLAYER

Location: http://www.lotus.com

Description
Lotus WebScreen Show Player is a plug-in for displaying Freelance Graphics presentations stored on the Web. You can view or print the presentations, or view them as you would a slide show. All animations, including page transitions, on-screen animations, and embedded video files, can be viewed. Presentations can include hyperlinks that take the browsing visitor to other Web pages or files.

Recommendation
You have to use this plug-in if your company uses Lotus Freelance Graphics for your presentations. But if not, and you or your company are in search of a great presentation program, I would strongly recommend taking a look at Astound's Studio M or PowerPoint 7 because both offer more features in an easier to use interface than Freelance. This is definitely a specific viewer, and not something a consumer would download unless he or she had a need to view such files.

NAME OF PLUG-IN: NEURON BY ASYMETRIX

Location: http://www.asymetrix.com

Description
Neuron is a plug-in is that displays Asymetrix ToolBook II files and files created by Asymetrix Instructor, Publisher, and Assistant. The Neuron plug-in allows end users to download and play presentations, kiosks, courseware, and other multimedia applications produced in ToolBook II over the Internet. Because the Neuron plug-in supports external multimedia files, users can access either complete titles or only the relevant portions of titles, providing streaming functionality. The Instructor can

automatically install the training application over the Web and assign courseware to students online. All sorts of scripting language options are used within this application, including Java, ActiveX, and Asymetrix Toolbook's own OpenScript.

Recommendation

If you do any type of electronic training and haven't checked into what Asymetrix's ToolBook offers, you should. It makes creating online and CD-ROM-based training much easier than using a conglomeration of other software programs. With the ability to create training that incorporates all sorts of Web-based technologies, such as ActiveX, Java, HTML, video, and audio, you can quickly create robust training applications with as much interactivity as you please. With Toolbook you can also include comprehension tests and track the results. Although the ToolBook application is expensive, it is really one of the best products on the market for creating instructional online materials. If you're involved in training of any kind, whether it's computer or human resource, I strongly suggest you download the plug-in, try out the test applications, then go out and buy it and start creating your own training online. For repetitive training, where you need to keep track of the results, this is the best way to go. No need to copy manuals, no need to pay a stand-up trainer, no need to have a clerk type in test results. All that can be done right in the Toolbook training application that you create. And better yet, with the interactive wizards that are included with the Toolbook application, you don't have to be a computer jockey to create relatively professional interactive training products.

NAME OF PLUG-IN: POWERPOINT ANIMATION PLAYER AND PUBLISHER

Location: http://www.microsoft.com

Description

The new Microsoft *PowerPoint Animation Player & Publisher* provides users with the fastest, easiest way to view and publish PowerPoint animations and presentations in your browser window. You can include animations, hyperlinks, sound, and special effects within your PowerPoint files to display through Web pages.

Recommendation

If you want to view PowerPoint presentations and don't want to pay for a conversion program, like PointPlus, to create Web-enabled PowerPoint files, this is the product you should consider downloading. It doesn't offer as many features, such as synchronization with Real Audio files, but it does offer a cheap and easy way to get your PowerPoint files out on a network. Definitely download it if you do a lot of presentations and want to share those across the Internet.

REMOTE APPLICATION & CONNECTION PLUG-INS

If you want to connect to remote computers, or even manipulate PCs on a network, these are the best plug-ins for the job. These plug-ins let you remotely control or view computers whether they are connected to the Internet or within your company's Intranet. There are two typical users who might use these plug-ins—those who provide computing support, and those who travel but still need access to their computer at home or at the office. With these plug-ins you can manipulate files and data on remote computers, and even use peripherals remotely attached to the systems you are connecting to.

NAME OF PLUG-IN: ALTiS BY EPICON

Location: http://www.epicon.com

Description

ALTiS is a plug-in that lets you access remote software applications over the Internet or an Intranet. Any Windows application can be ALTiS enabled, which means a user can click a link to the application from a Web page, then immediately begin executing the application on his PC. ALTiS delivers the application to the PC over the network, then caches the code needed for local execution. Applications can be ALTiS enabled to allow the network administrator to combine central control of applications with distributed processing, even when PCs have limited disk space.

Recommendation

If you have a need to deliver applications over the Internet, this is an excellent plug-in to use. With it you have full control over what applications, regardlesss of whether they be Internet aware or not, can be placed on your Intranet and accessed by your users. It's definitely a tool for those network administrators dealing with limited resources, constant problems with unauthorized use of licensed software, and problems tracking what computer has what software installed. You will have to purchase the ALTiS software that lets you turn any software program on your conputer's network into a clickable application, but for the costs of this software you'll save yourself hours and hours of hassles, and still be able to control what's installed where.

NAME OF PLUG-IN: CARBON COPY/NET BY MICROCOM

Location: http://www.microcom.com

Description
Carbon Copy/Net is a Netscape plug-in that lets you remotely control another PC over the Internet. You can run applications, access files, and view or edit documents on a remote PC as though they were on the PC in front of you. Carbon Copy/Net is an ideal tool for remote access to Windows applications, collaboration, remote software demonstrations, remote support, and remote access to CD-ROMs, printers, or other peripherals.

Recommendation
It's a solid product that has been around for years, first as a software package that allowed you to control a PC through a modem-to-modem connection. Now it's found it's way to the Internet and runs relatively well. I've used it on many occasions to help clients get out of a jam, even though I wasn't in town and able to sit in front of their computers. You do have to set up the remote PC for access, however, and that means the remote PC must have a sufficient amount of RAM in order to run the Carbon/Copy host software. It's a toss up really between this and Look@Me by Netopia. I actually prefer Look@Me, but only because the interface appeals to me a bit more than Carbon/Copy. You should see which works best for your particular installation.

Name of Plug-In: Citrix WinFrame by Citrix

Location: http://www.citrix.com

Description

The *Citrix WinFrame* Client enables you to work with any Windows application or file stored on a remote computer through a standard Web page. You can run applications remotely, from the WinFrame server through your Web browser, with full menu, mouse, and keyboard control. This is a different product entirely than either Carbon/Copy or Look@Me because you aren't controlling a remote computer, but rather running an application stored on the WinFrame server through a Web page. You use the server's horsepower to run the application, basically using the plug-in and browser as a window into the screen and keyboard. You can use this product with WinFrame-enabled dumb terminals such as Wyse terminals if you would rather not use a PC, thereby reducing the cost of offering access to a full spectrum of Windows applications.

Recommendation

I've used this product many times and have even installed the server, and I find it works as advertised. It's relatively slow over dial-up lines, however, so this is definitely a plug-in for Intranets. The best use of this product is to offer applications to those who either don't have the application installed, or for those machines on your network that simply don't have the capabilities to run the software. With WinFrame you can keep your investment in your older computers, offering access to newer Windows 95 applications that older machines may not be able to run. The only disadvantage is that you must also purchase a server, allocate at least 16MB of space to each remote terminal/PC you plan to offer on your network, and then install the application software on the server. The advantage, however, is that besides saving on hardware, you can also save on software site licenses.

NOTE

This company is partly owned by Microsoft. You never know what Microsoft might do with this product, but if I were to look in my crystal ball, I would say that you'll see this technology in Microsoft's WebTV products, or you may just see it die on the vine. Who can tell with Microsoft.

NAME OF PLUG-IN: LOOK@ME BY NETOPIA

Location: http://www.netopia.com

Description
The *Look@Me* plug-in allows you to view another Timbuktu/Look@Me user's screen remotely. It allows you to watch the activity taking place, letting you edit documents, view presentations, work with graphics, or provide online training and support through a remote computer. You can even use this software product to update software remotely or access other types of computers, such as Windows NT or Macintosh computers running the Timbuktu software. Security is built into the system, allowing you full control without having to worry about hackers.

Recommendation
Because it offers cross-platform compatibility, meaning you can control both PCs and Macs, that makes this product excellent for help-desk support people. You can remotely control the other computer as if you were sitting right in front of it. You definitely need a large amount of RAM on the host machine, as well as the control machine, in order to prevent potential problems when running more than one application remotely. It's an excellent product, but I recommend you test out both Carbon/Copy and Look@Me to see which one meets your particular needs.

NAME OF PLUG-IN: WEBTERM TOOLBOX BY WHITE PINE SOFTWARE

Location: http://www.wpine.com/

Description
WebTerm Toolbox offers full TN3270, TN5250, and VT420 terminal emulators that allow you to connect to remote computers, not PCs but larger systems such as UNIX or mainframe systems, through a Web browser. You can access remote computers using any terminal configuration you choose. Your keyboard is then mapped to match the keyboard for the terminal emulation you are using. You can copy and paste from the screen into other Windows-based applications. You no longer need a separate Telnet application to access remote computers that do not use graphical interfaces or Web forms for interaction.

TIP

*You have a built-in Telnet client with your Windows 95 operating system. Simply click the **Start** button in the **Taskbar**, then select **Run** from the pop-up menu. Next type TELNET or TELNET HOSTNAME, where Hostname is the name of the remote computer you want to connect to, then hit **OK**. You will immediately see the Windows Telnet client launch. It should then connect you to the remote computer.*

Recommendation

Finally, a plug-in that offers the capability that every browser should have built in access to remote computers through the Telnet client. If you're like me, someone who still loves PINE, an e-mail program that runs on Unix systems, you'll find this plug-in a godsend. Just load the browser, telnet to the remote computer, and you're instantly connected and the computer's terminal display pops up in your browser window. If you have any need to connect to remote computers, again, not PCs but computers larger than PCs that still run off text-based systems, you need this plug-in. Those who work a great deal with government computers, those who connect to mainframe systems, or even those like me who just like to go back to Unix once in awhile, this is the plug-in to have. You never have to leave your browser again, regardless of what type of connection you want to make. I would certainly spend the money to purchase this plug-in.

Name of Plug-In: VTX-Plug by Monaco Telematique

Location: http://www.windows95.com/apps/plugins-misc.html (in the U.S.) or http://www.mctel.fr/spd_vtxplug_fr.html (in France)

Description
VTX-Plug, a Minitel plug-in, will allow you to access the French Minitel services directly from within your Web browser. The software allows you to run a kind of terminal emulation, giving you access to all the features Minitel users have access to.

Recommendation
The only reason you would need to download this plug-in is if you wanted to access France's Minitel system. So if you are one of the millions and millions of French who simply don't want to give up your

Minitel unit, but want to incorporate both the Internet and the Minitel system together, this is the only plug-in you'll need. Or if you want to experience what the French have had for so long, and want to know what is making them so slow to move towards the Internet, download this plug-in and see for yourself.

NAME OF PLUG-IN: OpSESSION BY NetManage

Location: http://www.netmanage.com

Description
OpSession is a plug-in that allows all 32-bit Windows applications to be viewed and remotely controlled from within your browser window. You can control such applications as Microsoft Powerpoint, Excel, Word, Corel Presentations, Lotus Freelance, CAD/CAM tools, or any other application you might have on your computer. The OpSession plug-in occupies less than 250K and the plug-in allows for one file to be viewed concurrently with up to 64 others. You could use OpSession to present PowerPoint presentations, or to remotely control software, or to conference, train, or support others online interactively. You set up one system as the host, and the other users can then access the host system remotely. The host must be a Pentium, whereas the users can run on less powerful machines.

Soon OpSession will be available in the form of a Java applet. More and more plug-ins are coming as both plug-ins or ActiveX controls, and as Java applets. If you find a certain plug-in of value, but you don't want users to have to go through installation procedures, you may consider upgrading to the Java version. With Java the user simply needs a Java-enabled browser. Then like ActiveX, when the user runs across a page that offers the Java applet or script embedded, the script loads if the browser is capable of interpreting Java. There is no need to download anything, and once the applet or script has been loaded, it can read or view the data file specified to work in conjunction with the applet or script.

Recommendation
If you need to connect remotely to another computer either over the Internet or an Intranet, this is a compact plug-in that won't tax your system. Unlike most other remote viewing plug-ins, this one is compact and runs on Windows 3.11 computers, which many others don't. My

recommendation is to try this plug-in along with several others to see which works best within your system, and which has the features you need the most. Some don't allow for concurrent viewing, such as OpSession does. Others may provide for remote printing, while OpSession currently doesn't offer. Each remote plug-in offers different features, and it really takes time to know exactly which one offers the options you want.

UTILITY ORIENTED PLUG-INS

These plug-ins perform certain utilitarian functions either with your browser or with your computer. From unzipping files to helping you find files on your computer, these plug-ins offer more than just document viewing options.

NAME OF PLUG-IN: NETZIP BY SOFTWARE BUILDERS INTERNATIONAL

Location: http://www.softwarebuilders.com

Description
Tired of downloading files, then having to go through the unzipping process? If so, this plug-in is for you. You can quickly download and unzip files while you're online. Offering complete integration with Netscape Navigator and Netscape Communicator, you create, add to, and extract from ZIP and EXE compression formats, all within the browser window. Once unzipped, you can choose to install the file if it requires installation. The plug-in also offers 18 different viewers for Windows, including Word, ASCII, TIF, and BMP.

Recommendation
Download it now! It's an excellent plug-in that offers a feature that should have been included with every browser—the ability to unzip files quickly while still online. And if you send files back and forth, you don't have to leave your browser to zip them. You can download the free evaluation copy, but I highly recommend you invest in the commercial version because you'll find yourself using it again and again, and thanking yourself for all the time and hassle you'll save. It's a must-have utility on any corporate Intranet because it makes the rather confusing task of decompressing files as simple as clicking a button.

NAME OF PLUG-IN: SCRIPTACTIVE BY NCOMPASSLABS

Location: http://www.ncompasslabs.com

Description

ScriptActive lets you view ActiveX controls within your Netscape Navigator browser. Any ActiveX control can be viewed as if it were part of a Web page, and as if Netscape offered such abilities. ScriptActive also contains the features of DocActive, a plug-in integrated with Microsoft Office 95 and Netscape Navigator that allows users to open, view, edit, save locally, and print Excel, Word, and PowerPoint documents, as well as document object files from other software vendors.

Recommendation

Why Netscape doesn't make this a part of their browser is beyond me. If they did, they'd compete head to head with Internet Explorer. Since they don't, and since Internet Explorer can use Netscape Navigator plug-ins, the competitive advantage is still with Internet Explorer. It's silly for Netscape to forget that users of their browsers are most likely users of other Microsoft software such as Microsoft Office. If they included such a plug-in that could interact with ActiveX controls, they would offer up all sorts of developer options that would create a truly integrated desktop for those Windows 95 users.

   This is a must-have plug-in if you work on a network that utilizes ActiveX controls, or if you're a dyed-in-the-wool Navigator user and want to see what you've been missing and simply don't want to install the latest buggy version of Internet Explorer. The only problem is that you have to pay for the product; but it's worth every penny if you don't want to be left in the dust on the information superhighway.

NAME OF PLUG-IN: DATADETECTIVE PC SEARCH BY APPLETWARE

Location: http://www.appletsite.com

Description

DataDetective PC Search is a Netscape Navigator plug-in that can perform full-text, boolean, and proximity searches on any directory or drive on your PC. The search results are presented as hyperlinks that point to the files that satisfy the query. The search is done on an index to a database created by the indexing portion of Data Detective (a Windows 95 application). The product's function is similar to Alta Vista's Search My PC (Private Extension) product; however, Data Detective is only 600K in size (uncompressed) and is faster than Alta Vista both in indexing and searching.

Recommendation
I've tried it, but since I have no problem finding files on my lowly two gigabyte hard drive, it really did little for me. However, for those users who are scatterbrains, and can never find what they are looking for on their drive, this product may help. And anyone that has to deal with large drives or servers, or with files stored by other users on servers or networked computers, this is an excellent utility to find what you are looking for.

It was somewhat unstable, however, and gave my browser some fits off and on. Check to make sure you download the latest version and that your computer is in fine working order before you add this plug-in.

Name of Plug-In: Plugsy by Digigami

Location: http://www.digigami.com

Description
Are you having problems with the wrong plug-in coming up when you view Web pages? Do you find yourself constantly creating MIME types for files you thought you had already set up? With *Plugsy* you can easily manage your MIME types and plug-ins through a simple interface. Plugsy manages conflicts between plug-ins that handle the same MIME type. For example, with Plugsy you can select Digigami's CineWeb audio/video player plug-in to handle QuickTime, Video for Windows, MPEG, and Autodesk Animation files, and at the same time use LiveUpdate's Crescendo MIDI plug-in for MIDI playback.

Plugsy can also be used to disable individual MIME types in a particular plug-in. You could disable the audio/x-wave MIME type in NPAUDIO.DLL while continuing to use an existing external MIME handler for audio/x-wave.

Recommendation
I've never really had any plug-in conflicts even though I have hundreds installed on my system. But I'm pretty selective about what I install, and

if one plug-in can handle a whole bunch of file formats, I'll use that plug-in over a collection of others that handle just a few file formats. So I guess you could say I'm a little more cautious about my plug-ins than the average user. Plus, I know how to quickly create new MIME types and how to clean up old MIME no longer needed.

So should you download or purchase this plug-in utility? Only if you seem to have problems with the wrong plug-in playing files, or if you are a network administrator and want to corral all those plug-ins that users on your tend to install and download. Or if you simply don't know how to fix your plug-in problems, this plug-in may be useful. But for the average user who uses a few plug-ins, this is a little overkill.

NAME OF PLUG-IN: SIR BROWSE-A-LOT BY SOFTCOM, INC.

Location: http://www.softcom.com/sir/

Description
Sir Browse-A-Lot is a plug-in for the Windows versions of Netscape Navigator 3.0, and it brings all the functionality of Microsoft Internet Explorer to Netscape. It does so by embedding Internet Explorer as a plug-in within Netscape Navigator. With it embedded, you can easily view Internet Explorer-enhanced sites, run ActiveX controls, view enhanced style sheet sites, and run VBScripts without having to leave your Netscape browser.

Recommendation
It's free. It brings all the functionality of Internet Explorer to your Netscape browser, although it does have some limitations, such as printing. And yes, you should download it if you find yourself locked out of Internet Explorer-only sites, or if you want to use ActiveX controls. Again, why Netscape never offered this capability is beyond me, but with this plug-in you can see what you're missing.

NAME OF PLUG-IN: SCRIPTEASE BROWSERPLUGIN BY NOMBAS

Location: http://www.nombas.com/applet/applet.htm

Description

The *ScriptEase BrowserPlugIn* allows for live interaction with HTML forms and HTTP servers, responding to data input on both ends. For example, a page could be set up to show and continuously update stock prices, and ring an alarm if a stock falls below a certain level. This plug-in can also validate and encrypt data before sending it to the server, using the secured version of the plug-in. With Secure ScriptEase, you can specify which scripts and commands can be run by users.

Recommendation

You need the server if you want to use this plug-in. And this plug-in is more development oriented than consumer oriented. You really have to read through the documentation to understand all the features you could use to create truly interactive Web pages, with push-oriented technology through a Web page.

TIP

If you are looking for a great utility that can record your sites so you can easily view them offline, you might try Nearsite, located at www.nearsite.com. Although this product doesn't exactly fall into the plug-in category, it does offer the ability to create your own Internet library full of Web sites, and it does allow you to share Web sites with others through diskettes and Zip drives. It's great if you need to travel or demonstrate your Web site at a trade show but have no connection to the Internet.

NAME OF PLUG-IN: NAVIGATE WITH AN ACCENT ACCENTSOFT

Location: http://www.accentsoft.com/

Description

Now you can view pages in Russian, Chinese, Arabic, Polish, Japanese, and Korean without having to install the specific language version of Windows. When you view a Web page created with Accent Global Author, the Navigate with an Accent plug-in automatically detects the language of the page and displays it appropriately. With other Web pages, if the language is not detected automatically, Navigate with an Accent lets you select the language of your choice. Navigate with an Accent also lets you choose a preferred font for each language. Online help is available in five different languages, and Web pages can be read in more than 20 different languages.

Recommendation

This is about the only choice you need to view Web pages written in different languages. The only problem is that it works best when viewing Web pages created with the Accent Global Author software, which many Web page authors do not use. Nevertheless, it's easier than going through the hassle of installing multiple Windows languages. If you work within a mutlilingual company, you should seriously consider purchasing the entire product line so you quickly create pages that anyone in your global company can read and understand.

VIRTUAL WORLDS & 3-D VIEWER PLUG-INS

OK, I hate virtual worlds because I love living in reality. But I do have to mention a few here since they work as advertised, and since a good deal of content of virtual worlds is available. Sure, some of the virtual worlds you can cruise through are games, but others are actually online worlds that make it easier to browse through Web sites. And some virtual worlds may provide access to information in a unique way that gives the browsing visitor a better idea of how a product might work, before the actual prototype is built.

3-D viewers have great potential in the manufacturing world and in many large companies. When coupled with 3-D photographic images, they will provide inexpensive ways to actually get the feeling of being there, without having to pay the price. There is potential, so don't get frustrated. Fine-tuning your 3-D virtual world browser may take time, and if you don't have a relatively powerful PC, forget about this whole section. Although some of the 3-D browsers will work with 486 computers, you really need a Pentium and a fair amount of RAM memory to avoid the most common problems. Also make sure your system is in pretty good working order and you have chosen the right video drivers. Many common problems you run into can be tied to too little RAM memory or the incorrect video drivers selected in your operating system software.

NOTE

NAME OF PLUG-IN: INTERVISTA'S WORLDVIEW 2.1

This plug-in is available directly from the enclosed CD-ROM.

Location: http://www.intervista.com

Description

WorldView is a browser plug-in for viewing 3-D worlds. You can easily navigate at variable speeds, and select from either a joystick, mouse, or keyboard. You have full control of what types of controls you use. WorldView also has a quick "Go To" feature that lets you jump directly to a location in your 3-D world. Based on Microsoft's DirectX technology, this plug-in allows for very fast rendering of 3-D worlds. The plug-in also allows you to hear streaming audio, if such audio has been included in the 3-D VRML file. The 3-D sound capabilities allow you to hear sound based upon your position. The further you move away from a sound file anchored to a world, the more distant sounding the file will play. There is also support for JavaScript, so worlds can be scripted.

Recommendation

It's one of the fastest 3-D world viewers around, and it offers more built-in capabilities than just about any browser. With the JavaScript support and the fact that it's built on Microsoft's DirectX technology, you should see some amazing worlds built for this browser. As a matter of fact, you'll find tons to explore if you check out the Intervista Web site. If you are thinking about developing VRML worlds, you might consider using this product as your preferred viewer. It's excellent. Just make sure you have enough horsepower.

NAME OF PLUG-IN: PLATINUM WIRL

Location: http://www.vream.com/

Description

Platinum WIRL, a virtual reality Web browser plug-in, lets users experience VRML content over the World Wide Web. This plug-in works with both Netscape Navigator and Microsoft Explorer, and can be used with ActiveX container applications such as Microsoft Powerpoint and

Microsoft Excel. WIRL provides higher interactivity and faster performance than traditional graphics and animation plug-ins. With this plug-in you can view any VRML content that is based on nonproprietary VRML standards, regardless of the tool used to develop the content. This plug-in uses Microsoft's Direct 3-D for ultrafast frame rates and enhanced performance using popular 3-D graphics accelerator cards.

Recommendation

It's an excellent product and worth the download. It's also a product worth developing since it offers connections through ActiveX to other applications, thereby extending the audience on both the Internet and within corporate Intranets. You do, however, need a powerful PC to work with this product.

NAME OF PLUG-IN: COSMO PLAYER BY SILICON GRAPHICS

Location: http://webspace.sgi.com/cosmoplayer/

Description

Produced by Silicon Graphics, one of the graphics industry leaders, this player offers a VRML client with OpenGL, offering support for hardware acceleration. Cross-platform supports consistent appearance and behavior across platforms, and the plug-in offers full extensible options for developers through links to Java and JavaScript. The plug-in also offers basic media support without the need to download additional plug-ins or software.   The *Cosmo Player* 1.0 is actually a standard component shipped with Netscape Communicator. The new version 2.0, however, delivers many more features and more support for other video, audio, and graphic file formats including support for MPEG, WAV, AVI, AIFF, MIDI, QuickTime, GIF, JPEG, PNG, and animated GIF files. Other options include support for 3-D surround sound, and the ability to create hotspots that link to other Web pages.

Recommendation

Try it. It can't hurt, and the dashboard controls make this 3-D viewer easy to use. Plus, with the support of all the video and audio file formats, you'll see some pretty creative interactive content offered. The support for Netscape Communicator also makes this one of the preferred plug-in choices of 3-D world developers. Check Netscape's site for links to a whole bunch of VRML content that this plug-in can display. Just make sure you have the horsepower to run the plug-in; otherwise you'll be frustrated with the slow response.

VIDEO-ORIENTED PLUG-INS

In the past the connection speeds of the Internet prevented anyone from adding video to their Web sites. But with new compression techniques and a plethora of video players now available, more and more sites are adding full-motion video. If you haven't experienced the wonderful world of video, you need to look into some of these plug-ins. Although Netscape Communicator comes with some ability to view video files, several of the plug-in players listed next offer more features, more control, and better decompressors for faster playback.

TIP

*Before you install any of these plug-ins, make sure you don't already have them installed. You do this by going to the **Help** menu and selecting **About Plug-Ins**. This page will list all the plug-ins installed.*

NAME OF PLUG-IN: QUICKTIME BY APPLE

Location: http://quicktime.apple.com

Description
The Apple *QuickTime* plug-in lets you view QuickTime movies, an almost Internet standard and a file format that is now available on almost all platforms including Mac and Windows. This plug-in also lets you experience QuickTime animation, music, MIDI, audio, and video, including MPEG and VR panorama photo files if you also installed the QuickTimeVR plug-in. QuickTimeVR files let you move around in 360-degree mode, zooming in and out, panning, and clicking on hotspots that take you directly to other Web pages. With Apple QuickTime plug-in's "faststart" feature, you can start viewing the video while it's still downloading. Although it's not true streaming media, it does offer the ability to determine whether you want to download the entire file, before the download is completed. You don't need any specialized server software to add QuickTime to your site, and most Web servers are configured for storing QuickTime files.

Recommendation

You probably already have this capability installed in your browser, but you probably don't have the QuickTimeVR plug-in option. So I highly recommend that you download the latest version, and make sure you also get the QuickTimeVR plug-in. Tons of movies, music, and VR files are available, making this one of the most popular video plug-ins on the market. The product works well on all personal computer platforms, and since you download, not just stream, the files, you can save the movie files for later playback.

The only problem is that QuickTime video files are still relatively large, so for movies of any length you'll need to wait awhile for the file to download. Apple has helped the user along by offering the ability to start playing the movie almost the minute you start the download process. This will help you determine if you really want to wait the entire time to download the movie. Apple continues to update this technology too, so you will see a lot more changes in the future. Make sure you keep checking the QuickTime site for the latest news on this technology.

NAME OF PLUG-IN: INTERVU PLAYER BY INTERVU

Location: http://www.intervu.com

Description

The *InterVu Player* lets you play any industry-standard MPEG audio video file without using specialized MPEG hardware decoders or Web servers. The first frame of the file is displayed where you embed the file, and the file will stream the video while downloading, providing full-speed cached playback from your computer's hard drive. In addition, the InterVu plug-in player links you directly to the InterVu Network where thousands of videos are available. The accompanying SmartVu Network Optimizer also will connect you to the Internet site for fastest delivery of the video.

Recommendation

Many major companies, such as FAO Schwartz and Budweiser, and sites, such as CourtTV, Major League Baseball, and the Outdoor Channel, are now using InterVu on their Web sites to deliver fast video. And with MPEG, the most TV-like full motion video compression available included as part of the InterVu plug-in, you get amazing quality and excellent audio all downloaded to your computer relatively fast. Although I think other video plug-in formats, such as the RealPlayer, actually give you access to more content, I do recommend downloading and just playing around with the InterVu player. There is enough content to justify the time spent downloading, and the quality is relatively good. You might even consider offering InterVu videos of the kids or your latest corporate seminar, since there is no need for specialized servers, and the encoding software is free and extremely easy to use.

NAME OF PLUG-IN: NETTOOB FROM DUPLEXX SOFTWARE

Location: http://www.duplexx.com

Description
NetToob offers high quality, real-time streaming audio and video using the MPEG standard. No special server software is necessary to offer or play real-time streaming files over the Internet or through an Intranet. NetToob can also play all the standard file formats such as AVI, MOV, MPG, FLC/FLI, WAV, and MIDI, regardless of whether you download them from the Web or play them directly from CD-ROMs. You can also embed links to NetToob files from with most Internet HTML-enabled e-mail readers.

The player will automatically determine the available bandwidth and stream the best quality video. The plug-in also works with virtually all browsers including America Online's own Web browser and Internet Explorer. You can also use the videos you've downloaded as screen savers if you so choose.

Recommendation
This plug-in is the only one that plays virtually all digital video standards, making it a plug-in well worth downloading. It will even play QuickTime VR files. Plus, it operates using a standard VCR-like interface, making it very easy for just about any user to use.

Before you download other video players, download this one. It covers almost every video format, meaning you only need one plug-in to play virtually any video file you might run across.

TIP

NAME OF PLUG-IN: VDOLIVE BY VDONET

Location: http://www.vdolive.com

Description

VDOLive compresses video images without compromising quality on the receiving end. With the VDOLive plug-in the speed of your connection determines the frame delivery rate: with a 28.8 Kbps modem, VDOLive runs in real time at 10 to 15 frames per second, delivering live video and audio over the Internet to your Web browser.

Recommendation

Definitely download this product. There is a lot of content, including plenty of video files and streaming live files you can view; and the quality of both the sound and video is amazing when you consider exactly how much compression is necessary.

NAME OF PLUG-IN: VIVOACTIVE BY VIVO

Location: http://www.vivo.com

Description

The *VivoActive* Player, a streaming video plug-in for Netscape Navigator, is the simplest, fastest way to get video clips on your Web page. Video for Windows AVI files can be compressed up to 250:1. These files can then be viewed without having to download the file first. VivoActive videos are transmitted using HTTP, so anyone who can view your Web pages can see your video without the need for a special video server.

This company was recently purchased by RealNetworks, so you may or may not see this player available, or you may find all the features of the plug-in rolled into the RealPlayer. If the player is no longer available at the Vivo site, check RealNetwork's site at http://www.real.com for more information.

Recommendation

I would try it. Although the quality isn't as high as other streaming video products, the compression is amazing. You'll find lots of content particularly sex oriented materials and live streaming video show using the Vivo format. So you won't be left watching only a few videos if you download this plug-in. There are literally thousands of sites that use this plug-in to deliver quick streaming recorded or live video to Web pages. All the compression tools that help you compress AVI moving files are easy to use.

NAME OF PLUG-IN: CINEWEB DIGIGAMI, INC.

Location: http://www.digigami.com

Description

Digigami CineWeb a plug-in is for viewing CineWeb streaming files such as Quicktime, AVI, MPGE, or AutoDesk Animator files. Incorporating JetStream technology, CineWeb lets you view the content as it is sent to you, in streaming format, without waiting for long downloads. CineWeb also requires no proprietary codecs or video file formats. You can even save multimedia content directly on your computer for later viewing if the author of the file allows it. CineWeb allows you to view MPGEG, AVI, MIDI, QuickTime, and WAV files directly in your browser without making you configure special helper applications.

Recommendation

I would consider downloading this plug-in simply because it lets me view so many movie file formats without having to wait for the files to download. It's one of the top ten plug-ins that I use consistently on the Internet. There's plenty of content available, installation is relatively painless, and the ability to save video files directly to my hard drive is an added benefit.

NAME OF PLUG-IN: COM ONE BY VIEWCOM

Location: http://www.com1.fr/uk/demovideo/index.html

Description

The *COM One* plug-in displays video and sound through a Web browser. With the use of the View Com Modem Kit, you can capture images and sounds regardless of their distance from the server, and with the plug-in anyone can view these files. You can have up to 16 video files on one page, all playing from a standard Web server. There is no need for a specialezed video server it you want to deploy video. Plus you can create a single Web page that offers multiple video files all that play simultaneously or are controlled by the user.

Recommendation

This is a very interesting and well-designed plug-in, but you do need the COM Modem Kit in order to create the video files. I found the entire plug-in somewhat confusing, so prepare yourself for spending time viewing the examples, and reading the online documentation. My first reaction was, why? But the more I started to play around with the plug-in and create pages with multiple video files embedded in them, I started to see some possibilities especially when considering offering online training to users on an Intranet.

SUMMARY

There you have it—the big list of plug-ins. The best of the best plug-ins available on the Internet today are all listed here in one easy to find format. But don't spend all your time here; make sure you read the rest of the chapters in this book since they provide additional plug-ins, utilities, and links that simply wouldn't fit here. Chapter 3 and Chapter 6, for example, are worth a read since they offer a glimpse of real world examples of how many of these plug-ins are used.

If you have Internet Explorer, you probably want to know exactly what ActiveX controls are available for your particular browser. If so, turn to the next chapter where you'll find several ActiveX controls you can add to your browser or even to your own Web pages.

TIP

If you have any questions about any of these plug-ins or new ones that hit the market after this book hits the store shelves, I'd be happy to lend a helping hand, although I can't provide technical support. You can email me at ckirk@alaska.net or visit my main home page located at http://www.ptialaska.net/~ckirk.

10 The Big ActiveX List

T here are literally thousands of ActiveX controls, some commercially available, and there are about the same number of Web sites that employ this technology. In this chapter I've tried to create a complete list of some of the more useful ActiveX-enabled sites, commercially available controls, and many free controls, along with some controls you might find useful if you plan on developing Web pages. This list is by no means complete. If it were, you wouldn't be able to pick up this book, let alone afford all that paper. But this chapter will give you a good idea of where to go to see and experience many ActiveX controls, and it will give you a list of resources if you want to integrate ActiveX controls on your own Web sites.

New controls are created, added, and implemented almost every minute. You can use your favorite search engine to find controls. One such engine, HotBot, located at http://www.hotbot.com, lets you search not only for ActiveX controls but also for Java applets. Check the Help file of your favorite search engine to find out if it offers a specific searching feature for applets and controls.

The best way to use this list is to go directly to the section that bests suits your needs. For example, if you're a Web page designer, go directly to the section entitled **Web Page Development** and **Utility Controls**. If you're just interested in using ActiveX controls, go to the section labeled **Web Sites That Use or Work with ActiveX Controls**. Also check out the CD for links to my Web site, *www.ptialaska. net/~ckirk*, where I'll always try to post new sites and new information about controls as soon as I can. The following pages detail other locations you should check for the latest additions to ActiveX controls. Table 10-1 lists the major ActiveX sites you should visit on a regular basis. These sites contain links to all sorts of ActiveX controls.

Again, you'll find two types of controls—those that you use if you are a developer and those you use if you are a consumer. And in some of these lists you'll also find controls that may not be specifically Web browser-oriented. Instead, you may find controls listed that actually work with Microsoft applications such as Office 97 or VBScript. You have to look carefully in order to determine whether the control is developer oriented or not and is related to a Web browser or rather a control you could used within a Web page or entire site.

TABLE 10.1: *A list of sites offering ActiveX controls.*

Site	Location	Comments
BrowserWatch	http://www.browserwatch.com	Offers a large list of controls for both consumers and developers segmented out by category. Because of the length of the list, information is not always updated; so you may find that some links are out of date, and you may find more links for developer-related controls than consumer-related controls.
Microsoft's ActiveX Site	http://www.microsoft.com/activex or http://www.microsoft.com/msdn_isv	Check the **Library** link, then search the **Developer** resource catalog. Here you will find controls for both developing and using. Many of the links, however, point to ODBC-type controls rather than browser-based controls. You have to read the information carefully. At last count there were about 3,800 controls, but of those 3,800, only several hundred were really Web-related.
ActiveX.com	http://www.activex.com	ActiveX.com offers reviews and direct links to where the controls are. Most, however, are geared more toward developers than consumers. You will find a few links that no longer work. If you come across a link that doesn't work, just look for the company's name, then try their Web site instead.
ZDNet's Hot Files	http://www.zdnet.com or http://hotfiles.zdnet.com	Excellent resource for consumer-related controls. Although some of the links may be outdated, many of the controls are rated in terms of usability and functionality.
DaveCentral	http://www.davecentral.com	Although you won't find huge amounts of ActiveX controls, you will find some of the best.
Developer.com	http://www.developer.com/directories/pages/dir.activex.html	Excellent resource for all sorts of controls used in the development process.
Activate!	www.componentworld.com/activate	If you're looking for both freeware and "pay-for" controls, this is a great place to go.

Web Sites That Use or Work with ActiveX Controls

It doesn't take a genius to figure out that many sites that utilize ActiveX controls are done by Microsoft. But Microsoft does understand the technology they create and they have created some pretty elaborate sites that use ActiveX controls in imaginative and inventive ways. Here are some impressive sites that use ActiveX. Yet remember, sometimes you don't even know you're using it, since controls download directly to your computer without fanfare. The best way to see what these sites offer in the way of controls is to first visit them with your Netscape, non-ActiveX control enabled, then fire up your Internet Explorer browser, and view the difference. You'll be amazed at how many features are offered for Explorer browsers that aren't afforded to Navigator users. You'll run across more and more as the Internet Explorer browser and ActiveX controls become more popular. Right now you'll see more Java-enabled sites, than ActiveX-enabled sites, but they're out there. So fire up the browser and get going!

Name of Site: Headtrip—The Magic 8 Ball

Location of Site: http://www.wgn.net/~headtrip/activex/magic8.htm

Nifty Things on the Site
Need advice on a big business deal? Want to know if maybe he or she is the "right one?" Stop spending money on those psychic hotlines. Instead, point your browser to this site, ask your special question, then electronically shake the *Magic 8 ball* for the answer. Your answer will appear in the browser window within seconds.

Yes, this site is totally useless, unless you want to base your life decisions on a funky little 8 ball. But it does give you an idea of how you can use ActiveX technology to create interesting interactive sites. If you're interested in other nonsensical sites, full of entertaining little ActiveX controls, make sure you check out *ActiveX and More! A Beginner's Guide*, located at *http://www.geocities.com/SiliconValley/Park/3545*, and the *Brady Bunch Lineup*, located at *www.rollins-assoc.com/brady/vsbrady.htm*. You'll also find several other controls on this page that demonstrate how to use ActiveX controls to chart information.

Some of the sites done by individuals may come and go. If you find that a site is no longer available, feel free to e-mail me and I'll let you know about any updates of sites I have. My address is ckirk@ptialaska.net.

NAME OF SITE: MICROSOFT EXPEDIA

Location of Site: http://www.expedia.com

Nifty Things on the Site
You name it, this site has it, from authentication to an excellent use of cookies and other types of interactive server/Web page technology. Although I must admit, this site uses ActiveX technology somewhat sparingly when compared to other Microsoft sites.

   The *Expedia* site is a total travel site that helps you find the best airfares, hotel packages, car rental options, and sites to see, regardless of whether you are traveling in the U.S. or overseas. It will search through multiple databases to find you the least expensive travel options.

NAME OF SITE: MICROSOFT INVESTOR

Location of Site: http://www.investor.com

Nifty Things on the Site
In my opinion, this is by far the best example of a site deploying ActiveX technology. From being able to import data from your Quicken personal accounting program, to showing you real-time stock ticker information, to allowing you to set up a portfolio that automatically updates the minute you bring up the site, this is probably the first place I would point you to if you wanted to know exactly what ActiveX technology can do for you as a user or as a Web site creator. As a matter of fact, I recommend you view it first with Netscape Navigator, then see the difference by viewing it with Internet Explorer. You'll be amazed at what you're missing.

   It's also one of the few sites you'll see that interacts with your desktop files. You can save information that you set up in your portfolio directly to your computer. Or you can take information from your computer, in particular Quicken, and interface it with the portfolio you saved on the Web site. Also take notice of pop-up menu and drop-down menu options, and a wide variety of other interface controls this site incorporates.

Name of Site: MSNBC

Location of Site: http://www.msnbc.com

Nifty Things on the Site

This site changes a great deal because, well, it's a news site. Here you'll find all sorts of small ActiveX controls, such as pop-up menus, that enhance the user interface. Again, the best way to see the difference is to view it first with Navigator, then fire up Explorer and see what you're missing.

With ActiveX and a little Java and cookies, this site can also customize the type of news you see. You can actually create your own interactive news service, complete with stock and news tickers. Click the link from the main page that lets you customize your personalized news page.

This site also employs a fair amount of Java. So pay attention by looking at the status bar at the bottom to discern when you're viewing Java applets or ActiveX controls.

TIP

Name of Site: CyberGo

Location of Site: http://www.brlabs.com

Nifty Things on the Site

Remember the old game Go? Well now you can play it directly on a Web site. You can arrange for a match online, against any opponents worldwide. Brilliance Labs has created a very inventive and interesting site that brings Go into the twenty-first century. You can play against others or against the computer.

If Go is not your game, and you need something a lot less taxing, try the ActiveX puzzle page located at *www.radanmedia.com/activex/puzzle.htm.* It's a page devoted to those little moveable pieces puzzles, where you have to arrange the puzzle pieces in numerical order. It's not fancy, but it's fast.

INTRANET AND COLLABORATION CONTROLS

Does your company want to share data easily? Is your company spread across the country? Do you want to save money communicating with other workers across your network? Are you looking for an easier way to share data without having to have a computer science degree? The controls listed in this section outline exactly how you can share data over a network, regardless of whether that network is right in your office or spread across thousands and thousands of miles.

Although Chapter 6 covers Intranet-related ActiveX controls in detail, to make it easily accessible, I've included a list of controls here as well so all the controls are available in one easy reference. Intranet and collaboration controls work especially well within an internal network, when you are trying to communicate and share data at the same time. Some of these controls work best for those who are supporting networks, whereas others work best simply sharing your ideas.

NAME OF CONTROL: PCANYWHERE EXPRESS

Location of Control: http://www.symantec.com

What the Control Does
pcAnywhere Express, an ActiveX control, plug-in, and Java client, is Symantec's remote control program that helps you control a PC from anywhere on a network through an ActiveX-enabled browser. pcAnywhere Express is actually a collection of communication components that provides remote control capabilities within a browser interface.

How You Could Use This Control
With pcAnywhere Express, you can remotely access both data and applications on another PC. This means you can run applications, copy, delete, move, or add new files to a remote PC, or simply watch as the other person controls the PC. You can easily use this product to help support PC users, remotely install software, or collaborate on documents across a network.

NAME OF CONTROL: CARBON COPY

Location of control: http://www.microcom.com

What the Control Does

This control lets you control another computer over the Intranet, the Internet, or via dial-up options. You can view data, run applications, connect to network resources, exchange e-mail through your company's network, and do just about anything you could normally do on your computer remotely. With version 5.0 you can voice chat, transfer files, print to any remote printer, and let others on the Internet know your PC is available for remote connections.

How You Could Use This Control

This is a must-have commercial control if you travel or need access to a network from a remote location, or if you are a support technician. With *Carbon Copy* you can access and control your PC remotely as if you were actually sitting at your desk in front of your computer. It does take a considerable amount of memory, at least 32MB of RAM, to operate fast and error free. And it does take a little understanding of your computer to understand how to connect to remote resources, but it's a must have if you travel or need to support other computers. Not all machines on your network will need this application, so don't go hog wild installing it on every machine on your Intranet, but do install it on those that need it, especially those users who may be totally clueless and need a helping hand from time to time.

NAME OF CONTROL: INTRALAUNCH

Location of Control: http://www.particle.net/IntraLaunch

What This Control Does

IntraLaunch is an ActiveX control that lets you create an entire Web-oriented desktop. With IntraLaunch you can create links to executable programs through a Web page. As long as these executable programs reside on the user's computer or within a network drive, the user can access EXE, COM, BAT, LNK, PIF, and other types of Windows 95/98-accessible files by clicking links on a Web page. You can also display default directories, password protect menu items, attach sound events, and pass along parameters to programs.

How You Could Use This Control

Run, don't walk, to Particle Software's site and download a demo of this amazing set of controls. This is probably one of the most valuable Intranet controls you could use since it turns your Intranet and everything on it into one big clickable link. With IntraLaunch you can build a secure Web-based menuing interface for all the programs and files for all the users on your Internet. IntraLaunch lets you link and execute all sorts of files including EXE, COM, and LNK files from within your Web browser. You never have to leave your browser to access files not only on your desktop but on servers or other computers as well. You can password protect those files or programs you don't want others to have access to and you can attach sounds to certain types of events such as copying files so it alerts the user. Just think, you can pretty much throw away the user's desktop, replacing it entirely with Internet Explorer. Which means you could cut down on training the users on your Intranet how to find, use, or manipulate their desktop computers.

NAME OF CONTROL: FARALLON'S LOOK@ME

Location of Control: http://www.farallon.com

How This Control Works

This control displays the screen of another computer that is running either *Look@Me* or Timbuktu Pro, from Farallon Communications. Look@Me is compatible with Windows 95 and Windows NT, but Windows NT computers cannot be observed.

How You Can Use This Control

Of course the best use of this control is to control another PC, and thus this is an excellent way to provide technical support to users. This control also comes in the form of a plug-in; the full description of what this control offers is listed there.

NAME OF CONTROL: EARTHTIME ACTIVEX

Location of Control: http://www.starfishsoftware.com

What This Control Does

EarthTime gives you the correct time for up to eight cities around the world within your browser. EarthTime will calculate the time differences, show you the daylight and darkness of the cities, and will also provide information about the cities, including area codes, the local language, and the currency used.

How You Could Use This Control

If you travel a great deal or if your company is spread across the country, there is no doubt this control can help you keep track of the time, area code, or local language of those co-workers who might work worlds away. With a simple page and this control, everyone on your network will know exactly when it's a good time to call, whether it's dark or light, and what kind of currency the workers use.

NAME OF CONTROL: WINFRAME WEB CLIENT

Location of Web Site: http://www.citrix.com

What This Control Does

For the first time, you can work with any 16- or 32-bit Windows application embedded in or linked to a standard HTML Web page. With *WinFrame* you can enrich your Internet/Intranet Web pages by seamlessly integrating any off-the-shelf Windows-based application with WinFrame application server software and WinFrame Web Client from Citrix.

How You Could Use This Control

You can open up all those Windows applications to those users who may not have the necessary hard disk space or computer processing power. The server does all the processing, sending the information and screen back to the user. Citrix offers this control in the form of a plug-in. If you need other ideas on how to use this control, check out the description for its plug-in cousin.

NAME OF CONTROL: SCRIPTACTIVE PLUG-IN

Location of Control: http://www.ncompasslabs.com/scriptactive/
download.htm

What This Control/Plug-In Does

The *ScriptActive* plug-in lets anyone using Netscape Navigator 2.0 or above use ActiveX controls within Netscape Navigator. This is a standard plug-in that downloads and installs just like any other plug-in.

How You Could Use This Control/Plug-In

Can't convince some of your users to use Internet Explorer instead of Netscape Navigator? Would you like to implement ActiveX controls in your network, but are concerned about security problems regarding the Internet Explorer browser? If you've invested in both Netscape and Microsoft technologies and want to marry the two, this is the plug-in you could use to do just that. No longer do you have to isolate Netscape Navigator users simply because the browser they choose to use doesn't incorporate ActiveX technology. By installing this plug-in just about any control you've added to your site can be used by Navigator users.

I include this control/plug-in here because it's more likely you'll run into the need for this type of plug-in on a network more so than just with individual users. It's hard to wrestle software away from users, especially if they are familiar with the use of a certain software program. If the only thing holding you back in terms of upgrading your Intranet to utilizing ActiveX controls on your network is that a large percentage of users are still using Navigator, you now have no excuse. So start adding those ActiveX controls and get your Netscape users online with ScriptActive so they can see what they are missing.

Some of these controls could actually be considered development controls, but I'm putting them here in the Intranet section simply because they lend themselves so well to use on an Intranet, as well as across the Internet.

NAME OF CONTROL: NET2000 ACTIVEX CONTROLS

Location of Control: http://www6.zdnet.com/cgi-bin/texis/swlib/hot-files/info.html?fcode=000H4R or check Novell's Web site at http://www.novell.com

What This Control Does

Do you have a Novell network? Are you tired of getting up and going over to the server to do the network administration? Want to have quick access to those Novell tools from within a Web page? *Net2000 ActiveX* controls is a beta version of a suite of controls that lets you program into a Web page several Novell tools, including controls that will let you monitor servers, mount and dismount volumes, control user access, modify print queues, and load NLMs.

How You Could Use This Control

Access Novell network options from any computer on your network through a Web page? Just think, the next time you're paged, you can instantly jump to any computer and fix just about any minor Novell network problem you might run into, from clearing out print queues to changing user access options. But take that one step further. Say you're on call and you get a call in the middle of the night from a night worker who needs help clearing out a print queue. No need to drag yourself into the office. If your Intranet is connected to the Internet or if you have dial-up access, you can control just about any function on your Novell network. Net2000 gives you session, directory, and server control, which means you can do just about anything you'll ever need to do as a network administrator.

NAME OF CONTROL: ACTIVEX INTRANET SOLUTION

Location of Control: http://www.auscomp.com

What This Control Does

This turns your Intranet into an easy to navigate Web site, based on a "tree structure" metaphor, much like that seen in the old Windows 3.1 File Manager. Each directory on your Web site is turned into an icon of a file folder, a folder that lets you click to expand or collapse the view. When you expand the view of a directory, you see all the subdirectories and files inside that directory. Inside each folder you can see exactly what kind of files are stored in the folder.

How You Could Use This Control

Tired of setting up Table of Contents Web pages just so your Intranet site navigation is easier for all the users on your network? Want to use a simple expandable file folder metaphor? Do you have absolutely no programming experience but want to add such a feature? Intranet 3.0 offers an easy to understand navigational tool through the use of ActiveX (and Java). All you have to do is change a few text files and you'll have this feature up and running in no time. Plus, this product is free. To understand what this control offers, you have to experience it for yourself. And Auscomp uses it throughout it's own Web site so you can experience it for yourself without having to download a thing.

*Also check out SiteMapper, a similar ActiveX control available from Quiksoft, located at www.quicksoft.com. SiteMapper, like **ActiveX Intranet Solution**, creates an easy to use nested listing of pages on your site. Quiksoft also has several other ActiveX controls for use on both Intranets and the Internet.*

TIP

NAME OF CONTROL: DISABLE PRO

Location of Control: http://www.infinet.com/~adkins/

What This Control Does

This control disables certain features of Windows 95 (and 98), such as the Run option of the Start menu, the Shut Down option of Windows 95. It can also disable portions of the Control Panel, along with File Sharing, Printer Sharing, or the running of MS-DOS programs. These are controls you add to Web pages that, when viewed by the user, disable the options you include in the page itself.

How You Could Use This Control

Want to control a user's computer remotely and turn off certain features so you can troubleshoot or install certain software applications? This collection of controls lets you control a variety of Windows 95 features by simply viewing the Web page with the control embedded in it. Since these are kind of building block controls, the types of things you could do with these controls are entirely up to you. Say you want to turn off

File Sharing over your network. Simply create a Web page, include the control and then point your users to the site and File Sharing is immediately turned off.

Document Viewers

These controls offer you the ability to view documents saved in file formats that Web browsers can't understand and display. From PowerPoint, to Excel, to PageMaker, to Lotus 1-2-3, to AutoCad files, these controls let you view these types of files directly in Internet Explorer 4.0. Therefore all the existing information you might have on your network could easily be placed on your Web server, and with the help of these viewers that information can easily be viewed without conversion of any kind. Every network administrator should consider purchasing at least one, if not more, of these controls so viewing data over an Intranet is easy for every user on the Internet.

Name of Control: QuickView Plus

Location of Site: http://www.inso.com

What the Control Does
Voted PC Magazine's editor's choice in 1997, this ActiveX control lets you view over 200 different file types directly in your Web browser. With *QuickView* you can view Word, Excel, Freelance, Lotus, Outlook, Eudora, and a wide variety of word processing file formats. You can even view Macintosh word processing and spreadsheet file formats, and a wide variety of database file formats, including Access, FoxBase, Works, and R:Base. Graphic formats are also supported, including PC Paintbrush, Corel Presentations, and PowerPoint files.

What You Could Do With This Control
This is one of those controls you simply need to have on your system because it provides access to virtually any type of data on an Intranet or the Internet. With QuickView you can find, view, and print just about any type of document, even though you may not have the program that created the file. You see the file exactly as you would if you had the application installed. If you want to see the control for yourself in action, you can download a 30-day, full-working trial version from Inso's Web site.

If you are running an Intranet, or simply have lots of people send you documents, this is an excellent control to own. Virtually any type of file can be opened from some of the most popular applications. It's definitely worth the investment.

NAME OF CONTROL: FULCRUM DOCUMENT VIEWER FOR ACTIVEX

Location of Site: http://fulcrum2.fulcrum.com/

What the Control Does
The *Fulcrum Document Viewer for ActiveX* lets users view, navigate, and manipulate non-HTML-formatted documents without leaving their Web browser. Like Adobe Acrobat, with the Fulcrum FulViewer you can view files in their native formats with all fonts, graphics, and other features left intact. You can place Word, Corel WordPerfect, Microsoft Excel, Lotus 1-2-3, and PowerPoint documents on a Web server and enable the users of the network to view all the features of these files without having to have the application that created the file. In addition, users can cut and paste information from retrieved files and copy it to other applications, or even run applications such as PowerPoint directly from their Web browser. There is no need to convert documents to HTML or launch helper applications to access information.

How You Could Use the Control
How could you not use this product is the question. This control should be able to display just about any document your users might create. That means your users don't have to convert any files to HTML format, and you don't have to create numerous Web pages to link directly to the information stored on your server.

NAME OF CONTROL: AUTOCAD'S WHIP!

Location of Control: http://www.autodesk.com

How This Control Works
The *WHIP!* control allows AutoCad users to view, send, and share design content over an Intranet. Based on the same rendering technology as the high-performance WHIP! driver in AutoCAD Release 13, the

WHIP! control offers you the ability to view AutoCad files without having to convert them into bitmaps, JPGs, or GIFs. With Whip! you can pan, zoom, and embed URL Web page links directly in files.

How You Could Use This Control

Any engineering or architectural company needs this control, as does any company that has any type of AutoCad drawings. You could use this control to view AutoCad documents without having to have the expensive AutoCad software. If you are remodeling a house, need access to engineering drawings, or simply want to view AutoCad files, this is the control to use.

Name of Control: Acrobat Reader

Location of Control: http://www.adobe.com/

How the Control Works

The *Adobe Acrobat PDF* Control for ActiveX uses the Adobe Acrobat Reader to let anyone using Internet Explorer and view and navigate Adobe Portable Document Format (PDF) files just like the Adobe Acrobat Reader control does. You can create PDF files from virtually any application. And through the use of this control, you can search through various PDF document files for the text that meets your search criteria.

How You Could Use This Control

If you installed the Adobe Acrobat 3.0 on every machine in your Intranet, users could print to PDF files, placing those files on your Web server, instead of printing to paper. Then anyone who needed to print out these files, whether they be policy manuals, promotional brochures, forms, or even faxes, by simply firing up their Explorer browser and using the Acrobat PDF Control to view, then print the files. With such a control you really could create an almost paperless office, giving people the control to print information only on demand. No more memos, no more thick manuals nobody every reads, no more forms stacked up in a closet gathering dust or brochures that end up in the trash bin because the pricing information is no longer valid. Instead the most up-to-date information is always available at the click of a button.

TIP

More and more files are becoming available in Adobe Acrobat format on the Web. This is a must-have control if you use Internet Explorer and want to view forms, manuals, and other files in their native form.

CONFERENCING, COLLABORATION, AND CONNECTIVITY

Whether you're two doors down or thousands of miles away, these controls help you collaborate interactively by voice or text, or by transferring of files. For some you'll need a multimedia PC, for others simply your Internet Explorer or ActiveX-enabled Netscape Web browser. Some, like *CallWorks*, bridge the gap between the Internet and telephone networks, whereas others keep it strictly on the Internet. These controls can work not only within Intranets but also across the Internet.

NOTE

Just remember, any form of communication you do over the Internet is neither entirely secure, nor private.

NAME OF CONTROL: ONLIVE TALKER

Location of Control: http://www.onlive.com

What the Control Does
The *OnLive Talker* lets you hold real-time voice communications with others across a network or across the Internet. You can hear and speak to other conference members. Featuring H.323 interoperability, users can talk to others using other Internet telephony products as well.

How You Could Use This Control
Want to meet new people? Interested in talking to others across the globe? Need to communicate with a group of people, but want to save money in long-distance conference calling? This is an excellent application, although it does require a special server in order to use it within your own network. Instead of having to make long-distance calls, you could collaborate and talk to a group of people in real time. All the others need is the control and a multimedia-enabled PC. Within seconds of connecting to the server, attendees will be able to talk to each other. Facilitators can control who joins, who speaks at what time, and who needs to be silenced if need be. Save thousands of dollars the next time you want to conference call with others.

The sound quality of this product is fantastic. If you want to save money conference calling others across a network, this is a much better product than the one-on-one Internet telephony products like NetMeeting, Internet Phone, or others. Also, since this product utilizes the browser as the interface, the user can easily click to a page to participate in a conference, without having to launch a separate application.

NAME OF CONTROL: CALLWORKS CONTROL

Location of Control: http://www.callworks.com

What This Control Does

Working with Internet Explorer and the *CallWorks* ActiveX control you can make calls to any phone in the world over the Internet. You simply fill out the registration form from the CallWorks Web site, let the site transfer the control to your computer, then once given an account number, you can start making calls from your PC. You'll need at least 16MB of RAM memory, Internet Explorer 3.01 or above, and a sound card, speakers, and a microphone attached to your computer.

How You Could Use This Control

I'm a big cheerleader for saving money making long-distance calls, and being the author of the *Internet Phone Connection*, I can tell you that you can get very good sound quality making phones calls both to other PC users and to telephones over the Internet, depending on your Internet connection. But you must have a relatively good grasp of how to make your computer, microphone, sound card, and speakers work, and you must be ready to experiment with different microphone settings and software sound or codec settings. And be aware, you may get relatively good sound quality with one phone call and then awful sound quality the next. It all depends on your Internet connection and the congestion of the Internet. At 16 cents a minute for most U.S. phone calls, unless you can't get low-cost long-distance phone service in your area, this is well worth looking into; or if you travel and can't get good calling card rates, this is a decent service to use. But even I, who live in Alaska, can get ten cents a minute, so although the ActiveX control works great, the cost isn't that great.

TIP

For more information about Internet telephony, check out www.von.com, or my book, "The Internet Phone Connection." More information about how I use Internet telephony is available on my Web site at http://www.ptialaska.net/~ckirk/.

Name of Control: ichat

Location of Control: http://www.ichat.com/

How This Control Works

The *ichat* ActiveX control allows users to communicate via real-time chat through a Web page. Web sites which are chat-enabled with ichat's ROOMS software offer anyone with the Internet Explorer browser the ability to communicate with others in real time in a text-based format. You can create public and private chat rooms, letting in only those who need to be in.

How You Could Use This Control

Is your company spread across the country? Do you want to offer better customer support? Are you looking for another way to collaborate on things without having face-to-face meetings? With ichat you can create text-based conferences. Ichat lets you conduct text chats. Administrators can control the flow of the conversation, and other users can talk to each other privately while a public conference is being held. Transcripts of the chats can be saved and links to Web sites, e-mail addresses, files, etc. can be included within the chats themselves.

Of course the best thing you could use this control for is to replace face-to-face meetings, or to conduct electronic board meetings online. I volunteer for a nonprofit organization, and sometimes with the weather, people's schedules, and what not, having a face-to-face meeting is just not an option. So we decided a while back to conduct our meetings online. That way I can attend, regardless of where I might be. Our board president can attend while watching the kids, and other board members don't have to worry about being at a particular place. We simply schedule the meeting for a particular day and time, then all meet electronically. More board members attend and better still we have an instant transcript of who said what. No more need for the secretary to take notes, then transcribe them; and we can easily put up the notes online for those who may not be able to log in.

TIP

Ichat is a widely used chat control (and plug-in) that provides some relatively advanced features. By far, ichat offers the common user a much easier to use interface than most IRC clients. However, since it requires you to download a client plug-in or control if you are setting up a chat site for your Web site, you may find people somewhat reluctant at first. Because of this reluctance, more and more chat servers are beginning to use Java as the client, since Java is built into most browsers. The only problem is that Java is much slower than specific plug-ins/controls like ichat. If you're thinking of setting up your own server, you should take a look at some of the Java chat server/client options and compare them to what ichat has to offer. The first difference you'll notice is the speed ichat has over most Java-enabled systems.

One Java-enabled chat option that you can even add to your own Web page is offered through ParaChat, located at http://www.parachat.com. If you want to see the real differences, set up a Parachat page and compare it to an ichat room.

MULTIMEDIA AND TRAINING CONTROLS

Multimedia and training controls help you deliver real online training direct from a Web page. Like their plug-in cousins, these controls offer access to sound, video, and animation, or help you create interactive training Web pages. With some of these controls you can create slide shows, PowerPoint presentations, or simply add audio to your Web pages. Whatever feature they may offer, every company has a need to convert videos, stand-up and on disk training to their Intranet. If you are still wasting money and time trying to teach computing basics, safety information, or human resources, consider augmenting all types of training you do with interactive Web pages that utilize these controls. Not only can you replace some training, thereby saving you money, but also you can extend the training you do give by making it and additional supporting materials available on your Intranet, or by offering training remotely to those on the Internet.

Training is not the only thing you can use multimedia options for. Adding Real Audio or streaming video can jazz up any site and extend the content you have available. Although some products require specialized servers, some file types can actually be placed directly on a Web-based server. You should check the development sections of the sites offering these products for more information on exactly what is needed if you plan on offering specialized files on your site.

If you're a consumer and not a producer, definitely take a few minutes to download some of the recommended controls. Although the quality of the voice and video is based on the speed of your connection to the Internet, your Internet provider's speed and connection to the rest of the Internet, and the speed of your computer, I think you'll be surprised at how many of these products actually do work and work well.

NAME OF CONTROL: VIVOACTIVE PLAYER FOR ACTIVEX

Location of Control: http://www.vivo.com

What the Control Does
The *VivoActive Player* for ActiveX lets you view streaming Vivo videos from within a Web page. The video could be live video or recorded video coming from a Vivo streaming server.

How You Could Use This Control
If you want to check out training videos, or view movie clips, or maybe you missed a conference and want to check out the keynote speaker, this is an excellent control to use. From Bill Nye the Science Guy to movie trailers from FineLine Features, you'll find plenty of content for the Vivo control. This is definitely a control you could use for entertainment and business-oriented information.

TIP

This control is widely used for sex-oriented streaming video sites. Remember this if you plan on gathering the kids around the computer. There are literally hundreds of sites now offering live sex shows through streaming Vivo audio connections, so if you're into this kind of thing, this is the control you'll need.

NAME OF CONTROL: VDOLIVE

Location of Control: http://www.vdolive.com

What the Control Does
The *VDOLive* ActiveX control brings real-time audio and video right into Internet Explorer, without the need for a helper application. Video is downloaded progressively from a server. This type of download is called streaming and offers relatively good sound and video quality.

In order for you to offer VDOLive files, you'll need the VDOLive server software.

How You Could Use This Control

Like Vivo, VDOLive offers very good streaming audio and video which means you can watch television from other countries, view training videos, watch movie trailers, and view live streaming video from a variety of sources including trade shows, specialized seminars, and sex shows. You can even get the weather report from Israel's award winning Channel 2 weather program or watch France's television news station, France 3, broadcast live every day. VDOLive is also used at the SuperMarket of the Internet, a kind of Internet QVC that lets you watch and shop interactively. Visit the VDOLive site gallery, located at *www.vdoguide.com*, for more ideas on exactly what you'll see.

Although I think RealPlayer is really the winner in terms of quality and depth of content, for some reason the content providers that use VDOLive offer a very wide range of content, some of which you can't find with RealPlayer. This is definitely a must-see control. Take an evening out, download the control, and check out the content. If you have a slow connection, try connecting at a less busy time to give the control all the bandwidth it can get.

NAME OF CONTROL: REALPLAYER

Location of Control: http://www.real.com

What This Control Does

This control allows you to view and/or hear Real files, sometimes called Real Audio or Real Video files. *RealPlayer* files can either stream "live" through a Real server, or they can stream through a standard Web server. RealPlayer files can also link directly to Web sites.

How You Could Use This Control

Adding video or audio to any Web page makes that page stand out. But adding Real Audio or Video files to your Intranet goes beyond simply the entertainment value. This control could be easily used to create interactive training guides that work in conjunction with information stored on Web pages. Because you can link and time the changing of

Web pages with Real Video or Real Audio files, you don't have to know much more than how to create a page, copy and paste a link, and record a Real Audio file. For anyone who has ever ventured into creating multimedia digital training programs, you know it can be a long and arduous task. By recording videos, adding audio, and placing links within the audio or video RealPlayer files, you can quickly and easily create interactive training and communication applications.

That means you can add audio from the latest shareholder's meeting, or place video from a particular training video on a Web page. Your Web pages can now come to life, and offer more than just static text to your co-workers.

You also have access to thousands of radio stations, hundreds of television stations, movie trailers, audio books, training videos, and more. In essence, this product extends the content you can get on the Internet. No longer is it just boring text and graphics. Instead you have connections to the world that offer you real-time news, information, and entertainment, 24-hours a day.

TIP

Although Internet Explorer 2.0 and above contains the Real Audio control, you may want to upgrade to the latest version of the player/control so you can see some of the newer content developed for the latest RealPlayer control.

This is a must-have control. Every day I tune into radio stations around the world, including radio stations in my home town, Tulsa, Oklahoma, and my parents home town, Houston, Texas. I never have to ask Mom how the weather is, or wonder what's going on in the place I grew up in. Instead I just fire up my browser and tune in. I can even listen to the police scanner in Los Angeles, or the airline control tower in Houston. Sources of Real content include *www.policescanner.com*, *www.timecast.com*, and *www.audionet.com*. You'll find audio books, live broadcasts, links to radio and TV stations, and more. If you want to see how I've incorporated Real Audio files, check out *http://www.ptialaska.net/~radio/*.

NAME OF CONTROL: HTML SHOW ACTIVEX CONTROL

Location of Web Site: http://www.quiksoft.com/htmlshow/

What This Control Does
This control displays an HTML Web page in another Web page, creating a slide show effect out of multiple Web pages. Much like animated

GIFs, instead of displaying GIFs, a Web page displays standard HTML pages.

How You Could Use This Control

Do you go to trade shows and want to show off your Web site with a rolling demo? This is the perfect tool for doing this. Do you want to create a simple timed presentation that anyone could view from any Web site? Again, this is the perfect tool. Each HTML file can be programmed to display for a certain amount of time, and can run at certain times of the day, making it possible for you to have updated information on your site at a particular time of day. You can also scramble the sequence each time the site is loaded, making sure that viewers of the site see a new page at the beginning of the presentation each time they view the site. The things you could do are unlimited. You could have the stock price and news of your company scroll through your site. You could create a "Tip of the Day" page that rotates through multiple pages of tips for your users, essentially using it as an electronic ever-changing billboard.

NAME OF CONTROL: MICROSOFT POWERPOINT ANIMATION PLAYER FOR ACTIVEX

Location of Site: http://www.microsoft.com/mspowerpoint/internet/player/default.htm

What the Control Does

Coupled with the PowerPoint Publisher, the *Animation Player* is the quickest way to publish your PowerPoint presentations in Web pages. The PowerPoint Publisher compresses, then converts, your PowerPoint presentations into Web-accessible presentations via the PowerPoint Animation Player. You can also use the application to add Real Audio sound files so you can narrate or add music or sound to your presentation.

How You Could Use the Control

It's hard to find a conference, training session, or seminar where the presenters aren't using PowerPoint to present their ideas and information. Now anyone in your company can view and hear the PowerPoint presentations other employees and vendors have created. But it doesn't stop at just marketing or sales presentations. With PowerPoint presentations virtually anyone could create interactive training materials with all sorts of animations, photos, graphics, sound, voice, and links to Web sites.

Want to teach people how to use your e-mail program? Struggling with teaching a whole bunch of users how to use Lotus Notes? Planning on teaching an auditorium full of people the ins and outs of Microsoft Office, but also want to make that presentation available to those who cannot attend? This is the way to do it. Create a PowerPoint presentation, then turn it into a Web-enabled presentation with the PowerPoint Publisher. As long as the people viewing your presentation are using the PowerPoint Animation Player for ActiveX, they can see and hear everything contained in your presentation.

If you do a lot of presentations or go to a lot of seminars, this is an excellent control to have. You can quickly access presentations with a click of a button.

NAME OF CONTROL: ASYMETRIX'S NEURON

Location of Control: http://www.asymetrix.com/toolbook/neuron/

How This Control Works
If your company uses the Asymetrix ToolBook to create multimedia training projects, the *Neuron* control is the best solution to give Web-based access to all the projects produced with any of the Asymetrix ToolBook II authoring products. The Neuron control lets the user view and play presentations, kiosks, courseware, and other multimedia applications produced in ToolBook.

How You Could Use This Control
This is an excellent way to revamp the content your company might have had created with the Asymetrix ToolBook II training and multimedia program. As a matter of fact, this is about the only way you can revamp existing content into Web-based format. If you haven't checked out what Asymetrix ToolBook II can do in terms of online and interactive training, make sure you check out their Web site for more information. You can create and keep track of training records easily and create compelling training materials with the ToolBook II product.

Some other controls you should check out include the ShockWave ActiveX control, located at www.macromedia.com, and the VivoActiveX player, located at www.vivo.com. The ShockWave control, like it's cousin the ShockWave plug-in, lets you view ShockWave-enabled sites, which contain interactive multimedia. The VivoActiveX player lets you view Vivo video-enhanced sites. These sites offer streaming video through your Explorer browser. Both can provide great training tools online. You might also check out the Demo-X control, which will play Demo-X files.

WEB PAGE DEVELOPMENT AND UTILITY CONTROLS

There are plenty of ActiveX controls that help you, the developer of Web pages, integrate Web technologies with your existing network, and that make gathering data from users easier. One of the best places to find ActiveX controls is ZDNet's Software Library. If you search the library with the keywords "activex controls," you'll find hundreds of ActiveX controls you can download for free. Here are some controls you might consider downloading for use on your system. From controls that control users computers to controls that connect to data acquisition equipment and display data from that equipment through a Web page, you'll find several listed on ZDNet's site. If you are thinking of incorporating ActiveX controls into your site, you need to look here first so you don't reinvent the wheel.

In this section I provide you with the name, location and description of the control. But unlike in the previous sections I'm not including examples of how you could use the control, except in certain cases when its warranted. If you're a developer you probably already know what you're looking for and how you could incorporate it into your site. What you'll find here is that many of these controls are simply design-oriented controls that are relatively self-explanatory. For those that may not be as apparent as others, that's when I include some ideas of how the control could be used in the design of your site.

Remember, most of these controls are not like plug-ins where you download the plug-in, create the file, then have the user view the Web site with the data file and plug-in embedded in the page. Instead, think of many of these controls not as end-user programs, but building blocks for your Web site. You download the controls, embed the instructions into your Web site, place the controls on your server, then when the user runs across the page that contains the control, the control is sent to the user's system.

NAME OF CONTROL(S): DAMEWARE ACTIVEX COMPONENT PACKETS

Location of Control: http://www.dameware.com/controls.htm

What These Controls Do

From controls that let you control various Windows NT server options, to controls that let you dial the phone directly from a Web page, to controls that pop up calculators right from a link in a Web page, you'll find numerous solid development controls from *DameWare*. Although these are "pay-for" controls and not shareware or freeware, you can view the control online and see for yourself whether the control is what you need or want. Most controls cost less than $30 and contain less than several hundred K.

NAME OF CONTROL: BLUE SKY SOFTWARE'S SMARTHELP

Location of Control: http://www.blue-sky.com

How This Control Works

The *SmartHelp* control allows Web authors to place a help button on their pages. When the user clicks on the button, a Windows help file is brought up, offering the user the standard Windows help interface they are used to.

How You Could Use This Control

If you are developing any sites that require user input, additional plug-ins or software, or simply are somewhat elaborate, you should include help files. With this type of control you can easily create a simple Windows help interface that users are familiar with, providing them with all the information they need without having to move from one Web page to another.

TIP

If you are developing pages for an Intranet, you should really look into using this type of control. The more help you can provide a user, the less support you'll need to do in the long run.

Names of Controls: 3D BorderFrame, 3D Button, AVI Player

Location of Controls: http://www.microhelp.com

What the Controls Do

Mh3dFrame is a frame control that allows for the creation of a frame with several border options. It also allows bitmaps to be placed on the background of the control. This can provide a three-dimensional look to a framed site.

Mh3dButn is a command button that allows multiple line captions, up and down button states, and multiple bitmaps to be placed on the control to represent various states. These are mainly ActiveX buttons that you can place on a Web page.

MhAVI plays AVI files. The AVI files can include both video and audio. MhAVI supports a three-dimensional, optional play bar and complete programmatic control from within a Web page. Although Internet Explorer can play AVI files, this control gives you design control over the displaying and playing of AVI files.

Name of Control: Micrografx's ABC Quicksilver

Location of Control: http://www.micrografx.com

What the Control Does

The *ABC QuickSilver* control lets Web developers use Micrografx Designer to create and display vector graphics instead of raster graphics on the Web. You can use the output from ABC Flowcharter or Micrografx Designer to create Web content. The QuickSilver control then lets the user work with these files online. The advantage of vector graphics is that they can be resized and they can retain the format of the original graphic file as it was created.

Name of Control: InterCAP Graphics Systems, Inc.'s ActiveCGM

Location of Control: http://www.intercap.com

What the Control Does

The *ActiveCGM* control offers you the ability to open another page within a browser window and incorporate graphic files such as an MPEG movie file, or possibly an expanded view of a drawing. Using ActiveCGM, anyone browsing a Web page can zoom in and see the finest details of a drawing without losing the quality of the original. You can't do this with a traditional Web browser. If there are fine line details a graphic file needs to display in varying views, this is one control you could use for the zoom-in technique.

NAME OF CONTROL: ANIMATED BUTTON

Location of Control: http://www.microsoft.com

What the Control Does

The *Animated Button* control will display various frame sequences of an AVI. Depending on the button state, you can control which frame sequence is viewed and the state of that frame.

The AVI file must be RLE compressed or 8-bit compressed before this control can be used.

NAME OF CONTROL: NCOMPASS LABS' BILLBOARD MANAGER

Location of Control: http://www.ncompasslabs.com

What the Control Does

This control displays several bitmaps as billboards and performs inline transitions. The control supports a large number of transitions, all of which happen in the control as it's placed inside the Web page. If you want to use more than just the <Marquee> tag in Explorer, and want to present varying information in flashy style, you should try out this control. It's relatively small once loaded, and very quick to display the animation used.

NAME OF CONTROLS: KWERY CORP. CALENDAR, KWERY CLOCK, KWERY PREVIEW

Location of Controls: http://www.kwery.com

What the Controls Do

The *Kwery Calendar* control allows you to place a month-at-a-time calendar inside your Web page. The Calendar control allows you to save notes and bitmaps directly embedded in the days.

The *Kwery Clock* control provides a clock with an analog or digital display format. It can also hold up to nine alarms set by the developer or user; when an alarm time is reached, an event is triggered that can be detected with code.

If you need to use date and time options within your Web site, these controls work relatively quickly and are easy controls to add to your site.

The *Kwery Preview* control allows you to retrieve information stored in Microsoft Office document files' summary information fields. Such Office applications as Excel 95, PowerPoint 95, Project 95, and Word 95 contain summary information. You could use this type of control to give the browsing visitor more information about the file before the visitor opens the file with an application or another viewer control.

NAME OF CONTROL: PROTOVIEW DEVELOPMENT CORP.'S CALENDAR & DATE

Location of Control: http://www.protoview.com/

What the Control Does

This control displays a calendar for the browsing visitor. The calendar control allows the user to make date entries in an easy form format. The control has a dropdown calendar that can be used to select a date from the form. If you need to provide easy field entry and formatting for dates and times in a calendar form format, this is an excellent control.

NAME OF CONTROL: LIVEUPDATE'S CRESCENDO **PLUS**

Location of Control: http://www.liveupdate.com/crescendo.html/

What the Control Does
Crescendo is a MIDI music player for Web browsers. It will embed a CD-like control pane into the Web page. You can also make the control invisible, and set it to play music in the background as the page is loading. It's unique features allow for the music to stream in real time over low bandwidth connections. If you want better options for playing MIDI files other than those afforded the current Internet Explorer browser, you should consider using this control.

NAME OF CONTROL: IMAGEFX PLANETFX

Location of Control: http://www.imagefx.com

What the Control Does
PlanetFX provides the special effects for displaying images, text, and labels. The control offers over 100 special effects that add additional impact to your Web page with little effort and without having the user download elaborate plug-ins. The special effects include wipes, diagonals, pushes, splits, blinds, crushes, rolls, and many more. You can also control timing, placement, speed, and events tied to user interactions. If you don't want to create PowerPoint presentations but want to use the same type of animation features afforded in PowerPoint, you should consider adding this control to your site. Check out ImageFX's Web site for examples of how the control works.

Try downloading Microsoft ActiveX Controls Programming Reference from Microsoft's Web site or from Zdnet's Internet User area located at http://www.zdnet.com. Information for each of the ActiveX controls included with Internet Explorer 3.0 is provided in this reference. For each control, this Word file reference includes information on properties, methods, and events supported by the control.

NAME OF CONTROL: RUMBA OBJECTX

Location of Control: http://www.walldata.com

What the Control Does
The *Rumba ObjectX* control allows you to place host access or access to another server inside a Web page. With this control, Web authors and developers can offer host connectivity with much less code than is required with the EHLLAPI option. If you need to connect Web users to mainframe or server systems, consider adding this control to your site.

NAME OF CONTROL: STOCK TICKER

Location of Control: http://www.microsoft.com

What This Control Does
This control is used to display changing data continuously. It downloads the specified URL at regular intervals and displays that data. The data can be in a text or XRT format.

You can see this kind of control in action if you visit Microsoft's Investor site located at www.investor.com. At Investor.com a stock ticker control is incorporated when you customize your settings for the site.

NAME OF CONTROL: SURROUND VIDEO

Location of Control: http://www.bdiamond.com

What This Control Does
The *Surround Video*™ *SDK* is a collection of tools developers can use to add 360° panoramic images to a Web page. The Surround Video™ SDK offers progressive rendering and image hotspots that link to other Web pages. There are four components to Surround Video™ SDK: the *Surround Video Editor*, which allows authoring of Surround Video Images; the *Surround Video API*, the runtime component responsible for image display; the *Surround Video Link Editor*, which provides for the authoring of *Surround Video Images* suitable for use on the Internet; and

the *Surround Video Internet Control*, which is an Internet-aware OLE control.

What You Could Do with This Control/Development System
If you want to create online games, stunning backgrounds for your Web pages, or just realistic depictions of sites, sounds, and images, this control offers just that. If you are designing a site for a museum, a hotel, a travel destination, a building, or any location where you want to display the entire location in a surround-type view, this control offers that and is much faster than other surround video technology like QuickTime VR.

NAME OF CONTROL: SYLVANMAPS

Location of Control: http://www.sylvanmaps.com

What This Control Does
This control lets you view geographical data in the form of a map. The geographical information is stored in an ODBC-based GIS (Geographic Information System) Mapping database, and which is the ODBC-based GIS Mapping database engine ActiveX control. With this control you can display and analyze data geographically. All data, including mapping data, is stored in ODBC tables, however, and the map itself is regenerated when the information is called from the database.

NAME OF CONTROL: SYSINFO

Location of Control: http://www.aditi.com

What This Control Does
The *Sysinfo* control provides system information of the browsing visitor. The publisher of the page could use this information for statistical analysis to determine who is visiting, the operating system they are using, and even the amount of available drive space on the user's machine. This is an excellent control to use if you are developing pages on an Intranet and want to keep track of the users who access various pages within your site. If you don't have access to server statistics, this may be an excellent way to keep track of your users.

If you don't want to add a control, but want to keep statistics on your site, you can easily do that with a free service called FreeStats, at http://www.freestats.com. It will monitor all sorts of statistics about the visitors to your site.

CONTROLS YOU'LL FIND ON CERTAIN SITES

Tons of developers are toiling away late at night creating all sorts of controls that could help you reduce the development time of your own Web site or simply make your browsing experience easier. The best place to find most of these controls is at some of the most popular sites. I've added a small list of controls you might want to take notice of at two sites, *ActiveX.com* and *ZDNet's HotFiles HyperActiveX* section. Use the search option to find the direct links to these files.

You'll have to sign up for ZDNet's Hotfiles section. All it requires is a few pieces of information, but it's well worth it.

USER-ORIENTED CONTROLS FOUND ON ACTIVEX.COM

ActiveX.Com is one of the best places for both user- and developer-oriented controls. It also has a ton of information on how to add, program, and interface controls with other software applications. Plus, it offers the latest news about ActiveX development and deployment. You should make *www.activex.com* a permanent link in your Favorites or Bookmark list.

NAME OF CONTROL: BYTECATCHER ACTIVEX CONTROL

What the Control Does
The *ByteCatcher* ActiveX control lets you download files from file transfer protocol (FTP) servers. With this control you can resume a file download that has been interrupted. You control whether the resumption of the download is automatic or manual. You can also use this control to shut down your computer once all your downloads are complete. This trial version is fully functional but only connects to Download.com or Winsock-L file archives. Since this is a function not available in Internet Explorer, this is a valuable control to install and valuable if you have to pay for connection time.

NAME OF CONTROL: CPC VIEW

What the Control Does
CPC View is a viewer control that lets you view documents in CPC, TIFF (black and white), and PBM formats. The viewer offers document navigation, scaling, and antialiased image options in both a page view and a thumbnail view and additional graphical capabilities. TIFF images are widely used with scanners, so this control will provide you with quick access to scanned documents stored on a network server.

DEVELOPER AND USER-ORIENTED CONTROLS FOUND ON ZDNET'S HOTFILES ACTIVEX SECTION
ZDNet is probably the premiere source for up-to-date user and developer information. Culled from their print resources, like *Computer Shopper* or *Internet Computing*, along with a wealth of online resources, ZDNet offers a full-featured ActiveX site that also includes an online ActiveX tutorial. You can find the direct links to the Internet ActiveX site on ZDNet by pointing your browser to *http://www.zdnet.com/products/internetuser.html*. Direct links to many of these ActiveX controls can be found off the **Download** button from this main page. Here are some you should be on the look out for.

NAME OF CONTROL: ACTIVEUPLOAD

Type of Control: User

What the Control Does
Since Internet Explorer doesn't have this feature, this control is a must-have. With it you can easily drag-and-drop files to a site to upload those files. You can also download files by dragging and dropping them to your desktop. With the *ActiveUpload* control, you can FTP files by dragging them from your desktop and dropping them onto the ActiveUpload control. You can make your Web pages interactive by incorporating this control into any type of form you might create.

ActiveUpload supports UNC paths to transfer to network drives, and the latest version adds support for proxies and passive FTP servers.

NOTE

Name of Control: Active Desktop for AltaVista and Yahoo search engines

Type of Control: User

What the Control Does

When you install *Active Desktop* components or the ActiveX controls for AltaVista and Yahoo search engines, you can instantly search with either search engines directly from the component or control. This prevents you from having to go directly to a page, or open up a separate window just to search.

TIP

*Did you know you can also use the Run command to open up Web pages? It's true. Just select **Run** from the **Start** menu, then type the full URL for the site you want to open. This will automatically open your default browser and connect you to that site if you are currently online.*

Name of Control: MultiPage Browser Control by VivaTexte, Inc.

Type of Control: Developer

What the Control Does

The *Multipage Browser* is a programmable ActiveX control that lets a developer add multipage browsing to applications or Web pages. Multipaging means allowing the browser to simultaneously open and display multiple Web sites. The user can then use the tab key to move from open page to open page. You could use this control to offer help, link to pages for advertising, or show different sites that can't necessarily be shown well in frames.

Name of Control: ActiveX Stock Graph with Technical Analysis

Type of Control: User/Developer

What This Control Does

This control offers not only an interactive stock ticker but also six different kinds of charts to track your investments. The charts you can choose from include High/Low/Close, Log/Linear, Point and Figure, Candlestick, Equivolume, and 3D Representation. You can use this control at the bottom of a page, in a frame or in conjunction with the MultiPage browser control, to display real-time and delayed investment information on your desktop.

NAME OF CONTROL: NO CODE POKERAX

Type of Control: Developer

What the Control Does
Want to spice up your site? Why not add a little poker game. With *No Code PokerAX*, all the coding is already done for you. You simply drop this control on a form, and instantly you have a fully-functioning poker game. The user can then play by himself or with others. If you use a chat room in conjunction with this control, you can have virtual online poker games going all the time without the fear of being raided, or having to clean up a mess.

NAME OF CONTROL: PC-CILLIN HOUSECALL

Type of Control: User

What the Control Does
You can use the *PC-cillin HouseCall* to search for viruses on your computer. PC-cillin HouseCall will detect viruses seen "in the wild," along with macro viruses found in Word and Excel files. When it finds a virus, it lists the name of the virus along with the name of the infected file. All of this is done directly in the browser. As a matter of fact, this control cannot be run without the use of an ActiveX-enabled browser. With this type of application you can eventually turn your Web browser into your desktop, making all information and applications available from within a Web browser, regardless of whether those files and applications are stored locally or remotely.

NAME OF CONTROL: PHONEBOOK

Type of Control: Developer/User

What the Control Does:
Phonebook is an ActiveX control that lets you search a wide list of phonebooks in the United States and Holland. Much like the Yahoo and AltaVista controls, you could program this functionality into your Web site to give your browsing visitors quick access to phonebook-related information.

NAME OF CONTROL: TWINTALK X

Type of Control: Developer/ User

What the Control Does:
TWinTalk X is a terminal emulation package featuring full VT100/VT220 and Videotex (Minitel) emulation. TWinTalk X is a signed and ready-to-use ActiveX control for Web site building and application design, which means you can give quick access to remote computing systems that are still accessible only through a text-based interface. This is more a developer control than a user control. For user controls that offer terminal emulation, check the Intranet section listed previously in this chapter.

NAME OF CONTROL: ACTIVEX PERSONAL DIARY

Type of Control: User

What the Control Does
ActiveX Personal Diary is the easiest way to keep your diary, phone book, or appointments online. You can view your diary file within an ActiveX browser from anywhere on the Web. You save your file on a file transfer server. The control contains sound and help files to help alert you of meetings. It's an excellent control if you have to share your calendar with other users or your secretary, and if you travel frequently.

NAME OF CONTROL: AUDIO CASSETTE

Type of Control: User, but really lends itself to a Developer

What the Control Does

Audio Cassette is an ActiveX control that lets you organize RealAudio files into groups that resemble cassette tapes. You have to have the links or files stored locally. If you want to create your own online CD, so to speak, this is one way to do this.

The latest version of the RealPlayer offers this same type of feature. If you want to create something like this for your users, this may be the right way to do it. Otherwise you would have to instruct the users how to configure their RealPlayer for such access.

NAME OF CONTROL: CALADONIA COMMERCE CONTROL

Type of Control: Developer

What the Control Does

Caladonia Commerce Control offers Web designers and application developers the ability to add credit card validation to their Web pages and programs. This ActiveX control can validate all major credit card types while checking the validity of expiration dates. Card numbers are encrypted for secure transfer and storage.

Try downloading the ActiveXCavator control. Once installed ActiveXCavator, a separate application, not a control installed inside your browser, that lists all the ActiveX controls installed in your system used by Internet Explorer. With this small program you can see all the information about all the controls used, such as the name, size, and location of the file. You can easily delete those controls you no longer need. This is a great utility application to keep track of all those controls you run across.

Name of Control: WebScanX

Type of Control: User

What the Control Does
Whenever you surf the Internet, you're subjecting your computer to various security risks. Since ActiveX controls can be downloaded to your system without your knowledge and can wreak havoc on your system, you might consider adding *WebScanX* to your browser. WebScanX is designed to provide a safe computing environment for Internet users by scanning everything that wants to gain entry to your system. Although the security options with Internet Explorer offer some protection, it's easy enough to turn off this type of protection accidentally. With WebScanX installed, you will be alerted of potential problems even if the security feature is turned off.

Don't forget DaveCentral, another great place to find ActiveX controls and plug-ins. You'll find DaveCentral at www.davecentral.com. And of course there's always Download.com, located at www.download.com, and ShareWare.com, located at www.shareware.com. For the developer side of you, don't forget Developer.com, located at www.developer.com.

TIP

Summary

About the only way to keep up with the never ending stream of new controls hitting the electronic transom is to go out and find them on your own. Every day some smart programmer comes up with a new way of utilizing ActiveX controls to not only enhance Web pages, but also to interact with other applications and data on your hard drive or on your network.

This list is by no means a complete list. With thousands and thousands of controls available, there simply isn't enough room. However, this list should get you started, whether you simply want to see ActiveX controls in action, add controls to your Intranet, see how ActiveX controls could enhance your browsing experience, or if you want to develop Web pages or create new controls of your own. After reading through this list and the subsequent plug-ins list, you'll probably have a whole slew of questions about how to use, incorporate, or troubleshoot controls and plug-ins. If that's the case, the next two chapters should help answer some if not all of the questions you might have.

11

The Big Plug-In and ActiveX FAQs

Whether you're a rank novice to the world of plug-ins or an old hat, you're bound to have questions. This chapter will serve as your quick reference guide for just about every question you might have concerning the installation and use of plug-in technology. If you have a question about a particular plug-in, I recommend you check out the manufacturer's home page for more detailed technical information that may not be covered here. On most manufacturer's sites you'll not only find FAQs, but also updates, technical notes, and bug reports. For help using Netscape Navigator, you might try checking out Netscape's list of FAQs at *http://help.netscape.com/faqs/* or the Unofficial Netscape FAQ at *www.sousystems.com/faq/*.

I've organized this FAQ into several different categories so you can quickly find the information you need. The **General Plug-In FAQs** answers most of the standard questions people have about plug-ins. If you've skimmed through the other chapters, and jumped right in downloading and installing them on your own, you might skim through this section. It'll answer some question you probably have.

The **Explorer and ActiveX FAQs** section offers you insights into the glitches you might face using Internet Explorer and it's ActiveX technology. If you search most popular search sites for ActiveX FAQs, you'll find plenty more, although most center around programming, not using ActiveX controls, like this section does. One note: if you are having problems using ActiveX controls, make sure you are using at least version 3.02 or version 4.0 with the security patch installed. You can find both of these versions at *www.browsers.com*.

The **Troubleshooting FAQs** section is meant for those who are grappling with problems using Netscape Navigator and Communicator, or Internet Explorer. You'll find some common problems and resolutions listed here, along with some pointers of where to go should you require more advanced troubleshooting. You'll also probably find plenty of ideas on how you can fine-tune your browser for better plug-in performance.

Finally, the **General Third-Party Plug-In FAQs** section gives you a few FAQs for some of the most commonly used commercial and shareware plug-ins. Check Chapter 13 for more information, or the actual plug-in or ActiveX control software vendor's Web site for specific help.

GENERAL PLUG-IN FAQs

Q. How do I know which plug-ins are installed in my browser?

You can find which plug-ins are installed one of two ways. If you are using Netscape Communicator or Navigator, you can type "about:plug-ins" in the **Location** field of your browser, or select **About Plug-ins** from the **Help** menu (see Figure 11.1).

Or if you are using Internet Explorer or simply want to find out the manual way, you can open up the folder where the browser is stored and locate the **Plug-ins** folder, which should be on the same level as the application itself.

Q. What's the difference between a 16-bit plug-in and a 32-bit plug-in?

16 bits, I guess. Actually 16-bit plug-ins are for Windows 3.1 users and 32-bit plug-ins are for Windows 95 and Windows NT users. Make sure you install the correct version of the plug-in for your system. There is a difference in the way in which the plug-ins handle information. If

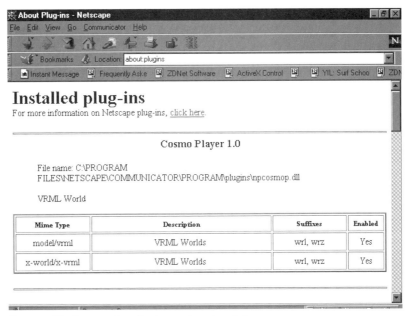

FIGURE   *Finding out what plug-ins you have installed.*
11.1

you install the wrong version, you may find the plug-in doesn't work or doesn't work properly with your system.

Q. What plug-ins come standard with Netscape Navigator?

The most recent version of Netscape Navigator, Communicator, will read the following data types:

- GIF
- JPEG
- XBM
- HTM
- HTML
- TXT
- AVI
- AIF

- AIFF
- AIFC
- WAV
- SND
- WRL
- QT
- MOV

Check Chapter 2 for more information on the plug-ins installed.

Q. When I try to view a page with a movie or video file, all I get is a black box. What's wrong?

Most likely the file didn't entirely stream or download to your computer. Try hitting the **Reload** or **Refresh** button on your browser to see if the data reloads properly. If you are still having problems, empty your browser's cache and history files. These files may be preventing you from seeing the movie or picture. If it still doesn't load, contact the Webmaster of the site and tell him your problems. You may need to upgrade to a newer version of your browser so it can work with the site and plug-in or ActiveX control used. You might also try exiting, then rebooting your PC, and trying the site again with your browser.

Q. How do I remove a plug-in I no longer want to use?

With most plug-ins all you have to do is remove the DLL files associated with the plug-ins. Those files are stored in your plug-in directory. Most plug-ins are actually comprised of only one or two DLL files. Also check **Add | Remove Programs** option in your **Control** panels. Some plug-ins can be uninstalled this way. However, some more elaborate plug-ins may require you to uninstall them. Check the vendor's support site for information on how to uninstall the program.

Q. When I try to use a plug-in it launches another application, such as Microsoft Word, which isn't close to what the plug-in reads. What's the problem?

Most likely either the MIME type is configured to launch Word, or in the case of using Internet Explorer, a Microsoft product will always try to launch a compatible Microsoft product. Double-check to make sure you have the right ActiveX control installed.

Q. How much memory should I have in order to use plug-ins?

You should have at least 16MB, and more if you plan on using lots of video- or audio-based plug-ins. The larger the plug-in, the more memory it will require when the browser calls it into action. 32MB is adequate for most browsing/plug-in activity, but the more you have, the smoother your system will operate (see Figure 11.2).

Q. Do plug-ins occupy much computer memory?

As detailed in Chapter 2, plug-ins occupy RAM memory only when they are being used to display or manipulate data. Once you move on, the plug-in unloads itself from your computer's turn-on or RAM memory. The amount a plug-in occupies in terms of hard disk or permanent memory is dependent upon the plug-in itself. The average size of a standard plug-in ranges from 50K to 5MB.

Q. When I loaded a page, it asked if I wanted to get the plug-in. I answered "no." Is there some way to have that dialog box show up again?

Simply click once on the box where the plug-in should be, where the puzzle piece is displayed. A dialog box like that shown in Figure 11.3 will pop up. You may also be able to click the **Reload** or **Refresh** option to have a dialog box display.

Q. Can I give plug-ins away? Or do I have to buy a license to distribute them on a network?

Although most plug-ins are meant to be freely distributed, you should first check with the software vendor before copying or posting their plug-in to other computers or to your Web site. The best way to distribute plug-ins to other users is by adding a link to the vendor's download site from your Web page. That way they will always have the latest plug-in, and you won't have to worry about updating anything.

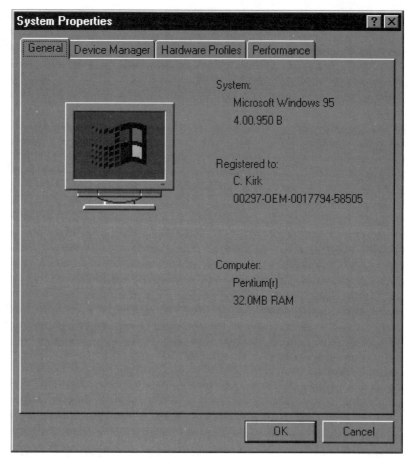

FIGURE   *To find out how much memory you have installed, open your Control Panel, then*
11.2   *open the System icon. You should see the amount of memory listed on the first*
tab.

**Q. I want to use ActiveX controls with my Netscape browser. How
do I do that?**

Currently you need a plug-in called Ncompass ScriptActive. As mentioned in Chapter 2, Netscape may offer this feature in future browsers, but for now you need a plug-in that can interpret the ActiveX technology. Check *www.ncompass.com* for more information on how this plug-in works.

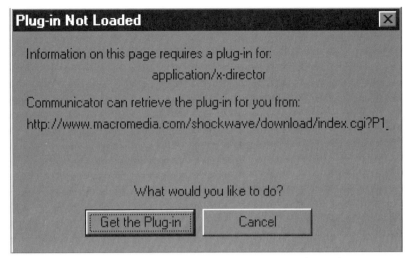

FIGURE   *Reloading a plug-in dialog option is as easy as clicking in the puzzle piece.*
11.3

Q. How can I tell if a plug-in has been installed?

The best way is to visit a page that uses that type of plug-in. Otherwise, you can select **About Plug-ins** from the **Help** menu in Netscape Navigator and see if the plug-in is listed. If it's not, most likely the installation did not complete properly. The best thing to do is try again.

Q. What's the difference between a helper application and a plug-in?

A helper application (as discussed in Chapter 2) is actually a separate program that opens and manipulates the data in its own window. In order to use a program as a helper application, you must assign it to the data type it will open within your browser application. A helper application can run independently of the browser, whereas a plug-in cannot. A plug-in displays the data within a browser window. During the installation process, plug-ins are automatically assigned to the data types they display.

Q. I'd like to include a link in my Web page so visitors can quickly go to the company that offers the plug-in that displays the data file I've embedded in my Web page. How do I do that?

You can quickly offer links to the company's Web page that offers the actual plug-in by using the PLUGINSPAGE parameter within the <EMBED> tag you use to specify the embedded data file. This is what it would look like if you wanted to point visitors to Adobe's Web site to download Adobe Acrobat when using embedding PDF files into your page:

<EMBED PLUGINSPAGE="http://www.adobe.com/">

This is how this tag works. If the browser can't find the plug-in installed within the browser, when it tries to load the Web page, it will alert the user, then let him go to the Web page specified in the EMBED PLUGINSPAGE parameter.

Q. Do I really have to restart Navigator every time I install a plug-in?

No, you really don't, but you should. But if you're too lazy to restart Navigator, you can try typing the following in the **Location** field of your Web browser once you've installed the plug-in:

Javascript:navigator.plugins.refresh()

Make sure you hit the **Enter** key after you type this command into the **Location** field of your browser. I don't recommend this for extensive, newly installed plug-ins such as QuickTime or Real Audio. To ensure the plug-in has been installed properly, it's really best to exit your browser, restart the computer, and restart the browser.

Q. I've run across a plug-in that says it requires the 32-bit version of Communicator. I have no idea what version I have. How do I find out?

If you have Windows 95 and have installed the Windows 95 version of Communicator, you have the 32-bit version. But if you're unsure, you can also check your list of plug-ins by selecting **About Plug-ins** from the **Help** menu (see Figure 11.4). Take a good look at the list of plug-ins. If the files that end in .DLL have the number 32 before them, you have the 32-bit version of Communicator. If you see a 16 before the name,

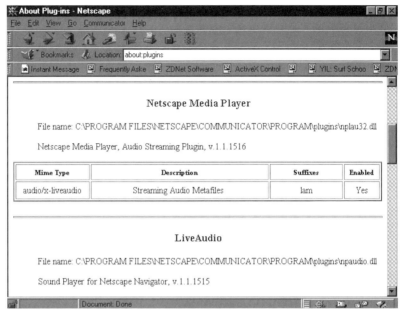

FIGURE   *You can find out if you have a 32-bit or 16-bit browser by the plug-in DLL files*
11.4   *installed. Notice the DLL file and where it's located.*

you have the 16-bit version. If you're using Windows 95, you need to install the proper version from Netscape's site.

Here's an example of what you might see:

NPSWF32.DLL—the 32 before the DLL file designator tells you this is a 32-bit browser.

Q. Is there a way I can speed up the loading of Communicator, so plug-ins such as Liveaudio load faster?

You can automatically load the Java Virtual Machine at the same time you launch Communicator. This will prevent Communicator from restarting the Java Virtual Machine each time you browse pages that have not only Java, but also audio files which the Liveaudio plug-in can play. To launch Communicator and the JVM at the same time, click the **Start** button, then select **Run** from the pop-up menu. Type the following on the command line field:

"C:\Program   Files\Netscape\Communicator\Program\netscape.exe" -start_java

This will launch Netscape Communicator, assuming it's stored in the **Program Files\Netscape\Communicator** folder. This option, however, will not work with the Windows NT version 3.51 version.

Q. How do I assign a data type to a particular plug-in?

From the **Edit** menu select **Preferences**, then click the **Navigator** tab, then click the **Applications** option. Locate the file type you want to assign to the plug-in, and choose the **DLL** file to use for the file type.

Q. Do I need a plug-in if I want to view files on my hard disk via my Web browser?

No. As a matter of fact, if you have the latest release of Communicator or Internet Explorer, you can even use these applications as a way to view Office 97 documents without a special plug-in, if you have the Office 97 application properly installed. If you want to see the files on your hard drive through your Communicator or Internet Explorer, simply type "C:\" in the **Location** field of your browser. Your browser will then display the files and folders on your hard drive as clickable links. You can easily navigate through your system by clicking the links for the folders. When you encounter a file you want to view, simply click the link for the file. If a plug-in is installed to view that particular data type, it will display the file within the browser window. If not, it will seek to launch a corresponding helper application. In the case of Office 95 or Office 97 documents, the latest versions of the browsers are already set to work properly with no configuration on your part (see Figure 11.5).

Q. Do I need to use WinZip to uncompress all the plug-ins I install?

No. Many plug-ins are compressed in self-extracting files, or EXE files. When you first try to download the plug-in, check the three letter extension. This tells you whether the file is a self-extracting files (.exe) or a zipped file (.zip).

Explorer and ActiveX FAQs

Q. What ActiveX controls come standard with Internet Explorer?

The following controls are installed with a standard installation of Internet Explorer:

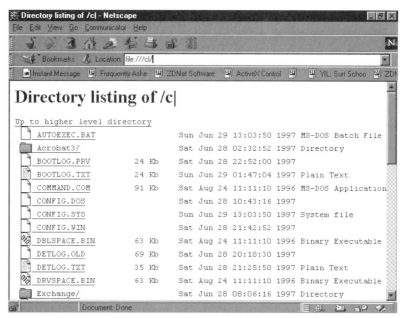

FIGURE *What you see when you view your computer files through a browser.*
11.5

- **Web Browser Control**—For displaying Web pages and other ActiveX controls.
- **Timer**—A control that can be programmed to execute a script or action at a particular time.
- **Marquee Control**—A control that allows you to scroll any HTML file in a horizontal or vertical direction.
- **ActiveMovie**—A control that displays streaming and nonstreaming media, such as video, sound, and synchronized slide shows containing both sound and video.

Q. Can I get more controls installed in my browser?

You sure can. As a matter of fact, there are more than a handful of controls you can download from the ActiveX gallery including controls that let you create charts, display a variety of labels, menus, or stock tickers directly into Web pages. You can find these controls at *www.microsoft.com/activex/gallery.*

Q. When I come across an ActiveX control, am I notified it's being downloaded?

You should be notified a component is being installed, and you should see the component's download progress in the status bar of your browser. If the control has been digitally signed, a certificate displaying the vendor's name and other information will be displayed. If you don't trust this company, you should refuse the download.

Q. I never see any notifications that ActiveX controls are downloading. Why?

If you have no security options turned on in Internet Explorer, you will not see any notifications. Check your **View | Options | Security** tab to ensure you have the proper level of security installed.

Q. I get a message saying my version of Authenticode is not updated. I get a screen asking me if I want to install and update it. What does this mean?

This means the version of security software you currently have installed with your Internet Explorer browser does not have the latest version of the Authenticode software responsible for checking the credentials of the sites offering you the ActiveX controls. When you get a message like the one shown in Figure 11.6, click the **Yes** button to update your security software. This should take a few minutes. It will allow you to view some sites you may not have been able to see before.

Q. How many ActiveX controls are there?

Currently there are 1,000 ActiveX controls commercially available. You can use a large majority of them on your own Web site without knowing anything about programming.

Q. Do I need to know how to program to use ActiveX controls?

Nope. All you need is a cursory knowledge of how to read and understand the constructs of a Web page and how to copy and paste. If you have experience using a scripting language, you'll have no problem with ActiveX.

Q. Where are ActiveX controls stored?

ActiveX controls are stored in the ActiveX control cache located in the \windows\occache\ directory.

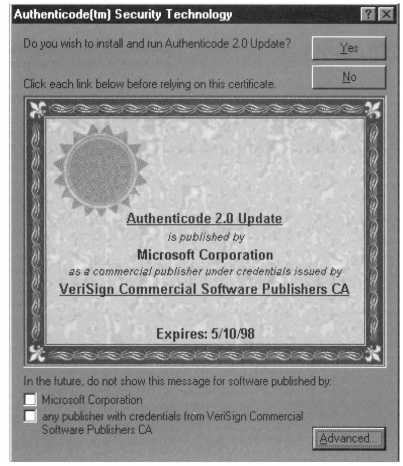

*Q. What happens if a new version of a control becomes available.
How does Explorer handle that?*

In Internet Explorer there is a feature called **Component Download
Service**, which supports versioning, the ability to detect the version of a
control and summon the download of the new control if necessary.

Q. Once I download a control, can I use it on my own Web page?

Controls can be distributed using either a developer license or a runtime license. With a runtime license, you can only view the control
within a Web page or application. You cannot insert that control into a

page yourself. With the developer license you can use, manipulate, and add to the control, placing it on whatever Web site you want. You should read the licensing agreement that accompanies each control before you decide to copy the control to your page.

Q. When I try to view an ActiveX control, it downloads fine, but then says it's from an unauthorized source and it won't show me the content. How do I get it to show me the content?

You have your security settings set too high to view the ActiveX control. If you are certain this control is from a reputable source and can be trusted not to harm your computer, select **Options** from the **View** menu, then click the **Security** tab. Select a lower security level from the list of security options, then click **OK**. Try reloading the page. The ActiveX control should then display properly.

Troubleshooting FAQs

Q. I'm getting Invalid Page Faults after installing a plug-in. What does this mean and what can I do to fix this?

Page Faults usually occur when your computer's processor tries to access a memory page that is not in RAM memory. You get this error when you have conflicting system or application resources. This means you may be using a plug-in that is conflicting with another plug-in or another application loaded in to memory. Try rebooting your system, and accessing the same information again. If you still get this error message, try downloading **Plugsy**, from **Digiami**, a plug-in utility to help resolve conflicts with other plug-ins. You can find **Plugsy** at *www.digigami.com/plugsy/*. Also make sure no other programs are running when you try to access the plug-in.

Q. The installer reports a "modifying .INI files" error, then stops the installation. What can I do to fix this problem?

This usually means your INI file is either missing, locked, or too big. If your Win.INI file is larger than 32KB, you may encounter errors installing plug-ins, such as QuickTime. You may want to remove references to postscript fonts, or other nonexistent applications. You could also try renaming the INI file, then rerunning the installation. After the installation is complete, you can boot up Notepad, then copy and paste the commands added to the INI file by the installation program to your old INI file. You should then rename the old INI file back to its original name, deleting the new INI file the installation program created.

Q. When I try to print, I get an "Out of Memory" error. What's up with that?

Most likely you are trying to print a page with a large data file embedded in it. You should try exiting all other applications and try printing again. If you still get this message, you might try saving the data file, and opening it up with a third-party application to print it. You usually can right-click in the embedded page, and select **Save As**.

Q. I've installed a plug-in, and it installed properly. But when I try to view a page that uses the plug-in, nothing happens. What could be wrong?

You might have multiple versions of a browser installed on your computer. Make sure you are using the browser you installed the plug-in for. For example, if you have upgraded from Navigator to Communicator, you may have directed the installation process to install the plug-in in the Navigator directory instead of the Communicator directory. Do a little sleuthing and you'll probably find the browser you installed the plug-in into.

Q. When I try to install a plug-in, it almost completes the installation, then stops. What's wrong? I can't seem to get it installed even though I've downloaded it several times.

Most likely the installation process created a temporary folder, and each time you rerun the installation program, it looks to this folder. You need to clean out this temporary folder, usually stored in the C:\TEMP directory, or in a temporary directory created by the program. Use the **Find** option to find any extraneous temporary files, then delete them.

Q. When I try to run a plug-in installation program, I get the error message, "Error during read of input file." What does that mean?

It means the installation file is probably corrupted. In this case you should remove the installation program and the compressed file, then redownload the file. Also double-check your C:\TEMP directory for any files the installation process may have left.

Q. When I try to click in an embedded application, I get a message prompting to download the file. What could be the problem?

You may have already assigned the file type to download to your computer. Check the **Preferences** of your browser and make sure you have not specified to save the file type to your hard drive. Also, the file type may not have been properly configured on the server. If your settings are correct but you still get this message, contact the Webmaster.

Q. I try to install a plug-in but I keep getting the error message, "Not enough free disk space." I think I have enough. What could be the problem?

You might have enough space for the plug-in itself, but the installation process may need double the space for it to install. The reason? The installation program may need to create temporary files to store various system software information, or to store uncompressed files it needs to fully install the plug-in. If you are running low on space, you should probably consider backing up your system, cleaning out your hard disk of any unnecessary files, and possibly getting a cartridge drive to store files you may not use on a frequent basis. Also consider adding another hard drive. The prices of hard drives have fallen substantially in the past few years. Now you can get multi-gigabyte drives for several hundred dollars.

Q. When I try to install a plug-in, I get an error message stating the application is being shared by another application. Why won't this plug-in install?

As the error message says, another application is probably using a file the installation process is trying to edit. Make sure you exit your browser and all other active applications before you install any plug-in. Also check your **System** tray for any other applications that may be preloaded at the time of your Windows startup. Many of these applications can be closed by right-clicking on the icon within the **System** tray and selecting **Exit** from the pop-up menu.

If you still get this message when you try to install the plug-in, your system may be using a DLL file the plug-in installation program is trying to access. Double-check the troubleshooting page of the software vendor and see if there is a work-around.

Q. I'm trying to install a plug-in, but it doesn't seem to install properly. Any suggestions?

You might first try booting Windows 95 in **Safe** mode. You do this by pressing **F8** while your system boots. After your system boots in **Safe** mode, try reinstalling the plug-in. If the plug-in still does not install, check the FAQ or troubleshooting page for more information about conflicts your system might be causing the installation program.

Q. When I try to view a page with a particular plug-in, it comes up and says, "Computer lacks sufficient memory." What does that mean?

You may simply not have enough memory or are trying to run too many programs in memory at a time. Launch only your dial-up networking software and browser, then try the page again. If this still doesn't work, check your local computer store for the cheapest prices for adding additional RAM memory. RAM memory is your turn-on memory, like your desktop. It's not storage memory like your hard drive.

Q. When I try to view a movie file, regardless of the plug-in, my screen locks up. What could be the problem?

You may have a problem with either the video driver you are using, or with the video settings. First check to see if it's the settings, by reducing the graphics acceleration through the **Control Panels | System | Performance | Graphics** option. Reduce the hardware acceleration from full to first. If that doesn't work, right-click anywhere on your desktop, then click the **Settings** button in the **Display Properties** window. Make sure you are using the right video driver and monitor. If not, change the settings by clicking the **Change Driver Settings** button. Make sure you reboot just as a precautionary measure so that the changes take effect.

If that still doesn't work, try changing the display driver to 640x480 with at least 256 colors or more.

Q. My Windows 95 computer seems to be freezing up on a regular basis. I'd like to say it's from all the plug-ins I've installed, but the problem started long before that. Any suggestions?

I'd first check out the latest Service Pack Upgrades available free for downloading on Microsoft's Web site, located at *www.microsoft. com/windows95/*. Click the **Support** or **Service Pack** link to find the latest updates available. Many novices, first-time users, or those unfamiliar with Windows have not upgraded their version of Windows 95 to at least Service Pack 1 or updated video or modem drivers. People are constantly discovering new bugs in the software. These Service Packs help to fix many problems, such as your machine crashing on a regular basis.

If you have updated your Windows 95 software and are still crashing, you may have Registry problems that are more complex. The easiest fix is to back up your data, reformat your drive, install a fresh copy of Windows, update it with any new Service Packs, and try again.

Q. I've set up a helper application, then downloaded and installed a wide variety of plug-ins. Now my helper application does not work. Why?

Plug-ins come first and override any helper applications you might have assigned to certain data types. If you want to use a helper application instead of a plug-in, you need to rename the plug-in that reads the same data type as the helper application as discussed in Chapter 2.

Q. I can't seem to see the list of plug-ins when I choose About Plug-ins from the Help menu. What's the problem?

Most likely you don't have Java turned on in your browser. Check the **Options | Network | Languages** option to turn on the Java language which is used by this menu option.

Q. I've assigned an application as a plug-in. Now I need to remove it. I've tried to change the Preferences under the Edit menu, but it still tries to load the application every time I encounter the assigned data type. What can I do to stop this?

First select **About Plug-ins** from the **Help** menu. Locate the reference to the application you've assigned as a plug-in, then write this down. Exit Navigator, then open the plug-ins folder and rename or delete the DLL file for the application you've assigned as a plug-in.

Q. After installing a plug-in from Asymetrix, I get the error message, "Bad MSVCRT.DLL." What happened?

Most likely you installed the Neuron plug-in which installs a newer version of the MSVCRT.DLL file on your computer. In order to get Navigator to work properly again, you'll have to rename the file, then reinstall Navigator.

Q. I'm getting all sorts of General Protection Faults after having installed a few plug-ins. What's wrong and what do GPFs mean?

General Protection Faults occur when a program attempts to access an area of memory that it's not assigned to use and may be used by another program, or when one program tries to pass information to another program and Windows is not able to interpret that data. To fix GPFs, follow the instructions found on Netscape's **Tech Support** page, located at *http://help.netscape.com/kb/client/970702-6.html*. There are detailed step-by-step instructions on how to resolve your GPF problems. Most likely it's an errant plug-in that is trying to pass data to Windows or is conflicting with another plug-in or application using the same memory.

Q. Suddenly Navigator has stopped playing WAV files. I've done some pruning and cleaning of my computer files. Could I have thrown away a file that affects the ability to play WAV files through my browser?

Most likely you've deleted the one DLL plug-in file that your browser uses to play WAV files. Make sure you have the file named NPAU-DIO.DLL in your Netscape plug-in directory. If you don't find this file, it might be a good idea to reinstall your browser, ensuring you backup your mail and newsgroup files stored in the User directory of your browser's folder.

Q. I downloaded a streaming video plug-in, but it doesn't seem to work on my company's network. What could be the problem?

Most likely your company's network firewall is preventing the plug-in from streaming the information to your computer. You need to do two things. First, contact the manufacturer of the plug-in to find out what port number, service type, and packet type the data file is. Then contact your network administrator. Tell him what you are trying to use, and the technical information the manufacturer gave you, then ask if that type of data can be transmitted to your network. Not all data types are allowed on internal networks due to security risks and network strain certain file types could cause.

Q. I've come across a page that offers Adobe Acrobat PDF files, but they don't seem to display. I can view them using the Acrobat program as a helper application, but not within a Web page. What's wrong?

Most likely these files are relatively large and have not been optimized for downloading over slow modem lines. This causes the Adobe Acrobat reader to time-out, thinking the page isn't going to be sent. You may see the first page of the file display just fine, but subsequent pages may not display at all. In this instance it may be better to simply download the entire file and save it to disk, then view it offline. Check the Adobe Web site for more information, or send an e-mail to the Webmaster of the site to let him know these files need to be optimized.

Q. I've updated my version of Netscape Navigator, but the plug-ins I installed previously don't appear to be working. What could be the problem?

According to Netscape, plug-ins installed into previous versions of Navigator are not automatically installed into the new version. With most plug-ins, all you have to do is copy all the DLL files stored in your old browser's plug-in folder to your new folder. However, more advanced plug-ins, such as QuickTime or Real Audio, require you rerun the entire installation program.

Q. I've downloaded a plug-in, but nothing seems to happen. What's wrong?

Most likely you downloaded a compressed file, that needs to be uncompressed, then installed. Try double-clicking on the file you just downloaded, and see what happens. If nothing happens, you may have downloaded a corrupted file. Try downloading the file again, then extracting and installing the plug-in.

Q. I've recently installed several plug-ins, now my computer crashes regularly. What can I do?

The first thing you should do is run the Windows ScanDisk program to ensure the computer system, application, and data files are still intact. You can locate ScanDisk by opening up the **My Computer** icon, right-clicking on the icon for your hard disk, then selecting **Properties** from the pop-up menu. You should see a tab labeled **Tools** in the **Properties** window. Click this tab, then click the **Check Now** button to run a thorough check of your system. If you have Norton Utilities or PC Tools, definitely run those system-checking applications as well.

Once you know your system is in proper working order, the next thing to do is isolate the culprit. One easy way to do this is to move all your plug-in files outside of the plug-in folder where they reside, then try normal Web browsing. If things work fine, then exit the browser and try adding them back in again one at a time, checking each time that things are still working by launching your browser.

If your browser crashes, the best thing to do is delete the suspected plug-in and try downloading, then installing it again. If the browser still crashes, check the manufacturer's support page if one is available, and see if the plug-in conflicts with other applications or software you have installed. If not, try reinstalling your browser again, and doing a clean install of each plug-in, checking as you go for any crashes.

Q. When I view a particular Web site, all I get is an icon which looks like a puzzle-piece. What does that mean?

It means you simply don't have the necessary plug-in installed. Check to see what plug-in is required, where to locate it, and how to install it. Once you've installed the plug-in, restart your system and try the page again.

Q. I've installed the plug-in, but I still get a puzzle-piece icon. What's wrong?

For some reason the browser isn't recognizing the plug-in. Try exiting the browser, restarting the computer, then trying the page again. If the plug-in still doesn't work, check to see if the data type is assigned to another plug-in or helper application. If it is, you may need to remove the plug-in or helper application, then try to reinstall the plug-in again.

Q. When I view a particular site, I see an empty box with a building block in it. What does that mean?

That means the site has an ActiveX control embedded in the page, and your browser either hasn't downloaded the control entirely yet, or you have elected not to install the control, previously leaving this page to only show the standard HTML. Try reloading the page, or exiting, then relaunching your browser again.

General Third-Party Plug-In FAQs

Q. I've installed the NetZip plug-in, but now every time I try to download a file by clicking on it, it doesn't work. What's the problem?

If you're using Netscape Communicator 4.0, you have to select the **Save** button in order to initiate the download. For more information on the NetZip plug-in check out the FAQ page at *http://www.netzip.com/*.

Q. I try to use the **File | Print** *menu option to print an Adobe PDF file, but it doesn't print. What's the problem?*

Make sure you click in the frame containing the PDF file, then use the Acrobat plug-in's **Print** option, not the **Netscape File | Print** option, to print the embedded file. Adobe Acrobat uses its own print engine to print files. Navigator cannot print a file handled by Adobe Acrobat.

Q. I'm trying to use the Real Player plug-in with my Netscape browser. But now it's giving me a security warning. What gives?

When Netscape gives you a security warning, then asks if you want to save the file, this means you simply need to reconfigure your Netscape browser so it can understand the MIME type for the Real Audio file. Try deleting, then reconfiguring your MIME types.

Q. I've downloaded the Ichat client to chat with others on the Internet. But I can't seem to connect to any IRC. What's the problem?

Make sure you are supplying a nickname, user name, and description. Otherwise, you won't be able to log on. Ichat requires you supply all this information.

Q. I'm trying to use the Ichat client with AOL. Nothing seems to work. It says the application can't load, although the installation process seemed to work fine. Why?

You need to use either Netscape Navigator or Internet Explorer to use Ichat. The Web browser option of the AOL software does not work properly with Ichat.

Q. When I'm trying to connect to an IRC server, all I get is a gray box. What does this mean?

First make sure you are running the right version of the chat software plug-in for your computer. Some 16-bit versions of chat client plug-ins won't work with Windows 95. Also make sure you are not behind a firewall. The firewall may be preventing you from connecting to an IRC server.

Q. I get the error message, "Program error. Your program is making an invalid dynamic link library call to a DLL file. Your program will close." What am I doing wrong?

Most likely you have two versions of the same plug-in, possibly QuickTime. What happens is these two programs/plug-ins' DLL files fight with each other causing the error. You should probably uninstall both versions, then reinstall the new version. If it asks to overwrite files, answer yes.

SUMMARY

Now that you have some answers, you're ready to get on the Internet to find more plug-ins or ActiveX controls. The next chapter is a list of just about every place that has anything to do with supercharging your browser. As you cruise through this list, which, by the way, is also available on the enclosed CD, remember new sites are added daily. Check out your favorite search engines for not only new plug-in sites, but also FAQ sites.

12 The Big Plug-In FAQs

This is a relatively short chapter for one simple reason: plug-ins are easy to install and use. If you've been following along, you should know by now that this is true. Most likely you've been able to install a wide variety of plug-ins with little or no problems. But you might be looking for just a few hints on how to tweak your system so your plug-ins or ActiveX controls work their best. If that's the case, then you've come to the right chapter. If you're in search of some quick tips or check lists of things you should do to prevent problems, or if you want to know the top ten plug-ins or ActiveX controls you should install to make your browser experience more fun and productive, this is the chapter to read. Here I list the top tips for using plug-ins; but also tips for uninstalling plug-ins, and ways to keep your system running at optimum speed.

If you have a specific technical question and are searching for answers, make sure you take a look at Chapter 11, as well as this chapter. And make sure you double-check the software vendor's home page for more specific answers to your more technical problems.

These tips are aimed at giving you some quick ideas on ways to optimize your system. Here you'll find tips for installing plug-ins, tips for using plug-ins, and tips for getting rid of plug-ins when you no longer need them. I've also included a few tips on using some of the more popular plug-ins. For more detailed information about installing plug-ins or specific technical information, check out Chapters 2, 3, 5, and 11. Consider this chapter just icing on the cake.

The Top Installing Tips

1. Backup your system before you install any plug-ins.
I can't stress this enough. Backup, backup, backup, or at least backup your Netscape or Internet Explorer directory and your Registry file. You *will* encounter problems. It may be a simple problem or it may be a problem that brings your system to its knees. When you install Windows 95 software, there are several locations where information could be updated or added. These locations include

- The **Registry** file
- The **System** folder
- The **Program Files** folder
- The **Win.ini** or **System.ini** file

Sometimes the additional files lines of code are easy to spot; sometimes they're not. Some may not cause you any problems at all, whereas others may cause all sorts of conflicts. By keeping a backup of your entire system, or at least the important files such as your Registry, Win.ini, and System.ini files, you can quickly rebuild your system and get it back to full working order by simply recopying these files into their original locations. If you don't have a backup device, get one. Check out the new removable cartridge drives that hold multi-megabytes of data, so you can quickly and easily back up and move files.

2.   Create a separate download folder for self-extracting or zipped files, and put it on your desktop. Then empty this folder on a regular basis.

I can't tell you how many people have called me saying they tried to download something, thought they had, but then saw no trace of what they thought they retrieved. When I get these kinds of calls, I usually recommend they save themselves a lot of wasted time and frustration by creating a download folder and putting it on their desktop. Then, every time they download a file, they save it in the download folder on their desktop. When the download is complete, they will instantly know where the file(s) went, and where they should go to run any self-extracting, uncompressing, or install programs.

Also, by creating a download folder and storing all your compressed or self-extracting files in it, you'll know exactly where to go when you need to do a little house cleaning and throw away all the extraneous files. Or you can easily back up this folder so you have all the compressed files handy in case you have to reformat your hard drive and start again. I can't tell you how many times I've had to do this. If I were smart, I'd follow my own advice and back up my download folder, so I wouldn't have to search all over the Internet for all those plug-ins recently installed.

3.   Update your Windows 95 software, and any outdated drivers for your video card and modem.

I host a radio call-in talk show on computers (check it out at *www.ptialaska.net/~radio/*) and I receive countless calls from people with problems that can easily be solved by updating their Windows 95 system software to the latest service pack upgrade. Microsoft calls them service pack upgrades; I call them bug fixes. These little self-extracting downloadable files fix the glitches inherent in the Windows 95 system. And believe me, there are plenty of bugs. These service pack upgrades fix everything from minor cosmetic fixes to the interface, to fixing the dreaded blue-screen errors. You can find them on Microsoft's Web site at *www.microsoft.com/windows95/*. Look for the link to the **Free Software/Updates**, which should lead you to the link for the service pack upgrades.

The upgrade itself is one simple self-extracting, self-installing file that usually is no more than 2MB in size and takes less than two minutes to install. Just remember, any time you upgrade your system you should close out all applications and back up any important data files.

While you're looking for the service pack upgrade, also look for new updated drivers—software that makes your hardware work together. The two most important drivers to look for are those for your video card and modem. Updated drivers can fix problems you might be experiencing with various types of hardware. For example, if you've been having problems with your new 56K modem getting slower and slower as you use it, an updated driver might fix the problem. The Microsoft Windows 95 Web site is probably the best place to check for updated drivers. If you can't find any updated drivers for your hardware there, check your video card or modem manufacturer's Web site. Again, like the service pack updates for Windows 95, these driver updates take a few minutes to download and only a few more minutes to install.

4. Make sure your computer is in fine working order before you start to use lots of plug-ins. Run ScanDisk and Defrag or a utility program before you install any plug-ins.

The Windows ScanDisk program checks your computer for file integrity and will clean up any problems with your computer's filing system, if you have set the option to do so. Before you install any new program, you should run ScanDisk, especially if your system has "bombed out" recently or has been acting up.

You find ScanDisk and its accompanying Defrag program by opening up the **My Computer** icon, then right-clicking on the hard drive you want to scan and defrag. This will bring up the **Properties** tab, as shown in Figure 12.1. Click the **Tools** tab, then select the option you want to use. You can also use programs like Norton Utilities, PC Tools, or other third-party applications. The idea is that you make sure your system is in proper working order. Programs like ScanDisk can help ensure it is.

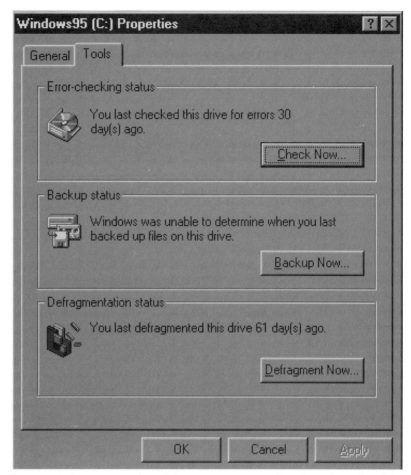

FIGURE *Defragmenting and scandisking your computer is relatively painless and can help*
12.1 *you avoid installation problems.*

5. *Install a virus-checking program or plug-in so all files you download are checked. More importantly, keep this software updated.*

Viruses abound, although you're much more likely to get them from a diskette than from most of the files on the Internet, particularly if you only download files from a reputable source. But keeping a virus-checking program running while you download files, and checking the files you download with a virus-scanning program can help save you hours of frustration should you run across an infected file. *MacAfee* and *Norton* are two companies that make virus-scanning programs, but you can also get virus checkers that check the file before you download it. *VirusSafe Web* is one such program. You can find it by searching the index at *www.shareware.com*, or you can download it directly from the company Web site at *www.eliashim.com*.

I've always been a little skeptical of viruses and what they really could do to your computer, until I finally was infected with one myself. I've been downloading software for years, and never once ran into a single virus, until one day when it struck. And the timing couldn't have been any worse—the deadline of my last book was just a few days away. It wasn't a virus that took over my whole system; instead it was an annoying little Microsoft Word macro virus that only appeared on the 30th of the month, then began to eat away at my Control Panel, until I had virtually no control left. So let this be a lesson to you—any virus-checking program should also incorporate Microsoft Word and Excel macro virus protection as well. Those viruses can do as much harm to your system as the plain vanilla operating system viruses.

6.   *Make sure you have enough memory to run the wide variety of plug-ins you'll want to download or use.*

This is probably the most important thing you should take note of when downloading and using plug-ins or ActiveX controls. You need memory. Not hard disk space, memory. You must have enough memory not only to load your operating system, but also your browser, the plug-in, and the data. All of these will take space in your computer's electronic desktop. And the more elaborate the plug-in, such as Adobe Acrobat, the more memory it will hog, not to mention the memory required by the file the plug-in is showing you.

You should have at least 16MB of space, but actually 32MB would be much better; and 64MB is even better than that. Netscape's latest Web application, Netscape Communicator, hogs a large amount of memory. If you're trying to run a plug-in and Netscape Communicator using only 16MB of memory, you most likely will find your system sluggish and more prone to crashing and freeze-ups. If you find this happening, spend a few bucks and get more memory. It will not only help you with your browsing activities, but also with everything else you do on your computer, from playing games to creating spreadsheets. The golden rule of computers is "You can never have enough memory."

7. Make sure your Win.ini file is small enough to accommodate new entries.

Even though Windows 95 is a hundred percent better than Windows 3.1, we're still dealing with INI files. A few programs still write to and use the Win.ini file, the initialization file Windows references every time you boot or reboot your computer into Windows 95. This file is still used primarily to offer backward compatibility to 16-bit applications that don't know about the Windows 95 Registry file, and must rely upon this file for their initialization settings. This file should not be larger than 32K, otherwise Windows 95 may not be able to read it.

If you've upgraded from a previous version of Windows to Windows 95, and have lots of fonts or are using 16-bit applications on your Windows 95 computer, you may be a prime candidate for a bloated Win.ini file and troubles. Various system and program settings are stored in this file, and so are all the fonts from your older system. A long list of fonts can mean problems with your system and should be deleted if possible. Win.ini files list font information from each printer that has ever been installed in your system. This causes most Win.ini files to be relatively large. To check your Win.ini file, you'll need to look in the Windows directory. Right-click your mouse on this file and you should see a screen like that shown in Figure 12.2.

If the file size is larger than 32K, make a copy of it, then double-click the original Win.ini file to open it. Delete some of the references to the fonts to pare down the size. You should then reboot your system in order for the changes to take effect.

8.   Check your system's Virtual Memory and Swap file to ensure things are set properly there, or to ensure your Swap file isn't corrupted.

You may not know it, but your swap file is consuming space on your hard disk and this could prevent a plug-in from installing correctly. Windows 95 uses Virtual Memory to optimize the performance of the operating system. When you run out of real, physical RAM memory, Virtual Memory takes over using your hard disk and the assigned Virtual Memory swap file as a kind of RAM memory. Windows 95 lets you control three settings for virtual memory: where you place your Virtual Memory swap file and the minimum and maximum size of the Swap file.

You get into problems with Virtual memory and your swap file when you start running out of space on your hard drive. You can also run into problems when you set your swap file too low to accommodate the

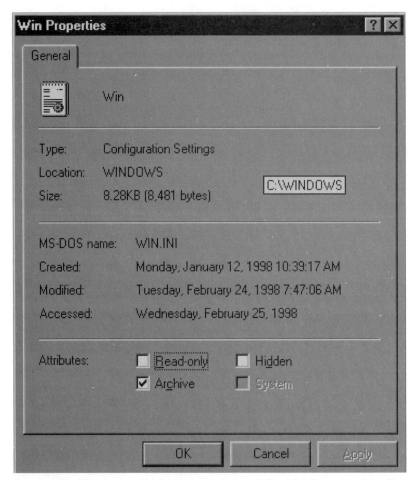

FIGURE   *The file size is listed in the Properties dialog window. If it's larger than 32K this*
12.2   *might be a source of problems.*

amount of space needed to swap computer programming code back and forth between the hard drive and RAM memory. Although Microsoft strongly recommends letting Windows 95 handle the setting of Virtual Memory, you can adjust this if you're running out of space on your drive, or if you would like to set a secondary drive to handle your swap file. To set or adjust Virtual Memory settings, open your **Control Panel,** then double-click on the **System** icon. This will bring up the **Systems Properties** window. Click the **Performance** tab. You should see a window like that displayed in Figure 12.3. Click the **Virtual Memory** but-

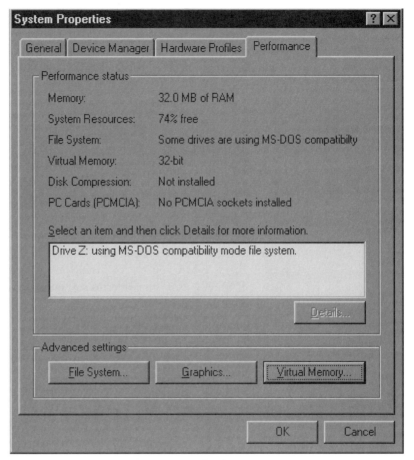

FIGURE   *The Systems Properties dialog window lets you set your Virtual Memory options.*
12.3

ton. You can adjust your settings from the Virtual Memory dialog window.

9. If you are having problems installing an upgraded plug-in, make sure you uninstalled previous versions.

If you try to install an updated version of a plug-in, but end up with nothing but problems, it may be because the remnants of the old plug-in are causing problems with the installation program. Try deleting the old plug-in entirely, or moving it to another location.

If you are still having problems, check to make sure the installation program isn't stuck trying to recover from a failed installation attempt.

For example, if you are trying to install the Real Audio plug-in, remove all references of Real Audio, with the exception of the installation program. Real Audio will create a folder, C:\Real. If the installation process is stopped or crashes for some reason, you'll need to delete this folder and start again.

THE TOP USING TIPS

1.   Check your plug-ins folder or temporary folder for errant zipped or compressed files that may be clogging up your system.
If you're having problems installing plug-ins or you need to do some house-cleaning, check out your plug-ins folder for errant zipped files that might have found their way into the plug-ins folder. Also, double-check your c:\windows\temp folder for extra files that might be causing you problems when you try to install new plug-ins. When a plug-in installs, it usually uses this folder to store temporary files it uses to put all the pieces together.

To keep your system running at optimum speed, clean out the temporary folder on a regular basis. But be forewarned, if you have applications open at the time, you may not be able to throw away all the files in this folder. You should exit all applications before you go rooting around and throwing things away. Keeping this folder clean can solve lots of installation problems.

2.   Set the Security options of your Internet Explorer to ensure you have enough security to protect you but not so much you can't download certain ActiveX controls that may not have authentication.
When using Internet Explorer, it's a good idea to set the security settings so you have enough flexibility to download unsigned ActiveX controls, but not so lax that you let any old control download to your system. Many authors of freeware- and shareware-based controls have created great ActiveX controls, but have not completed the necessary authentication process that would allow you to set the security options on High. For this reason you may need to set the security level to Medium, or in some cases None, if you know the company offering the control is reputable.

If you are getting lots of error messages indicating controls are not being properly downloaded and installed, check to make sure you have the latest version of the browser and the most recent version of the authentication/verification software to go along with the browser. Check the Microsoft Internet Explorer Web page every so often to ensure you have the latest updates for your browser software. You'll find this Web page at *www.microsoft.com/explorer/*.

3.   *Regularly check for updates to your browser, security software, and plug-in or ActiveX control by checking the software manufacturer Web sites.*

Let's face it. These days software is created so quickly there just isn't time to test every possible configuration. The combination of browser, security software, and/or plug-in or ActiveX control could be causing you fits, and an upgrade may be available. Make sure you bookmark the locations from which you've downloaded various plug-ins and make sure you visit either the Netscape plug-ins or Microsoft ActiveX gallery sites, or check BrowserWatch's Plug-in Plaza for a list of plug-ins that have recently been upgraded or added.

Also make sure you keep updated on the latest information about security options, particularly if you are using the Internet Explorer browser. Because ActiveX technology opens up all sorts of security issues, new security holes are discovered almost monthly. A good source for information on security issues is *www.news.com* or *www.browserwars.com*.

But be cautious of all upgrades. Although upgrades or updates to plug-ins, browser or security options will fix conflicts with other software, take it slow when it comes to upgrading your browser. Let other people work out the problems with new browser upgrades. Oftentimes having the latest doesn't necessarily mean having the greatest. Proceed with caution, but at least proceed.

4. *Set your browser's cache to the right setting so it is working at optimum speed.*

You can set your browser to cache or store pages and graphics from Web pages you've visited in memory and/or on your hard disk, so the next time you go to one of the sites you've previously visited the site will load faster. It's a good idea to set your browser to cache documents according to the amount of memory and hard disk space you have. Here are some guidelines:

Memory (RAM) cache:
- 8MB of RAM-1024
- 8-16MB of RAM-2048

- Over 16MB of RAM-2048 to 4000

Disk (hard disk) cache:
- This setting really depends on how much space you have available on your computer. Anything less than 5,000 is not worth setting. More than 10MB (10,000) is a waste of space and could actually slow down your system.

You can set these options through the **Edit | Preferences | Advanced | Cache** option in Netscape Communicator, or through the **Options | Network Preferences | Cache** option in Netscape Navigator 2.0 or above. Figure 12.4 is an example of Communicator's preferred settings for a machine with 16MB of RAM memory.

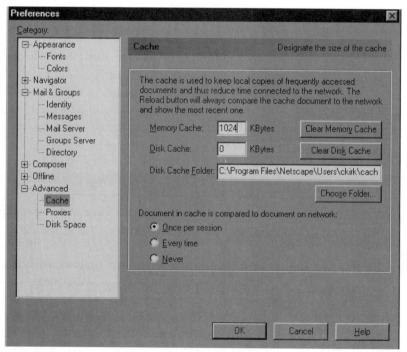

FIGURE *Communicator's Cache options should be set according to the capabilities of your*
12.4 *computer.*

5. Clean out your browser cache on a regular basis. This will clean up lots of problems.

When your browser starts to slow down, it may be because the cache is full and is trying to swap things between the disk cache and memory cache. When this happens, you need to clean out your cache, both hard disk and memory, so your browser will perform better. You can clean out the caches through the **Edit | Preferences** menu option in Netscape Communicator, the **Options | Network Preferences** in Netscape Navigator 2.0 or above, or the **View | Options | Advanced** option in Internet Explorer.

You can have your browser clean these files out every time you exit your browser, or you can clean them out manually. It's entirely up to you, but for optimum performance you should clean out your cache at least once a week.

6.   Check to make sure you have sufficient system resources to use the plug-in and browser.

You may be sucking down your system's resources without even knowing it. The more applications you load, then unload, the more memory resident programs use. And the more applications which you have load automatically every time you start your computer, the less space you allow for your browser and its plug-ins to work. Take a look at your system tray and see how many icons you have other than your volume and date icons. If you have several that span your taskbar, your system is being tasked. Also take a look at the taskbar itself. Do you see lots of items on it? If so, more memory is being consumed, which means less memory for your browser, plug-ins, and data files.

The easiest way to check to see how many resources are being consumed is by opening the **Control Panel**, double-clicking on the **System** icon, then clicking the **Performance** tab in the **System Properties** dialog window. Notice the **System Resources** option listed in the **Performance Status** area. You should see a dialog window like that shown in Figure 12.5.

If it's less than 60 percent, you can bet you'll probably run into problems soon, including your system freezing, running sluggishly, and possibly causing you to hit the **Control-Alt-Del** keystroke combination. Exit out of any programs you aren't using, and close any windows that might be consuming resources. Then check your resources again. The more you can reclaim the better. If you can't reclaim any resources, try restarting your system and investigating the **StartUp** folder and **Win.ini**

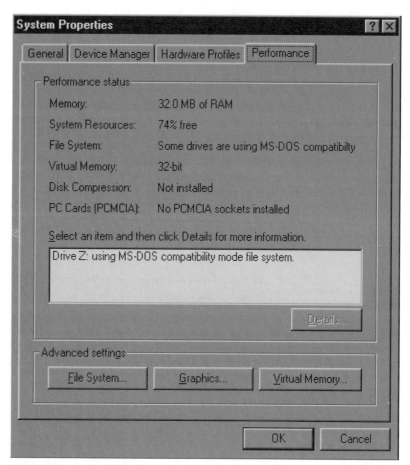

FIGURE *System Properties window shows you the percentage of resources remaining.*
12.5

and **System.ini** files to see what programs are loading automatically. If you can reduce what's loaded, you'll be able to reclaim more resources, and this will help your plug-ins operate smoothly.

7. *Make sure you have sufficient hard disk space for any temporary files that your plug-ins might create.*

If you are getting lots of invalid page faults or out-of-disk error messages, or if your system seems to hang or freeze while viewing large data files over the Web, you may not have enough free space for Windows 95, your browser, and accompanying plug-ins to write temporary files to. Although most temporary files are deleted once the program or data file is closed, Windows, Netscape, and/or Internet Explorer need space to write to, and this space is usually on your hard drive in your c:\windows\Temp directory. As a good rule of thumb, you should have at least three times the size of the data file you want to work with available as free space on your hard disk.

To check the amount of available hard disk space, open the **My Computer** icon, right-click on the hard drive you want to check the space for, then select **Properties** from the pop-up menu. Click the **General** tab in the **Hard Disk Properties** window, like that shown in Figure 12.6.

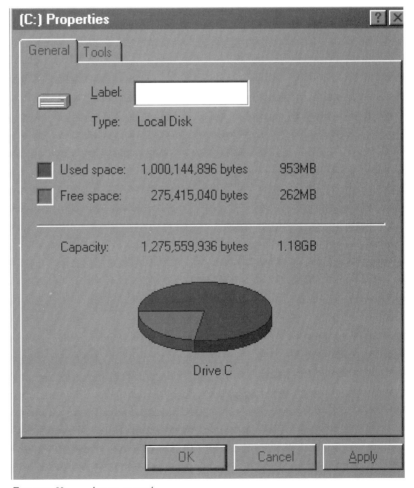

FIGURE *You need room to work.*
12.6

8. *Download (or buy) Plugsy to help you avoid plug-in conflicts.*
If you're having problems with plug-in conflicts, you may want to download *Plugsy*, a plug-in utility that can eliminate conflicts between plug-ins, and between plug-ins and helper applications. With Plugsy you can set specific MIME types to be associated with specific plug-ins, thereby allowing you to mix and match which plug-in or helper application does what with which data type. This means you can have one plug-in to play MID music, while another plays WAV files.

Besides helping you sort out what plug-ins do what, Plugsy also helps you avoid potential conflicts by making sure multiple plug-ins don't try to load when you come across a data type that could be read by more than one plug-in. You can also use Plugsy to disable certain MIME types. This means that if you've downloaded the Shockwave plug-in, but you want to browse sites quickly without waiting for the Shockwave files to load, you can use Plugsy to turn this particular MIME type off for the moment. You can find Plugsy at *www.digigami.com.*

THE TOP UNINSTALLING TIPS

1. *Check the Help | About Plug-ins option before you start to uninstall plug-ins.*
You should check to see what the plug-in's name is, where it's installed, and what MIME types it reads before you uninstall it. You can do this by selecting the **Help | About Plug-ins** menu option. This will help you locate the plug-in and ensure you don't uninstall or delete the wrong one. You also won't know what MIME type your browser will be able to read until you install a new plug-in that will read that same MIME type. Consider printing out this list of plug-ins you have installed to keep handy in case you need to do some housecleaning and want to clean out your plug-ins folder.

2. See if the plug-in can be removed through the Add/Delete Programs option through the Control Panel.
With many well-designed software programs, including plug-ins, you can now go to the **Control Panel | Add/Remove Programs** option to remove not only the program from your hard disk but also any INI files from the system **Registry** database. If your plug-in is listed in the **Control Panel | Add/Remove Programs** option, use this option to delete the plug-in, rather than deleting it from the plug-in folder. This will ensure all remnants of the plug-in will be removed. Figure 12.7 is

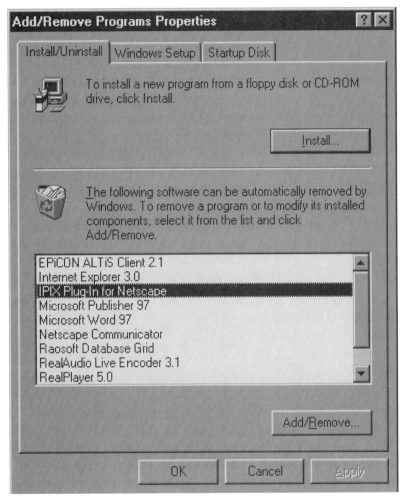

FIGURE   *See if your plug-in can be removed through this option first.*
12.7

an example of what you might see when you double-click the **Add/Remove Programs** icon in the **Control Panel** folder.

3. Make sure you are not running your browser when you start to uninstall the plug-in.

Although this may sound simplistic, I can't tell you how many times I've installed or uninstalled a plug-in while my browser was still running. I then ran into all sorts of problems, including crashing my browser, which in turn forced me to reinstall it so it would work properly again. Never delete, move, or uninstall a plug-in while your browser is running; double-check your taskbar before you start doing any cleanup work.

4. Clean out the plug-in folder, but don't delete the plug-in just yet.

Before you start deleting plug-ins, you should first move them to another folder, not directly to the recycle bin. This way you can test the usability of your browser without the plug-in to see if it functions properly. If it does, you can be relatively sure deleting the plug-in will cause no ill effects to your browser and system.

You may want to create a cleanup folder on your desktop for those plug-ins you eventually want to clean. Then if your browser operates properly without them, you'll know exactly where to go to remove them. To make a folder on your desktop, simply right-click anywhere on an empty spot of your desktop, then select **New | Folder** from the pop-up menu.

5. Consider purchasing an uninstalling program like CleanSweep or Uninstall. These may help you clean out your system more completely.

Commercially available software programs like CleanSweep or Uninstall oftentimes can help you fully clean out your system. They not only help you uninstall plug-ins, but also clean up your hard disk so you'll have more space for additional plug-ins. These cleanup programs usually start by removing program files, DLL, VBX, and INI files that can find their way into directories other than your plug-in folder.

Programs like CleanSweep can not only remove unwanted files from programs you want uninstalled, but can also seek out those files you don't need that were installed with the normal Windows 95 installation. You could do what these programs do, but you would have to know where the superfluous files are located, what their names are, and what files you can delete without crippling your system. Programs like CleanSweep can do all that for you. You'll find CleanSweep at Quarterdeck's Web site at *www.qdeck.com*.

6. Make sure you read the instructions on how to uninstall the program if such instructions are available in the ReadMe or Installation instructions.

Amazing, but true, **ReadMe** files were written to be read! And many ReadMe files have specific instructions on how to uninstall plug-ins properly. Make sure you keep these files just in case you will need to uninstall the software; they do have gems of information in them.

VARIOUS PLUG-IN TIPS

Although most of the tips listed previously pertain to just about every plug-in, there are some specific tips you might take advantage of for certain popular plug-ins. I've listed the four most popular plug-ins, *Adobe's Acrobat Reader*, the *Crescendo* plug-in, the *Real Audio* plug-in, and *Macromedia's Shockwave* plug-in.

MACROMEDIA'S SHOCKWAVE

1. Use the right version with the right version of your browser, and make sure you are using the latest version of Internet Explorer, Netscape Navigator, and Shockwave.

This may not sound like much of a tip, but it is. Most of the problems that occur with *Shockwave* are related to using an older version of Shockwave or an older version of your browser. Also make sure you have downloaded the right "bit" version of the plug-in with the browser you are using. The 32-bit version of Shockwave will not work with the 16-bit version.

2. Change the disk and memory cache settings.

If you are getting poor performance, try setting your browser's memory and disk cache to at least 15MB. Check Netscape's **Edit | Preferences | Advanced** tab or select **Options | Network Preferences** to set your disk and memory cache for your browser. In Internet Explorer, check the **View | Options** setting.

3. If you get a SWA Decompression error, your computer may not have a Floating Point Unit.

If you get an error message that mentions *SWA Decompression*, you either are using an old version of Shockwave or your computer was not equipped with a *Floating Point Unit*, a special chip that handles advanced mathematical computations. Check your computer's hardware manual for information on whether you can add this chip.

4. Update your virus protection software.

Update your virus-protection software, particularly if you are using McAfee's **WebScanX** software. Some virus-checking software can interfere with how a plug-in functions, because the virus-checking software is running in memory at the same time the plug-in runs.

5. Check your video settings and update your video driver.

If you are getting *General Protection Faults*, or if you are having problems running any Macromedia files, double-check to make sure you are using the standard Microsoft video drivers. Set your video settings to at least VGA, which is 16 colors, or SVGA. If you are not using the standard Microsoft video drivers or your video driver is not working properly, either set your settings to the standard Microsoft drivers or download an updated driver for your video system.

To switch your settings, right-click on your **Desktop**, then select **Properties** from the pop-up menu. Click the **Settings** tab in the **Properties** dialog window. Under the **Color Palette**, select the **256 Color** option. Under the **Desktop** area, move the slider to **640x480** setting. Click **OK**, then restart Windows.

6. Double-check your printer drivers. They may be causing conflicts.

Your printer causing you problems? It's possible. You might check your printer manufacturer's Web page for any updates to your printer driver, especially if you have problems printing a Web page with a plug-in embedded in the page. You might also change the default printer to no printer, then restart your computer. The printer driver loads into memory and could be causing a memory conflict with the plug-in you are using.

ADOBE ACROBAT READER

1. Device drivers may be giving you installation problems.

If you are having problems installing the *Acrobat Reader*, disable all your device drivers by restarting Windows in **Safe** mode. You do this by pressing the **F8** key when your Windows 95 computer boots. Once the system boots in **Safe** mode, try installing the plug-in, then rebooting in **Normal** mode.

2. Save large PDF files so you can read them offline.

Some PDF files may not be optimized. And that means you may have problems reading large files. If your system freezes while reading a large

PDF file, save the file to your hard drive, then try to read the file off-line.

3. If the text is blurry, change the settings.

Acrobat Reader 3.0 offers an option to smooth text and images, but this option may cause some blurring. To disable Acrobat Reader's smoothing option, select **File | Preferences**, then select **General**. In the **General Preferences** dialog box, deselect the **Smooth Text** and **Monochrome Images** option. Click **OK**, and reload the page with the file to see if the images and text are less blurry.

4. "Out-of-Memory" errors when printing? Check your printer driver and try printing with limited fonts or a lower resolution setting.

If you get "Out-of-Memory" errors when you try to print, you should check to make sure you have the latest printer drivers installed on your system. If you know your printer driver is the most up to date, then try to reduce the amount of memory required to print the file. You do this by opening your Acrobat Reader, then selecting the **File | Preferences** option, then selecting **General.** From the **Substitution Fonts** pop-up menu select either **Sans** or **Serif**, then click **OK.** If that still does not solve the problem, try printing at a lower resolution.

CRESCENDO PLUG-IN

1. If you don't hear any sound, check your Multimedia icon to ensure everything is working properly.

If you are having problems hearing sound coming from the MIDI *Crescendo* plug-in, you may not have your MIDI mapper set to have all 16 MIDI channels directed to the same MIDI output device. Check your **Control Panel | Multimedia** icon, check the settings to make sure all 16 channels are directed to the same output device.

2. To avoid conflicts with other plug-ins, have the Crescendo plug-in load first.

Navigator 3.0 activates plug-ins in the reverse order they appear in the plug-ins folder. The last plug-in in the plug-ins folder will always activate first if there is another plug-in that can play or display that same MIME type. So if you have a plug-in that can play MIDI files, other than the Crescendo plug-in, you must make sure Crescendo is the last one added to your plug-ins folder. Here's what you do.

Create a temporary folder on your desktop. Call it something like "plugintemp." Open the **\Program Files\Netscape\Plugins** folder, and copy all the plug-ins in the plug-ins folder to the new plugintemp folder. Delete all the files in the **\Program Files\Netscape\Plugins** folder. Next, copy all the files except *npmidi32.dll* from the plugintemp folder back into the empty **\Program Files\Netscape\Plugins** folder. This is the Crescendo plug-in. Once you have all but this plug-in in the **\Program Files\Netscape\Plugins** folder, then copy the *npmidi32.dll* file individually. This will make it the last plug-in added to your plug-ins folder, and thus it will load first when a MIDI file is encountered.

You could also rename the other plug-ins that are conflicting with the Crescendo plug-in. For example, if the Netscape plug-in is being loaded each time instead of the Crescendo plug-in, rename the *Npaudio.dll* file to something like *Xnpaudio.dll*. This will prevent this plug-in from loading, and will allow the Crescendo plug-in to play MIDI files.

Real Audio

1. No sound? Check your sound card settings.
Since most embedded Real Audio files you'll run across don't give you too many controls, if you don't hear any sound when your browser runs across a Real Audio file, first check the **Volume Control** in the **System Tray** to ensure you have the sound turned up. Also, if you have an external speaker control volume knob, make sure that's turned up as well.

2. If after reconfiguring your browser, the Real Audio file is not recognized, manually configure your browser so the Real Audio plug-in will be recognized.
Oftentimes when you reconfigure, reinstall, or move your browser to another location, the Real Audio plug-in may no longer be associated with RAM and RA files. In that case, you may have to reconfigure your browser manually so the file types are recognized. To do that, follow these steps:
1. Select the **Preferences** setting from either the **Options** or **Edit** menu.
2. Click the **General Preferences** option if you are using Navigator 3.0 or below, or the Navigator option to expand it, then click the **Applications** subsection.
3. Click the **New** or **New Type** button.

4. Enter the following information in the fields provided:
   - **Description**: audio/x-pn-realaudio
   - **MIME type**: audio/x-pn-realaudio
   - **Suffixes**: rpm, ram, rm, ra
5. Click the **Plug-in radio** button and select the **Real Audio** plug-in from the pull-down menu, or click the **Browse** button and locate the **Real Audio** player.
6. Click **OK**, then **OK** again to close the **Preferences** dialog window.

3.   If you encounter an error saying something like, "Could not load plug-in for MIME type," and then your plug-in doesn't load.
If you get this error message, most likely the Web server is not configured properly to understand what kind of file the Real Audio file is. Therefore it cannot pass along the information about the file to your browser. The best thing to do in this case is to send an e-mail message to the Webmaster of the site, or the system administrator of the network, and let him know the server is not configured properly. Tell him to check the following Real Audio technical note which outlines exactly what he needs to do to their server so Real Audio files can be downloaded, then played:

http://service.real.com/solutions/ras00029.htm

4. Having problems playing a Real Audio file from Internet Explorer?
Most likely the file is stored in a password-protected directory on the Web server. Tell the Webmaster to remove the password protection, and your Real Audio plug-in will play the file just fine. There seems to be a problem in the way in which Explorer uses the authentication process which interferes with the way in which the Real Audio plug-in links to the actual file. By the time you read this, this problem may have been solved; but you may need to update your Real Audio plug-in or your Explorer browser.

SUMMARY

By far the best plug-in tip is to visit the software manufacturer's Web site on a regular basis and download, then install, any updates to the plug-in. The name of the game in the software business is update, update, update. Many times those updates will fix problems in previous versions. Also, be aware when you update your Web browser: many new plug-ins may be part of your browser's update, meaning you may not have to add plug-ins on your own. Always check the plug-ins folder or the **About Plug-ins** option every time you update your browser, so you know exactly what plug-ins came with the new browser update.

Above all, remember this: plug-ins make your browsing life more exciting and are about the easiest way to supercharge your browser!

CHAPTER

13

Plug-Ins and ActiveX Online Resources

I've cruised the Internet for some of the best resources relating to plug-in and ActiveX technology and in this chapter I list them all. If you thought you should have taken note of them before, while you were reading through others chapters, don't despair—they are all here. Be forewarned, however; Web sites have a tendency to change on a regular basis. By the time you read this, some of these sites may have changed. If you're having a problem locating a particular Web site, feel free to contact me directly at *ckirk@alaska.net* or check out my Web site at *www.alaska.net/~ckirk* for more plug-in related information.

I've divided this chapter into two main sections—online resources for plug-ins and online resources for ActiveX controls. Plug-ins are relatively easy to find, whereas ActiveX controls may be more difficult to locate. At the time of this writing there were some 180 different plug-ins available, and a recent keyword search located about 108,000 different pages listing the keyword **Plug-in** and some 60,879 pages listing **ActiveX**. I strongly encourage you to do some regular sleuthing on your own by searching some of the more robust search engines and directories.

*Make sure you use the keyword **Plug-in** as well as **Plugin**, since the spelling of plug-ins varies from manufacturer to Web site. Also realize there are plug-ins for Photoshop, a popular photoediting program, as well. You will run across numerous sites offering plug-ins; just make sure the plug-ins they are offering are for your browser, not for Photoshop.*

Some of the more popular search engines are listed in Table 13.1. I've commented on the options each site has to offer, and that you might consider using. The key to a successful search is knowing exactly how to narrow your search down to find the information you need. Many search engines and directories also allow you to search within your search results. Make sure you use this option frequently to narrow down the number of links you have to review.

*One other thing to remember when searching for articles on plug-ins. Many sites, such as CNN Interactive, may display lots of pages that use the keyword **Plug-in**. Although the keyword is listed on the page, it refers to which plug-in the browsing visitor needs to use in order to experience the site fully.*

TABLE 13.1: *Search sites for finding plug-ins.*

Site	Location	About the Search Engine
HotBot	www.hotbot.com	Click the **SuperSearch** button and check **ActiveX** if you want to search for just ActiveX controls.
AltaVista	www.altavista.digital.com	Use the search string, "title:plug-in", in order to find only those pages that include the word plug-in in the title of the Web page itself. You can also use the search string, "applet:keyword" to search for Java applets with the keyword specified.
DogPile	www.dogpile.com	Use this MetaSearch site to search multiple search engines and directories at once, and to search file repositories along with news wires.
DeJaNews	www.dejanews.com	Offers the ability to search newsgroups. Use the keyword "plugin" to find discussion groups about plug-ins.
InfoSeek	www.infoseek.com	You can type in a question, like "Where do I get plug-ins?" Infoseek has also segmented out a wide variety of topics in its Computer Channel.
Netscape's Support Site	http://help.netscape.com	You can search the FAQs or the knowledge base for information pertaining to any of Netscape's products.
Microsoft's Knowledge Base	www.microsoft.com/kb/	You can search the knowledge base for ActiveX support.
Search.com	www.search.com	Search a wide variety of indices all at one time. Excellent site for finding shareware sites containing plug-ins. Currently houses links to over 250 search sites.
WebSitez	www.websitez.com	Find Web sites whose domain names contain the keywords, "plugin" or "plug-ins." Gives you a complete listing of all sites relating to plug-ins. Good for finding other Web sites as well. Not every site containing the word "plug-in" in the domain name caters to Netscape plug-ins, but many do.

(Table 13.1 continued)

Reference.com	www.reference.com	An excellent site to search for mailing lists and newsgroups pertaining to browsers, Web page development, and plug-ins.
NewsBot	www.newsbot.com	If you're looking for a search engine to search computer news stories, this is the place to go.

Finding Plug-Ins and ActiveX Controls

Of course the best place to find the perfect plug-in or Active X control is at the software manufacturer's Web site. But unless you know exactly what you're looking for, knowing which vendor's site to go to is next to impossible. Therefore, many Web sites create links for plug-ins and even

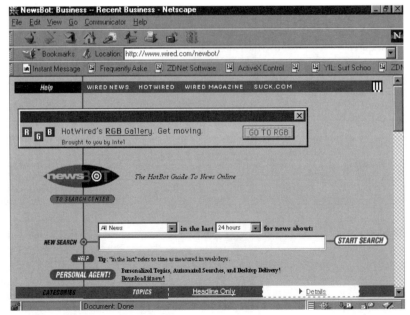

FIGURE   *NewsBot, a news search engine, is just one of many specialized search engines*
13.1   *available.*

store them directly on their server, so you don't have to go to the manufacturer's site to get the plug-in.

Table 13.2 and 13.3 list some of the best sites available for finding, then downloading, plug-ins and ActiveX controls directly to your computer. I've listed the site, along with some general comments about what the site offers. As you can tell, there is a pretty lengthy list of sites to choose from, which can be somewhat overwhelming. Which site is the best for what you're looking for? Well, I've made it a little easier by ranking the sites in terms of overall content and depth of plug-ins offered. Some sites are simply links to the plug-in files, whereas others offer complete reviews or even demonstrations of the plug-ins in action.

I'd recommend checking out these sites for a list of plug-ins or ActiveX controls that suits your needs. But I would also recommend checking the manufacturer's site once you've located the plug-in you're looking for. Although most of these sites keep their files updated, by checking out the manufacturer's site you can do the following:

- Avoid downloading outdated files
- Usually register your e-mail address with the manufacturer so you can be notified of updates
- Avoid possible infections with viruses from plug-ins that have been uploaded from other sources
- Have the ability to read about the plug-in's capabilities
- Usually have immediate access to frequently asked questions about installation and operation
- Get an idea of what other products are offered that may work in conjunction with the plug-in
- Can usually view documentation on how to implement the plug-in right on Web pages of your own

New plug-ins are created almost monthly. So it's really a good idea to check these sites on a regular basis if you are looking for ways to supercharge your browser continually .

TABLE 13.2: *Where to find plug-ins to download. Rating is out of five.* ★★★★★ *equals excellent.*

Site	Location	Comments	Rating
Browsers.com	www.browsers.com	Offers links to sites offering some of the best plug-ins available. Also offers links for direct downloading of the latest browser software.	A "Must Visit" site for up to date information on everything relating to Netscape and Internet Explorer browsers. *Content:* ★★★★★ *Depth:* ★★★★

(Table 13.2 continued)

BuyinGuide	www.buyinguide.com	You can search for plug-ins you can buy. This site gives you side-by-side comparisons of products, along with prices and product information.	Not a bad site for locating commercial plug-ins or ActiveX controls. *Content:* ★★★ *Depth:* ★★★★ (for commercial plug-ins)
Dave Central	www.davecentral.com/Websurf.html	Offers not only links to downloading popular plug-ins but also some more esoteric plug-ins. Site is displayed much like the Windows Explorer or File Manager displays information. Very easy to find what you want.	Could combine all plug-ins under one category. But does offer quick and easy access to plug-ins. Excellent reviews however. You should go here if you simply want down to earth information about what plug-ins do. *Content:* ★★★★ *Depth:* ★★★★
Download.com	www.download.com	A great search site to find demos of pay-for plug-ins. Works much like Shareware.com.	*Content:* ★★★★ *Depth:* ★★★★
Netscape Helper Applications	Home.netscape.com/assist/helper_apps/index.html	Although not plug-ins, helper applications work in conjunction with Netscape and Internet Explorer, this is a great place to find a list of browser-friendly, helper-related applications.	The definitive guide to all the Netscape Helper Applications. The site takes some time to load, but is segmented into several different categories. *Content:* ★★★★★ *Depth:* ★★★★★
Netscape Inline Plug-Ins List	Home.netscape.com/comprod/products/navigator/version_2.0/plugins/index.html	The definitive list of inline plug-ins available for all levels of Netscape Navigator, starting at version 2.0. Segmented out by category, you can read about the plug-in, then click the link to download the plug-in or connect to the company's Web site.	The definitive guide to all the Netscape Plug-ins. This is where you should go first if you are looking for a plug-in to suit your needs. *Note: You never know when this site's location will change. If this link does not work, search the main Netscape site.* *Content:* ★★★★★ *Depth:* ★★★★★
Plug-In Gallery & Demo Link	www2.gol.com/users/oyamada/index.html	An excellent site for finding and demo-ing plug-ins. You select the type of plug-in you want to see, such as video or document viewers, and the site returns not only the company site that offers the plug-in, but also links for sites that implement that particular plug-in.	If you have a hard time connecting to the Netscape site, or want to access a long list of plug-ins this is the best place to go. *Content:* ★★★★★ *Depth:* ★★★★★

(Table 13.2 continued)

Plug-In Plaza	www.browserwatch. com/plug-in.html	An excellent site for both plug-ins and ActiveX controls. Actually has more plug-ins listed than the official Netscape page. Also offers easy search options.	Rivaling the Netscape Site, Plug-in Plaza and ActiveX Plaza has just about every link to every plug-in and ActiveX controls. Many offer cursory reviews and are categorized by operating system and type. *Content:* ★★★★★ *Depth:* ★★★★★
Pop Rocket's Plug-In Paradise	www.poprocket.com/ paradise/	Specializing mainly in multimedia plug-ins, this site will demonstrate a wide variety of multimedia plug-ins, including Talker, Sizzler, Shockwave, and Viewmovie.	Good site for finding multimedia plug-ins. *Content:* ★★★ *Depth:* ★★★★
Shareware.com	www.shareware.com	Not actually a site that contains plug-ins, but rather a shareware search site that points you to the right location to find any file you are looking for. Make sure you check out the new picks each week. Plenty of new shareware programs are listed each week.	This site has no files, but is a good place to search for sites that offer plug-ins for downloading. If you don't want to go through a long list, trying to find the plug-in that meets your needs you can search using keywords. You can search by operating system,keyword or most popular downloads. *Content:* No real content *Depth:* ★★★★★
Stroud's Consumate Winsock Applications Site	www.wlyn.com/stroud/ 32plugin.html	Gives you a good list of commonly used plug-ins, with links and ratings, listing the pros and cons of each one. Also includes full reviews of the most popular plug-ins available.	Definitely worth checking out if you want to read up on what works and what doesn't. *Content:* ★★★★ *Depth:* ★★★
The ShockeR List	www.shocker.com/ shocker/	If you're into the ShockWave plug-in and want to see it demoed in all its glory, this is an excellent source for finding ShockWave-enabled sites.	Only relating to Shockwave sites. *Content:* ★★★★ *Depth:* ★★★
TuCows Windows 95 Plug-In Repositories	www.tucows.com or tucows.Web4all.net/ plug95.html	Doesn't contain all plug-ins, but is an excellent repository for finding the latest and greatest. Check the main TuCows site if the Web4all link does not work.	If you can't find it at Shareware.com, you can usually find it at TuCows. Reviews and more in depth information is provided than Shareware.com. *Content:* ★★★★ *Depth:* ★★★

(Table 13.2 continued)

Windows 95 Web Browser Plug-Ins	www.windows95.com/ apps/plugins.html	As the name implies, this site specializes in Windows 95 oriented software. Easy to navigate system helps you find files fast. A complete listing of plug-ins segmented out by category. Doesn't contain as many links or downloadable files as either Netscape or BrowserWatch, but does offer quick access to most of the popular plug-in titles.	This link takes you directly to the list of plug-ins this site offers. New links are added weekly. *Content:* ★★★★ *Depth:* ★★★
ZDNet Software Library	www.hotfiles.com	An excellent source for finding hundreds of plug-ins and ActiveX controls.	Some of the links are inactive, but overall a good list of plug-ins and reviews. *Content:* ★★★★ *Depth:* ★★★★
Virtual Software Library	http://castor.acs. oakland.edu/cgi- bin/vsl-front	Very fast index that searches many different software repositories.	Not as fancy as others, but very fast. *Content:* ★★★★ *Depth:* ★★★

FIGURE **13.2** *Dave Central is a great place to find plug-ins offering plenty of straightforward advice.*

TABLE 13.3: *Where to find ActiveX controls to download.*

Site	Location	Comments
ActiveX.com	www.activex.com	Go here first if you are looking for ActiveX controls, ActiveX assistance, or development information for ActiveX options.
ActiveX—The Unofficial Guide	www.shorrock.u-net.com/index.html	An excellent resource for developers and consumers as well.
ActiveX Resource Center	www.active-x.com	Definitely a place to look for controls, although the site does not appear to be updated frequently.
Gamelan	www.gamelan.com or www.developers.com	Excellent source for everything ActiveX oriented.
Active Web Design	www27.pair.com/pixman1/	Excellent location for finding ActiveX controls examples and code. Be forewarned—you need to be using Internet Explorer or Netscape with Ncompass installed in order to view many of these pages.
ActiveX Developer's Support Group	http://activex.adsp.or.jp/Public/default.asp	A great resource for lots of ActiveX development issues.
Active Xpress	www.techWeb.com/activexexpress.com	Although heavy on the Java side, this site, definitely for developers, gives you good resources and plenty of articles to help you bone up on creating your next ActiveX control.
Active Desktop Gallery	www.microsoft.com/ie/ie40/gallery/	If you want to add Active Desktop content to your Internet Explorer 4.0-enabled computer, this is the place to go. Be careful, however; some Active Desktop content can be dangerous to your desktop.
ActiveX Gallery	www.microsoft.com/activex/gallery/	Links to sites that are employing the ActiveX technology.

(Table 13.3 continued)

The Development Exchange	www.windx.com	If you are a developer, you need to check out this site. Plenty of good development information is listed here.
ZDNet Software Library	www.hotfiles.com	One of the more robust software search engines, containing more ActiveX controls than you probably imagined existed. Contains both user and developer controls.
Virtual Software Library	http://castor.acs.oakland. edu/cgi-bin/vsl-front	Very fast index that searches many different software repositories.

Figure   *ZDNet gives you quick access to plenty of files.*
13.3

WEB SITES AND ARTICLES ABOUT PLUG-INS AND ACTIVEX CONTROLS

Plug-ins haven't really taken the computer press by storm. It's an innovative technology, alright, but it's a technology that actually has been panned by many of the major computer media sources. Most of what you'll find in terms of informative articles focus on what this or that plug-in will do for you. But there are several good articles out there that can offer you more insight and up-to-date information on new plug-ins and enhanced plug-in technology. Table 13.4 gives you a list of some of the more interesting plug-in articles available on the Internet.

ActiveX controls, on the other hand, have garnered some press, mainly because of the security risks they pose and because, Microsoft makes them. You can find links to almost every positive article written about ActiveX controls from the main Microsoft ActiveX Web site located at *www.microsoft.com/activex/*. Table 13.5 lists some of the more worthwhile articles you might want to read if you are planning on using or developing sites that incorporate ActiveX controls.

TABLE 13.4: *Sites where you can read about plug-ins.*

Site	Location	Comments
C|Net Central's Netscape Navigator Plug-Ins by Daniel Will-Harris	www.cnet.com/Content/ Reviews/Compare/Plugin/	Although somewhat outdated, still an excellent article about plug-ins—what they are, how they work, and where to get them.
ZDNet's Internet Channel	www.zdnet.com/products/ internetuser/	An excellent source for all sorts of browser and Internet-related articles.
Official Netscape Plug-In Book	www.vmedia.com/books/ plugin	After reading *this* book, I'm sure you'll have all your questions answered. But if you have an insatiable desire for more books to read on the subject, check out this online version of the *Official Netscape Plug-In Book* by Shannon Turlington.
Macmillian's Computer Book Site	www.mcp.com	Yet another location where you can read online books about plug-ins. You have to register for the site, and then you can choose.

(Table 13.4 continued)

ZdNet's Web Plugin User	www.zdnet.com/products/ webpluginuser.html	Not only a list of the best plug-ins according to ZiffNet editors, but also a list of other links specific to plug-ins.
News.com	www.news.com	Use the search option to search for the keyword, "plug-in." At last count, about 300 different articles offered information on plug-ins.
Sympatico's Plug-in Site	www.ns.sympatico.ca/ Sympatico_Help/Software/ Plugins/index.html	A Web service provider in Canada that offers some very interesting information on plug-ins.
WebReview	www.webreview.com	If you're interested in designing sites with plug-ins, this is an excellent site for all sorts of articles on plug-in technology.
Byte's Virtual Press Room	www.byte.com or www. byte.com/art/9703/sec5/ art5.htm	This is an excellent article on how to write Java code to work and operate a plug-in within Netscape. Worth reading if you plan to develop and connect your Javascripts to plug-ins.
CMP's Tech Search	www.techweb.com	A great resource for the more technically inclined. Stories center more on corporate computing information, rather than on the consumer market. This site is a combination of all the CMP publications, including *Communications Week, Computer Reseller News, Home PC, Information Week, Network Computing,* and *Windows Magazine.* Use the search feature to search all the publications. You can also find a link to search the CMP Tech site through www.search.com. Currently they have over 600 stories that contain the word "plug-in" in them.

(Table 13.4 continued)

Wired's WebMonkey	www.webmonkey.com	If you are a developer or simply want to learn how the pros do it, you need to read *WebMonkey* on a regular basis. *WebMonkey* not only tells you about the hottest new Internet technology, but also shows you how to implement it.
ZDNet's ActiveX 101 Channel	www.zdent.com/products/ activexuser/intro.html	A great place for articles, reviews, and links to ActiveX-enabled sites.

TABLE 13.5: *Sites where you can read about ActiveX controls.*

Site	Location	Comments
Browsers.com's Survival Guides	www.browsers.com	Click the link for the Internet Explorer guide. You'll find everything you'd ever want to know about Internet Explorer, and a search engine that will search for all Internet Explorer plug-ins and ActiveX options.
ZDNet's Browser Lab	www.zdnet.com/products/ browseruser.html	An excellent source for all sorts of browser and Internet-related information.
Inquiry.com	www.inquiry.com	Use the search options to search for ActiveX articles. Also make sure you check out the link to DevEx, the Developer's Exchange, a great resource for developers.
WebTechniques	www.webtechniques.com/ features/1997/02/cornell/ cornell.shmtl	Excellent article on writing ActiveX controls with VBScript. Also includes archives from the magazine by the same name.
Byte Magazine	www.byte.com/art/9709/ sec5/art1.htm	ActiveX controls demystified. An excellent collection of articles on ActiveX written from the developer's perspective.

(Table 13.5 continued)

ActiveX Journal	www.folkarts.com/journals/ activex	A pay-for subscription site for Web site developers. Free access is granted for you to look at the site, but you must be using Internet Explorer to view the pages.

NEWSGROUPS FOR PLUG-INS

There are several newsgroups that offer some great banter about plug-ins. Most are browser- or platform-specific. If your service provider doesn't carry these, ask them to, or check out *www.dejanews.com* or *www.zippo.com*. These are free Web-based newsgroup services. Remember, newsgroups are populated by all types. Not all the information comes from experts. You'll find plenty of people willing to help, but you have to take the information you receive in these newsgroups with a certain amount of caution. If it doesn't sound right, don't try it. Also, don't let anyone talk you out of your credit card number, your password, or any other personal information. Because of the anonymity of newsgroups, people aren't always who they say they are.

Table 13.6 lists some of the best newsgroups you should be on the lookout for:

TABLE 13.6: *Newsgroups offering conversation about plug-ins.*

Newsgroup	Overview of Newsgroup	Average Number of Messages
Plug-Ins	THE newsgroup for asking, learning about, and staying on top of plug-ins. If you're having a problem with a particular plug-in, this is the place to post your question. The participants are relatively quick to answer.	From 10-100
Comp.infosystems. www.browsers. ms-windows	The main newsgroup for Windows-based browsers. It's a relatively active newsgroup with plenty of knowledgeable participants. It comprises any Web-based browser, so you may need to search through lots of messages for the information you need.	From 30-200

(Table 13.6 continued)

Alt.security.pgp	Interested in privacy on the Internet?	From 20-100
Comp.graphics.apps	This newsgroup centers around computer graphic applications. Regular postings about graphic-oriented plug-ins appear. *Note: You'll also see postings about Photoshop plug-ins. These are not browser-based plug-ins.*	From 50-200+
Comp.lang.javascript	Mainly about writing Javascript applets, you'll also occasionally find references to using plug-ins and Javascript together. I would categorize this newsgroup into the developer's end.	From 100-300
Comp.lang.vrml	If you're into virtual realities or using virtual reality plug-ins, this is the place to check out not only solid developer information, but also new sites and products.	From 50-100+
Comp.infosystems. www.authoring.html	If you plan to set up Web pages using plug-ins, and are having problems embedding them into your pages, this is a good place to solicit help.	From 20-100+
Microsoft.public. inetexplorer.ie3 (or microsoft.public. inetexplorer.ie4)	If you are using Internet Explorer version 3.0 or 4.0, you can go here to ask questions about plug-ins as they relate to Explorer.	From 100-300+
Comp.text.pdf	Using the Adobe Acrobat plug-in? Have questions about it? This is an excellent place to go to ask those questions.	From 10-50
Rec.video.desktop	When you install streaming video plug-ins, you may run into problems. This newsgroup can answer most recreational desktop video questions.	From 20-100
Secnews.netscape.com/ netscape.navigator	The official secure Netscape news-group for Netscape Navigator.	From 100 to 1000

(Table 13.6 continued)

ecnews.netscape.com/ netscape.communicator	The official secure Netscape news-group for Netscape Communicator.	From 100 to 1000
Comp.infosystems.www.browsers	A good place to go if you have a specific browser-related question.	From 100 to 1000
Comp.infosystems.www. browser.misc	If you have an off-the-wall browser or a question about non-standard browser utilities, this is a good resource to post.	From 100 to 500
Alt.fan.mozilla	A newsgroup for all those nutty Netscape groupies.	From 50-500

TABLE 13.7: *Newsgroups offering conversation about ActiveX controls and development.*

Newsgroup	Overview of Newsgroup	Average Number of Messages
microsoft.public.activex. authoring.html	Public newsgroup centered on authoring Web sites with ActiveX controls.	50-100
microsoft.public.activex. controls.activemovie	Public newsgroup specifically about the ActiveMovie ActiveX control.	20-100+
microsoft.public.activex. controls.chatcontrol	Public newsgroup sponsored by Microsoft and centered around using the ActiveX chat control.	20-300
microsoft.public.activex. controls.usage	Public newsgroup sponsored by Microsoft and centered on sites using ActiveX controls.	100-200
microsoft.public.activex. controls.Webbrowser	Public newsgroup sponsored by Microsoft and centered on Web browsers who use the ActiveX controls.	100-200
microsoft.public.activex. programming.control.dev	ActiveX development newsgroup. May not be available on every service provider.	50-100

(Table 13.7 continued)

microsoft.public.activex. programming.control. licensing	Newsgroup centered on licensing ActiveX controls.	50+
microsoft.public.activex. programming.control. safety	Discussion group centered on the security issues ActiveX poses, along with security breaches, fixes, patches, and updates.	100+ depending upon security breaches found
microsoft.public. inetexplorer. ie4.activex_contrl	Newsgroup about using ActiveX controls within the Internet Explorer 4.0 browser.	75+
tw.bbs.comp.activex	Non-Microsoft-based ActiveX newsgroup. Oftentimes free wheeling with comments, techniques, and ideas.	50-100+

*You can use your Web browser to summon up newsgroups. Just make sure you have your Newsgroup server settings listed correctly in your **Preferences** or **Options** menu listing. You summon up a newsgroup, much as you would a Web page. In the **Location** field where you would normally type the Web page, type "**news://newsgroup.name** where newsgroup name" is the full complete name of the newsgroup you want to go to. For secure newsgroup servers, such as Netscape's, you would type an "s" before the newsgroup protocol designator. For example, if you wanted to go to the Netscape Communicator newsgroup, which is stored on a secured newsgroup server, you would type*

Snews://secnews.netscape.com/netscape.communicator

By the way, if you know the type of server you want to connect to, you can use your Web browser to summon up the site by supplying the full directory or path name. Here are some common protocols you can use:

- FTP://—for connecting to file transfer servers
- HTTP://—for connecting to Web servers
- HTTPS://—for connecting to secured Web servers
- NEWS://—for connecting to newsgroup servers
- SNEWS://—for connecting to secured newsgroup servers
- MAILTO://—for summoning up your e-mail application

PLUG-IN AND ACTIVEX E-MAIL LISTS

You can find plenty of mailing lists that discuss the concept of browsers, but only one specific to plug-ins. In tables 13.8, 13.9, and 13.10 I've listed some you might want to subscribe to. Subscribing to any of these costs nothing. And most are relatively low-volume lists, offering less than 20 messages flowing through the electronic transom per day. Since new lists are added almost daily, you might want to check one of the following mailing list search engines for more plug-in related e-mail lists:

TABLE 13.8

Site Name	Location	Options
Find Mail	www.findmail.com	Mainly oriented towards commercial mailing lists, this site looks to be promising for subscribing and searching for mailing lists.
Liszt.com	www.liszt.com	Probably one of the largest search/index sites for locating mailing lists of all kinds. Most results will include instructions on what the mailing list offers and how to subscribe.
Reference.com	www.reference.com	Rivaling Liszt.com, this site also lets you search mailing list posting archives, along with newsgroup postings. Not all mailing lists available are archived, but what is accessible is the most popular.
Tile.net	www.tile.net	A very fast search engine for finding mailing lists. Also lets you search for files and news group postings simultaneously.

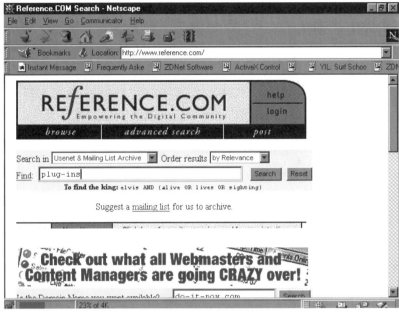

FIGURE
13.4
Reference.Com offers a quick way to search mailing list archives.

TABLE 13.9: *E-mail lists specializing in browser and plug-in technology.*

Mailing List	Subscribing Instructions or Location	Special Instructions
A list of mailing list databases.	www.emailtopics.com	Go to the Web site, then read the instructions for subscribing.
HTML—A discussion about HTML and browser-related issues.	Send an e-mail to Listserv@listserv.aol.com	In the body of the message include "Subscribe HTML FIRST NAME LASTNAME"
Lightwave—For people using and developing for the Lightwave plug-in.	Send mail to listserv@listserv.rc.arizona.edu	In the body of the message include "Sub LW-PLUGIN FIRSTNAME LASTNAME"
C|Net Central's Browser Alert for people who want to keep up on the latest browser news C|Net Central has to offer.	Send mail to Listserv@dispatch.cnet.com	In the body of the message include "Sub BROWSER-ALERT-PC FIRSTNAME LASTNAME"

(Table 13.9 continued)

TileNet's Informational Announcement Lists—For those who want to know what's happening commercially. An excellent source if you need to keep up to date on new products.

Use your Web browser to go to http://tile.net/signup/

Enter your e-mail address and zip code, then check the types of informational mail-lists you want to be added to.

PostMaster Direct—A commercial announcement list you can sign up for to get information about new products and services.

Use your Web browser to go to www.postmasterdirect.com

Click the link entitled *Join Our List,* then select the mailing lists you want to join. Very low volume on most of the lists.

TABLE 13.10: *E-mail lists specializing in ActiveX technology.*

ActiveX-Dispatch is a mailing list that centers on discussion of development of ActiveX controls. This mailing list is sponsored by C|Net Central. Although developer-related, the mailing list also informs the readers of newly available ActiveX controls.

Send mail to Listserv@dispatch.cnet.com

In the body of the message include "Sub ACTIVEX-DISPATCH FIRSTNAME LASTNAME"

ActiveX controls is run by the Microsoft Netowrk and offers a whole host of valuable information on controls and development.

Send mail to Listserv@listserv.msn.com

In the body of the message include "Sub ACTIVEXCONTROLS| FIRSTNAME LASTNAME"

ActiveXScript is mainly for the developer writing ActiveScript applets.

Send mail to Listserv@listserv.msn.com

In the body of the message include "Sub ACTIVESCRIPT FIRSTNAME LASTNAME"

IE-HTML is a discussion list about creating Web pages specifically for use with the Internet Explorer browser and its tags and capabilities.

Send mail to Listserv@listserv.msn.com

In the body of the message include "Sub IE-HTML FIRSTNAME LAST NAME"

When you sign up for any mailing list, make sure you either print out or keep the instructions the automatic e-mail server sends you. This initial message usually provides you information on how to unsubscribe, get help, query the list for other members, or read the mailing list archives.

Remember too, mailing lists work off two different addresses. The first address, where you send the request, is the mailing list administrator address. This address is not usually where you send messages to other list members, rather it is where you query the list manager software for information about the list. A second address is the actual "posting" address, where you post messages. The help file sent to you when you initially subscribe will tell you what the posting address is, along with other helpful hints. See Table 13.11 for a list of other helpful sites.

TABLE 13.11: *Other sites offering help or specializing in plug-ins and ActiveX.*

Site	Location	Comments
Compuserve's Internet Explorer Help Central	www.iehelp.com	Offers support and discussion groups about all versions of Internet Explorer.
IE4 Central	www.barkers.org/ie/	Good site for IE4 information.
ClubIE	www.clueie.com	A decent assortment of tips, tricks, and discussion groups about Internet Explorer.
Compuserve's Netscape Help Central	www.netscapehelp.com	Offers support and discussion groups centering around all flavors of Netscape Navigator.
IE 4 Daily Tips	www.WebsiteConcepts.com/IE4/	Plenty of tips, mainly focusing on the using aspect, not necessarily ActiveX or development options.

SUMMARY

Remember, the Internet is constantly changing. By the time you read this, another 50 or 100 sites specializing in plug-in and ActiveX technology will have sprung up. If you would like to know what those new sites are or have a particular question, feel free to e-mail me at *ckirk@ptialaska.net*. I'll be happy to point you in the right direction. And make sure you check Netscape and Microsoft's Web pages frequently for more information and links to new plug-ins and ActiveX controls.

Index

About the CD-ROM

THE CD: INFORMATION & INSTALLATION INSTRUCTIONS

The CD contains over 35 megabytes of plug-ins and a complete Web site to help you instantly locate plug-ins from the Web. You most likely won't have to type a single URL because I've tried to include not only links to the plug-ins but also plug-in resources as well. Here is some valuable information you should read before you pop-in the CD.

I cannot provide you with technical support on any of these plug-in products. Please contact the individual software vendors for specific technical support on the plug-ins themselves. If you are having problems with the CD, however, please feel free to e-mail me at ckirk@alaska.net or ckirk@ptialaska.net. I'll be happy to answer any questions you might have about the files and the CD itself.

DESCRIPTION OF THE CD

The CD is meant to provide you with quick access to some of the best plug-ins available, and instant access to plug-in resources on the Internet.

System Requirements. You should have the following hardware in order to run this CD:

- 16MB of RAM
- 100MB of free hard disk space
- Windows 95 Operating System (There are links to Windows 3.1 plug-ins in the Web Site folder.)
- Sound Card, Speakers, and Microphone if you want to use the sound/Internet telephony plug-ins
- Netscape Version 2.0 or above (Version 3.0 and Communicator are recommended versions)
- Internet Explorer
- WinZip
- CD-ROM drive with at least 2X capabilities

There are no ActiveX controls on this CD. They are best experienced directly from the Web sites that offer them.

What's on the CD and How to Install the Software

When you first pop-in the CD, you'll notice a folder entitled OpenMe. Double-click this folder and inside this folder you will find three items. They include:

- Plug-Ins
- ReadMe.doc
- Website

Plug-Ins Folder

This folder contains the top 10 plug-ins you should install. With the exception of one plug-in, all are self-extracting files. Here is a list of the plug-in installation applications on the CD.

Make sure you exit your browser application before you install any of these plug-ins. Also make sure no other applications are running either on your TaskBar or in your System Tray.

CalQuick—Calendar Quick (Calendar Quick Calendar Files)

There are two files in this folder. The first, Calqck32.exe is the application that allows you to create CalendarQuick files that can be embedded in a Web page. This application has a time-limit imposed and is used for evaluation purposes only. If you find this application worthwhile you can purchase the application from the Calendar Quick Web site.

CQPlug32.exe—Calendar Quick Plug-In

This is the installation program for installing the CalendarQuick Plug-in. Double-click the self-extracting file and follow the on-screen prompts to install the software.

CSWL—Dr. DWG NetView (AutoCad Files)

There is one file in this folder, and it contains a Zipped file, so you must have WinZip installed on your computer in order to uncompress this file. You can get a beta or evaluation copy of WinZip at *www.winzip.com*. Double-click to unzip the files. There are two files that create a disk image that allows you to install the NetView plug-in. Simply double-click the first uncompressed file to install the NetView plug-in.

IPIX—IPIX Viewer (3D Photo Files)

There is only one file in this folder, IPXSet32.exe. This is a self-extracting file. Simply double-click and follow the onscreen instructions for installing this plug-in. Then check out the IPIX home page for demonstration files you can view.

PCInstall—(PCInstall from a Web Page)

There are two files in this folder. One, the NPINST.exe file is the self-extracting file for installing the PC Install plug-in within your Netscape browser. The other, PCIv6Man.pdf is the complete manual for using PCInstall. You must have Adobe Acrobat in order to view the manual. You can get Adobe Acrobat at *www.abode.com*

Scream—(The Awesome Scream Plug-In)

In this folder is one zipped file entitled Getit.Zip. If you have Winzip you should be able to simply double-click and have this file launch the WinZip application. Within the WinZip application the installation program should start, asking you if you want to Scream! and install the Scream plug-in. Make sure you check out the amazing demos from the Scream Web page.

SPCO—Software Publishing Company's Active Presenter WebShow

In this folder is one file, WS2NAV95.exe. This is a self-extracting file. Simply double-click on it, and the installation software will start. Follow the installation wizard. You can view demos from Software Publishing's Web page.

SVF—SoftSources SVF Plug-In for Viewing AutoCad Files

There are three files in this folder. FAQ.HTML offers answers to your most frequently asked questions about the SVF plug-in. Help.HTML provides quick ready access to instructions and help on how to use and install this plug-in. Both files require a Web browser or HTML viewer. The final file, VI32V16.exe is the self-extracting installation program for installing the plug-in with either a 32-bit or 16-bit viewer.

Valis—The Valis Group's FlexViewer

This folder has one file, Flxinst.exe, which is a self-extracting file that will automatically install the Viewer into your Web page. Make sure you check out their web site at *www.valisgroup.com* for demonstrations on the viewer and their other amazing products.

Verity—KeyView Pro 6.0 Multiple File Type Viewer

In this folder there are two files, the license agreement which you should read, and the actual plug-in installation program. 32KVPRO60.exe is a self-extracting file. Simply double-click on this file to install all the components of the KeyView Pro viewer. Once installed you'll be able to view just about any file type ever created for a computer. You can purchase the product if you find it worthwhile online from their Website, which is located at *www.verity.com*

WrldView—Intervista's WorldView 3D VRML World Browser plug-in

There is one file and two folders in this folder. The file, License is a HTML file you should read before you agree to test drive this plug-in. The two folders, one Explorer and the other Netscape, contain the self-extracting files for installing this plug-in in either Internet Explorer or Netscape Navigator.

Check their Web site for information on the latest versions for Communicator.

README.DOC

This document pretty much says what this chapter outlines, only more briefly. You can read it with any text editor or Word processor.

WEBSITE

This is the most time-saving folder of the entire CD because it contains all the links listed in the book, categorized by the type of plug-in information you are looking for. As long as you have a Web browser installed, all you have to do is double-click to open this folder, then locate the INDEX.HTM file and double-click it. This file is the main index that links to all the other files in the Website folder on the CD. You can also double-click on any of the .HTM files if you want to view their pages individually. All links should take you directly to the Web sites containing either plug-ins or information about plug-ins. The folder contains these files:

• **Activex.htm**—The Big List of ActiveX controls.

- **Aolusers.htm**—The information you need if you are using America Online or CompuServe.
- **Biglist.htm**—The Big List of Netscape Plug-Ins with links to the companies offering these plug-ins. This list offers ALL the plug-ins available, not just the plug-ins listed in this book.
- **Creating.htm**—The page listing resources for creating your own Web pages and embedding plug-ins within those pages.
- **Index.htm**—The main page that links to all the rest of the pages on the CD.
- **Installing.htm**—This page offers resources and links to helping you install and find out what plug-ins are installed within your browser.
- **Intranets.htm**—If you want to implement plug-ins on an Intranet this page contains all the links listed in Chapter 6. Not only are there links to the plug-in sites, but also Intranet resources and articles.
- **Manpoint.gif**—A graphic to adorn the various pages.
- **Me.gif**—A graphic to adorn the various pages.
- **Penpaper.gif**—A graphic to adorn the various pages.
- **Plugins.htm**—The big list of plug-ins listed in the book, complete with descriptions of each plug-in.
- **Pointwmn.gif**—A graphic to adorn the various pages.
- **Resources.htm**—The big list of plug-in resources, magazine articles, Web sites, development sites, and more.
- **Soundcards.htm**—A list of soundcard companies in case you need to upgrade your computer to make it sound capable.

SUMMARY

If you have any problems with the CD let me know by e-mailing me at *ckirk@alaska.net* or *ckirk@ptialaska.net*. I strongly encourage you to test out each plug-in, and use the Website as your quick reference guide as you sit down with the book and read through all the options you can install that Supercharge your browser! Thanks for buying the book, and let me know what you end up doing with the plug-ins you install.

—Cheryl

Ask a Tough Question. Expect Solid Direction.

Help on the Horizon. Arnold Information Technology points corporations and organizations to information that get results. Access our experienced professionals who can help senior managers identify options and chart a course.

Since 1991, we've proven we can help in a range of capacities:

BUSINESS DEVELOPMENT
- Knowledge Management
- Competitive Intelligence
- Marketing & Sales
- Acquisitions & Mergers
- Patent Evaluations
- Technology Startups

INFORMATION TECHNOLOGY SERVICES
- Intranets, and Extranets
- Web-based Technologies
- Database Management
- Digital Work Flow Planning
- Information Engineering

ACTION FROM IDEAS. We helped build the service known as the Top 5% of the Internet, found at www.lycos.com. Our latest competitive intelligence tool can be explored at abcompass.com. It builds a personal daily news feed that only you receive.

A TEAM WITH STRATEGIC VISION. Our seasoned consultants can build, research, prototype, budget, plan, assess, and tackle some of the toughest jobs in information technology. Our managers have taken a leadership role in U.S. corporations and elsewhere in the world.

GET WHERE YOU WANT TO GO. TODAY.
We move corporations and organizations into the future. Our work spans a variety of industries, including publishing, telecommunications, government agencies, investment banks, and startups. We welcome confidential, informal discussions of your challenges and opportunities.

CONTACT:

Stephen E. Arnold, President
Arnold Information Technology
P.O. Box 320
Harrods Creek, Kentucky 40027
Voice: 502 228-1966
E-Mail: ait@arnoldit.com
Facsimile: 502 228-0548

MICROSOFT INTERNET EXPLORER, VERSION 4.0, AND SOFTWARE RELATED COMPONENTS.

END-USER LICENSE AGREEMENT FOR MICROSOFT SOFTWARE

IMPORTANT-READ CAREFULLY: This Microsoft End-User License Agreement ("EULA") is a legal agreement between you (either an individual or a single entity) and Microsoft Corporation for the Microsoft software product(s) identified above which may include associated software components, media, printed materials, and "online" or electronic documentation ("SOFTWARE PRODUCT"). By installing, copying, or otherwise using the SOFTWARE PRODUCT, you agree to be bound by the terms of this EULA. If you do not agree to the terms of this EULA, do not install or use the SOFTWARE PRODUCT. If the SOFTWARE PRODUCT was purchased by you, you may return it to your place of purchase for a full refund.

The SOFTWARE PRODUCT is protected by copyright laws and international copyright treaties, as well as other intellectual property laws and treaties. The SOFTWARE PRODUCT is licensed, not sold.

1. GRANT OF LICENSE. The SOFTWARE PRODUCT is licensed as follows:

* Installation and Use. Microsoft grants you the right to install and use copies of the SOFTWARE PRODUCT on your computers running validly licensed copies of the operating system for which the SOFTWARE PRODUCT was designed [e.g., Windows(r) 95; Windows NT(r), Windows 3.x, Macintosh, etc.].

* Backup Copies. You may also make copies of the SOFTWARE PRODUCT as may be necessary for backup and archival purposes.

* Components. Certain software components of the SOFTWARE PRODUCT are subject to the following additional provisions:

DCOM95. You may only use copies of the DCOM95 component on computer(s) for which you have licensed Microsoft Windows operating system platforms.

NetMeeting. NetMeeting contains technology that enables applications to be shared between two or more computers, even if an application is installed on only one of the computers. You may use this technology with all Microsoft application products for multi-party conferences. For non-Microsoft applications, you should consult the accompanying license agreement or contact the licensor to determine whether application sharing is permitted by the licensor.

Internet Assistants and Internet Viewers: You may reproduce and distribute an unlimited number of copies of these components of the SOFTWARE PRODUCT; provided each copy shall be a true and complete copy, including all copyright and trademark notices, and shall be accompanied by a copy of this EULA. Copies of these components may be distributed as a standalone product or included with your own product.

Microsoft Agent. You may distribute Microsoft Agent and its associated characters and speech engines in accordance with terms of a separate end user license agreement. See the "EULA.htm" file located at http://www.microsoft.com/workshop/prog/agent/ for further details.

2. DESCRIPTION OF OTHER RIGHTS AND LIMITATIONS.
* Maintenance of Copyright Notices. You must not remove or alter any copyright notices on all copies of the SOFTWARE PRODUCT.
* Distribution. You may not distribute copies of the SOFTWARE PRODUCT to third parties.
* Prohibition on Reverse Engineering, Decompilation, and Disassembly. You may not reverse engineer, decompile, or disassemble the SOFTWARE PRODUCT, except and only to the extent that such activity is expressly permitted by applicable law notwithstanding this limitation.
* Rental. You may not rent, lease, or lend the SOFTWARE PRODUCT.
* Transfer. You may permanently transfer all of your rights under this EULA, provided the recipient agrees to the terms of this EULA.
* Support Services. Microsoft may provide you with support services related to the SOFTWARE PRODUCT ("Support Services"). Use of Support Services is governed by the Microsoft polices and programs described in the user manual, in "on line" documentation and/or other Microsoft-provided materials. Any supplemental software code provided to you as part of the Support Services shall be considered part of the SOFTWARE PRODUCT and subject to the terms and conditions of this EULA. With respect to technical information you provide to Microsoft as part of the Support Services, Microsoft may use such information for its business purposes, including for product support and development. Microsoft will not utilize such technical information in a form that personally identifies you.
* Compliance with Applicable Laws. You must comply with all applicable laws regarding use of the SOFTWARE PRODUCT.

3. TERMINATION. Without prejudice to any other rights, Microsoft may terminate this EULA if you fail to comply with the terms and conditions of this EULA. In such event, you must destroy all copies of the SOFTWARE PRODUCT.

4. COPYRIGHT. All title, including but not limited to copyrights, in and to the SOFTWARE PRODUCT and any copies thereof are owned by Microsoft or its suppliers. All title and intellectual property rights in and to the content which may be accessed through use of the SOFTWARE PRODUCT is the property of the respective content owner and may be protected by applicable copyright or other intellectual property laws and treaties. This EULA grants you no rights to use such content. All rights not expressly granted are reserved by Microsoft.

5. U.S. GOVERNMENT RESTRICTED RIGHTS. The SOFTWARE PRODUCT is provided with RESTRICTED RIGHTS. Use, duplication, or disclosure by the Government is subject to restrictions as set forth in subparagraph (c)(1)(ii) of the Rights in Technical Data and Computer Software clause at DFARS 252.227-7013 or subparagraphs (c)(1) and (2) of the Commercial Computer Software Restricted Rights at 48 CFR 52.227-19, as applicable. Manufacturer is Microsoft Corporation/One Microsoft Way/Redmond, WA 98052-6399.

6. EXPORT RESTRICTIONS. You agree that you will not export or re-export the SOFTWARE PRODUCT to any country, person, entity or end user subject to U.S.A. export restrictions. Restricted countries currently include, but are not necessarily limited to Cuba, Iran, Iraq, Libya, North Korea, Sudan, and Syria. You warrant and represent that neither the U.S.A. Bureau of Export Administration nor any other federal agency has suspended, revoked or denied your export privileges.

7. NOTE ON JAVA SUPPORT. The SOFTWARE PRODUCT may contain support for programs written in Java. Java technology is not fault tolerant and is not designed, manufactured, or intended for use or resale as on-line control equipment in hazardous environments requiring fail-safe performance, such as in the operation of nuclear facilities, aircraft navigation or communication systems, air traffic control, direct life support machines, or weapons systems, in which the failure of Java technology could lead directly to death, personal injury, or severe physical or environmental damage.

8. NO WARRANTIES. Microsoft expressly disclaims any warranty for the SOFTWARE PRODUCT. THE SOFTWARE PRODUCT AND ANY RELATED DOCUMENTATION IS PROVIDED "AS IS" WITHOUT WARRANTY OF ANY KIND, EITHER EXPRESS OR IMPLIED, INCLUDING, WITHOUT LIMITATION, THE IMPLIED WARRANTIES OR MERCHANTABILITY, FITNESS FOR A PARTICULAR PURPOSE, OR NONINFRINGEMENT. THE ENTIRE RISK ARISING OUT OF USE OR PERFORMANCE OFTHE SOFTWARE PRODUCT REMAINS WITH YOU.

9. LIMITATION OF LIABILITY. To the maximum extent permitted by applicable law, in no event shall Microsoft or its suppliers be liable for any special, incidental, indirect, or consequential damages whatsoever (including, without limitation, damages for loss of business profits, business interruption, loss of business information, or any other pecuniary loss) arising out of the use of or inability to use the SOFTWARE PRODUCT or the provision of or failure to provide Support Services, even if Microsoft has been advised of the possibility of such damages. In any case, Microsoft's entire liability under any provision of this EULA shall be limited to the greater of the amount actually paid by you for the SOFTWARE PRODUCT or US$5.00; provided however, if you have entered into a Microsoft Support Services Agreement, Microsoft's entire liability regarding Support Services shall be governed by the terms of that agreement. Because some states and jurisdictions do not allow the exclusion or limitation of liability, the above limitation may not apply to you.

10. MISCELLANEOUS.

This EULA is governed by the laws of the State of Washington, U.S.A.

If you acquired this product in Canada, this EULA is governed by the laws of the Province of Ontario, Canada. Each of the parties hereto irrevocably attorns to the jurisdiction of the courts of the Province of Ontario and further agrees to commence any litigation which may arise hereunder in the courts located in the Judicial District of York, Province of Ontario.

If this product was acquired outside the United States, then local law may apply.

Should you have any questions concerning this EULA, or if you desire to contact Microsoft for any reason, please contact the Microsoft subsidiary serving your country, or write: Microsoft Sales Information Center/One Microsoft Way/Redmond, WA 98052-6399.

Si vous avez acquis votre produit Microsoft au CANADA, la garantie limitée suivante vous concerne:

EXCLUSION DE GARANTIES. Microsoft exclut expressément toute garantie relative au LOGICIEL. Le LOGICIEL et la documentation y afférente sont fournis "en l'état", sans garantie d'aucune sorte, expresse ou implicite, y compris, de manière limitative, sans aucune garantie de qualité, d'adéquation à un usage particulier ou de non-contrefaçon. Vous assumez l'ensemble des risques découlant de l'utilisation ou des performances du LOGICIEL.

Pas de Responsabilité pour les Dommages Indirects - Microsoft ou ses fournisseurs ne seront pas responsables en aucune circonstance pour tout dommage spécial, incident, indirect, ou conséquent quel qu'il soit (y compris, sans limitation, les dommages entrainés par la perte de bénéfices, l'interruption des activités, la perte d'information ou toute autre perte pécuniaire) découlant de l'utilisation ou de l'impossibilité d'utilisation de ce LOGICIEL ainsi que pour toute disposition concernant le Suport Technique ou la façon dont celui-ci a été rendu et ce, même si Microsoft a été avisée de la possibilité de tels dommages. La responsabilité de Microsoft en vertu de toute disposition de cette convention ne pourra en aucun temps excéder le plus élevé entre i) le montant effectivement payé par vous pour le LOGICIEL ou ii) US$5.00; advenant que vous ayez contracté par entente distincte avec Microsoft pour un Support Technique étendu, vous serez lié par les termes d' une telle entente.

La présente Convention est régie par les lois de la province d'Ontario, Canada. Chacune des parties à la présente reconnaît irrévocablement la compétence des tribunaux de la province d'Ontario et consent à instituer tout litige qui pourrait découler de la présente auprès des tribunaux situés dans le district judiciaire de York, province d'Ontario.

Au cas où vous auriez des questions concernant cette licence ou que vous désiriez vous mettre en rapport avec Microsoft pour quelque raison que ce soit, veuillez contacter la succursale Microsoft desservant votre pays, dont l'adresse est fournie dans ce produit, ou écrivez à : Microsoft Sales Information Center, One Microsoft Way, Redmond, Washington 98052-6399.